STATE PARKS OF
NORTH CAROLINA

STATE PARKS OF
NORTH CAROLINA

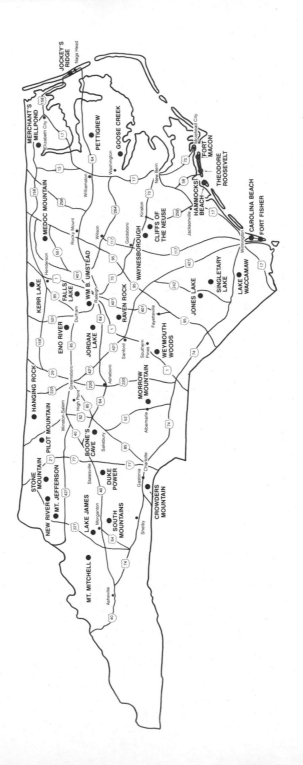

STATE PARKS OF
NORTH CAROLINA

by

Walter C. Biggs, Jr., and James F. Parnell

John F. Blair, Publisher
Winston-Salem, North Carolina

Cover photographs
left to right, top to bottom:

High Shoals Falls, South Mountains State Park
Raccoon, Merchants Millpond State Park
American lotus bloom, Lake Waccamaw State Park
Gulls flying above the surf, Fort Macon State Park
Shaded creek along Fern Trail, Crowders Mountain State Park
Cypress trees and Merchants Millpond, Merchants Millpond State Park
Sand dunes and sea oats on Bear Island, Hammocks Beach State Park
Great egret, Hammocks Beach State Park
Rhododendron blooms, Mount Mitchell State Park
The Blue Ridge at sunset, from Mount Mitchell State Park

Library of Congress Cataloging in Publication Data

Biggs, Walter C.
  State parks of North Carolina.

  Bibliography: p.
  Includes index.
  1. Parks—North Carolina—Guide-books.   2. North Carolina—
Description and travel—1981-   —Guide-books.   I. Parnell, James
F.   II. Title.
F252.3.B44   1989   917.5604'43   89-6976
ISBN 0-89587-071-1

Contents

Foreword

North Carolina's state parks system offers a wide variety of opportunities for visitors to and residents of the Tar Heel State. The state's scenic beauty and diversified natural resources are on display every day in our state parks, recreation areas, and natural areas.

The parks system's facilities spread from the top of Mount Mitchell, the highest peak east of the Mississippi, to Jockey's Ridge, the highest sand dune on the east coast.

State parks and recreation areas offer all citizens the opportunity to get away from it all and become one with nature. Whether you are an avid camper, hiker, boating enthusiast, or just someone who enjoys watching a magnificent Tar Heel State sunset, the North Carolina state parks system caters to a myriad of recreational needs.

The wide variety of recreational opportunities and natural resources featured throughout the state parks system, from the mountains to the sea, provides substantial evidence to support the claim that North Carolina is a "variety vacationland."

As stewards of an important part of the state's and the nation's natural heritage, the North Carolina Division of Parks and Recreation invites you to discover North Carolina's state parks. They belong to everyone.

William W. Davis, Ph D.
Director, North Carolina
Division of Parks and Recreation

Preface

The three years during which we prepared this book were a time of discovery, a time during which we discovered the exceptional beauty and the diversity of the parks, natural areas, and recreation areas that have been established for the people of North Carolina. Our knowledge of these special places is personal and direct. The information we present is derived from our experiences and observations while traveling more than 9,000 miles throughout the state, visiting nearly every unit of the state parks system, and hiking an estimated 120 miles of trails. We also gained information from conversations with parks personnel, from printed material produced by the Division of Parks and Recreation, and from a variety of published literature. It is our hope that this book will lead other people to share our discovery of the rich environment of our parklands, guide them on their visits, and encourage greater public support for legislative and administrative action for the benefit of the state parks of North Carolina.

Visitors to the state's parklands may experience both physical recreation and spiritual re-creation. They may come away with a collage of lasting impressions—mountain peaks, ridges, and promontories silhouetted in the glow of a brilliant sunset; ocean waves crashing against the shore, and the pungent smell of salt marshes teeming with living organisms; woodlands in shades of green quilted with the bright colors of spring flowers; flowing streams producing musical sounds along their rock-strewn channels; and tree-lined lakes and rivers shimmering beneath a midday sun. The protection of such scenic beauty and environmental diversity is a primary function of the parks system. The conservation of parkland promotes enjoyment of the natural environment; teaches stewardship of the land; enables visitors to better understand the intricate relationships among organisms within natural communities; provides opportunities for solitude and the rejuvenation of the spirit; and preserves resources that help to provide clean air, an unpolluted water supply, and habitat for diverse living creatures. As the population of North Carolina continues to grow, and as more and more land undergoes commercial and residential development, the need to conserve land becomes increasingly imperative. Not too many generations ago, most folks could walk "out back" to find the peace of a quiet woodland when the pace of life became too frantic. A lucky few still can. For most, however, the parks and other protected lands have become their refuge.

Visitors to state parklands should realize that their enjoyment of the parks is directly related to the quality of the physical environments they encounter and that the protection of those environments and the living creatures that make them their home is paramount. We must not love our parks to death, and we must not permit visitors to abuse them. If the protection of park resources comes into conflict with visitor activities, concern for the environment must always prevail.

This book is intended as a guide for visitors and as a source of information about each park, natural area, and recreation area in the North Carolina state parks system. Each major unit of the system is discussed in a separate chapter. The parks are grouped according to the physiographic province of the state in which they are located, whether coastal plain, Piedmont, or mountain. Within each of the three provinces, the parks are presented alphabetically. The natural areas and recreation areas are fewer in number than the parks; discussions of these places are arranged alphabetically also, but without being divided by physiographic province.

Chapters begin with a summary of basic data, followed by a description of the principal physical features of the park units, an account of the historical background of the areas within which park units are located, and a summary of events that led to the establishment of individual parks. Geological, ecological, and biological information relevant to an appreciation of the parks is provided. We have not attempted a comprehensive discussion of plant and animal life; references have been limited to the common and conspicuous organisms that park visitors are most likely to encounter or seek out. The common names of plants and animals are used in the text, while their corresponding scientific names are provided in the appendix. We have included detailed descriptions of hiking trails in park units to encourage visitors to explore a variety of environments and to find places of special beauty and significance away from crowded, easily accessible sites. We have also provided descriptions of the visitor-use facilities and identified special activities available at individual parks, natural areas, and recreation areas. For most park units, a map shows the location of roads, hiking trails, visitor-use facilities, and other features; the maps have been redrawn from those produced by the North Carolina Division of Parks and Recreation. Places of interest located near units of the state parks system are briefly discussed.

It is our hope that the people of North Carolina will visit their parks and that this book will help to enrich their experiences.

Acknowledgments

This book could not have been produced without the cooperation and assistance of personnel of the Division of Parks and Recreation of the North Carolina Department of Natural Resources and Community Development. Dr. William W. Davis, division director, supported our efforts, and Mr. Donald G. Reuter, public information officer, and Mr. Michael L. Dunn, head of interpretation and education, made available sources of information, expedited our work in the parks, and aided us in many other ways. We are also grateful for the enthusiastic cooperation of superintendents, rangers, and other persons throughout the parks system who talked with us, aided us on visits to parks, and reviewed portions of the manuscript.

Significant contributions to this project were made by Mr. David M. DuMond, Ms. Eloise F. Potter, Dr. David J. Sieren, and Dr. W. David Webster, who read part or all of the manuscript and provided helpful suggestions for improvement. Whatever merit is achieved by this book is due in part to the dedication and industry of the production staff of John F. Blair, Publisher: Ms. Margaret Couch, Mr. Steve Kirk, Ms. Carolyn Sakowski, and Mrs. Debbie Hampton, who drew the maps.

Contributions made by all these persons have been invaluable; however, errors and omissions that inevitably remain in this book are the responsibility of the authors alone.

The University of North Carolina at Wilmington, through its Department of Biological Sciences, provided a professional base for our work and assisted us in numerous ways. We also acknowledge the support and encouragement of our wives, especially for companionship while hiking some long park trails.

All photographs were taken by the authors using Kodachrome 64 film. The black-and-white photographs in this book were printed from original color transparencies. On visits to state parklands, more than eighty rolls of film were exposed to create a file of approximately three thousand images.

Introduction

North Carolina's varied landscape extends from the Atlantic Ocean to the Great Smoky Mountains. A journey along the 543 miles between Manteo and Murphy leads from the sand dunes of the Outer Banks, across the rolling countryside of the state's midregion, to mountain peaks more than 6,000 feet above sea level. Three physiographic provinces are recognized—coastal plain, Piedmont, and mountain.

Nearly one-half of the state is within the coastal plain, which varies in width from 100 to 140 miles between the Atlantic Ocean and the Fall Line at its boundary with the Piedmont province. The coastal plain is often subdivided into tidewater and inner coastal-plain regions. The tidewater region includes the Outer Banks, the coastal capes, and the area bordering coastal sounds; much of it lies at elevations of 20 feet or less. The inner coastal-plain region extends westward to the Fall Line, reaching elevations of 400 to 600 feet above sea level.

The Piedmont province, approximately equal in area to the coastal plain, lies between the Fall Line and the escarpment of the Blue Ridge Mountains in the west. It reaches elevations of 1,500 to 2,000 feet above sea level. Characterized by rolling hills and red clay soils, the Piedmont also contains a series of low, isolated peaks and ridges that includes the Uwharrie Mountains, the Sauratown Mountains, the Kings Mountain range, and outliers from the Blue Ridge such as the Brushy and South mountains.

The mountain province contains approximately 12 percent of the area of the state. It is from 15 to 50 miles in width, lying along the state's western boundary. The province includes two highly dissected chains of mountain ranges, the Blue Ridge Mountains along the eastern perimeter and the chain containing the Unaka, Great Smoky, and Unicoi mountains, which roughly parallels the Blue Ridge to the west. Elevations of mountain peaks range from 3,000 to more than 6,000 feet above sea level. The two principal chains of mountain ranges are connected by several cross-ridges; among them are the Black Mountains, with a dozen peaks that exceed 6,000 feet, and the Pisgah, Balsam, and Nantahala mountains. The eastern continental divide follows the crest of the Blue Ridge Mountains.

The state parks system protects natural resources in each of the three physiographic provinces. North Carolina's parklands, therefore, offer a variety of experiences. Visitors may stand upon the highest sand dune on the east coast or the highest mountain east of the Mississippi River. Fishermen may cast for trout in cool mountain streams, for largemouth bass in the still waters of a man-made reservoir, or for bluefish in the surf of the Atlantic Ocean.

Canoeists may experience the quiet beauty of New River, the rocky rapids of the swift-flowing Eno, or the placid waterway of Lassiter Swamp. Hikers may follow winding trails through spruce/fir forests on mountain peaks, deciduous hardwood forests of the Piedmont, or swamp bottomlands near the coast. The seasons introduce additional variety to the parks—wildflowers in spring, dense, wind-stirred foliage in summer, palettes of red, orange, and yellow in autumn, and bare, mist-shrouded branches in winter.

Forty-one state parks, natural areas, and recreation areas encompassing nearly 135,000 acres were established between 1916, when 795 acres on Mount Mitchell were purchased to create the first state park, and 1987, when land was acquired on the shore of Lake James for the state's newest park. Because of a policy initiated in 1929 that dictated that state funds could not be appropriated for the purchase of parkland, land for approximately half the parks, natural areas, and recreation areas of the state parks system was donated by public-spirited citizens and agencies and by the federal government. Parkland was also procured with the assistance of the Nature Conservancy, with matching-fund grants from the federal Land and Water Conservation Fund, and by lease from the United States Army Corps of Engineers. The state policy on land acquisition changed in 1969, when land was purchased with state funds for Carolina Beach State Park. Several other parks have subsequently been added to the system with state appropriations.

Between 1934 and 1941, most park development, including the construction of visitor-use facilities, was undertaken by the Civilian Conservation Corps, the Work Projects Administration, and other federal public-works programs that operated in cooperation with state agencies. These sources of money and labor were terminated at the beginning of World War II, and modest funds for the development and maintenance of facilities have since been provided by the state and the Land and Water Conservation Fund.

A set of principles adopted in 1955 states that "the purpose of the North Carolina State Parks System shall be . . . to serve the people of North Carolina and their visitors by (1) preserving and protecting natural areas of unique or exceptional scenic value for the benefit and inspiration of the present generation, as well as for generations to come; (2) establishing and operating state parks that provide recreational use of natural resources and outdoor recreation in natural surroundings; (3) portraying and interpreting plant and animal life, geology, and all other natural features; and (4) preserving, protecting, and portraying scientific sites of statewide importance."

The state parks system includes units of three types, which operate according to different principles and objectives. **State parks** preserve and protect distinctive areas of natural beauty that would not be accessible to the public if they were under private ownership. They provide recreational opportunities for camping, picnicking, hiking, and nature study, so long as such activities do not harm the natural environment. A minimum of 400 acres is required for the establishment of a state park. **State recreation areas** provide outdoor recreational opportunities as their major function, though the conservation of natural resources remains a concern. Recreational activities usually include camping, picnicking, boating, fishing, and swimming. **State natural areas** focus on resource preservation, education, and interpretation. Recreational activities are restricted to hiking and nature study.

Rules and regulations governing the use of parklands have been established by the North Carolina Division of Parks and Recreation. They are intended to ensure the safety of visitors and to protect park resources. Rules and regulations applicable to individual park units are posted prominently. Parks, natural areas, and recreation areas are open year-round, though heavy snowfall may force the closure of mountain parks on occasion. Some facilities within park units may not be available in the winter. A schedule of events such as guided walks and interpretive programs is provided at most units of the state parks system; information about events may be obtained from the park offices.

While present parklands possess outstanding scenic, natural, and recreational values and are places to be treasured, many problems exist, primarily due to lack of adequate funding for the system. This book does not present a litany of specific problems and needs; instead, it focuses upon the resources present and the potential of the parks for the future. Nevertheless, if the system is to realize its potential for the people of the state, needs must be recognized and addressed. A commitment by the state to maintain our parks and provide meaningful experiences for visitors is essential. Some needs requiring attention are acquisition of land for new parks and enlargement of existing parks, as specified in various master plans; provision of adequate visitor facilities that safeguard the natural character of the parks; hiring of additional personnel to assist in operating and maintaining parks; and appropriation of funds for the repair and maintenance of facilities.

In 1987, the North Carolina General Assembly adopted the State Parks Act, which mandated the preparation of a statewide plan for the parks system that will be reviewed and updated every five years. The *Systemwide Plan for the North Carolina State Parks System* was released in December 1988 by the Division of Parks and Recreation. It describes park resources and needs and recommends solutions to problems, including substantial additional funding for the development, operation, expansion, and staffing of the parks system. Implementation of specific recommendations contained in the plan will be vital to the future of the system. Most parks came into existence because of the foresight and initiative of North Carolinians who recognized the value of parklands in conserving a portion of their natural heritage and in providing sanctuary from the overdeveloped world in which they lived. The people of the state must demand that the material resources necessary for the realization of the full potential of the parks system be provided.

The North Carolina Natural Heritage Program was established in 1976 as part of the Division of Parks and Recreation. Its primary purpose is to compile the North Carolina Registry of Natural Heritage Areas. The registry catalogs rare plants and animals of the state, lists exemplary or unique natural communities and ecosystems, and seeks their protection in a variety of ways ranging from the registration of sites by private owners to public acquisition. The state natural areas discussed in this book are included in the registry; ecologically significant portions of most state parks have also been registered as natural heritage areas. Many other natural heritage areas lie within public holdings, such as national forests or state game lands, and are managed by landholding agencies. Many small natural areas and those under private ownership are open to public visitation. A *Directory to North Carolina's Natural Areas* (Roe 1987) provides an excellent introduction to the program as well as a directory of 108 natural heritage areas. For additional information, write: North Carolina Natural Heritage Program, P.O. Box 27687, Raleigh, N.C. 27611.

The North Carolina Wildlife Resources Commission is a state agency devoted to conservation of the state's wildlife and other natural resources, conservation education, enforcement of laws and regulations governing hunting and fishing, and management of inland fisheries. Its monthly magazine, *Wildlife in North Carolina*, contains excellent articles concerning the flora, fauna, and natural environments of the state. It often features articles about state parks, state natural areas, and state recreation areas. To subscribe, write: *Wildlife in North Carolina*, 512 North Salisbury Street, Raleigh, N.C. 27611.

Several organizations promote the conservation of North Carolina's natural resources.

Friends of State Parks is of special interest to citizens who support the state parks system. It is an advocacy group that works to protect and upgrade the parks, to increase public enjoyment of parklands, and to promote the formation of support groups that assist park personnel at the local level. For additional information, write: Friends of State Parks, 4204 Randleman Road, Greensboro, N.C. 27406.

The Nature Conservancy's stated goal is "to find, protect, and maintain the best examples of communities, ecosystems, and endangered species in the natural world." It is a private organization that secures land and either manages it and protects its natural values or transfers it to public land-managing agencies. The Nature Conservancy has frequently assisted the state in the acquisition of parkland. For additional information, write: The Nature Conservancy, North Carolina Field Office, P.O. Box 805, Chapel Hill, N.C. 27514.

The North Carolina Conservation Council, the North Carolina Wildlife Federation, the Council of Garden Clubs, and many regional and local organizations have also made significant contributions to the protection of the state's natural resources.

STATE PARKS
Coastal Plain

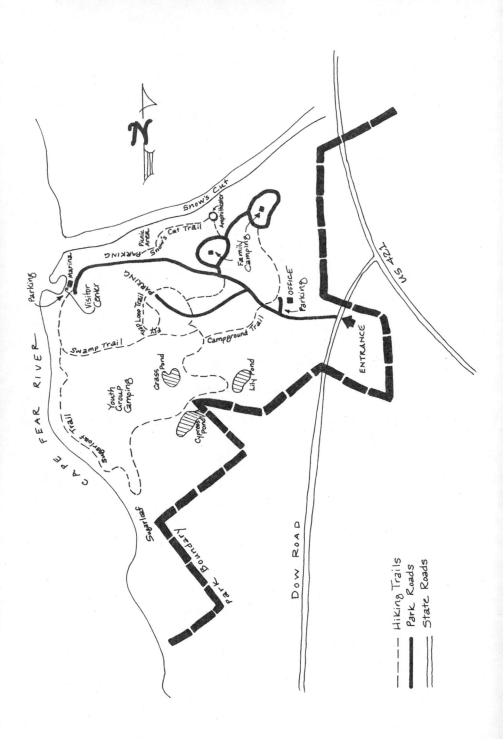

CAROLINA BEACH
STATE PARK

Address: P.O. Box 475
            Carolina Beach, N.C. 28428

Telephone: (919) 458-8206 (office)
            (919) 458-8207 (marina)

Size: 1,773 acres

Established: 1969

Riverbank, Cape Fear River

Location: New Hanover County, 10 miles south of Wilmington; follow U.S.
            421 to Carolina Beach city limits, then turn right onto Dow Road (SR
            1573) for 0.3 mile and follow the signs. The park may also be reached
            from the south (Brunswick County) by way of the Southport–Fort
            Fisher ferry, which crosses the Cape Fear River near its mouth; from
            the ferry landing at Fort Fisher, follow U.S. 421 north to Carolina
            Beach.

Principal Attractions: Cape Fear River and Snow's Cut (Intracoastal Water-
            way); Sugarloaf, a relict sand dune 50 feet in height; variety of coastal
            habitats; Venus' fly trap and other carnivorous plants; proximity to area
            beaches and Fort Fisher State Recreation Area.

Visitor Activities: Hiking and nature study; fishing and boating; family and
            group camping; picnicking.

Season: Open year-round.

The southern tip of New Hanover County is a triangular finger of land lying
between the Atlantic Ocean and the Cape Fear River. It became an island
(known in tourist advertising as Pleasure Island) after the 1929 dredging of
Snow's Cut, which connects Masonboro Sound to the Cape Fear River.
Snow's Cut is part of the Atlantic Intracoastal Waterway, which provides an
inland passageway for boat traffic along the Atlantic coast of the United States.
Carolina Beach State Park is located in the northwestern corner of Pleasure

Island, where Snow's Cut enters the Cape Fear River. Thus, the western boundary of the park is washed by waters coming down from the North Carolina Piedmont and mountains, while the saline waters of the Intracoastal Waterway flow along its northern boundary.

Carolina Beach State Park was established to preserve a portion of the unique natural environment along the Intracoastal Waterway and to allow opportunity for public recreation at nearby beaches. Part of the land for the park (437 acres) was purchased by the state, and the part adjacent to Snow's Cut (135 acres) was received from the United States Army Corps of Engineers; additional land was leased from the army. A prominent physical feature of the park is Sugarloaf, a relict sand dune 50 feet in height near the bank of the Cape Fear River. It appeared on navigational charts as early as 1738 and was an important landmark for river pilots. The dune was also of strategic significance during the Civil War. As part of the Confederates' defense of the port of Wilmington, about five thousand troops were camped on or near Sugarloaf at the time of the siege of Fort Fisher.

The engrossing historical record of the region around Carolina Beach State Park and Fort Fisher State Recreation Area, 5 miles to the south, spans more than four centuries. Before exploration and settlement of the area by Europeans, the Cape Fear Indians, of the Siouan language group, lived along the river and its tributaries. They farmed communal fields, fished the streams, and hunted the abundant game of the woodlands. The small and relatively weak tribe grew hostile to early settlers, who reportedly abused them. In 1715, the tribe participated in a general uprising against Europeans in the area; the Indians were defeated and reduced in number. The Cape Fear tribe was also victimized by other tribes, and they left their homes by 1725, never to return. Artifacts of this native culture, including pottery fragments, arrowheads, and mounds of oyster shells, have been found, primarily south of Carolina Beach.

European exploration began in 1524 when Ian Verrazano, in the service of France, visited the lower Cape Fear River area. In 1526, Lucas Vasquez de Ayllon from Santo Domingo arrived in "Florida" for the purpose of establishing a Spanish settlement. He explored the Cape Fear area but did not remain, moving farther south to Winyaw Bay. Over 150 years later, attempts at colonization were begun by the English. In 1662, Puritans from Massachusetts settled on the river near its mouth, but they soon departed, leaving a sign that advised others to stay away. A second unsuccessful English settlement, known as Clarendon County, was established in 1664 on the west side of the river by colonists from Barbados. The settlement flourished for a time but was abandoned in 1667, due in part to conflicts with the Indians.

Permanent settlement along the lower Cape Fear River was achieved in

1726 by persons who moved south from an established colony in North Carolina located between the Albemarle and Neuse rivers, along with a second group that moved north from the South Carolina colony established around the mouths of the Ashley and Cooper rivers. North Carolina acted to create New Hanover Precinct (or County) from the newly settled land. A dispute over the boundary between the North and South Carolina colonies and the jurisdiction over the lower Cape Fear region was resolved when the English king drew the line at its present location, including Cape Fear in North Carolina. Between 1735 and 1875, five new counties were formed from land originally included in New Hanover, establishing the county's present limits.

The Cape Fear River was one of five official North Carolina ports of entry designated by the English crown. The town of Brunswick was established by Maurice Moore in 1726. Located on the west bank of the river about 12 miles upstream from its mouth, opposite present-day Carolina Beach State Park, Brunswick became the center of trade for the area and, in 1729, the seat of New Hanover County. In 1733, New Town (or Newton) was begun on the river's east bank, 15 miles farther upstream. The two towns became rivals, and in 1740, after Newton was incorporated as the town of Wilmington, the county seat was moved there.

Agricultural and timber products, naval stores, and shipping and trade formed the basis of the economy of the region. The principal transportation route was the Cape Fear River; by small river craft from inland areas, Brunswick and Wilmington received goods to be shipped overseas and to other coastal ports. Sandy roads made overland travel difficult whether by horse, carriage, or stagecoach, leaving the area relatively isolated.

On occasion, events outside the region intruded upon the lives of Cape Fear people. Pirating along the Carolina coast was a common practice during colonial times. Stede Bonnet, an ally of Edward Teach (or Blackbeard), entered the lower Cape Fear River in 1718, was trapped there by two ships from South Carolina, and was later tried and hanged for his crimes. In 1748, during King George's War, Spanish privateers attacked Brunswick and inflicted damage; one of their ships was sunk in the river. In 1765, in response to imposition of a stamp tax on the colonies by the English Parliament, men of the region demonstrated against the tax in both Wilmington and Brunswick, defying British authority. During the Revolutionary War, British forces under Lord Cornwallis and Sir Henry Clinton entered the Cape Fear River. Raiding parties attacked Brunswick and burned the evacuated town, which never regained prominence and was in total ruin by 1830. In January 1781, the British occupied Wilmington, and Cornwallis made his headquarters there for a brief time that April. British forces left the city in November, following the defeat of Cornwallis at Yorktown, Virginia.

As Brunswick Town declined, the port of Wilmington assumed greater importance as a center of trade and shipping. In 1817, the first steamboat entered the Cape Fear; later, other such vessels were added, making regular runs to Southport and Fayetteville in North Carolina and, by the 1850s, Charleston in South Carolina. In 1840, the first railroad line into Wilmington was completed. The economic, cultural, and recreational development of the lower Cape Fear has continued to the present, and the region has assumed an increasingly significant role in the affairs of the state.

Cape Fear country played a significant role during the Civil War; Wilmington, a vitally important port for the Confederacy, was defended by Fort Fisher and other fortifications on the river. Some of the events of that period are discussed in the section on Fort Fisher State Recreation Area.

PLANT LIFE

Several coastal ecosystems are present within Carolina Beach State Park. Most notable are forests dominated by longleaf pine, turkey oak, and live oak, which occupy dry, coarse soil on a series of relict sand dunes. In some swales between dunes there are dense shrub swamps, called pocosins, dominated by pond and loblolly pines, sweet bay, yaupon, and evergreen shrubs. There also is a small swamp forest with a canopy of black gum and red maple. Mixed pine/oak forests dominated by loblolly pine and laurel oak occupy less elevated, more mesic uplands, while open longleaf pine/wiregrass savannas are present on drier sites. Brackish marshes dominated by cordgrass and sedges occupy the area between the uplands and the Cape Fear River.

Several small, shallow upland ponds are densely vegetated, each with an interesting and distinctive plant community. The most unusual is Cypress Pond, which is occupied by a dwarf cypress forest. In summer, Lily Pond is dominated by the broad, oval leaves and beautiful white flowers of water lilies floating on its surface. A variety of herbaceous aquatic plant species grow in Grass Pond, while carnivorous sundews and butterworts thrive in the boggy soil around its edge. These ponds generally lack inlets and outlets and are dependent upon local rainfall.

Venus' fly trap

Their origin is uncertain but appears to be related to the slumping of underground substrates, which leads to the formation of shallow, bowl-shaped depressions.

The shallow ponds, pine savannas, and pocosins provide habitat for several carnivorous plants of special interest. These plants grow in acid, mineral-poor soils, where they trap and digest small animals, mostly insects. They acquire necessary minerals and other nutrients from digested matter absorbed into their tissues.

The most familiar and spectacular carnivorous plant in the park is the Venus' fly trap. These plants die back in winter; new traps develop from underground stocks in spring and usually remain active into November. A single plant consists of a rosette of leaves; each leaf has a short blade and a trap which, like a clamshell, is bivalved. The two valves of the trap are hinged by a stiff midrib. Stiff hairs line the edge of each trap half. The interior surface of the trap is colored pale yellow to bright red, and it has three fine trigger hairs arranged in a triangular pattern; when the trigger hairs are touched, the valves of the trap close and the guard hairs mesh, entrapping the animal. The trap becomes a flattened, stomachlike pouch, and digestive fluids are secreted. After nutrients have been absorbed, usually within three to five days, the trap reopens. The natural distribution of Venus' fly traps is within a 60- to 75-mile radius of Wilmington, and their numbers are declining. Protection of their habitat is vital to their survival. Controlled burning, which discourages competing species, is beneficial to fly traps as well as other kinds of carnivorous plants; this management practice is employed at Carolina Beach State Park.

Pitcher plants are rare in the park. They are relatively large and conspicuous carnivorous plants that arise from underground stems in early spring. Their prominent leaf traps are tubular, like elongated funnels, with a hood or lid overhanging the open end. Although the hood does not close the opening, it may help prevent the dilution of the fluid contents of the tube by rainwater. The colorful hood and secretions of nectar seem to attract prey, which either crawl or fall into the trap. The smooth wax coating of the pitcher's interior allows insects to enter but prevents their escape. Animals trapped in the fluids at the base of the tube are digested. Some organisms are resistant to the digestive mixture of the pitcher; some other animals, such as spiders, snails, and small frogs, often seek cover within the plant or make a meal of prey attracted there.

Sundews, which grow along the boggy margins of ponds and other wet areas in the park, are small and often inconspicuous. Their leaves are arranged in a rosette pattern, each with a short stem and a spatula-shaped blade modified into a trap for tiny prey. Numerous bright red, stalked glands are on the upper surface of the blade; each glistens with a drop of dewlike secretion. Prey attracted to the plant and insects seeking a place to alight become mired in the sticky substance and entrapped by the stalked glands, which bend inward and hold the animal in the digestive area at the center of the trap. Sundews are highly adaptable and vigorous plants that can withstand environmental disturbances better than most other carnivorous plants. Butterworts are similar to sundews in that (unstalked) glands on the leaf surface produce a secretion that immobilizes prey until digestion can occur. Growing prostrate on the ground, their pale yellow-green leaves are flat with rolled edges. Both sundews and butterworts produce flowers on stalks that grow high above the rest of the plant; sundews have five to thirty blooms ranging from white to rose pink, whereas butterwort flowers grow singly and are blue or yellow.

ANIMAL LIFE

Carolina Beach State Park is a good place for bird-watching at all seasons. Painted buntings, common yellowthroats, and prairie warblers can be found in summer in the thickets and forest edges around the marina parking lot, and ospreys are always in Snow's Cut in summer. Brown pelicans can be seen at all seasons, and waterfowl are present along the river, and sometimes on the ponds, in winter. In addition to providing habitat for the abundant resident land birds that can be seen in summer and winter, the park, which lies along an important migration corridor, attracts many other land birds during their autumn journey southward. Northwesterly winds and the northeast-to-southwest orientation of the nearby beaches combine to concentrate migrants along North Carolina beaches in the fall, often filling the forests and thickets of the park with warblers, finches, woodpeckers, and other species in September and October. Visitors should bring binoculars and field guides for bird-watching at all seasons of the year.

Many other animals common to the lower coastal plain may be observed in the park. Gray squirrels are present, and eastern cottontails and marsh rabbits, along with an occasional Virginia opossum, gray fox, or river otter, may be encountered.

The small ponds are home to numerous frog species, including the rather uncommon gopher frog. Carolina anoles, five-lined skinks, and six-lined racerunners may be found in appropriate habitats. An alligator is sometimes seen in the marina, and a variety of snakes, including the colorful scarlet snake, inhabit the woodlands.

HIKING TRAILS

The five miles of winding trails are relatively flat and easy, allowing a leisurely pace and time to observe the diversity of habitats and organisms present. The only impediments are biting insects during warm months; hikers should come equipped with insect repellent.

Fly Trap Nature Trail is a pleasant 0.5-mile loop through pocosin, savanna, and longleaf pine/turkey oak communities. The trailhead is at a parking lot reached by a side road that turns to the left between the park office and the campground. A brochure available in the park describes the plant communities encountered along the trail. Venus' fly traps can often be seen along the edges of the pocosins; their small white flowers, which grow in a cluster at the end of a tall stalk, are usually present in May, but the plants can be found from early spring until frost. Several native orchids bloom along the trail—grass pinks and white ladies' tresses in June and white-fringed orchids in August. Part of the trail is over three short wooden boardwalks; hikers must stay on the trail to avoid damaging small and fragile plants and refrain from removing plants from this and other parks.

Sugarloaf Trail begins at the marina parking lot and is marked by yellow blazes painted on tree trunks. The first mile of the trail passes briefly through a pine forest, then follows the river's edge to Sugarloaf. En route, the trail crosses several tidal marshes on wooden boardwalks; depending on the tide, hikers may get their feet wet. Along the shoreline and in the marshes adjacent to the trail are dense growths of cordgrass, saw-grass, and black needlerush; fiddler crabs, snails, and other aquatic invertebrates live in these marshes. Visitors may also see the tracks of raccoons, gray foxes, marsh rabbits, and white-tailed deer along the shoreline. This is an excellent place for watching waterbirds. Yaupon, wax myrtle, and yucca grow along the trail, and large live oaks dominate the forest at Sugarloaf. An easy climb to the top of the dune is rewarded with a scenic view of the Cape Fear River and its adjacent marshes, islands, and shoreline. Vehicles were once allowed to drive over Sugarloaf, but they are now banned from the area. Only footprints should be visible there.

The trail continues to the left from Sugarloaf, away from the river, through a sand-ridge plant community. Cypress, Grass, and Lily ponds are located on this portion of the path and may be explored by hikers. The trail is intersected by Campground and Swamp trails near its end at the Fly Trap Nature Trail parking lot.

Campground Trail, marked with blue blazes on trees, begins at the family campground, crosses the paved road near the park office, and joins Sugarloaf Trail. **Swamp Trail**, marked by red blazes, begins and ends at points along Sugarloaf Trail (see map), providing access to two youth group camping areas.

Snow's Cut Trail leads along the edge of Snow's Cut from the family campground to the picnic area. This is fiddler crab habitat; large numbers of their burrows can be seen in the mud near the water, and "armies" of the small crustaceans forage over the mud flats.

FACILITIES AND ACTIVITIES

The **park office** is located a short distance past the entry gate; information may be obtained there or at the temporary **visitor center** near the marina and parking lot at the end of the park road. There are plans to replace the building at the marina with one that will include an office and a camp store equipped to sell refreshments and camping and boating supplies. A turnoff to the right past the access road to Fly Trap Nature Trail leads to the **family campground**. Eighty-three campsites are well-shaded beneath pine and oak trees along two loop drives; each site has a table and a grill, and drinking water is available throughout the area. Two centrally located washhouses provide lavatories, toilets, and hot showers. Most campsites will accommodate either tents or trailers; there are two dump stations for RVs, but electrical hookups are not available. A fee is charged, and sites are made available on a first-come basis. An **amphitheater** is close to the family campground. During the summer, interpretive programs are provided at the amphitheater and on hikes led by rangers. Groups may schedule special programs; requests should be made at least a week in advance.

Youth group camping areas, one on each side of Swamp Trail, are available by advance registration. A fee is charged. Equipment and supplies must be packed to the sites. The camping areas provide tables, fire circles, hand pumps, and pit toilets. Each area can accommodate a maximum of thirty-five persons. For additional information, contact the park office.

A **picnic ground** for day visitors is located near the bank of Snow's Cut between the campground and the marina. Nineteen tables and five grills are widely spaced in the shade of large oaks. Drinking water and modern restroom facilities are provided. A small parking area serves visitors to the area.

Boating and fishing are popular activities at Carolina Beach State Park. Snow's Cut provides an interesting variety of fish, including spot, flounder, sheepshead, and striped bass. Visitors may fish from the bank or from boats launched at the marina. The **marina**, situated at the confluence of Snow's Cut and the Cape Fear River, is at the terminus of the park road. There are sixty-five boatslips and two launching ramps; fuel for boats is available. The marina provides access to the river, the estuarine waters of Masonboro Sound, and the Atlantic Ocean via the mouth of the Cape Fear River or Carolina Beach Inlet. These waters may be rough at times; seaworthy boats and skill at boating in large, open tidal water are necessary.

NEARBY

Carolina Beach State Park is at the gateway to the southern beaches of New Hanover County. Within a few miles are Carolina Beach, Wilmington Beach, and Kure Beach, each with an extensive sandy shoreline for swimming, surfing, sunbathing, beachcombing, and other water-related activities. There are excellent opportunities for saltwater and freshwater fishing from surf, pier, boat ramps, and commercial boats.

Brunswick Town State Historic Site, in Brunswick County, is reached by N.C. 133 west of Wilmington. The site preserves the remains of the colonial port founded in 1726 as well as the earthen mounds of Fort Anderson, built by the Confederates at the old town site during the Civil War to help protect the approach to the port of Wilmington. A hiking trail loops through the site past the excavated foundations of many of the town's sixty dwellings and historic St. Phillips Church, then along the earthworks of the fort. Part of the trail provides a scenic view of the Cape Fear River. At the visitor center are displays of artifacts found in the ruins and interpretive exhibits that tell the history of Brunswick Town and Fort Anderson. A picnic area is provided. For more information, write: Site Manager, P.O. Box 356, Southport, N.C. 28461 (919/371-6613).

The **historic district of Wilmington** features historic churches, public and commercial buildings, and restored homes. Visitors may take walking or driving tours of the district and a river tour on the Cape Fear; several buildings, including Thalian Hall, Burgwin-Wright House, and Zebulon Latimer House, are open to the public for a fee. The USS *North Carolina* **Battleship Memorial** is located across the river from the downtown waterfront. It may be toured by the public; a fee is charged. The memorial is reached by U.S. 74/76 or by river taxi. A city park, **Greenfield Gardens**, is reached from South Third Street (U.S. 421); the 20-acre park offers playground and picnic facilities in addition to a 5-mile scenic drive and hiking trail around Greenfield Lake. The park is beautifully landscaped, primarily with azaleas, which provide a spring display of colors. For additional information, write: New Hanover Convention and Visitors Bureau, Box 266, Wilmington, N.C. 28402.

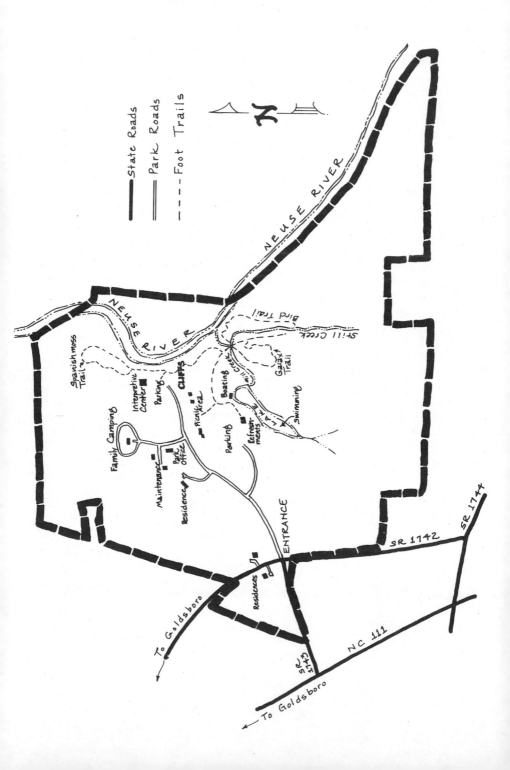

CLIFFS OF THE NEUSE STATE PARK

Address: Route 2, Box 50
            Seven Springs, N.C. 28578

Telephone: (919) 778-6234

Size: 748 acres

Established: 1945

Location: Wayne County, along the banks of the Neuse River, 14 miles
            southeast of Goldsboro on N.C. 111. The community of Seven Springs
            is nearby on N.C. 55.

Principal Attractions: Colorful 90-foot cliffs carved by the Neuse River;
            diverse plant and animal life; 11-acre lake; interpretive museum.

Visitor Activities: Nature study; fishing, swimming, and boating; family and
            group camping; picnicking.

Season: Open year-round.

River otter

The Neuse River, its banks overhung with the branches of countless trees and shrubs, flows placidly seaward through Cliffs of the Neuse State Park. Over many millions of years, the river cut its course through layers of sediment deposited by a succession of shallow seas that had earlier covered the present coastal plain. The segment of the river now included within park boundaries bent broadly against its west bank and slowly carved the Cliffs of the Neuse, a formation rising 90 feet above the water. The erosive action of the river exposed the multicolored layers of sediment that form the face of the cliffs, a time capsule in which is recorded and preserved the geological and biological history of the land. This geological treasure is protected within the park and is its principal scenic attraction.

The cliffs formation extends about 600 yards along the Neuse. A path and a rail fence follow the cliffs' edge, which is lined by oaks, dogwoods, and other trees, some with long, flowing beards of Spanish moss shielding portions of the river from view. At the lower end of the cliffs is a wooden observation deck; the view to the left is back along the cliffs, and visitors may enjoy an unobstructed look at the layered and streaked face. The forces of erosion that created the formation continue to remove the land bit by bit, as the Neuse curves against the cliffs' base and water runs down the face during periods of rain. The layers of sediment are composed of multicolored sands, sandy clays, small gravels, shale, and seashells; their colors include white, tan, yellow, and brown.

The human history of the area is inextricably bound to the river. Indians of the Tuscarora and Saponi tribes once occupied much of the land between the Neuse and Pamlico rivers, as evidenced by remnants of their villages and campsites in Wayne County and elsewhere. The present park area, known to the Indians as Sapony Hills, was a ceremonial ground and a gathering place for hunting forays. The river served as a vital avenue for travel into the Neuse wilderness. Early explorers along the Neuse were Thomas Hariot and Captain Arthur Barlowe, sent by Sir Walter Raleigh in the late sixteenth century, and John Lawson, a colonial surveyor who died at the hands of Tuscarora Indians in the early eighteenth century. Lawson reported the presence of European traders and trading cabins at Whitehall (now known as Seven Springs), which was perhaps the earliest English settlement in the area. William Whitfield II is considered the first permanent settler of Whitehall, and the cliffs area was part of a 5,000-acre grant to Whitfield by King Charles II through the Lords Proprietors. After the Revolutionary War, a stagecoach line and river traffic promoted the growth of the town. Agriculture was the principal occupation of residents.

As a navigable waterway that flows into the Pamlico Sound and hence the Atlantic Ocean, the Neuse River played a role in Civil War history. An ironclad ramming vessel, the CSS *Neuse*, was built at Whitehall as part of an effort by the Confederate navy to challenge the control of North Carolina's coastal waters by the Union. The ship ran aground in the river in 1865 and was destroyed to prevent its capture. The town itself was bombarded by Union cannons, and much of it was destroyed.

At the turn of the present century, Whitehall grew into a mecca for society; on summer weekends, hundreds of visitors lodged at Seven Springs Hotel, Ninth Springs Hotel, and other establishments to drink mineral water and take riverboat excursions to the cliffs. The seven springs, each said to produce water with a different chemical content, are located within an area of a few square feet. A gallon a day of the waters was prescribed for a long list of ills. The waters may have been more effectively used at whiskey stills along Still Creek (now within the park boundary); local sages explained that if mineral water could not cure people's ills, corn whiskey would make them forget what ailed them. The town was briefly a thriving community again, but it was damaged by fire in the early 1920s and never fully recovered.

In March 1944, Lionel Weil proposed that the cliffs area along the Neuse River be preserved as a state park. Establishment of the park came in 1945 on land on the west side of the river donated by Weil and other individuals through the Wayne Foundation. The contribution of approximately 200 acres from the Whitfield Plantation by Alonzo James and Elizabeth Whitfield Davis extended the park boundary east of the river. Additional purchases and donations of land enlarged the park to its present size.

PLANT LIFE

The flora protected within the park is abundant and highly diverse; 425 plant species in ninety-two families have been recorded there. Due in part to a variety of distinctive habitats—river margins, flood plains, rolling uplands, and ravines—an unusual mixture of trees, shrubs, and herbaceous plants is found in the park. A pine forest similar to that in the Sandhills region is adjacent to a Piedmont-type oak/hickory forest, with a cypress swamp nearby. Live oaks, characteristic of the coastal plain, grow down the slope from red oaks and Virginia pines, typical of habitats farther west.

Underscoring the biological diversity of the area is the presence of Spanish moss, which is common in eastern North Carolina but is at the western limit of its distribution at the Cliffs of the Neuse, and galax and trailing arbutus, which are most often associated with cool mountain slopes. Spanish moss is a misnomer, because the term is applied not to a moss but to a rootless flowering plant in the pineapple family. It grows draped from the limbs of cypress, oak, and other trees in the park, primarily in moist areas along or near the river and creeks. The plant is an epiphyte that directly absorbs rainwater and dew, along with minerals, through stems and leaves covered by minute scales that open when wet, giving the plant a greener appearance than at other times; nutrients come from dust that collects on its surface. Galax is a low-growing broadleafed evergreen that is abundant on well-drained slopes in the park and often forms a solid mass of green on the forest floor; small white flowers are produced in the spring and summer along slender spikes that extend 8 to 14 inches above the rootstalk. Trailing arbutus is a prostrate woody plant that in the very early spring displays beautiful, fragrant white or pink flowers along runners that creep through the forest duff.

Several different plant communities exist within the park. The most wide-spread is the mixed pine/hardwood community that is found in relatively dry upland areas and in moist, well-drained ravines. The forest canopy is mainly loblolly pine and oaks of several species; sweet gum, red maple, and beech appear in moister areas. Flowering dogwood, American holly, hickories, and various shrubs intermingle in the understory. Yellow jessamine and Japanese honeysuckle are common vines.

A deciduous hardwood community occupies bottomlands on the east side of the river opposite the cliffs, the area south of the cliffs along the river and Mill and Still creeks, and the area north of the interpretive museum along Spanish Moss Trail. Included in the forest canopy are sweet gum, red maple, black walnut, beech, hickories, and several species of oaks. Smaller trees in the understory include sourwood, sweet bay, flowering dogwood, and ironwood; common herbs are galax, partridge berry, heart leaf, and ferns.

The river-margin community found in small, narrow parcels of land that border the Neuse is characterized by the presence of bald cypress, river birch, sycamore, black willow, black gum, and red ash. Other trees are also present; species composition varies in relation to the degree to which the habitat is covered by standing water.

Typical Sandhills vegetation makes up the xeric, coarse sand community that is found on relatively high, level surfaces in the park, such as the area near the campground. The dominant trees are longleaf and loblolly pines and turkey oaks, with a scattering of oaks of other species and many different shrubs. The forest canopy is relatively open. The soil is sandy and dry.

ANIMAL LIFE

Animal life is abundant in Cliffs of the Neuse State Park. The diversity of plant communities provides many different types of habitats for animals. Birds are abundant at all seasons. Breeding species include the northern parula, which, in the coastal plain, nests only in clumps of Spanish moss, and the prothonotary warbler, which lives along the river and its tributaries. During fall and winter, mallards and other species of waterfowl augment populations of wood ducks, which nest in hollow trees along the river. The red-crested, crow-sized pileated woodpecker is a permanent resident.

Many mammals are also present, but they are not as easily observed as the birds. Visitors may see Virginia opossums, raccoons, foxes, and gray squirrels in the campground or along hiking trails, and a muskrat or river otter along the waterways. White-tailed deer are common, as are several species of small, secretive, nocturnal rodents, which are important components of the park fauna, though they are seldom seen.

The park provides habitat for many kinds of reptiles. Skinks and Carolina anoles range throughout the park, and the snapping turtle and several species of "terrapins" or "sliders" are present. Snakes encountered will most likely be nonpoisonous species, but visitors should be aware of the presence of cottonmouths in the lowlands and of copperheads throughout. Amphibians are abundant in wetland and aquatic habitats.

Great blue heron

The Neuse River and its tributaries are home to the familiar bluegill and largemouth bass, several species of catfishes, and other species that are encountered less often. White and hickory shad migrate up the Neuse through the park each spring.

HIKING TRAILS

Park trails are easy, well-marked, and accessible from the parking lot at the interpretive museum. Some sections of the trails may be muddy, especially after a rain.

Spanish Moss Trail begins at the rear (north side) of the interpretive museum and descends steeply into a ravine filled with large and beautiful hardwood trees. The 0.5-mile loop returns to the trailhead and parking lot. Short spur trails can be followed to the edge of the river.

Galax Trail and **Bird Study Trail** begin near the observation deck that overlooks the cliffs and the river. A path to the right of the deck descends 350 yards to the trailhead. After crossing a short boardwalk over Mill Creek, hikers may turn right onto Galax Trail or left onto Bird Study Trail. Galax Trail, approximately 0.5 mile in length, loops through a hardwood forest and returns; Bird Study Trail, 0.75 mile in length, passes in view of the riverbank, loops across Still Creek, and follows the stream back to Mill Creek and the trailhead. **River Trail**, a spur off Bird Study Trail, leads along the river's edge for a short distance. It is a quiet place where visitors may "wet a line" and test their fishing skills. The creeks along these trails have been important in local history; each was used in the processing of corn—a gristmill on Mill Creek ground grain into meal, while two federally operated whiskey stills on Still Creek distilled grain into moonshine.

FACILITIES AND ACTIVITIES

A spacious, well-maintained **family campground** is located in a beautifully wooded area near the **park office**. There are thirty-five tent/trailer camp-sites, each with table and grill; there are no water or electrical outlets at individual campsites, but running water is provided at several locations in the campground. There is a centrally located washhouse with hot showers and electricity. A dump station is provided. A primitive **tent camping area for youth groups** is available in an undeveloped area of the park, accessible via Spanish Moss Trail; contact the park office for additional information.

An **interpretive museum** at the northern end of the cliffs contains ex-hibits that explain geological and natural history and the history of both native American and early European inhabitants of the area. The exhibits interpret the complex forces and processes that, over vast geological time, shaped the land. An outdoor **amphitheater** is next to the interpretive museum; there, rangers offer programs to enhance knowledge of the park. Drinking water and restrooms are provided at the museum building.

Recreational activities center on an 11-acre **man-made lake**. Swimming facilities include an attractively graded, sandy beach, a diving platform, and a bathhouse. There also is a snack bar. Rowboats can be rented for use on the lake; private boats are not permitted. Fishing from the banks of the nearby Neuse River is permitted; a state fishing license is required.

Visitors may picnic in the shade of huge pines at the excellent **picnic ground** located near the lake. A hundred outdoor picnic tables and ten grills are provided; a large shelter contains an additional twelve tables and two fireplaces. Drinking water and comfort stations are on the grounds.

NEARBY

The massive, 500-ton hull of the CSS *Neuse* was excavated from the Neuse River in 1963 and is on display at a state historic site west of Kinston on U.S. 70. A visitor center tells the story of the ill-fated vessel. At the same site is the **Richard Caswell Memorial**, where the first governor of the inde-endent state of North Carolina is buried; a small museum details his military and political career.

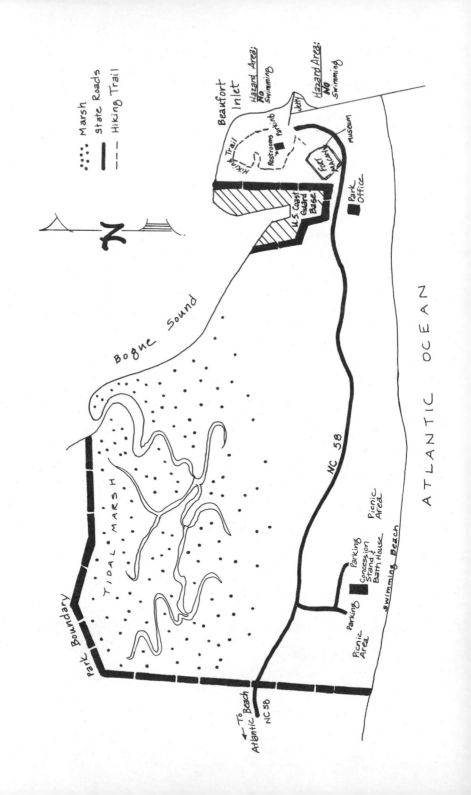

FORT MACON STATE PARK

Address: P.O. Box 127
             Atlantic Beach, N.C. 28512

Telephone: (919) 762-3775

Size: 389 acres

Established: 1924

Location: Carteret County, at Beaufort Inlet on the eastern end of Bogue
            Banks; Shackleford Banks (part of Cape Lookout National Seashore)
            and the town of Beaufort lie across the inlet from the park. To reach the
            park, turn south off U.S. 70 in Morehead City, cross the bridge over
            Bogue Sound to Atlantic Beach, and turn east on SR 1190; you may also
            follow N.C. 58, which crosses Bogue Sound at the western end of the
            island, to Atlantic Beach and SR 1190.

Principal Attractions: Restored Fort Macon; Atlantic Ocean and Beaufort
            Harbor; coastal environment.

Visitor Activities: Touring Fort Macon; fishing and swimming in the Atlantic
            Ocean; bird-watching and nature study; picnicking.

Season: Open year-round; bathhouse and refreshment stand open from June
            to Labor Day.

Aerial view of Fort Macon

Fort Macon State Park, including restored Fort Macon, was the second park to be established by the state. The fort and surrounding land were given to North Carolina by an act of Congress in 1924, and except for the brief time when it was garrisoned during World War II, the park has been a popular and significant unit of the state park system.

The park is located at the eastern end of Bogue Banks, where the fort overlooks Beaufort Inlet, the towns of Beaufort and Morehead City, and the North Carolina State Port. Bogue Banks is one of a series of barrier islands along North Carolina's coast. Barrier islands are sandy strips of land usually separated from the mainland by broad salt marshes and estuaries. Lines of dunes covered by sea oats are typically found behind the beaches of these islands; shrub thickets and occasional woodlands may be present if the land is sufficiently high and protected from salt spray. Barrier islands are often subjected to the forces of erosion and overwash, especially when northeast winds blow or severe storms or hurricanes strike from the sea.

Fort Macon State Park is unique within the park system in providing visitors opportunities both to explore a portion of the state's coastal environment and to become acquainted with a vital period in the history of the state and the nation. Visitors may experience the inshore ocean and its open beach, high barrier dunes, and rich, productive marshes and estuaries. They can also relive, in their imaginations, the experiences of soldiers garrisoned in the fort and their Civil War battle against Union forces.

In the days of small sailing ships, North Carolina inlets and sounds attracted seafarers, including pirates like Edward Teach (Blackbeard) who sought safe haven. In 1747, the Spanish attacked English colonists at Beaufort, captured the town, and held it for several days. As a result, funds were appropriated in 1748 for the construction of four forts along the coast, one of which was to be Fort Dobbs at Old Topsail (now Beaufort) Inlet. Fort Dobbs was begun in 1756 but was never completed. The harbor remained without defenses until 1808, when a small masonry structure, Fort Hampton, was built. Located about 300 yards east of the present site of Fort Macon, Fort Hampton was lost to the forces of erosion in the early 1820s.

Construction of the present Fort Macon began in 1826, and the fort was garrisoned in 1834. It was named for North Carolina Senator Nathaniel Macon, who was responsible for procuring approximately $463,700 to build the fort. A system of stone jetties was constructed in and adjacent to the inlet in the 1840s in an effort to control the continuing loss of land to erosion; Robert E. Lee engineered and supervised the project.

The fort was seized from Federal control by the state in 1861, at the beginning of the Civil War. A Confederate force of 450 men under the command of Colonel Moses James White was attacked and heavily bombarded on

April 25, 1862. After eleven hours of fighting, the fort was surrendered to Union forces. There were few casualties, and the Confederates were paroled to their homes. The fort served as a coaling station for Union ships for the duration of the war and was a Federal prison until 1876.

Fort Macon was closed on April 28, 1877, garrisoned briefly from June to September of 1898 during the Spanish-American War, and then closed again until it was turned over to the state in 1924. Reconstruction of the fort was begun during 1934 and 1935 by the Civilian Conservation Corps, and additional work was done in the 1950s. The North Carolina General Assembly appropriated $367,000 in 1974 for repairs and reconditioning. Much of the original structure of the fort has been painstakingly restored, preserving both its architecture and the record of a significant period of history.

The beautifully designed, five-sided fort is constructed of brick and stone. Enclosed by outer walls 4.5 feet thick are twenty-six vaulted rooms (or casemates); several smaller rooms that served as offices, powder magazines, storage areas, and so forth; an inner court or parade ground; and a wide moat that, formerly, could be flooded with water from Bogue Sound. Four counterfire rooms with cannon emplacements are within the outer wall. The wide covertway around the fort provides excellent views of Bogue Sound, Bogue Inlet, Shackelford Banks, the Atlantic Ocean, and the surrounding area. Entrance to the fort on the north side is by way of a plank walk across the covertway and moat and through the sally port. The arches of the sally port, as well as the doors and windows of the casemates, open onto the parade ground. Visitors reach the fort entrance by way of a short path from the parking lot. A printed guide is available at the sally port; it directs your self-guided tour of the fort and describes the uses of each of the rooms during the Civil War period.

PLANT LIFE

The dune fields adjacent to the ocean are vegetated primarily by sparse stands of sea oats. The interior of the park, including the area around the fort, is covered mostly by dense thickets of wax myrtle, yaupon, red cedar, live oak, and other small trees and shrubs. A dense tangle of greenbrier is interwoven through much of this thicket. The regularly flooded marshes along the edge of Bogue Sound are dominated by smooth cordgrass, while the less frequently flooded upland margins are covered with saltmeadow cordgrass and a variety of other grasses and sedges.

ANIMAL LIFE

Fort Macon State Park is an excellent place to be introduced to the abundant and varied animal life of the coast.

Birds are present at the beaches, the inlet, and the inshore ocean at all seasons. In summer, gulls and terns of several species may be found feeding over the rich marine waters or resting on the beaches. Many nest on nearby islands, and visitors may have an opportunity to witness the spectacular courtship flights of royal terns or to see young laughing gulls begging for food as they follow harried parents on feeding forays.

In late summer, shorebirds begin their southward migration, and beaches may be occupied by flocks of sanderlings, dunlin, and many other species. Land birds also begin moving down the barrier islands, and the thickets around the fort may be alive with warblers, sparrows, and other migrants.

Winter is also a special time to see birds at Fort Macon. In addition to witnessing the winter gulls that frequent the beach, observers may find rare northern visitors feeding along the rock jetties that guard the inlet. These jetties are one of the places that attract such regional rarities as purple sandpipers and common eiders, birds usually associated with rocky coasts farther north.

Bottle-nosed dolphins are permanent residents in the marine environment around the park and may be seen at any season. Other whales may occasionally be seen at sea from the beach, and, rarely, a loggerhead turtle may crawl ashore in June or July to lay its eggs on the beach.

Fish are abundant in the local waters, and fishing in the inlet or ocean waters may be excellent. Flounder, bluefish, spot, croaker, sheepshead, and whiting are commonly sought during summer and fall.

A visitor may encounter many interesting invertebrates by exploring the base of the jetty at low tide or by walking the beach and searching for mollusc shells washed up by the last storm. Sea urchins, corals, and sea stars may be observed on or under jetty rocks or other objects in shallow water. Ghost crabs venture from their burrows in the beach sand at night or late in the day but scurry to cover when disturbed.

Although most people spend their time at Fort Macon on the beach or at the fort itself, a walk along the marsh edge on the backside of the island can reveal many interesting animals that may be unknown to visitors from inland regions. Visitors may encounter clapper rails, several species of herons and egrets, and other marsh birds. In summer, diamond-backed terrapins, the only reptiles to regularly inhabit estuarine waters along our coast, may be seen in the tidal creeks. At low tide, oysters may be observed growing along the edges of these creeks, and with perseverance and the dexterous use of fingers and toes, visitors may be able to locate beds of clams in a muddy creek bottom. These are good examples of the rich, regularly flooded salt marshes that are vital to coastal ecosystems. They are veritable food factories for marine organisms, and they serve as nurseries for many important marine animals like the economically valuable shrimp, crabs, shellfish, and finfish that may be sampled at nearby seafood restaurants.

HIKING TRAIL

The **Elliott Coues Nature Trail** is an easy 0.4-mile loop that winds through a dense shrub thicket and over low sand dunes to the edge of Beaufort Inlet. The trail begins on the right side of the entrance into Fort Macon and ends at the parking lot. Some trees and shrubs along the trail are live oak, yaupon, cedar, beach holly, and black locust. Elliott Coues was an ornithologist, historian, and scientist who served as physician at Fort Macon in 1869 and 1870; he published numerous articles describing the flora and fauna of the area.

FACILITIES AND ACTIVITIES

A side road immediately past the park entrance leads to the picnic grounds, bathhouse, and public beach. The **bathhouse** is located between two large, paved parking lots behind the frontal dunes bordering the beach. Restrooms are at ground level; steps lead up to a large, open pavilion, where visitors may relax in the shade and enjoy an excellent view of the ocean and the sand dunes. Dressing rooms and showers are provided for a fee. Cold drinks and snacks may be purchased at the **refreshment stand**. A boardwalk leads from the bathhouse area to the oceanfront dunes, from which there is access to the protected **public beach**, where swimming, sunbathing, and surf fishing may be enjoyed. These facilities are open from June 1 through Labor Day. The two **picnic grounds** are also near the bathhouse, one on the far side of each

Interior of Fort Macon

parking lot. There are sixteen shelters with thirty tables and four grills; drinking water and rinse-off showers are provided. The beach is accessible from each picnic area.

Within Fort Macon itself, casemates 2 through 5 now serve as an **interpretive center** for park visitors. A **bookstore** has for sale an extensive selection of books on the Civil War and North Carolina history, as well as on topics pertaining to the natural history of the coast. A **museum** interprets the history of Fort Macon and the Civil War by means of displays, exhibits of artifacts, and a narrated slide program. Casemate 4 is a restoration of typical living quarters of enlisted men. Furnishings, artifacts, and a taped narration provide insight into the daily life of soldiers garrisoned at the fort. Similarly, casemate 5 is a restoration of the private quarters of Colonel White, commandant of Fort Macon from 1861 until its surrender in 1862; a recording describes his wartime experiences.

There is no campground within the park. Several commercial campgrounds are located along N.C. 58 on Bogue Banks.

NEARBY

Beaufort, settled in 1708, is the third oldest town in the state. Its early history included use of its harbor by pirates and an attack by Spanish privateers. The historic district of the town features examples of eighteenth-century coastal architecture and an interesting colonial cemetery. The waterfront was recently restored, and vessels of many types anchor in the harbor and moor along the town docks. The **North Carolina Maritime Museum** and its **Watercraft Center** (a branch of the North Carolina Museum of Natural Sciences) are located on the waterfront in Beaufort. The museum offers exhibits and programs that reflect the themes of maritime history and coastal natural history.

On Piver's Island, between Beaufort and Morehead City, are located the **United States National Marine Fisheries Service Laboratory**, the **University of North Carolina Institute of Marine Science**, and **Duke University Marine Laboratory**.

Cape Lookout National Seashore includes Shackleford and Core banks and Portsmouth Island; access is via ferry or boat from Harkers Island.

Theodore Roosevelt State Natural Area, a 265-acre preserve, is the site of the **North Carolina Aquarium at Pine Knoll Shores**; it is located 7 miles west of Atlantic Beach.

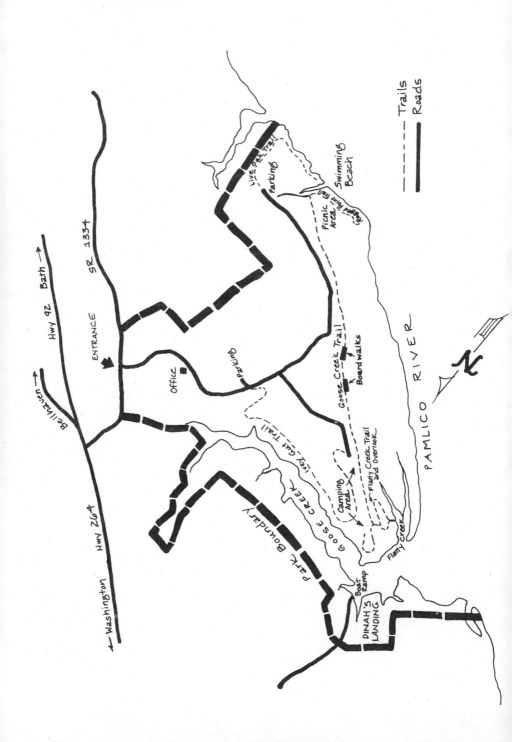

GOOSE CREEK STATE PARK

Pamlico River from Live Oak Trail

Address: Route 2, Box 372
             Washington, N.C. 27889

Telephone: (919) 923-2191

Size: 1,327 acres

Established: 1974

Location: Beaufort County, on the north side of the Pamlico River; from
Washington, North Carolina, follow U.S. 264 for 10 miles, then turn
onto SR 1334 for 2.5 miles to the park entrance. The historic town of
Bath is 6 miles to the east of the park on N.C. 92.

Principal Attractions: Pamlico River and a major tributary, Goose Creek,
with approximately 9 miles of combined shoreline; varied plant communities, with large oaks, cypresses, and pines draped in Spanish moss.

Visitor Activities: Picnicking, swimming at protected beach, boating, fishing, hiking, nature study, and primitive camping.

Season: Open year-round.

The southern boundary of Goose Creek State Park lies along the Pamlico
River in an area of sandy beaches, rich marshlands, and, behind them, evergreen shrub bogs and hardwood swamp forests. Goose Creek, broad and
slow-moving, joins the river at the western edge of the park; the creek's
banks are lined by a dense growth of tall, overhanging trees that reflect

dramatically from the water's surface. Graceful waterbirds frequently patrol the shoreline of the creek, and occasional fishing boats move downstream, their occupants intent upon casting baited lines into shaded nooks. Shrub thickets, swamp forests, and the pine forests on higher ground collectively form a natural garden with diverse and distinctive species of plants. In Goose Creek State Park, rich rewards come from hiking the trails, experiencing the bogs and swamps, and discovering the creatures that make them their homes.

The park is located in a rural, sparsely populated region of the coastal plain that, prior to settlement by Europeans, was occupied by Secotan and Pamlico Indians. The Tuscarora tribe was the dominant Indian power in eastern North Carolina during the colonial period, and serious conflicts arose between Tuscaroras and white settlers along the Pamlico, Neuse, and Trent rivers in 1711. Early explorers of the area around the Pamlico River were Captain Thomas Blount, who on May 21, 1701, came ashore at Ragged Point, now within park boundaries, and John Lawson, surveyor general for the colony in the early eighteenth century, who resided for a time in Bath. Land that Lawson owned in the vicinity of Goose Creek may now be included in the park. Other well-known inhabitants of Bath were several royal governors, including Charles Eden, and the notorious pirate Blackbeard.

The recent history of the Goose Creek area has centered around subsistence farming, timber production, and commercial fishing in the Pamlico River. Evidence of these activities includes abandoned fields now returned to forestland, remnants of old loading docks and piers along the river, and a railroad bed, now trackless, along which logs were hauled shortly after the turn of the century. Logging soon came to be the principal industry in the area; operations begun by the Eureka Lumber Company were taken over by the Weyerhaeuser Corporation, which acquired extensive acreage around Goose Creek, including most of the land that ultimately became parkland.

The initiative for the establishment of a state park along the Pamlico River came from local citizens. At their request, the North Carolina Division of State Parks investigated potential park sites in 1969 and 1970 and determined that the Goose Creek area was the most suitable. Negotiations with the Weyerhaeuser Corporation resulted in a park plan approved by the North Carolina Conservation and Development Board on May 13, 1972. Local support for the plan was expressed in a resolution addressed to Governor Robert Scott and adopted on October 18, 1972, by the Southern Albemarle Association, which represented the six-county region around the proposed park site. Goose Creek State Park was officially established on September 25, 1974; 1,208 acres of land were purchased from Weyerhaeuser at a cost of $1,115,000.

PLANT LIFE

Brackish marshes adjacent to the Pamlico River and its tributaries contribute significantly to the scenic beauty of the park. The soil in these low-lying areas is waterlogged, and the water is slightly saline. The dominant species in this community are large grasses and sedges, such as saw-grass and black needlerush, which may grow to 8 feet. These plants produce a food supply for waterfowl and other birds. Evergreen shrubs, such as wax myrtle, red bay, and groundsel tree, and small bald cypress, red cedar, and loblolly bay trees grow along ecotones between marsh and swamp or on slightly elevated hummocks. Many wildflowers add color along the waterways; the pink blossoms of seashore mallow appear on summer mornings, and the blooms of rose mallow, morning glory, cardinal flower, and climbing hempweed may be seen in late summer.

Evergreen shrub thickets in low, boggy, freshwater areas of the park are characterized by dense growths of woody plants. Within the thick understory of this community is an abundance of wax myrtle, along with gallberry, groundsel tree, red bay, and sparkleberry. The density of the shrub growth is enhanced by a tangle of greenbriers. The canopy, or overstory, is formed by loblolly bay, which may reach up to 40 feet in height, and by black and tupelo gums, red maple, sweet gum, and bald cypress. The diverse herbaceous flora in the bogs includes marsh pennywort, arrowheads, and ferns.

Swamp forests occur in the interior lowlands and along those stretches of the creeks where there is fresh water. Cypress is relatively abundant along Goose and Mallard creeks. Tupelo gum and red maple mix with cypress along the swamps' edges, and large loblolly bays and shrubby black willows are present in their interior. Spanish moss hangs profusely from much of the vegetation throughout the park but is especially abundant here.

Loblolly pines dominate the upland regions of the park. In areas not recently disturbed by logging or agriculture, impressive specimens standing 100 feet or more are present. In the shade beneath the pines, a diversity of hardwoods— mockernut hickory, sweet gum, and live, water, white, and southern red oaks—form a secondary canopy about 30 to 50 feet aboveground. These hardwoods will ultimately replace the pines through the process of natural succession. Many shade-tolerant shrubs, including red bay, wax myrtle, flowering dogwood, sweet pepperbush, and beautyberry, thrive beneath the hardwoods. Bracken ferns, pipsissewa, and a host of other species grow on the forest floor.

ANIMAL LIFE

The animal life in the park varies dramatically with the seasons. Nearby Pamlico Sound is a major wintering area for waterfowl. Ducks, including

White-tailed deer, buck

bufflehead, scaup, and canvasback, may often be seen in the open water adjacent to the park; tundra swans and Canada geese may also be present. Black ducks, mallards, wood ducks, and other dabbling ducks frequently inhabit the creeks and flooded swamps.

Fish are abundant in the Pamlico River and its tributaries, and fishing success may be good during the warmer months of the year. Game species present include largemouth bass, bluegill, and white and yellow perch.

Brackish marshes are home to marsh wrens, rails, and several species of herons and egrets. Mink, raccoons, muskrats, and river otters live there, and water snakes are present even though the water is slightly saline.

Wooded swamps and shrub thickets provide excellent habitat for wildlife. Some species of birds, such as pileated and red-headed woodpeckers, barred owls, red-shouldered hawks, and wood ducks, are year-round residents, but mallards are present mainly in winter. A host of summer residents arrive from the south to nest in spring; breeding birds include prothonotary and parula warblers, red-eyed and yellow-throated vireos, and blue-gray gnatcatchers.

The swamps are also home to gray squirrels, raccoons, Virginia opossums, and white-tailed deer, which find abundant food and protective cover throughout the park. Marsh rabbits are present in the marshes and swamps, while eastern cottontails occupy drier uplands. The tracks of elusive bobcats and gray foxes provide evidence of their presence in the area. Numerous salamanders, frogs, turtles, and snakes, including the cottonmouth, are common in the wetlands of the park.

Upland forests provide habitat for animals typical of the coastal plain. The presence of the endangered red-cockaded woodpecker in mature pine trees within the park is of special interest. A detailed discussion of this rare bird is included in the chapter on Weymouth Woods/Sandhills State Nature Preserve.

HIKING TRAILS

Hikers may experience most areas of the park by way of 6.9 miles of winding, well-marked trails. Hikers should have sturdy footwear that can withstand getting wet and a supply of insect repellent in the warmer months. A path from the parking area at the end of the main park road leads to the picnicking and swimming area on the Pamlico River. The trailheads for Live Oak Trail, Ragged Point Trail, and Goose Creek Trail are located there.

Live Oak Trail, at 1.2 miles, is perhaps the most scenic trail in the park. It begins at the east side of the beach, passes large, spreading live oak trees draped in Spanish moss, and then follows the riverbank with its sandy shoreline and a view across the broad expanse of water flowing slowly toward Pamlico Sound and the sea. Near the park boundary on the east, the trail turns left and passes through forests of hardwoods and pine before ending at the parking area.

Ragged Point Trail, at 0.25 mile, begins near the picnic area; a boardwalk over marshland leads to an elevated wooden observation deck that affords a view of the marsh and Pamlico River. As a sign along the trail states, "Violent storms have given this area a ragged appearance. Salt water killed most of the cypress that grew on this point. The result is a changing landscape of ghostly snags and vegetation adapted to slightly brackish water. The trail passes through zones where different habitats meet—forest, thickets, marshes, and the Pamlico River."

The trailhead for **Goose Creek Trail** is on the path between the picnic area and the beach; the one-way trail leads west for 2.9 miles to the tip of the peninsula at Goose Creek through swamp forest and shrub thicket. Two boardwalks at 1.4 miles carry hikers over small streams and swampland, beyond which the trail continues past the entrance to the camping area. A junction with **Flatty Creek Trail** is reached at 2.3 miles; this is a side loop trail 0.7 mile in length that leads to a short boardwalk over the marsh and an elevated wooden observation deck. The view from the deck is of beautiful, serene Flatty Creek, which enters Goose Creek near its mouth, and the adjacent marshland community. Goose Creek Trail continues to the east bank of Goose Creek at a point opposite Dinah's Landing, where boats may be launched. The bluff overlooking the calm waters of the creek is a peaceful, remote spot. Hikers may retrace their steps to the swimming beach, arrange to be picked up at the campground parking area, or hike via Ivey Gut Trail to the main park road.

Ivey Gut Trail, at 2.1 miles, extends one-way from the campground to the main park road, where cars may be parked in a clearing in the woods. The trail leads through the swamp forest adjacent to the east bank of Goose Creek; excellent views of the creek appear through the trees and at turnoffs. The vegetation is often dense, and ground duff is thick; watch carefully for trail blazes.

FACILITIES AND ACTIVITIES

An attractive **park office** building is located a short distance past the entry gate. Information is available there, and rangers will interpret natural features of the park for visitors. The paved road continues to parking areas near the picnic ground.

The **picnic ground** is in a pine/oak forest and is equipped with running water, grills, and twenty tables; restrooms are nearby. A short path leads to the protected **beach** along the shore of the Pamlico River; swimming is restricted to this area. There are additional picnic tables at the beach.

A primitive **family campground** is located in a heavily wooded area near Goose Creek and is reached by way of an unpaved side road to the right between the park office and the picnic area. There are twelve tent sites, each with a table and a grill. Pit toilets and a manually operated water pump are provided. A fee is charged for camping privileges. The campground is a quiet, isolated site for those wishing a true outdoor experience.

Goose Creek State Park provides excellent opportunities for **canoeing, boating**, and **fishing**. The unhurried creeks are ideal for canoeists; visitors must bring their own canoes, as none are available for rent in the area. Powerboats are allowed in the river, and a boat ramp is located at Dinah's Landing on the west side of Goose Creek, an area accessible from outside the park; no launch fee is charged. Visitors may fish in both the creeks and the river, in accordance with North Carolina fishing regulations. Both freshwater and saltwater fish may be caught in these waters, and fishing is generally excellent.

NEARBY

Historic Bath, now a state historic site, was founded in 1705 and is the state's oldest incorporated town. It is located on the bank of Bath (Old Town) Creek, where it is joined by Back (Adam's) Creek before flowing into Pamlico River. The site began attracting French and English settlers in the 1690s. John Lawson, explorer and surveyor general to the crown, designed and laid out the town and was one of several prominent early residents. Bath was the seat of government for three proprietary governors and a base of operations for the pirate Blackbeard. Its long and colorful history is summarized in *Bath*

Town, a beautifully illustrated guide booklet available at the site. Preservation of the town's historic district was begun in the late 1950s by the Beaufort County Historical Society and the Historic Bath Commission. Today, the walking tour that begins at a visitor center includes five restored buildings, one of them St. Thomas Episcopal Church. Built in 1734, it is the oldest church in the state still in use. The outdoor drama *Blackbeard, Knight of the Black Flag* is presented during the summer. For information, write: Historic Bath State Historic Site, P.O. Box 124, Bath, N.C. 27808.

Historic Washington was founded by James Bonner in the 1770s on his farmland on the banks of the Pamlico and Tar rivers. In 1776, it became the first town to be named for the Revolutionary War general and first president of the new nation. The town has had an interesting history, especially during the Civil War period. Its historic district, listed in the National Register of Historic Places, is distinguished by a variety of architectural styles. A 1.9-mile historic walking tour includes twenty-three sites. It begins at the Old Seaboard Coastline Railroad Depot at Main and Gladden streets. For information, write: Historic Washington, P.O. Box 1988, Washington, N.C. 27889.

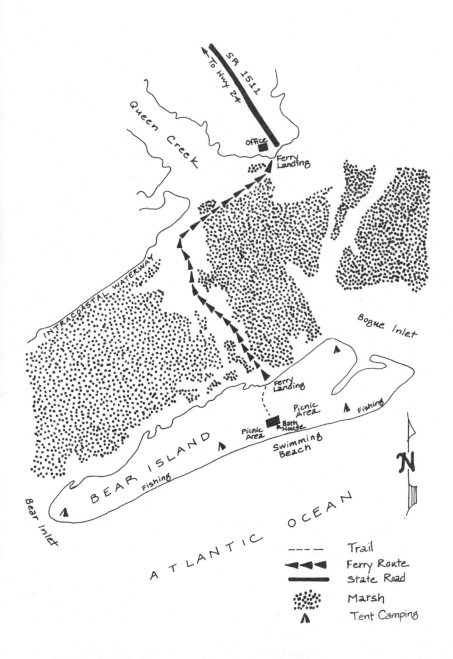

To Hwy 24

SR 1511

Queen Creek

Office

Ferry Landing

INTRACOASTAL WATERWAY

Bogue Inlet

Ferry Landing

Picnic Area

Picnic Area

Bath House

Swimming Beach

Fishing

BEAR ISLAND

Fishing

Bear Inlet

ATLANTIC OCEAN

N

- - - - Trail

◀◀◀ Ferry Route

━━━ State Road

Marsh

∧ Tent Camping

HAMMOCKS BEACH STATE PARK

Address: Route 2, Box 295
             Swansboro, N.C. 28584

Telephone: (919) 326-4881

Size: 892 acres on Bear Island; 35 acres on mainland

Established: 1961

Location: Onslow County, between Jacksonville and Morehead City; on east side of Swansboro, turn west off N.C. 24 onto SR 1511 and proceed 2.1 miles to parking lot and ferry landing. Bear Island is reached via a 2.5-mile ride on a passenger ferry available daily June 1 through Labor Day and weekends in May and September, or year-round by private boat.

Principal Attractions: Atlantic Ocean and barrier island with unspoiled beach, high dunes, maritime forests, salt marshes, and tidal creeks; varied and abundant marine life. The site is a national natural landmark.

Visitor Activities: Swimming at protected beach; sunbathing, walking, and bird-watching along 3.5 miles of oceanfront; surf fishing; photography and nature study; picnicking; primitive camping among sand dunes.

Season: Open year-round, though most facilities and services close in winter.

Visitors to Hammocks Beach State Park carry away vivid and lasting memories—sunlight reflected from the surface of a restless sea and countless waves crashing on the wide, windswept beach; graceful sea oats with long, slender stalks bending in gentle breezes on tops of rounded dunes of white sand; shorebirds with long, matchstick legs racing to and fro with the waves and probing the wet sand for a hurried meal; a distant, solitary figure patiently casting a baited hook beyond the rows of foaming breakers; and the distinctive smells, sights, and sounds of salt marshes and shallow tidal pools, with their countless tiny creatures and acres of high grasses that color the area brilliant shades of green and gold. Images such as these are the dividends earned on the investment of time by persons who venture to this special place.

Except for a 35-acre parcel of land on the mainland near Swansboro, the park occupies Bear Island, 892 acres in size and one of the chain of barrier islands that extends along the Atlantic coast from New Jersey to Florida. The

Salt marsh behind Bear Island

island is more than 3.5 miles in length and about 0.75 mile in width; it is bordered to the southeast by the Atlantic Ocean and to the northwest by extensive salt marshes, tidal estuarine creeks, and the Atlantic Intracoastal Waterway, which separate the island from the mainland. At the northeast end of Bear Island are Bogue Inlet and, beyond, Bogue Banks; to the southwest are Bear Inlet and, beyond, Browns Island.

Undeveloped Bear Island retains a wilderness quality and illustrates the dynamic natural forces that shape barrier islands. Distinctive vegetational zones include oceanfront dunes with sea oats and other grasses; flats among the dunes covered by grasses and shrub thickets; maritime forests of live oak, red cedar, and pines; and broad salt marshes. Because overwash has not occurred here in recent years, large dunes and sand ridges are present. Some of them tend to migrate gradually over portions of the maritime forests. Bear Island is a place of tranquility and relative isolation, free from the commercial pressures common along many other areas of the North Carolina coast.

The human history of Bear Island is as relevant to an appreciation of the park as is its natural history. Woodland Indians in dugout canoes used the vast coastal waterways as avenues of travel between the islands in the area and the mainland. Although the sandy soil of Bear Island was not suitable for growing crops, the Indians obtained an abundance of food by fishing, by gathering shellfish, fruits, and berries, and by hunting deer, bear, birds, and other animals.

The three Indian language groups along coastal North Carolina were the Algonkian, Siouan, and Iroquoian. The area on and around Bear Island was inhabited by the Neusick (or Neuse) Indians, an Algonkian tribe with a village at the mouth of White Oak Creek opposite Bogue Inlet, and by the Coree Indians, an Iroquoian tribe. Both groups participated in the Tuscarora wars of 1711 and 1713 against colonists in the region, and they continued guerrilla-type hostilities from hideouts around the island until the middle of the eighteenth century, when they joined the Tuscaroras in a northward migration.

The island was identified as Bear (or Bare) Banks in colonial records as early as 1713, when Tobias Knight, secretary to Royal Governor Charles Eden, acquired a land patent for the property. Eden and Knight are best remembered for their alleged dealings with notorious pirates Blackbeard and Stede Bonnet. They protected the pirates for a price and granted them pardons for crimes in 1718. The inlets along the North Carolina coast, including Bogue and Bear inlets, and the shallow waterways behind the barrier islands provided havens from which pirates could prey upon merchant vessels and in which they could hide and repair damage to their ships.

Spanish privateers also created problems for colonists in the area. In the 1740s, ships from Florida roamed north along the coast and made attacks in the vicinity of Bogue Inlet, Bear Inlet, Ocracoke Inlet, Core Sound, the Cape Fear River, and elsewhere, killing several people, burning ships and buildings, and carrying off slaves. Several forts were subsequently built for protection, including one on Bear Island in 1749; it has since disappeared.

Until the late eighteenth century, the island was owned by John Starkey, a prominent citizen of Onslow County who held important state and colonial governmental offices. A whaler from Core Banks, Captain Daniel Heady, acquired the island early in the nineteenth century, and it remained in his family for four generations. During that period, whales beached onshore and porpoises caught off the island were processed to obtain oil from their blubber and to make a variety of other commodities.

During the Civil War, Bear Island and White Oak River were on the boundary between Confederate forces positioned at Jacksonville and Wilmington and Union forces occupying Bogue Banks and New Bern. Confederate pickets were placed on Bear Island opposite a small fort at the entrance to Bogue Inlet; the fort was evacuated and destroyed in 1862. A Union gunboat entered Bear Inlet in March 1864, burned a vessel, and rescued slaves hiding on the island. Nearly a century later, during World War II, the island again assumed military importance; a Coast Guard station was located there to help maintain the security of the coast and to monitor German U-boat activity offshore.

Dr. William Sharpe of New York, a pioneer in neurosurgery, visited the area to hunt ducks and geese early this century and acquired Bear Island as a place for retirement. He planned to will the property to John Hurst, his longtime boatman, guide, and friend, but Hurst persuaded him to donate the island to the North Carolina Teachers Association, an organization of black teachers, as a summer retreat. The property was deeded to the group in 1950, and the Hammocks Beach Corporation was founded for the purpose of development; in 1961, however, due to limitation of funds and to the island's inaccessibility, the group donated the island to the state of North Carolina for a park. Hammocks Beach State Park was initially planned for use by black citizens, but subsequent to the Civil Rights Act of 1964 it was opened to all citizens.

PLANT LIFE

The open, sandy beach is bordered by tall sand dunes, most of which are vegetated by sea oats and American beachgrass. Behind the dunes are large sheets of sand that may be relatively flat and covered by a mixture of grasses and forbs, such as saltmeadow cordgrass and seaside goldenrod, or occupied by large, unstable dune fields as high as 60 feet that are either devoid of plants or vegetated by sea oats and other scattered forbs.

Small units of maritime forest occur at each end of the island, where loblolly pine, red cedar, and live, laurel, and water oaks are found along with red maple and red bay. Yaupon and flowering dogwood are important understory species. Facing the ocean, these forests have characteristic sheared canopies, shaped by salt spray brought in by onshore winds. Salt droplets carried on the wind are deposited on leaves and twigs, causing the death of buds facing the sea.

Shrub thickets have developed on other sites that offer adequate protection from wind and salt spray. These thickets are usually dominated by such species as wax myrtle, yaupon, and red cedar. Dense tangles of poison ivy, Virginia creeper, Smilax, and other vines sometimes make these thickets nearly impenetrable.

Grasslands and thickets on the northwest side of the island grade into marshes. Upper portions of the marsh where flooding is infrequent are dominated by saltmeadow cordgrass and black needlerush, whereas the portions of the marsh that are flooded regularly are dominated almost completely by smooth cordgrass. Visitors pass through large stands of smooth cordgrass as they ferry from the mainland to the island.

ANIMAL LIFE

The fauna of barrier islands is usually limited with regard to species associated with freshwater habitats. This is especially true at Bear Island, where there is no permanent source of fresh water. Amphibians are few in number. Although Carolina and squirrel treefrogs live most of the year in the thickets and forests, they breed in rain pools in spring and summer.

Terrestrial reptiles are also relatively uncommon, but anoles, glass lizards, and several species of snakes, including the canebrake rattlesnake, may be encountered.

Two species of turtles are of special interest. The diamondback terrapin, whose dorsal shell (or carapace) may measure up to 9 inches in length, lives in estuarine environments and is found in tidal creeks between the island and the mainland. Loggerhead sea turtles nest on the island beach in summer. Female loggerheads come ashore under cover of darkness between mid-May and late August to nest above the high-tide line on the beach strand. Contrary to legend, females will come ashore any time during the nesting season, not just on a full moon. Females nest every three or four years, laying up to six nests a year at approximately two-week intervals. Their pear-shaped nests are 10 to 20 inches deep and usually contain about 120 eggs similar in size and shape to Ping-Pong balls. After about two months of incubation, the hatchling turtles emerge from the nest cavity at night and race toward the sea. Hatchlings that reach the sea swim out to the Gulf Stream, where they remain for fifteen to twenty years until they reach maturity. Loggerheads can live seventy or eighty years, at which time males might weigh 400 pounds; most nesting females, by contrast, weigh 150 to 250 pounds. Turtles are subjected to predation throughout their lives. Eggs are dug from nests by raccoons, foxes, and other animals; hatchlings are taken in large numbers by ghost crabs and other nocturnal animals that feed on the beach. Many sea-dwelling predators prey upon young turtles in the ocean, and adult populations have been adversely affected by humans.

Loggerhead sea turtles are included on the federal list of endangered and threatened species; they were designated as threatened in 1978. Persons who

Loggerhead turtle at nesting site

disturb or harm adults, nests, or hatchlings are subject to severe legal penalty. Activities on the beach at night during the nesting season are regulated, and camping is not permitted during peak egg-laying periods. Inquire at the park office for more specific information.

Mammal life on Bear Island is not abundant, but house mice live in the dunes, and eastern cottontails, gray foxes, raccoons, and white-tailed deer are encountered occasionally. Bottle-nosed dolphins are frequently seen offshore. Several other species of whales are reported on rare occasions.

Birds are the most abundant vertebrates on the island. Laughing gulls are common along the beaches in summer, and least, royal, common, and gull-billed terns are often present. Willets and American oystercatchers nest in the grasslands and feed along the beaches, and brown pelicans feed offshore at all seasons. There is usually a heavy migration of birds along the coast in fall, and thickets and forests may be alive with transient warblers, thrushes, sparrows, and hawks from August to October. During both spring and fall, shorebirds rest on the beaches and feed in the tidal marshes on their journey between winter and summer homes. Herons and egrets feed along tidal creeks, and ospreys may be seen plunging for fish or feeding on elevated snags. Clapper rails, more often heard than seen, are abundant in the marshes.

In contrast to the paucity of freshwater habitats for animals on Bear Island is the abundance of estuarine and marine environments that surrounds it. Visitors can fish in the surf and inlets for bluefish, Virginia mullet, and puppy drum or in tidal creeks and the Intracoastal Waterway for spot, croaker, and flounder. Fishermen who camp on the island can cast their lines in relative solitude on the beach, in the soft, golden light of dusk and dawn.

Strollers on the beach are likely to find the empty shells of many species of marine molluscs, cast up by the action of waves and tides, and the burrows from which elusive ghost crabs scurry briefly to feed. A dinner of blue crabs can be caught from tidal creeks, or, on low tide, visitors can search for oysters and clams on the mud flats. An excursion about the island may become a rich educational experience, as an abundance of interesting marine invertebrates is there to be discovered. A little digging in the intertidal zone may uncover various crustaceans, polychaete worms, and molluscs living just beneath the surface of sand and mud. Adventuresome explorers who don't mind a little mud on their shoes may find live conchs, mussels, sea stars, crabs, and a host of other marine life exposed at low tide.

FACILITIES AND ACTIVITIES

From Swansboro, SR 1511 leads to the Hammocks Beach State Park entrance and 35 acres of parkland on the Intracoastal Waterway adjacent to Queen Creek. A large paved parking lot accommodates both cars and boat trailers. The **park office** and **ferry dock**, as well as a ramp for launching private boats, are located there; use of the ramp is restricted, and visitors must check with the ranger on duty. A shelter with benches and restrooms is provided.

Two pontoon ferries with canvas covers provide free transportation to Bear Island. Each boat can accommodate up to thirty-six passengers. A pier leads visitors to steps for boarding the vessels. The ferries operate daily except during inclement weather from June 1 through Labor Day and on weekends in May and September. The schedule is from 9:30 A.M. to 6:00 P.M.; a boat embarks each hour on Monday and Tuesday and each half hour Wednesday through Sunday. On peak visitation days during summer months, it may be necessary to wait in line for a considerable time, and it is wise to arrive early in the day. Private boats may be used to reach the island, where they may be beached onshore or tied at the island dock when ferries are not operating; docking space is limited.

The 2.5-mile, twenty-five-minute ferry ride to Bear Island is a pleasant experience. The route is southwest along the Intracoastal Waterway, then southeast through the shallow water of Cow Channel. The channel, along which cows were once herded to the island to graze, passes through an expanse of salt marsh; graceful wading birds either flying or feeding along creek edges, clumps of oysters exposed at low tide, and other inhabitants of the wetland environment are often observed along the way. The profile of the island as it is seen from the ferries is one of low-growing vegetation and prominent sand dunes.

Passengers disembark onto a pier that leads to a shelter, which has benches but no restrooms or drinking water, and to the head of a 0.5-mile trail that crosses the island to the beach. The trail passes through deep sand that is usually quite hot on a summer day; visitors are advised to wear comfortable shoes for this fifteen-minute walk among the dunes. Hikers pass a building that serves as an **interpretive center** and a barracks for workers on the island. The trail ends near the ocean at the bathhouse.

The **bathhouse** is a large structure elevated on pilings behind the frontal dunes that parallel the beach. Restrooms and showers, available to picnickers, swimmers, campers, and other park visitors, are below the building. Steps lead to a spacious upper level that is open at each end, allowing a flow of cool ocean breeze; the changing rooms, showers, and restrooms on the upper level are available for a fee. A **refreshment stand** offers cold drinks and snacks. An open deck with benches and a scenic view extends toward the ocean. A naturalist is on hand to interpret the cultural and natural history of the island during summer months.

A path across the dunes leads to a protected section of the beach, marked by prominent signs, which is reserved for swimming and sunbathing. A life-guard is on duty during the summer, and swimming outside this area is prohibited. Visitors may walk along the beach and fish in the surf. There are no established trails, but hikers may explore the dunes and the interdunal flats as well as the edges of inlets, lagoons, and tidal creeks. A stroll to Bogue Inlet is an especially rewarding experience; extensively developed commercial property can be seen across the inlet on Bogue Banks, and park visitors can appreciate anew the wisdom of the state in preserving such special places of unspoiled natural beauty as Bear Island.

Picnic areas are located behind the frontal dunes on either side of the bathhouse. There are a total of six picnic shelters, each with tables and grills.

Primitive **camping** on the island is restricted to numbered sites that provide space to pitch tents among sand dunes near the beach and the inlets. Campers must obtain permits at the park office before going to the island; a fee is charged. Family campsites can accommodate up to six persons each; twelve sites are northeast of the bathhouse, along the beach and Bogue Inlet, and two additional sites are southwest at Bear Inlet. Three group campsites, each of which can accommodate up to twenty persons, are located between the bathhouse and Bear Inlet. Advance reservation for group campsites is necessary and can be made by writing or telephoning the park office. Drinking water is available during summer months, and restrooms and cold showers are available to campers at the bathhouse. Use of these facilities requires a hike of a half mile to over a mile, depending on the location of the site. No fires are permitted, and campers must remove all trash from their sites when leaving the area. The island is closed to camping at specified times during June, July, and August to minimize disturbance of nesting loggerhead turtles; inquire at the park office.

NEARBY

Croatan National Forest encompasses 155,000 acres in Carteret, Jones, and Craven counties. It is bounded by the Neuse, Trent, Newport, and White Oak rivers and, to the south, by Bogue Sound and the Atlantic Ocean. The area is part pine timberland and part pocosin or evergreen shrub bog. Five major spring-fed shallow-water lakes within the national forest range in size from 500 to 2,600 acres. Recreational activities in the forest include hunting, fishing, boating, swimming, picnicking, camping, and hiking. More than 22 miles of hiking trails are maintained by the National Forest Service, and visitor facilities are provided at the Neuse River, Cedar Point, Fisher Landing, and Flanner's Beach recreation areas. The national forest provides habitat for a rich diversity of plants and for many kinds of wildlife. For information and maps, write: District Ranger, Croatan National Forest, 435 Thurmond Road, New Bern, N.C. 28560.

Theodore Roosevelt State Natural Area, the **North Carolina Aquarium at Pine Knoll Shores**, and **Fort Macon State Park** are nearby in Carteret County and should be included in a visit to the area. They are discussed in detail elsewhere in this volume.

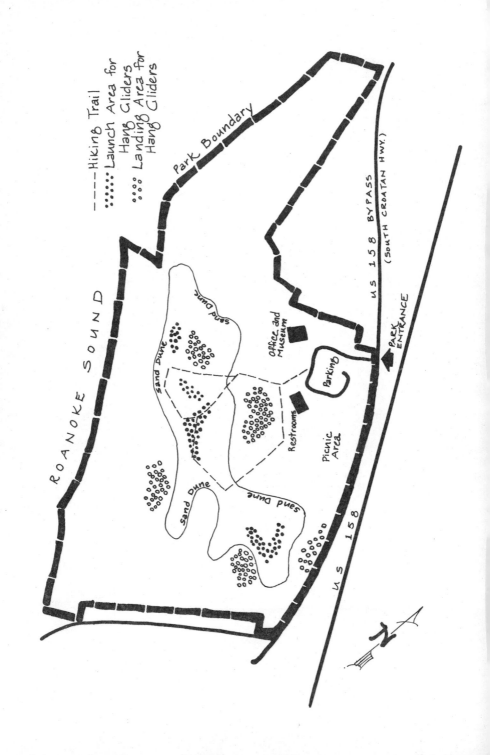

Hiking Trail
Launch Area for Hang Gliders
Landing Area for Hang Gliders

Park Boundary

ROANOKE SOUND

Sand Dune
Sand Dune
Sand Dune
Sand Dune
Sand Dune

Office and Museum

Parking

Restrooms

Picnic Area

PARK ENTRANCE

US 158 BYPASS (SOUTH CROATAN HWY.)

US 158

N

JOCKEY'S RIDGE STATE PARK

Jockey's Ridge looking west toward Roanoke Sound

Address: P.O. Box 592
            Nags Head, N.C. 27959

Telephone: (919) 441-7132

Size: 393 acres

Established: 1975

Location: Dare County, on the Outer Banks of North Carolina; turn west off U.S. 158 bypass at the town of Nags Head at the entry gate. The park is reached from the north via N.C. 168 and U.S. 158, from the east via U.S. 64/264 across Croatan and Roanoke sounds and Roanoke Island, and from the south via N.C. 12 across Ocracoke and Hatteras islands.

Principal Attractions: Jockey's Ridge, the highest system of unstabilized sand dunes in the eastern United States, a national natural landmark; nearby maritime forests; surrounding coastal environments.

Visitor Activities: Hiking on the dunes; photography; nature study; picnicking; hang gliding, model-plane soaring, and kiteflying from specified locations on the dunes. Camping is not permitted in the park.

Season: Open year-round; this is a day-use park, and daily closing times are posted at the entry gate.

Jockey's Ridge is the highest active sand dune along the Atlantic coast of North America and is a dominant feature of the landscape of the Outer Banks of North Carolina. The bare ridge of shifting sand is easily visible to travelers approaching Nags Head from bridges across Croatan and Roanoke sounds, up to 8 miles distant, and across Currituck Sound, 5 miles to the north. The dune eclipses the western horizon from the town of Nags Head and U.S. 158 along the narrow strip of land that is Bodie Island. The topmost elevation of Jockey's Ridge is from 110 to 140 feet, but the figure cannot be determined with accuracy because prevailing winds of varying speed and direction continually change both the shape and the height of the dunes. Jockey's Ridge is the largest and most imposing of eight prominent, named dunes in the area.

The dunes have been compared with the barkhans, or marching dunes, of North Africa. Jockey's Ridge is an example of a medaño—a massive, asymmetrical, shifting hill of sand lacking vegetation. The dunes are of recent origin, resulting from complex geological processes not well understood. An excess sand supply reached the beaches from offshore and was pushed inland by onshore winds, evolving gradually into the system of dunes now stretching for many miles along the coastline.

The Nags Head/Jockey's Ridge area and the entire Outer Banks region have a rich and fascinating history that spans more than four centuries. Several Indian tribes were present in the region long before the arrival of European settlers. Croatan Indians lived in villages at Cape Hatteras and befriended Roanoke Island colonists. Other tribes were not permanent inhabitants of the Outer Banks, but traveled there seasonally from nearby islands and the mainland; among these were the Corees, Machapungas, and Poteskeets. The Corees and Machapungas participated in the Tuscarora uprisings of 1711 and 1713, attacking settlements on Roanoke Island and the mainland and warring against the more peaceful Hatteras (Croatan) tribe. In time, and for a variety of reasons, the tribes were diminished and ceased to be a significant factor in the region.

Between 1713 and 1718, many notorious pirates roamed the Outer Banks. They attacked coastal shipping and found safe haven along the uninhabited barrier islands. That colorful period of history effectively ended on November 22, 1718, when Blackbeard's ships were attacked at Ocracoke Inlet by two sloops from Virginia under the command of Lieutenant Robert Maynard; Blackbeard was killed and his severed head displayed at Bath on the bowsprit of Maynard's ship.

Jockey's Ridge became an important landmark for mariners following early Spanish and French exploration of the coastline. Land grants for portions of the Outer Banks were recorded in the late seventeenth and early eighteenth centuries, and an early reference to "Jockey's Hill" appeared in a grant to John

Campbell in 1753. Among the early inhabitants of the area were hermits, castaway seafarers, pirates, and, later, fishermen, hunters, whalers, and persons rearing livestock.

By the early nineteenth century, the Nags Head area began attracting summer visitors from the mainland seeking to escape outbreaks of malaria, which seems to have been absent on the Outer Banks. In the 1830s, a Perquimans County planter bought 200 acres of land on the shore of Roanoke Sound near Jockey's Ridge and built a summer house; others followed, and a resort community developed. The need for a public house was recognized, and in 1838 the first Nags Head hotel was built, accommodating two hundred guests. The building was enlarged through several changes in ownership, and by 1852 it was served by a railroad and a boardwalk that stretched 800 feet to the ocean. Because the only access to the island was by boat, a wharf was built that extended 0.5 mile to the deep waters of the sound. During the 1850s, Nags Head was a popular resort that attracted many notable visitors. By January of 1862, however, the Civil War had reached the Outer Banks, and the Confederate army took over the hotel as a headquarters; when forced to retreat, the Confederates burned the building. A second hotel was constructed after the war, but by 1900 a new community had developed on the oceanfront. The site of old Nags Head was soon reclaimed by the sands of Jockey's Ridge.

The problem of access to the barrier islands was solved by a series of bridges constructed, in 1928, from Roanoke Island to Nags Head; in 1931, across Currituck Sound; in 1957, across Croatan Sound; and in 1963, across Oregon Inlet. Concurrently, rapid development led to the present-day resort town of Nags Head.

There are many legends about the Nags Head/Jockey's Ridge area. Some say that Nags Head was named for a beach in England, while others claim that an early mapmaker saw a resemblance between the outline of the Carolina coast and that of a horse's head. A more enduring tale is that the name was derived from trickery carried out by castaway pirates, men who attempted to lure unsuspecting ships to the beach by means of a light fixed on the head of a nag hobbled on the crest of a sand ridge. Another tale is that of a horse that caught its head between the limbs of a tree and hanged itself, the head remaining in place within the tree for many years. Whatever its origin, the name appeared on maps as early as 1738. Legend also accounts for the name Jockey's Ridge. Early inhabitants captured wild ponies and raced them on a flat surface of sand at the base of the ridge. The steep sides of the dune served as a grandstand for spectators from nearby communities.

Even though privately owned before establishment of the state park, Jockey's Ridge has always been considered public domain. As the development of

Nags Head proceeded, many local people desired protection for the dune area. Action was precipitated in the summer of 1973, when bulldozing was begun on the sound side of Jockey's Ridge. Carolista Golden, a resident who lived nearby, confronted the operator of the machine and successfully demanded that it be shut down. There followed petitions to "Save Our Sand Dune," appeals to local and state government officials, the organization of People to Preserve Jockey's Ridge, and a request that the threatened dune be designated a state park. A study of the feasibility of establishing a park, initiated by the North Carolina Board of Conservation and Development, received a favorable report in October 1973, and the North Carolina General Assembly appropriated $500,000 for land purchase in 1975. With matching funds from the United States Bureau of Outdoor Recreation, approximately 152 acres were acquired; additional land was purchased and donated to the state by the Nature Conservancy. Thus, action begun by Carolista Golden culminated in 1975 in the establishment of Jockey's Ridge State Park.

PLANT LIFE

While Jockey's Ridge State Park is considered to be an area essentially devoid of vegetation, that is not the case. Even though the shifting sands do provide an inhospitable environment, several distinct plant communities are present. Small pockets of grasses occur along the bases of the dunes, and sea oats and American beachgrass grow on more stable sites. Shrub thickets dominated by wax myrtle, red cedar, live oak, and red bay are found in protected dune pockets and near the picnic/parking area. To the west of the high dunes is a small forest that consists of live and southern red oaks, hickories, sweet gum, and loblolly pine; dogwood, sassafras, and other small trees form a subcanopy. The margins of the forest, adjacent to Jockey's Ridge, are often covered by windblown sand.

The forest gives way to brackish marshes adjoining Roanoke Sound. The upper, less frequently flooded portions of the marsh are dominated by saltmeadow cordgrass, cattails, and sedges. As the open sound is approached, these give way to giant cordgrass, smooth cordgrass, and other species adapted to longer and more frequent periods of inundation.

ANIMAL LIFE

The open, unvegetated dunes are not places where one expects to encounter great numbers of animals. Nevertheless, animals of many species are present in the dunes area, as evidenced by a surprising abundance of tracks and other signs left in the sand during the night. Early-morning hikers may see places where white-tailed deer, rabbits, foxes, lizards, beetles, and other animals walked under cover of darkness. Sea gulls and other birds are often present; they use deflection currents rising above the dune faces to obtain lift for soaring, much like hang-glider pilots.

The forest and the marshes to the west of the dune fields provide the best habitats for animals; numerous small mammals, including white-footed mice, rabbits, foxes, and raccoons, live there. Muskrats may be encountered in the marshes, as may the similar, larger, round-tailed nutria, a South American species introduced along the Outer Banks.

Bird life is most abundant in the park in late summer and fall, when large numbers of migrants funnel southward along the Outer Banks. Warblers, flycatchers, sparrows, and many other species may be seen in shrub thickets and forests. In winter, waterfowl are often present in the waters of the adjacent sound.

While Jockey's Ridge is not noted for its wildlife, it is near one of the best places in North Carolina to observe a rich variety of birds and other coastal animals. A visit to Pea Island National Wildlife Refuge should be included in a trip to this region of the state. Pea Island National Wildlife Refuge is described in the **Nearby** section below.

FACILITIES AND ACTIVITIES

Entry to the park is from U.S. 158 bypass at milepost 12. The entry road passes the **park office** on the right and leads into a large, paved parking lot. Personnel at the office provide information about facilities and activities; hang-glider pilots must register there. A **natural history museum/interpretive center** is located in the office building. Exhibits explain the physical and biological features of Jockey's Ridge and the surrounding area, and programs are presented by park rangers throughout the year. A visit to the park should begin there.

A **picnic area** is adjacent to the parking lot. Eight picnic shelters provide shade from the sun and are spaced among small sand dunes with low-growing vegetation. Each shelter has two tables and a grill; drinking water and modern restrooms are nearby. A path leads south from the parking lot past the restrooms to Jockey's Ridge. Several benches along the path allow visitors to relax and enjoy a beautiful view of the high dunes ahead.

There are no marked hiking trails on the dunes or in the park, but hikers should follow the designated routes indicated on the park map to avoid specified landing areas for hang gliders. The route to the left passes to the side of the dune system and leads to the top of the highest ridge. Visitors are free to explore the massive dunes and other areas of the park and to enjoy spectacular views of the Atlantic Ocean to the east, Roanoke Sound to the west, the nearby maritime forest, and the length of the Outer Banks to the north and south. In summer, temperatures are in the mid-80s, milder than on the

Hang gliding on Jockey's Ridge

mainland, and southwesterly winds often sweep across the rounded contours of the dunes; consequently, a walk through this remarkable domain of sand, sea, and sky becomes a pleasant and unique adventure. The view from the high ridges is especially beautiful in the soft light of early morning or late afternoon, as the sun rises above the sea or sets behind the mainland horizon across the quiet waters of the nearby sound.

Hikers share the dunes with persons engaged in other recreational activities, including **hang gliding, model-plane soaring,** and **kiteflying.** Conditions on Jockey's Ridge are ideal for these sports. The configuration of the dunes and the year-round winds from the southwest and northeast that blow up the slopes of the highest ridges are often in the optimal range of 10 to 15 miles per hour. Similar conditions at nearby Kitty Hawk attracted Orville and Wilbur Wright from their Dayton, Ohio, cycle shop to test their theories on powered flight.

Next to hiking, hang gliding is the most popular activity on Jockey's Ridge, and it draws many pilots and spectators to the area. The activity is regulated by the park staff to assure the safety of participants and to minimize interference with the rights of other park users. Specific areas for launching and landing gliders have been designated, as indicated on the park map. Experienced pilots launch their flights into the wind from the peaks of Jockey's Ridge and land on relatively level areas near its base. Beginners and inexperienced pilots usually launch from lower levels. The modest height, gentle slopes, and loose sand make it a relatively safe site for gliding, even though a total of fourteen injuries did occur in 1987.

Regulations governing hang gliding are posted at the park office. Pilots must apply for permits to fly from Jockey's Ridge, and they must have a membership card from the United States Hang Gliding Association (USHGA). It is necessary to register before each day's flights, and permits must be displayed. Flights must cease at least one hour before the park's posted closing time for the day. A concessionaire has operated a USHGA-certified flight school at Nags Head since 1974. The concessionaire offers lessons for beginners and sells and services equipment; for information, write: Kitty Hawk Kites, P.O. Box 240-E, Nags Head, N.C. 27959.

Radio-controlled model airplanes launched from the peaks of Jockey's Ridge soar at altitudes ranging from 50 to 200 feet, sustained by rising air currents produced by winds of 10 to 15 miles per hour. Because planes can be landed at the discretion of pilots, they are not a danger to other park visitors. Use of the park for this activity is minimal and attracts few spectators. Kiteflying from the dunes is a pleasant activity for the family and is fully compatible with other park uses.

The use of park facilities for hang gliding and model-airplane soaring causes concern for persons who feel that such activities damage resources and interfere with hiking on the dunes. It is important that all visitors be considerate of the rights of others and abide by park rules.

NEARBY

There are no camping facilities at Jockey's Ridge State Park, but commercial campgrounds are located in nearby communities on Bodie, Hatteras, and Roanoke islands. The National Park Service operates five campgrounds in Cape Hatteras National Seashore to the south, as described below.

The Outer Banks of North Carolina is a popular destination for vacationers, sportsmen, nature enthusiasts, history buffs, and persons with a variety of other interests. Visitors to Jockey's Ridge State Park should consider stops at many of the other special places in the region.

Fort Raleigh National Historic Site is the place where settlers sent out by Sir Walter Raleigh in 1585 and 1587 attempted to establish the first English colony in the New World. It is located off U.S. 64 on 144 acres of land at the north end of Roanoke Island, across Roanoke Sound from Bodie Island and Jockey's Ridge. The story of the ill-fated colony that Governor John White found abandoned upon his return from England in 1590 is told by displays, exhibits, and film at the visitor center. Fort Raleigh, an earthen structure surrounded by a moat, has been reconstructed at the site of the colony. The outdoor Wayside Theater on the shore of Roanoke Sound is the setting for *The Lost Colony*, a drama written by Paul Green and produced each summer since 1937 by the Roanoke Island Historical Association. In the evenings, the sixteenth-century colonists come to life through drama, song, and dance, though their disappearance remains a mystery. The **Elizabethan Gardens,** created by the Garden Club of North Carolina, are near the fort and the theater. Beautifully landscaped with ornamental plants and herbs, the gardens exemplify the exquisite English gardens of the Elizabethan period. Thomas Hariot Nature Trail, 0.3 mile in length and named for the natural scientist on the 1587 expedition, leads from the visitor center to the edge of Roanoke Sound; signs interpret plant life along the trail.

Wright Brothers National Memorial near Kitty Hawk marks the site of the first successful sustained, powered airplane flight in history, which took place on December 17, 1903. Orville and Wilbur Wright experimented with gliders at Kitty Hawk from 1900 through 1902, making more than a thousand flights from Kill Devil Hill. In 1903, a small gasoline engine and propellers were added, and on an area of level ground north of Kill Devil Hill, they succeeded in flying the craft 120 feet in twelve seconds. Three additional flights of 175, 200, and 825 feet followed, ushering in the age of aviation.

Entry into the memorial is from U.S. 158 bypass into a paved parking lot. A visitor center contains excellent exhibits that tell the story of the Wright brothers and replicas of their 1902 glider and 1903 powered airplane. Nearby is their reconstructed 1903 camp—two wooden buildings that served as hangar, workshop, and living quarters. At the site of the first powered flights, a granite boulder marks the spot where the flights began; additional markers are positioned where each flight ended. The Wright Memorial Shaft, a pylon of granite 60 feet in height, stands on the top of Kill Devil Hill, a dune 90 feet in elevation. A road from the parking lot encircles the dune; paths lead from parking areas at the base to the monument. A picnic area is nearby.

Cape Hatteras National Seashore extends along portions of Bodie, Hatteras, and Ocracoke islands south of Whalebone Junction. Access from the north is by N.C. 12 and a free ferry across Hatteras Inlet and from the south via toll ferries from Cedar Island and Swanquarter to Ocracoke Island. The narrow barrier islands of North Carolina's Outer Banks offer long stretches of marshes, sand dunes, open beaches, and woodlands. Recreational opportunities include swimming, sunbathing, boating, fishing, picnicking, hiking, and nature study. There is an abundance of marine organisms to be discovered, and a rich diversity of wildlife, especially birds. The maritime heritage of the area is evident in small seaside villages along the highway, historic lifesaving stations at Rodanthe and Avon, and storied lighthouses at Ocracoke, Cape Hatteras, and Bodie Island. The waters off the coast of these islands are known as the Graveyard of the Atlantic, where more than six hundred ships have wrecked.

Information about the Cape Hatteras National Seashore and exhibits on its natural resources are available at an information center at Whalebone Junction and at visitor centers at the south end of Bodie Island and at Cape Hatteras. There are nature trails at several locations within the park. Coquina Beach on Bodie Island has a bathhouse and picnic ground and is a popular stop for visitors. There are five campgrounds operated by the National Park Service: Oregon Inlet, Cape Point, and Ocracoke campgrounds are open from mid-April to mid-October; Salvo and Frisco campgrounds are open from mid-June until late August. Because they are near the shore, campsites are exposed to wind and sun, and they are usually in deep sand. Campers should be properly equipped for such conditions. Cold showers, modern restrooms, and drinking water are provided, but there are no hookups for RVs. Reservations for campsites during summer months may be made through Ticketron; otherwise, they are assigned on a first-come basis. A camping fee is charged. For additional information about the park and public campgrounds, write: Cape Hatteras National Seashore, Route 1, Box 675, Manteo, N.C. 27954 (919/473-2111).

Pea Island National Wildlife Refuge, at the north end of Hatteras Island, stretches from Oregon Inlet to near Rodanthe. It is an excellent place to observe many species of resident and migrating waterfowl. Of particular interest are the breeding pied-billed grebes, common moorhens, gadwalls, blue-winged teals, and black-necked stilts. American avocets are present year-round. Trails and observation platforms provide views of bird habitats. For additional information, write: Pea Island National Wildlife Refuge, P.O. Box 1969, Manteo, N.C. 27954 (919/473-1131).

Elizabeth II State Historic Site presents a replica of a 69-foot, square-rigged sailing vessel (the *Elizabeth II*) representative of the sixteenth-century ships of the type that brought colonists to Roanoke Island in 1587. The ship is docked at Manteo and may be toured for a fee. Tours begin at a visitor center, where exhibits, special programs, and dramatizations explain shipboard life and the voyages to Roanoke. For information and a brochure with a diagram of the ship, write: Site Manager, P.O. Box 155, Manteo, N.C. 27954 (919/473-1144).

North Carolina Aquarium at Roanoke Island, one of three aquaria operated by the state, is located 3 miles northwest of Manteo off U.S. 64. Exhibits interpret the coastal environment, and living marine organisms may be viewed in large tanks. Field trips, films, and other programs are available to the public. For information, write: Director, North Carolina Aquarium, P.O. Box 967, Manteo, N.C. 27954.

Nags Head Woods, a national natural landmark, encompasses approximately 1,000 acres of land along the shore of Roanoke Sound between Jockey's Ridge State Park and Wright Brothers National Memorial. The area includes ancient dunes up to 60 feet in elevation, a well-developed maritime forest, more than thirty freshwater ponds in swales among the dunes, and expanses of both saltwater and freshwater marshes, with small tidal creeks and pine hammocks within the wetlands. This is a distinctive resource with a forest of oaks, beeches, hickories, and hollies three hundred or more years old.

The **Nags Head Woods Preserve**, created cooperatively by the Nature Conservancy and local citizens, protects 680 acres of maritime forest and related habitats. A visitor center is located at the end of Ocean Acres Drive, west off U.S. 158 bypass. Trailheads for two hiking trails are near the visitor center; Central Trail is 0.25 mile in length, while Sweetgum Swamp Trail is 2.25 miles in length. For information, write: Nags Head Woods Preserve, P.O. Box 1942, Kill Devil Hills, N.C. 27948.

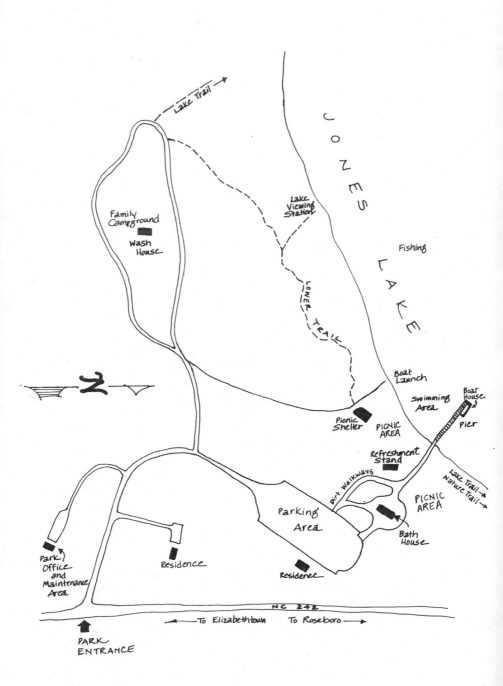

JONES LAKE STATE PARK
SINGLETARY LAKE STATE PARK

Carolina Bay Lakes

Aerial photographs reveal a concentration of elliptical or oval depressions in the surface of the coastal plain of the southeastern United States from northern Virginia to southern Georgia. It has been estimated that at least 500,000 such depressions, or bays, exist; most are small, but perhaps 140,000 are greater than 500 feet in length. "Carolina bays" are distinctive in that they generally run parallel to each other in a northwest-to-southeast orientation. Most are filled with wet organic soils and are overgrown with swamp-type vegetation; in the past, however, nearly all contained lakes. A few open-water bay lakes remain in North Carolina, and among them, Jones, Salters, Singletary, and Waccamaw lakes in Bladen and Columbus counties are within state parks.

The origin of Carolina bay lakes has long been a subject of speculation and debate. Unlike many other groups of lakes in the Northern Hemisphere, they did not result from glacial action, for the immense ice sheets of the Pleistocene period did not reach this far south. Several hypotheses have been proposed implicating underground springs, dissolution of subsurface minerals, wind and wave action, meteorite showers that penetrated the atmosphere and struck the uncompacted sandy soils of the coastal plain, and combinations of other factors. No explanation has gained universal acceptance.

The structure of a typical Carolina bay lake, as shown on the next page consists of a sand rim or ridge from 1 to 10 feet in height surrounding a bay; the sand rim is usually best developed at the southeast end of the oval depression, where it forms a natural sand beach. A layer of relatively impervious clay underlies the bay, above which, lining the lake bottom, is a layer of sand continuous with the rim. Over an extended period of time, dense vegetation growing around and within the bay has produced peat deposits that vary from a few feet to 40 feet in thickness. Peat usually extends onto a portion of the lake bottom, overlying the layer of sand. Carolina bay lakes are shallow, ranging from approximately 8 feet (Bay Tree Lake) to nearly 12 feet (Singletary Lake) in depth. With the exception of Lake Waccamaw, the bay lakes of the region are not fed by streams or springs but are dependent upon rainfall and runoff from the surrounding land; water levels, therefore, fluctuate with local precipitation. In general, the deepest water is at the southeast end of the lakes, adjacent to the beaches. Within state parks, visitor access and recreational activities usually are concentrated in beach areas. The water in bay lakes is reasonably pure, usually darkcolored, highly acidic, and deficient in essential plant nutrients.

TYPICAL BAY LAKE GEOMORPHOLOGY

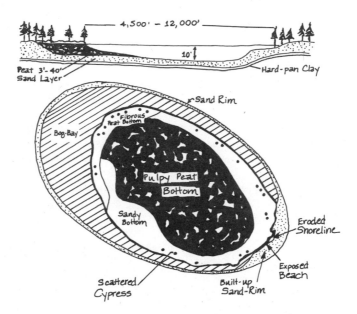

Vegetation tends to become established around the margins of bay lakes, but it usually is most dense at the northwest ends of the bays. Trees and shrubs along lake perimeters reduce wave and current action, permitting sediments to accumulate and encouraging new plants to become established. Thus, peat is produced gradually from dead organic matter, and forests grow out into the lake. The process slowly reduces the size of the lakes; for example, Jones Lake is presently only 34 percent of its original size. Ultimately, bay lakes may be reduced to moist bogs.

Legislation enacted in the 1827–28 biennium and in 1911 established that "land now covered by the waters of any of the lakes of the state" could not be recorded for private ownership and that any lake in Bladen, Columbus, and Cumberland counties containing 500 or more acres "shall always be and remain the property of the State of North Carolina for the use and benefit of all the people of the State." Additional legislation in 1929 established state ownership of lakes of 50 or more acres and gave administrative responsibility for these recreation areas to the North Carolina Department of Conservation and Development.

The bay lakes region of Bladen, Columbus, and Cumberland counties was settled during colonial times. The land was used primarily for subsistence farming, while the extensive pine forests were exploited for naval stores (primarily turpentine and pitch) and timber. By 1935, the land was exhausted, and most forests had been cutover. Much of the submarginal land in the bay lakes area of Bladen County was acquired by the federal government in 1936; it was managed by the Resettlement Administration until 1939. Administrative headquarters were constructed at Jones Lake and Singletary Lake. At Jones Lake, a bathhouse, a refreshment stand, picnic grounds, and a swimming beach were built. These facilities and land at Jones Lake were turned over to North Carolina in 1939 to be used as a state park. Land at Singletary Lake became a recreational demonstration project of the federal government, a program in which submarginal agricultural land was utilized for recreation, education, and resource conservation. The land was deeded to the state in 1936. Between 1936 and 1939, workers of the Resettlement Administration constructed the Singletary Recreation Center, which included an office and recreational facilities. Later, Singletary Lake Group Camp was built to accommodate approximately one hundred persons, with cabins, dining and recreation halls, and an infirmary. It was recently renamed Singletary Lake State Park.

Jones Lake State Park

Address: Route 2, Box 945
           Elizabethtown, N.C. 28337

Telephone: (919) 588-4550

Size: 2,208 total acres
           (1,669 acres of land and 539 acres of water)

Established: 1939

Location: Bladen County, 4 miles north of Elizabethtown on N.C. 242.

Principal Attractions: Jones Lake (224 acres), Salters Lake (315 acres), and associated Carolina bay environment.

Visitor Activities: Visitor use is concentrated at Jones Lake and includes swimming, boating, water-skiing, fishing, picnicking, hiking, nature study, and family camping; access to Salters Lake is restricted.

Season: Open year-round; most recreational facilities available during summer months.

Jones Lake State Park is located in a quiet, rural setting adjacent to Bladen Lakes State Forest. The park consists of 1,669 acres of land and two Carolina bay lakes, Jones Lake and Salters Lake. Visitor-use facilities are located at the southeast end of Jones Lake. Salters Lake, managed as a natural area, remains undeveloped and has restricted public access. Both Jones Lake and nearby White Lake attract large numbers of summer visitors, especially on weekends. The state park provides facilities for family picnicking, swimming, camping, and other forms of recreation. The beach and picnic area are often crowded, but elsewhere the natural environment of the park is relatively undisturbed.

The lakes are named for early prominent residents of the area. Jones Lake was once known as Woodward's Lake for Samuel Woodward, a justice of the peace in the mid-eighteenth century; it was renamed for Isaac Jones, a landowner who donated the tract of land on which Elizabethtown was established in 1773. Salters Lake derived its name from William Salter II and from Sallie Salter, a Revolutionary War heroine who spied on the Tories encamped in the town.

PLANT LIFE

Jones Lake State Park features open lake, bay-bog, and sand-ridge plant communities typical of Carolina bay environments. Longleaf pine forests and cypress swamps typical of the coastal plain are also in evidence.

The Carolina bay-bog community around Jones Lake is subject to periodic flooding when the water table rises near or above ground level, and it is subject to drought when precipitation levels are low. Vegetation, therefore, must be resistant to both conditions. In addition, bay vegetation must be able to withstand fire and the low nutrient content of the deep peat soil in the area. Characteristic canopy trees include pond and loblolly pine, Atlantic white cedar, cypress, black gum, and sweet gum. Dense understories of low trees include loblolly, red, and sweet bay, with their showy white flowers. Under the low trees, pepperbush, leatherwood, bitter gallberry, fetter-bush, wax myrtle, and wild huckleberry form a thick layer of green often interwoven by bamboo briers. The insectivorous Venus' fly trap and pitcher plant may be found in the more open portions of the bog communities at Salters Lake.

Arid conditions exist in the sand-ridge environment; soil water is low, and the coarse, gray-white, sandy surface reflects heat, making the area just above ground level hot and dry. The soil is quite sterile and low in some of the nutrients essential for the growth of many plants. Vegetation is lacking in both abundance and diversity. The most prevalent trees are longleaf pine and turkey oak; loblolly pine and scrubby post oak may also be present. Scattered within the sparse wiregrass ground cover are such plants as bayberry and dangleberry. This community is an extension of the longleaf pine forests that cover much of the uplands outside of the bays.

Where there is a high water table in low-lying areas outside the bay, swamp forest communities are present. Such forests are dominated by tupelo gum, black gum, ash, bald cypress, and red maple.

ANIMAL LIFE

Few fish species are present in these acidic, nutrient-poor bay lakes. The most abundant game fish are yellow perch, but chain pickerel, bullhead catfish, chub suckers, and the diminutive blue-spotted sunfish are also present. Few amphibians are able to tolerate the acidic waters of these lakes, but cricket and carpenter frogs may be present. Reptiles are represented by several species of water snakes and turtles, which may be seen sunning on fallen logs or at the bases of trees along the shorelines. Most water snakes are non-poisonous, but visitors should beware of the dangerous cottonmouth. The open lakes do not attract many birds. Occasional flocks of ducks are present in fall and winter, and wood ducks may be seen along the wooded edges at all seasons. Barn swallows nest beneath the boathouse roof and forage for insects over the lake.

Bay forests are home to many interesting animals, although the acidic waters that saturate their soils also exclude some species. These dense forests often provide habitat for bobcats and black bear; white-tailed deer may be common. Although gray and fox squirrels build their nests along the edges of these forests, they do most of their foraging in the adjacent uplands. Nesting birds present in mature bay forests may include the uncommon black-throated green warbler, a species also found in high-elevation mountain forests.

Bullfrog, a common resident

Upland forests within the park are home to many species of animals typical of coastal-plain forests. Of special interest is a population of black vultures that resides in the park; a roosting site for these large scavengers is on the north side of Jones Lake along Lake Trail. "Park vultures" sometimes visit the picnic area looking for an easy meal among the garbage cans. Other residents of the uplands include eastern bluebirds and the endangered red-cockaded woodpecker. Drier areas, especially the sand ridge, are home to several species of common lizards such as Carolina anoles, six-lined racerunners, and fence lizards.

Swamp forests are less acidic than bogs and generally have a greater abundance of wildlife. Red-shouldered hawks and barred owls prey on frogs, snakes, birds, and small mammals that are present.

HIKING TRAILS

Lake Trail, a self-guided 3-mile loop around Jones Lake, enables park visitors to experience the Carolina bay environment. The trail, well-marked and easy to follow, leads through dense vegetation, often over boggy soil. At intervals, short side trails lead to the margin of the lake, where large bald cypress trees laden with Spanish moss line the shore or grow in shallow water. Overhanging the water's edge are leatherwood (titi) plants with delicate white flowers and other bay shrub species. When the water level is low, hikers can explore exposed sand flats and look for animal tracks. Hikers may begin the trail at either the north or west side of the picnic area. To the north, hikers first enter **Nature Trail**, a self-guided 1-mile loop adjacent to the lakeshore that features markers that identify many of the plants along the way; Lake Trail continues from the far end of the loop. To the west, adjacent to the large picnic shelter, **Lower Trail** enters the bay forest, extends through a sand-ridge community to the lower end of the family campground near campsite #8, and then continues as Lake Trail around Jones Lake.

Bald cypresses at edge of Jones Lake

FACILITIES AND ACTIVITIES

A paved road leads from the park entrance to a parking lot with access to the picnic area, bathhouse, and beach. The **picnic ground**, shaded by pine, cypress, and other kinds of trees, is an open, well-kept grassy area adjacent to the beach. Numerous grills and approximately seventy-five tables are scattered throughout the area. A large picnic shelter with two fireplaces is at the southwest side of the area; it can accommodate up to three hundred persons and may be reserved for a fee by contacting the park office. Six small shelters, each with a table and grill, are available on a first-come basis. A **refreshment stand** is open during summer months for light snacks.

The sandy **beach** is ideal for sunbathing, and the shallow water is a safe and delightful place for swimming. The swimming area is supervised by lifeguards from June 1 until Labor Day. The bathhouse provides changing rooms, clothes baskets, showers, and restrooms; a fee is charged. A pier extends into the lake and to a boathouse.

Boating and **fishing** are popular activities at Jones Lake. The launch ramp at the west side of the picnic area is reached by a short, unpaved road from the campground entrance. Because the lake is shallow, it may be difficult to launch large boats when the water level is low. The maximum number of powerboats permitted on the lake is fifteen. Canoeing, sailboating, water-skiing, and wind-surfing are popular activities. Rowboats are available for rent at the boathouse from June 1 until Labor Day. There is a small parking and boat-launch area at Salters Lake; use of the lake is restricted to boating and fishing, and permission for access must be obtained from park personnel.

A small family **campground** with twenty tent/trailer sites is open from March 15 through November 15. The spacious and well-maintained sites are in a beautiful wooded section of the park; each is equipped with a table and a grill. Drinking water is provided, but there are no water or electrical hookups for trailers. A modern washhouse with hot showers and flush toilets is centrally located for all campers. Campsites are available on a first-come basis, and a fee is charged. Facilities for group camping are not available.

Ranger-led programs are offered on weekends during the summer months and at other times to groups on request. Visitors may join guided hikes. The 1-mile self-guided nature trail provides opportunity for independent study. Plans for the park include an interpretive center with exhibits, to be located in the bathhouse building.

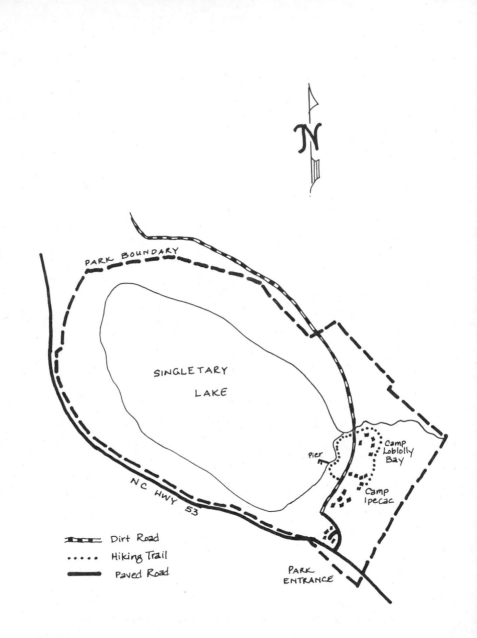

N

PARK BOUNDARY

SINGLETARY
LAKE

NC HWY 53

Pier

Camp
Loblolly
Bay

Camp
Ipecac

Dirt Road
Hiking Trail
Paved Road

PARK
ENTRANCE

Singletary Lake State Park

Address: Route 1, Box 63
            Kelly, N.C. 28448

Telephone: (919) 669-2928

Size: 1,221 total acres
            (649 acres of land and 572 acres of water)

Established: 1939

Location: Bladen County, 14 miles southeast of Elizabethtown on N.C. 53.

Principal Attractions: Singletary Lake (572 acres) and associated Carolina
    bay environment.

Visitor Activities: Group camping; swimming, hiking, fishing, boating, and
    nature study for groups renting camps.

Season: Open year-round for groups.

Singletary Lake derived its name from Richard Singletary, who received a
grant of land in Bladen County in 1729. The history of the area and the park is
similar to that of Jones Lake State Park. The lakes and the Carolina bay
environments within the two parks share the characteristics discussed above.
Singletary Lake is a beautiful, peaceful place where nature prevails. Much of
the lakeshore is bordered by huge pond cypress trees, some of which are
reported to be four hundred years old. Located within the park is Turkey Oak
Natural Area, so designated by the Society of American Foresters. It consists
of a coarse sand ridge at the southeastern end of the lake, a portion of the bay
bog, and the ecotone between the two. Insectivorous sundews and Venus' fly
traps grow in the area.

HIKING TRAIL
Singletary Lake Trail is an easy 1-mile hike that begins at the lakeshore
near the pier and passes through a forest of bay shrubs, juniper, cypress,
gum, and poplars. The return segment takes hikers through turkey oak and
longleaf pine to the main camp road. The trail offers an excellent opportunity
for visitors to study a relatively undisturbed Carolina bay environment and its
plant and animal life.

FACILITIES AND ACTIVITIES

Within the park are two organized group camps that are available to non-profit youth and adult organizations, including civic clubs, church and school groups, Boy Scouts, Girl Scouts, YMCA, YWCA, 4-H Clubs, and others. **Camp Ipecac**, built in 1939, has space for up to eighty-eight people; it is closed during the winter. **Camp Loblolly Bay**, opened in 1984, can accommodate up to forty-eight people and is open year-round. Each camp has camper and counselor cabins, a washhouse with showers, and a mess hall with a well-equipped kitchen and a dining area. The camps may be rented weekly from June to August; during the other months, groups may rent for periods of less than one week. Daytime access to the group camps by individuals is currently prohibited when groups are present. Reservations and detailed information about accommodations and rental fees may be obtained from the superintendent. Plans for the state park include construction of public, day-use facilities.

The two group camps are located within the sand-ridge environment of the park. The forest consists of turkey oak and longleaf pine trees, and the soil is coarse, gray-white sand. The areas around the cabins are relatively open and suitable for group activities and games. A path that begins on the camp road near Camp Ipecac leads through a bay-bog community, encircles the lake, and ends at the lakeshore. A pier more than 500 feet in length extends into the lake into water up to 12 feet deep. The pier is ideal for sunbathers and swimmers. There is no other development on the lake.

Singletary Lake has a large population of yellow perch, and fishing may be more productive than at Jones or Salters lakes. Groups using the camps are permitted to fish in the lake and to bring their boats. Other visitors may use the lake for fishing only when the camps are not rented.

NEARBY

There are other state-owned Carolina bay lakes in the region. The best known is **White Lake** on N.C. 53, 1 mile south of its intersection with N.C. 41 east of Elizabethtown. White Lake is 1,068 acres in size and is clear because the dark water of the bordering bay bog drains away from the lake. It is one of the most faunally diversified of the bay lakes with its twenty-two species of fish, though the fish are present in relatively small numbers. There is virtually no state-owned public access to the lakeshore, since the land is privately owned and densely developed. Swimming, boating, and water-skiing are popular activities, and the lake is often crowded; access is by way of private beaches and commercial facilities. **Bay Tree Lake** and **Bushy Lake** are discussed elsewhere in this volume.

Moore's Creek National Battlefield, located on N.C. 210 near Currie, was the site of a brief battle on February 27, 1776, early in the Revolutionary War. A patriot force defeated a larger loyalist force at Moore's Creek Bridge, preventing a rendezvous at the coast with an expeditionary army under Lord Cornwallis. The 86-acre park preserves the site of the battle. Reconstructed earthworks are present, but probably not at their original locations. A boardwalk across the creek was constructed in late 1988 upstream of the battle site to allow visitors access to the west side of the stream, where the loyalists encamped. An authentic reconstruction of Moore's Creek Bridge is planned. A visitor center offers exhibits that interpret the battle and the events that preceded it. **History Trail**, 0.7 mile in length, loops from the visitor center to the battle site and passes several monuments to participants. A picnic ground with two shelters is provided. One of the shelters is known as Freedom Hall, and it may be reserved by groups. For additional information, write: Superintendent, Moore's Creek National Battlefield, P.O. Box 69, Currie, N.C. 28435.

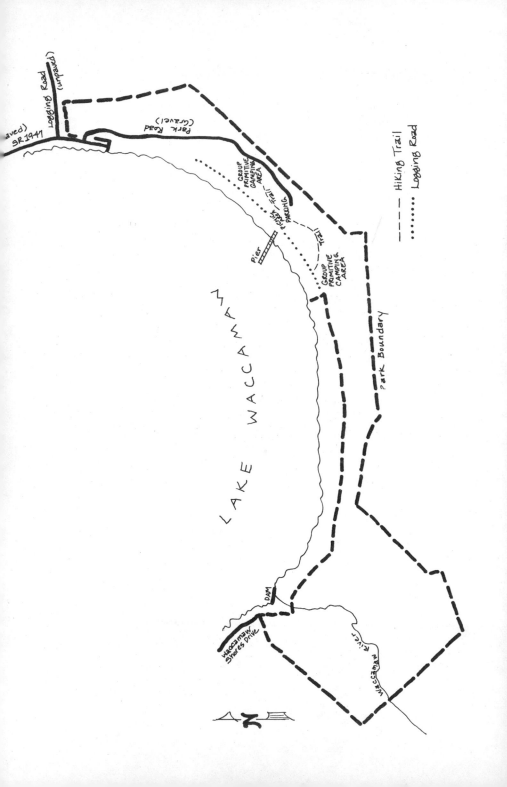

LAKE WACCAMAW

Logging Road (unpaved)
SR 1947
(paved)
Park Road (Gravel)
GROUP PRIMITIVE CAMPING AREA
PARKING
Pier
Picnic Trail
Trail
GROUP PRIMITIVE CAMPING AREA
Park Boundary
DAM
Waccamaw Shores Drive
Waccamaw River

Hiking Trail
Logging Road

LAKE WACCAMAW STATE PARK

Address: c/o Singletary Lake State Park
             Route 1, Box 63
             Kelly, N.C. 28448

Telephone: (919) 669-2928

Size: 10,446 total acres
             (1,508 acres of land and 8,938 acres of water)

Established: 1976

Location: Columbus County, 38 miles west of Wilmington and 12 miles east
of Whiteville. From the park sign on U.S. 74/76, turn south toward the
town of Lake Waccamaw on SR 1740 for 0.3 mile; turn east onto N.C.
214 for 1.1 miles; turn south onto SR 1757 for 1.2 miles; turn east onto
SR 1947 for 2.6 miles, past North Carolina Wildlife Resources Commission boat access area; and turn left onto Martin Road, a gravel road, for
1.1 miles to park entry gate. The park road continues 0.8 mile to a
parking lot.

Principal Attractions: Lake Waccamaw, a Carolina bay lake with access by a
boardwalk and pier; associated Carolina bay and sand-ridge plant communities; headwaters of Waccamaw River.

Visitor Activities: Swimming; fishing; boating; picnicking; primitive group
camping; hiking; nature study.

Season: Open year-round.

Lake Waccamaw near mouth of Waccamaw River

John Bartram of Philadelphia, America's first great botanist, included south-eastern North Carolina in his extensive travels along the Atlantic coast as he studied and collected plants. After visiting Lake Waccamaw, on the northern border of the Green Swamp of Brunswick and Columbus counties, Bartram declared it to be "the pleasantest place that ever I saw in my life." His view of the broad expanse of glistening water, lined by huge, moss-draped cypress trees, came after a journey through the wilds and the mosquitoes of the great swamp, an area with a rich diversity of plant and animal life. The Green Swamp, some 140 square miles of wilderness, was and remains a true botani-cal paradise. Bartram saw vast forests of cypress, gum, beech, maple, ash, poplar, white cedar, and longleaf pine that served as habitat for black bear, cougar, white-tailed deer, wild turkey, and a host of other wildlife. Though the swamp and the lands adjacent to Lake Waccamaw have since been greatly altered by human enterprise, they continue to be a natural resource of im-mense value and significance.

Archaeological evidence indicates continuous habitation of the lands around Lake Waccamaw for several thousand years. Among the peoples who lived there before the arrival of European settlers were the Waccamaw-Siouan Indians. Artifacts and other reminders of Indian cultures have been found at such locations as Jones Ridge, also known as the Indian Mounds, on the lake's east shore. Jones Ridge is now included in the park. Private ownership of the Green Swamp began in 1797, when the state deeded 170,120 acres to Stephen Williams, Benjamin Rowell, and William Collins for the grand sum of $7,100. In the 1850s, geologist Ebenezer Emmons saw agricultural potential in the land and advocated that it be drained and "put to work"; the swampland remained relatively intact in 1900, however, due perhaps to the immensity of the task.

In 1904, the land of Williams, Rowell, and Collins was bought by the Wac-camaw Land and Lumber Company, and for the next thirty-four years the virgin forest was cut to supply logs for the company's sawmill at Bolton. Lake Waccamaw had become a regular stop on a railroad line between Wilmington, North Carolina, and Florence, South Carolina, in the nineteenth century, and the lumber company laid additional rail lines, including short spurs into the swamp, to transport timber. Closely placed logs served as crossties across the wetlands, and loggers often worked in water to fell the great trees. The mature forests seen by Bartram and other early visitors to the Green Swamp were virtually gone by the 1930s. The timberland was sold to the Riegel Paper Corporation (now Federal Paper Company), from which a portion of the land now included in the state park was obtained.

In 1869, the production of cypress shingles was begun by Charles Beers on the south shore of Lake Waccamaw and by Henry Short on land south of the lake. The two enterprises were merged in 1879, giving rise to the North

Carolina Lumber Company. Shingles were transported across the lake on flatboats, loaded onto rail cars that were pulled by teams of mules to the town depot, and then shipped to market by freight train. Later, all transport of logs and shingles was by rail. This was made possible by a rail spur built along the west side of the lake. The track crossed the Waccamaw River just below its outlet from the lake and the site of the present-day dam. Some remnants of the river crossing remain. Part of the area was obtained in 1987 from the Georgia-Pacific Corporation and is now parkland.

Drainage of sections of the swamp, especially to the north, was under way by 1914, fulfilling the 1850s wish of Ebenezer Emmons. Huge steam-powered dredges cut many miles of canals through the soft, wet soil, producing farmland. Fortunately, much of the magnificent Green Swamp survives.

Lake Waccamaw State Park includes the lake and 1,510 acres of land on the south and southeast shore. Lake Waccamaw is a Carolina bay lake (see the description of bay lakes in the account on Jones Lake State Park, page 59). It is 8,938 acres in size, with approximately 14 miles of shoreline, an average depth of 7 feet, and a maximum depth of 10.8 feet. It is part of the Waccamaw River system. Water enters the lake from the north by way of Big Creek, then flows southward from the lake to the sea by way of the dramatically scenic Waccamaw River. Sand composes 64 percent of the lake bottom and completely encircles the shoreline; the remainder of the bottom is covered by peat, which is confined to the lake's interior.

In contrast to bay lakes that are relatively barren of life due to their acidity, Lake Waccamaw has neutral water that supports numerous aquatic plants and an abundant fauna that includes several fishes and molluscs that occur only in or immediately around the lake. The unique chemistry of the water is due primarily to the presence of limestone outcrops along several miles of the northeast shore.

The lake, with its clear, shallow water and beautiful tree-lined shore, has attracted visitors since the late nineteenth century. The public beach, a sandbar 950 feet in length, was dedicated to the "good citizens" in 1853 by Josiah Maultsby, who first owned the land where the town of Lake Waccamaw was built. Early this century, the lake and beach became a popular tourist attraction; hundreds of people came for recreation, especially on holidays and weekends. Charter trains brought vacationers from faraway places. A bathhouse, pavilion, pier, and picnic ground were provided at Weavers Beach, as the area came to be known. Use of the beach declined, and the facilities are now gone; a controversial housing development is under way at the site. Approximately three-fourths of the lakeshore has undergone residential or commercial development that limits public access to the lake. The state park, therefore, meets a vital need for visitors to the area.

State ownership of Lake Waccamaw and other natural lakes 50 acres or more in size was established by legislative action in 1827–28, 1911, and 1929. Suggestions that a state park be created on Lake Waccamaw were made as early as 1925. In October 1964, the North Carolina Board of Conservation and Development began an effort to obtain land on the lakeshore for this purpose. The proposal was supported by the town board of Lake Waccamaw and other agencies, and in 1969 the North Carolina General Assembly appropriated $50,000 for land acquisition. A 273-acre tract was purchased in May 1976 by the North Carolina Division of Parks and Recreation to establish the park. Additional funds appropriated by the state in 1985 were earmarked for land acquisition for the park; purchases made in 1986 and 1987, including those of land owned by Federal Paper Company and Georgia-Pacific Corporation, increased the park to its present size. The most recent purchase included a large area of wetland at the headwaters of the Waccamaw River. At present, the park includes about 2 miles of the lakeshore. The Nature Conservancy has assisted the state in the acquisition of land.

PLANT LIFE

Several terrestrial and aquatic plant communities are present within the boundaries of the park. The uplands consist primarily of dry sand ridges covered by second-growth longleaf pine, with an understory of scattered turkey, post, and laurel oaks. Huckleberries grow within the shrub layer, and the ground is usually covered by a carpet of wire grass.

Sites in topographic depressions are generally occupied by dense, wet shrub thickets or low forests. The assemblage of plants found there is referred to as pocosin, or bay, vegetation. The canopy usually consists of pond pine and sweet, red, and loblolly bay, but Atlantic white cedar may also be present. Beneath this low canopy, an almost impenetrable tangle of such shrubs as fetterbush, gallberry, and titi may be woven together with bamboo briar. Where openings occur within pocosins, ferns flourish and insectivorous pitcher plants may grow.

Open, parklike savanna communities develop on slopes between dry sand ridges and pocosins; longleaf pine and pond pine may both be present. Adequate sunlight and moisture in the soil allow a diverse herbaceous flora to develop, and showy wildflowers are often present. It is here that the insectivorous Venus' fly trap may be seen.

A ribbonlike stretch of swamp forest borders the shoreline of Lake Waccamaw; cypress trees are most evident, but black gum, red maple, and other species are also present. Vines, including poison ivy, rattan vine, and cross vine, are abundant, and Virginia tea, swamp alder, swamp dogwood, and other wetland shrubs occur in scattered thickets. Wetland herbaceous plants such as maiden cane often form emergent beds along the forest edge.

Surrounding the mouth of the Waccamaw River is a diverse and distinctive swamp forest. Large cypress trees border the river where it drains away from the lake below a small concrete dam that helps to control lake water levels. The flood plain is occupied by a mixture of red maple, sweet gum, American elm, and other deciduous trees. The understory is sparse and the aspect is quite open, owing largely to frequent flooding.

The lake bottom slopes gradually downward from its perimeter, and emergent beds of maiden cane grass extend for 100 feet or more into the lake. Beds of yellow cow lilies also extend well into the open lake. Other species of both emergent and submerged wetland plants abound, including American lotus, pickerel weed, and cattail.

ANIMAL LIFE

Animal life in upland habitats of the park is typical of such forest communities. Among the birds, yellow-throated warblers are summer residents in the dry longleaf ridge forests, and pine warblers and brown-headed nuthatches are permanent residents. Rufous-sided towhees are present all year in pocosins, and common yellowthroats and other thicket-lovers occur in summer. Curious naturalists should be able to find large, coppery broad-headed skinks in the pine forests, and black racers and other reptiles can sometimes be observed. Although becoming scarce in eastern North Carolina, fox squirrels may be encountered occasionally in open pine forests. White-tailed deer may be seen in the woodlands, as may gray squirrels, which are more abundant than fox squirrels.

While the animal life of the uplands is rather typical of coastal-plain habitats, life in the lake is very special. Lake Waccamaw has a good population of game fishes and is a popular destination for fishermen, who commonly catch white perch, yellow perch, largemouth bass, chain pickerel, and several species of sunfishes. An occasional American alligator is seen in the lake or in the river, and waterfowl are usually present in winter.

In addition to the more common species, Lake Waccamaw and the immediately surrounding swamps and streams are unique in that they provide habitat for several species of endemic animals found nowhere else in the world. Endemic fishes include the Waccamaw silversides, Waccamaw darter, and Waccamaw killifish. The Waccamaw silversides was recently listed as threatened by the United States Fish and Wildlife Service, meaning that it receives additional protection provided by federal law. All three species are very small and are commonly referred to as "minnows." The darter is primarily a bottom-dweller, whereas the silversides occurs in schools in the open lake; the killifish is a top minnow and usually stays near shore except in winter, when it is found farther out in the lake. Endemic freshwater molluscs (clams and snails) that are found only in the lake and nearby waters include the Waccamaw lance, Waccamaw spike mussel, Waccamaw helix, Waccamaw mucket, and Waccamaw snail. Several other rare or poorly known organisms are also present. Lake Waccamaw is therefore one of the most biologically significant bodies of water in North Carolina. The reasons for this unusual assemblage of animals in a lake generally considered to be of fairly recent origin are not understood.

HIKING TRAIL

Visitors may hike on abandoned logging roads that parallel the lakeshore inland from the swamp forest and on **Sand Ridge Nature Trail**, which is 1.5 miles in length. Completed in early 1988 by Chris Blasky of Whiteville as an Eagle Scout project, the trail begins at the west side of the picnic ground and extends along the sand ridge to its terminus near the group camping area. Hikers may return to the picnic ground by way of a logging road. Markers identify many of the prominent trees and shrubs along the trail.

FACILITIES AND ACTIVITIES

Lake Waccamaw State Park is relatively undeveloped. Some facilities are provided for day visitors, however, and others are scheduled to be added. The gravel park road extends for approximately 2 miles along a sand ridge to an unpaved parking lot. Paths lead to an adjacent **picnic ground** in an area of white sand, wire grass, huckleberries, and woodlands consisting of turkey and live oaks and longleaf pines. The larger oak trees, draped with flowing beards of Spanish moss, create a dramatic backdrop for an afternoon family picnic. Tables and grills are distributed about the area beneath the trees. Restrooms and drinking water are available near the picnic area.

A gravel path leads from the parking lot through the picnic ground to a nearby **boardwalk** that crosses the swamp forest bordering the shoreline. The boardwalk, approximately 1,000 feet in length, is an excellent vantage point from which to observe the distinctive vegetation of this plant community. It joins a **pier** that extends 375 feet over the shallow water of the lake, allowing access for swimming and other activities. The addition of a sun shelter on the pier is planned. The pier provides a magnificent view of the lake and its tree-lined shore, especially in the light of early morning or late afternoon.

A grant from the United States Bureau of Outdoor Recreation obtained by the Columbus County Department of Parks and Recreation, in conjunction with the North Carolina Division of Parks and Recreation, financed construction of the picnic ground, boardwalk, and pier. These facilities were built by the county with the assistance of state personnel.

Two primitive **group camping areas** are located within the park. The larger, which can accommodate up to forty persons, is approximately 1 mile west of the picnic ground and is reached by way of an old logging road. The area is within a pine/oak forest. Tables, a fire circle, and pit toilets are provided. Nearby, a short path off the logging road leads to the lakeshore. This narrow window to the lake offers a beautiful view of the broad expanse of water. Several tables are available for picnicking visitors. A smaller camping area approximately 200 yards northeast of the picnic ground is also reached by a former logging road. Bordered by bay vegetation, the area provides a table and a fire circle. All supplies, including drinking water, must be packed to the camping areas. A fee is charged. For additional information, contact the park superintendent.

The portion of the park at the mouth of the Waccamaw River is reached by way of a perimeter road leading west from town. Waccamaw Shores Drive ends at an informal parking area on private land adjacent to a concrete dam at the outlet from the lake into the river. This is a beautiful area with an extensive bed of emergent grasses and large cypress trees extending into shallow water. It is a popular area for fishermen, and canoe trips on the river begin below the dam. The only access into this portion of parkland is by canoe or other small boat.

There is no boat access to the lake from the park. Two free, public **boat-launch areas** are maintained by the North Carolina Wildlife Resources Commission. One is on SR 1947 at the northeast side of the lake near the park entrance, and the other is on Lake Shore Drive at the northwest side of the lake near the Waccamaw Sailing Club. Powerboats and sailboats may be launched at these access areas, though parking space is limited.

Fishing is a popular activity on the lake, in Big Creek, and in canals along perimeter roads; forty-eight species of game and nongame fishes have been recorded. Fishing may be from the shore, from small boats along the shoreline and in open water, or by wading along the shallow lake perimeter, where emergent aquatic plants provide cover for fishes. The North Carolina Wildlife Resources Commission stocks the lake with largemouth bass, bluegill, shellcracker, and redbreast sunfish. Applicable state fishing regulations are enforced.

NEARBY

A number of other Carolina bay lakes are located in Columbus, Bladen, and nearby counties. Jones and Salters lakes (within Jones Lake State Park),

Singletary Lake (within Singletary Lake State Park), White Lake, Bay Tree Lake, and Bushy Lake are discussed in this volume.

The Green Swamp, featuring what are perhaps the most outstanding examples of pine savannas, bay forests, and pocosins surviving in the Carolinas, is a natural area of major biological significance. In 1974, the United States Department of the Interior designated 24,800 acres of the swamp a national natural landmark. In 1977, the Federal Paper Board Corporation donated 13,850 acres of property to the Nature Conservancy "to be held in perpetuity for the people of North Carolina." With the acquisition of additional land, the conservancy's **Green Swamp Preserve** now comprises 15,722 acres. The preserve is located in Brunswick County 5 miles north of Supply on N.C. 221 and is open to the public. Access to the area is provided by a boardwalk into interior savannas; visitor trails are planned. The preserve features the principal plant communities of the swamp. Plant life is highly diverse, especially in moist savannas, where up to fifty different species per square meter have been recorded. At least fourteen species of carnivorous plants, such as pitcher plants and Venus' fly traps, may be found in the Green Swamp Preserve, as may numerous wildflowers including the endangered rough-leaf loosestrife. The swamp is also home to a diverse fauna that includes the American alligator, the eastern diamondback rattlesnake, Bachman's sparrow, and the endangered red-cockaded woodpecker. It is, however, an easily disrupted environment that requires protection not only by its managers but also by its visitors. For additional information, write: Nature Conservancy, Box 805, Chapel Hill, N.C. 27514 (919/967-7007).

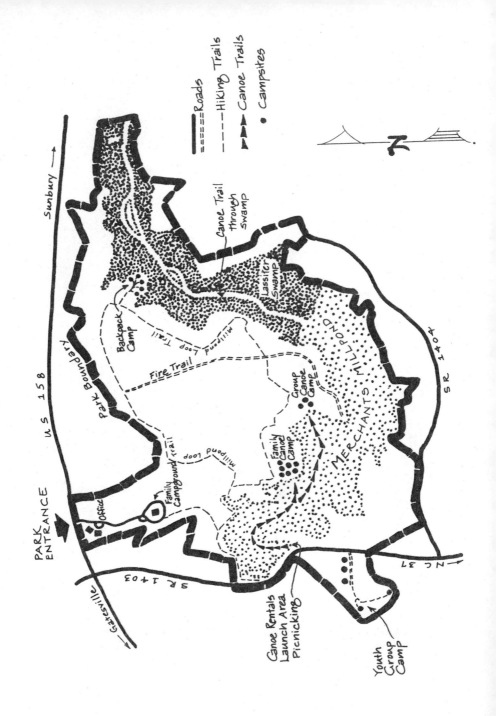

Legend:
- ═══ Roads
- --- Hiking Trails
- ►►► Canoe Trails
- • Campsites

Sunbury →

U.S. 158

PARK
ENTRANCE

← Gatesville

SR 1103

Office

Family Campground Trail

Millpond Loop

Family Campground

Park Boundary

Backpack Camp

Millpond Loop Trail

Fire Trail

Lassiter Swamp

Canoe Trail through Swamp

Group Canoe Camp

Family Canoe Camp

MERCHANTS MILLPOND

Canoe Rentals
Launch Area
Picnicking

Youth Group Camp

← NC 37

SR 1404

N

MERCHANTS MILLPOND
STATE PARK

Address: Route 1, Box 141-A
              Gatesville, N.C. 27938

Telephone: (919) 357-1191

Size: 2,659 acres

Established: 1973

Boardwalk at Merchants Millpond

Location: Gates County. Main entry gate is 4.5 miles west of Sunbury and
            4.3 miles east of Gatesville on U.S. 158; turn off at sign to reach park
            office and family campground. Proceed 0.3 mile west on U.S. 158 to
            Eason's Crossroads and turn south on SR 1403 for 1.5 miles to Millpond
            Access Area.

Principal Attractions: Merchants Millpond, an impoundment on Bennetts
            Creek approximately 760 acres in size, and Lassiter Swamp; a southern
            swamp forest dominated by massive bald cypress and tupelo gum trees.

Visitor Activities: Canoeing; fishing; hiking; nature study; picnicking; family
            and group camping.

Season: Open year-round.

Coastal pond and southern swamp forests mingle within Merchants Millpond State Park, one of North Carolina's rarest ecological communities. Bennetts Creek, a slow-moving, dark-water, coastal-plain stream, flows through
starkly beautiful Lassiter Swamp and past massive gum and cypress trees,
some of which are from five hundred to a thousand years old. The creek then
enters the placid millpond, which has shallow water dotted with gums and
cypresses that often display growths of Spanish moss and resurrection ferns.
The swamp and pond environments, together with the hardwood and pine
forests covering the slopes and ridges above the lowlands, create a diversity

of habitats for many kinds of animals, making the park a wilderness sanctuary into which humans may intrude only briefly.

Settlement of the territory that now includes Gates County and the park began about 1660, first at Corapeake and later at the present sites of Gatesville and Sunbury. The earliest recorded visit to the vicinity of the present state park was in 1672 by Quaker clergyman George Fox, who camped at Bennetts Creek. The area was also explored by Richard Bennett, governor of Virginia from 1652 to 1655, for whom the creek is named.

People of the rural communities that developed in the area depended upon farming and lumbering for their livelihoods, and they required mills and other means of processing and marketing their products. Hunters Millpond was built at the head of Bennetts Creek before 1720; it was destroyed in 1922 during highway construction. In 1811, Kincken Norfleet built Norfleets Millpond (later to be called Merchants Millpond) downstream; gristmills for corn and wheat and a sawmill were completed at the site in 1812, and the first corn was ground into meal. After several changes in ownership, the complex of mills was the largest in the area at the turn of the century. By 1908, the wheat mill was no longer in operation, but two gristmills had ample business, as did the sawmill located beneath a shelter extending from the millhouse. A mercantile store where farmers could buy supplies and other commodities was built nearby, and the area became the chief trade center of Gates County; consequently, the pond became known as Merchants Millpond. Local people congregated at the pond to socialize, picnic, and fish, and perhaps to sample the apple brandy made at a nearby still.

The rustic millhouse, approximately 25 by 30 feet, stood on cement pilings over the water. A dam across Bennetts Creek along the east side of present-day SR 1403 formed the millpond. The flow of water from the millpond into lower Bennetts Creek was regulated by seven wooden gates. Gates beneath the millhouse, protected against damage from floating debris by logs chained together across their openings, allowed water into the millrun and over the mill wheel; the flow of water powered the millstones of the gristmill and the saws of the sawmill. A covered wooden bridge passed in front of the millhouse and over the dam, allowing horse- or mule-drawn carts to reach the mill with their cargos of corn to be ground. Farmers usually paid for this service by allowing the miller to take a "toll" of their corn, several quarts per bushel, and by helping to maintain the mill whenever repairs were required.

The pond, millhouse, sawmill, and store were owned by Charles Lawrence from about 1910 until 1944, and the mill remained in operation until shortly before World War II. The millpond was sold in 1944 to H. P. Foxhall of Virginia and in 1951 to B. Howell of West Virginia. Foxhall and Howell had plans to develop the area that never materialized. The property was acquired over a decade later by A. B. Coleman of Moyock, North Carolina. In June 1973, Coleman donated 919 acres including the millpond and some adjoining land to the state. This generous donation led to the establishment of the state park. In December 1973, the Nature Conservancy contributed an additional 925 acres of woodlands north of the pond to the park. Later purchases by the state have enlarged the park to its present size.

PLANT LIFE

Several distinct plant communities occur in the park, but most visitors will first encounter those of the millpond itself. The pond is over 175 years old, and it has had sufficient time to develop into complex, mature ecosystems. Its dark, acidic waters are shaded by old, massively buttressed cypress and tupelo gum trees that form a high canopy. Numerous species of herbaceous aquatic plants inhabit the pond water. The yellow cow lily and other floating emergents are present, as are submerged aquatic species such as parrot feather. At times, much of the surface of the pond is covered by a green and reddish layer of floating and unattached duckweeds, water fern, and liverworts. These floating mats, moved about by wind and current, create a constantly changing mosaic of colors and patterns on the water. Many plants not adapted for growth directly in the water take hold in the crevices and hollows of growing trees, the rotting trunks of fallen trees, and stumps left behind by loggers. Swamp rose, Virginia tea, royal fern, and red maple seedlings thus grow just above the surface of the pond, adding colorful diversity to its flora.

At the head of the pond and along its shallow edges, the open water meets a swamp forest that is flooded most of the year. Cypress and tupelo gum still dominate, but other species such as red maple, ash, and water hickory are also important components of the community. At slightly higher elevations, and as flooding during the growing season becomes less frequent, the swamp forest changes to a bottomland hardwood forest; cypress and ash are less common, and sweet gum, water oak, black gum, and red maple appear, trees that are adapted to moist soil that is subject to infrequent flooding.

Relatively well-drained slopes are occupied by sweet gum, oaks, and loblolly pine; stands of American beech occur in a few locations. The highest elevations are vegetated by mixed stands of loblolly pine, sweet gum, yellow poplar, and other upland species. Much of this community has been logged in recent years and is in the process of redeveloping a forest cover. Several successional stages ranging from dense mixtures of grasses, shrubs, and pine saplings to well-developed pine forests may be distinguished.

ANIMAL LIFE

Merchants Millpond State Park is home to an abundance of wetland wildlife. The millpond itself provides good habitat for many important game fishes, including largemouth bass, bluegill, warmouth, and crappie, as well as for nongame species that add to the diversity of the fish fauna. Long-nosed gar and bowfin, primitive species that have existed relatively unchanged for millions of years, are of particular interest; both are rather large and important predators in blackwater habitats of the coastal plain.

Frogs are plentiful in this water-dominated environment. Bullfrogs may be heard on warm summer evenings as they call to potential mates and challenge other males. After spring or summer rains, a mixed chorus of frogs adds to the special charm of coastal ponds. A cacophony of calls is produced by carpenter frogs, leopard frogs, bullfrogs, cricket frogs, toads, and species of tree and chorus frogs.

Reptiles, including turtles and water snakes, are also abundant in wetland environments, especially where protection prevents the incidental shooting that so often occurs at unprotected sites. Several species of pond turtles, often called cooters or sliders, may be seen on warm days as they bask on fallen logs or stumps. Most are vegetarians or scavengers, but the snapping turtle is an able predator on other aquatic creatures.

Most of the water snakes at the millpond are nonpoisonous, although they are frequently misidentified as moccasins, a local term for the cottonmouth. Poisonous cottonmouths are present, and any snake that does not quickly retreat upon encounter should be treated with caution and respect. Water snakes often lie in the sun at the water's edge, but they are generally secretive, hiding under logs or mats of vegetation. They are adept swimmers and divers. They feed on a variety of water-dwelling prey, including frogs, crayfish, and small fishes.

Birds abound in the millpond and swamp. In summer, it is an excellent place to see nesting prothonotary warblers and northern parulas. Prothonotaries nest in crevices or holes in logs and stumps; parulas place their nests in clumps of Spanish moss. Both warblers add much to the attraction of coastal swamp environments. Waterbirds also are plentiful. Green-backed and great blue herons, great egrets, and other waders are seen occasionally. Ospreys fish in open waters, and wood ducks nest in hollow trees and raise their broods in the pond. Barred owls live as waterbirds in such environments, as they feed on frogs and even fish in the shallow, flooded swamplands.

Autumn brings migrant waterfowl to the park; dabbling ducks such as mallards, black ducks, and wigeon are often seen, as are divers such as scaup and ring-necked ducks. Visitors may also see the spectacularly beautiful hooded merganser, a small fish-eating duck whose males display a magnificent, black-bordered white crest.

Merchants Millpond is an ideal place to encounter several species of interesting mammals, especially while paddling quietly through the pond and creek. Beavers have returned to the area; even though the animals themselves are rarely seen, their dams or lodges are in evidence. Stumps of small saplings cut by beavers for food and construction materials and bearing their teeth marks protrude from swampy soil around the pond. Mink, river otter, and bobcats are occasionally sighted, and white-tailed deer, raccoons, Virginia opossums, and other common coastal-plains mammals are present. Bats roost in clumps of Spanish moss, feed on insects high over the pond, and dip to the surface to drink. They may be sighted at dusk; different species may be distinguished by variations in size and flight patterns.

Although most visitors come to Merchants Millpond State Park to explore and to enjoy the millpond and the swamp, the park also features several upland forest communities. A quiet walk along a trail may provide an opportunity to see and hear wildlife typical of relatively dry coastal-plains habitats.

HIKING TRAIL

The trailhead for the 6.7-mile **Millpond Loop Trail** is off SR 1403 at the north end of the bridge over Bennetts Creek. From the parking lot at Millpond Access Area, cross the bridge to the trail sign; the dam and the concrete pilings that served as the foundation for the old millhouse may be observed en route. The trail enters the forest, following the bank of the pond and then following a ridge through upland hardwoods. At 0.5 mile, Millpond Loop Trail is joined by a trail from the family campground. At 0.8 mile, the trail forks; hikers may elect to follow the loop by proceeding north, away from the pond and across a series of ridges and ravines through upland hardwoods and mixed pine/hardwood forests, or south, along the edge of the millpond and through sections of both lowland and upland hardwoods.

Hikers who proceed north cross, at 2.2 miles, a broad fire lane that transects the loop trail and may be followed as a shortcut return to the trailhead. A short side trail, at 3 miles, leads to the primitive backpack camp, which overlooks Lassiter Swamp. The trail turns south, parallels Lassiter Swamp with excellent views of the "enchanted forest" at intervals from a ridge above the swamp, continues around Merchants Millpond to complete the loop at 5.9 miles, and returns to the trailhead.

FACILITIES AND ACTIVITIES

There are two points of entry into the park.

An attractive sign is at the main entry gate on U.S. 158; a paved road leads to the **park office**, a new building where park personnel provide information and assist in planning visits. The road continues to the **family campground**, located in a pleasant mixed pine/hardwood forest. There are twenty tent/trailer sites, each with a table and grill; electrical and water hookups for trailers are not provided. A centrally located washhouse has drinking water, modern toilets, hot showers, and a sink for washing clothes. A fee is charged at the family campground, and sites may be occupied on a first-come basis. A trail, 0.5 mile in length, leads from the campground to Millpond Loop Trail. Access to the primitive **backpack camp** is provided by a short side trail off Millpond Loop Trail. There are five sites. A pit toilet is provided. All supplies must be carried to the area.

Millpond Access Area is reached via SR 1403. Near the parking lot are the picnic ground, boat ramp, and trailheads for both canoe and hiking trails. A trailer serves as a temporary **interpretive center** and contains exhibits. A staff member is on duty during the summer to interpret the cultural and natural history of the park.

A **picnic ground** is near the boat ramp and in view of the millpond. There are seven tables and grills without shelters but in the shade of large trees; pit toilets and drinking water are provided. A loop trail, 0.3 mile in length, passes through the picnic area and around a small peninsula extending into the pond.

A **boat ramp** and a wooden **pier**, easily accessible from the parking area, facilitate the launching of canoes and small fishing boats (with trolling motors only) into Merchants Millpond. **Canoe rentals** are made from a preserved tobacco barn that stands near the water's edge; the barn is typical of those commonly used in the past in rural North Carolina for curing tobacco leaves for market. Canoes, life preservers, and paddles may be rented on a first-come basis by persons at least fifteen years of age for use in Merchants Millpond and Lassiter Swamp. Rentals are by the hour or by the day; daily rental is from 8:00 A.M. until one hour before the posted gate-closing time, or it may include overnight camping at one of the canoe campgrounds. For information about rental fees and regulations on use of canoes, contact the park superintendent.

The beauty and distinctive features of Merchants Millpond State Park are perhaps best appreciated while paddling a canoe among the great trees that grow above the smooth, dark surface of the slow-moving waters. In the stillness of the forests, the fortunate observer may witness the wind stirring the branches, the song of an unseen bird, the splash made by a turtle disturbed from its spot in the sun, the color of a swamp rose growing on a stump hummock. This is a special and beautiful place, a sanctuary from the modern world.

Canoeists may explore the relatively broad expanse of Merchants Millpond, moving quietly among towering bald cypresses and tupelo gums, with their massive, swollen trunks and luxuriant growths of Spanish moss, and around islands of vegetation clinging to life on old stumps left behind by loggers' saws. The millpond narrows gradually and the forest closes in as the mouth of Lassiter Swamp is reached. The creek channel through the swamp is often indistinct and may be difficult to follow; only a few feet above sea level, the water moves sluggishly, and the direction of the current may best be determined by observing objects floating on its surface. Relatively few visitors enter Lassiter Swamp, but those who do share an uncommon experience. In this remote and undisturbed swamp, there is an abundance of wildlife, especially animals adapted to life in aquatic or wetland habitats. There is greater plant diversity in the swamp than in the millpond, with ashes, red maple, and swamp hickory intermingled with cypress and gum. Within this ancient swamp is a stand of tupelo gum, part of what has been called an "enchanted forest," with trunks and branches distorted by numerous burls and knobs caused by the presence of American mistletoe, a common plant parasite. The roots of the mistletoe penetrate the tissues of deciduous trees and absorb nutrients. The host tree produces a woody growth that surrounds the parasite, apparently isolating the affected area. Large masses of mistletoe, with its leathery, oval leaves and white berries, may be seen at the tops of the trees.

Two canoe trails lead from the boat ramp to primitive canoe camping areas on the north side of Merchants Millpond. Orange markers lead to the **family canoe camp**, with seven sites, and yellow markers lead to the **group canoe camp**, with three sites. Sites are available on a first-come basis, except that organized groups that provide their own canoes may make advance reservations. Pit toilets are provided. All supplies must be carried to the sites. A fee is charged. For additional information, contact the park superintendent.

Fishermen have been attracted to Merchants Millpond since early in its history. Today, **fishing** for largemouth bass, bluegill, chain pickerel, and black crappie is perhaps the most popular activity on the millpond. Fishermen may cast their lines either from the bank (usually in the vicinity of the dam on SR 1403) or from boats that drift idly among the gum and cypress trees. The parking area and boat ramp provide easy access to the pond. The North Carolina Wildlife Resources Commission stocks the pond with game species and regulates water level in the millpond. All state fishing regulations are enforced, including possession of a valid fishing license.

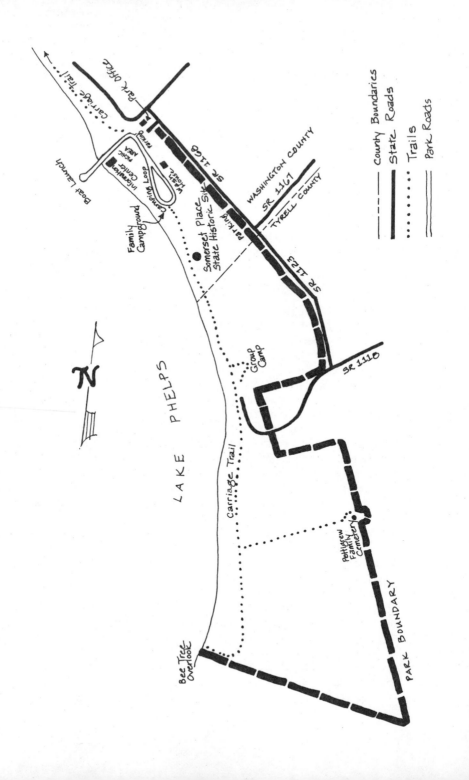

County Boundaries
State Roads
Trails
Park Roads

Carriage Trail
Park Office
SR 1160
WASHINGTON COUNTY
SR 1167
TYRELL COUNTY
SR 1123
Parking
Boat Launch
Picnic Area
Information Center
Camping Loop
Wash House
Parking
Family Campground
Somerset Place State Historic Site
N
SR 1110
Group Camp
LAKE PHELPS
Carriage Trail
Pettigrew Family Cemetery
Bee Tree Overlook
PARK BOUNDARY

PETTIGREW STATE PARK

Address: Route 1, Box 336
             Creswell, N.C. 27928

Telephone: (919) 797-4475

Size: 17,449 total acres
             (849 acres of land and 16,600 acres of water)

Established: 1939

Location: Washington and Tyrrell counties; turn south off U.S. 64 at Cres-
            well and follow park signs for 7 miles on SR 1142, SR 1160, and SR 1168
            to entry gate.

Principal Attractions: Lake Phelps, a Carolina bay lake; Somerset Place, a
            state historic site, the plantation home of Josiah Collins III built in the
            late eighteenth and early nineteenth centuries.

Visitor Activities: Fishing and boating on Lake Phelps; touring Somerset
            Place; picnicking; hiking and nature study; family camping.

Season: Open year-round.

Pettigrew State Park is the largest of North Carolina's parks. Located on
16,600-acre Lake Phelps, it includes the lake, 349 acres of land on the lake's
northeast shore, where visitor-use facilities are concentrated, and 500 undeveloped acres of land on the south side of the lake. The park provides for
diverse visitor interests, including water-related recreation on Lake Phelps,
nature study in the forests and along hiking trails bordering the lake, and
exploration into the social and agricultural history of the area at Somerset
Place, a preserved plantation site encompassed by the park.

Lake Phelps is a Carolina bay lake; such lakes are described in the section
on Jones Lake State Park. With approximately 25 square miles of water
surface, Lake Phelps is the second-largest natural freshwater lake in the
state. Fed by precipitation and springs, it has an average depth of 4 feet and a
maximun depth of 8 feet. Lake Phelps is situated on a broad, flat peninsula, an
area of the lower coastal plain bordered by Albemarle Sound to the north,
Pamlico River to the south, and Croatan and Pamlico sounds to the east. This
low-lying landmass is characterized by numerous bays, rivers, lakes, bogs,
and swamps, features that have greatly influenced the history of the area and
the use of the land.

Artifacts found in the vicinity of Lake Phelps document the presence of Indians as early as 8,000 B.C. It is not clear whether the Indians established permanent villages or came to the area only seasonally to hunt and fish in the lake. Pottery, projectile points, and other objects have been recovered, but the approximately thirty dugout canoes discovered sunken in the lake are of greatest interest to archaeologists. The dugouts range in length from 24 to 37 feet and are varied in style, some with blunt and some with pointed bows or sterns. The 37-foot vessel is the longest Indian dugout canoe discovered in the South. Radiocarbon dating of nineteen of the canoes has shown them to range in age from 550 to 4,380 years, with six being over 2,000 years old; the 4,380-year-old canoe is the second oldest to be discovered in the United States. The canoes found at Lake Phelps were made by burning out the interior of cypress logs and scraping away the charred wood until only a shell remained. If the Indians camped in the area seasonally, they may have stored and protected their boats by purposely sinking them in the shallow water.

Prior to 1755, the wilderness swampland in the region around the lake was considered by European settlers to be a "haunt of beasts" and the "Great Eastern Dismal," a forbidding and mysterious place rarely entered. Tradition credits a group of hunters seeking suitable land for hunting and farming with the discovery of the lake. Josiah Phelps, the first man to reach the water, claimed the right to name it for himself. Following the discovery of the lake, the surrounding land was transformed into productive agricultural fields and prosperous plantations.

Development of the area was initiated by a group of businessmen led by Josiah Collins, Sr., an Edenton merchant who immigrated to America from Somersetshire, England, in 1773. The Lake Company was formed in 1785; over 100,000 acres of swampland around Lake Phelps were acquired, and efforts were begun to drain the area for farming. An estate was cleared, mills were constructed, and a canal 6 miles in length was cut by slaves to connect the lake with the Scuppernong River. Completed in 1788, the canal served not only for drainage and irrigation but also for transportation to ports on Albemarle Sound, as supplies were received and farm products carried to market via the waterway. In time, an extensive system of canals with locks was developed to facilitate the production of rice and corn.

Collins ultimately became sole owner of the Lake Company and continued to develop the enterprise in association with his son, Josiah Collins, Jr., who managed the farm after his father's death. Somerset Place, named for the family's home county in England, was inherited by Josiah Collins III, who completed construction of the fourteen-room mansion. He and his wife began their occupancy in 1830. The plantation flourished and landholdings increased during the next thirty years. The mansion became a favorite gathering place for the planter aristocracy of the area. The Collinses were generous hosts to great numbers of house guests, who often stayed for extended periods of time.

The Civil War brought an end to the prosperity and the elegance of Somerset Place; with the coming of Federal troops to the area, the Collins family fled to Hillsborough, North Carolina, where Josiah Collins III died impoverished in 1863. His widow was forced to sell the plantation, which changed hands several times before it was acquired by the United States Farm Security Administration in the 1930s.

Bonarva, home of the Pettigrew family, neighbored Somerset Place. Bonarva plantation was established in 1789 by Reverend Charles Pettigrew, the first Episcopal bishop-elect of the state; his son was a congressman, and his grandson, James Johnston Pettigrew, for whom the state park is named, was a Confederate general who gained fame at Gettysburg. All three men are buried in the family cemetery within the park. The last Pettigrew home on the plantation was destroyed in 1953, and only a few bricks remain to indicate the site.

Pettigrew State Park was established in 1939 as a result of a ninety-nine-year lease of land by the United States Department of Agriculture to the North Carolina Department of Conservation and Development. After selling federally owned land adjacent to the park at auction, the Department of Agriculture deeded approximately 203 acres to the state in 1947, giving it permanent ownership of established parkland. An additional 66 acres were purchased between 1952 and 1961, and 500 acres on the south shore were acquired in 1963; 80 acres were added by purchase during 1986–87.

Colony House (left) and the Collins mansion, Somerset Place

SOMERSET PLACE STATE HISTORIC SITE

Somerset Place State Historic Site occupies 8 acres of land within Pettigrew State Park and is managed by the Division of Archives and History of the North Carolina Department of Cultural Resources. The site may be reached via SR 1168 a short distance past the main entry gate of the park, or by a brief hike from the parking lot at the park office. The Collins mansion and gardens and several outbuildings have been beautifully preserved. Visitors may imagine what life on a nineteenth-century plantation in eastern North Carolina was like.

The restoration of buildings and gardens was begun in 1951 and is continuing. The refurbishing of the interior of the Collins mansion was completed in 1969. The stately mansion, constructed of heart cypress grown on the plantation, features elements of the early Greek Revival style in combination with a traditional coastal style that is most evident in the large, double-deck verandas, across which blow cool breezes from Lake Phelps. Even though few pieces of original furniture remain, the great house is filled with furnishings dating from 1810 to 1860.

There were at least twenty outbuildings near the Collins mansion. Those restored and still standing are the kitchen, kitchen storehouse, smokehouse, icehouse, and Colony House. The bathhouse and overseer's house have been rebuilt. Colony House, said to have been the residence of Josiah Collins III and his wife while the mansion was being completed, later housed their sons and their tutors and served as a guesthouse; today it is a visitor information center. A residence for the park superintendent was constructed in 1954 on the former site of the plantation overseer's house. The sites of other outbuildings, including slave quarters, hospital, chapel, and woodhouse, have been subjects for documentary and archaeological research. The foundation of one of these structures survives. Restoration of additional buildings is planned. The visitor center has preserved plantation slave records for genealogical research.

The spacious lawn and formal gardens are adjacent to the mansion. The grounds and buildings are bordered by picturesque white wooden fences, and brick walks crisscross the area and lead to the big house. A carriage drive lined by huge cypress trees leads to the front entrance of the mansion, alongside Somerset Canal, which was dug to its 20-foot width by slaves in the 1780s.

When occupied by the Collins family, the mansion stood close to the lake, and the view of the water was unobstructed; only great cypress trees grew at the water's edge. Today, due to a reduction in the size of the lake, the shore is farther from the house, and the view is obstructed by vegetation. One can still imagine the serene beauty witnessed from the Collinses' veranda on a cool spring evening as the sun set behind Lake Phelps.

Somerset Place is open daily; guided tours of the Collins mansion are provided, and admission is free. For additional information, including schedules and a printed guide to the site, write: Site Manager, Somerset Place, P.O. Box 215, Creswell, N.C. 27928.

PLANT LIFE

The flora of Pettigrew State Park is characterized both by its diversity and by the large size of many trees in the forest bordering Lake Phelps. The dominant plant community on the north side of the lake is an impressive fringe of deciduous forest with stands of large bald cypress, sweet gum, sycamore, tulip poplar, sugarberry, shagbark hickory, swamp tupelo, and laurel, swamp chestnut, and cherrybark oaks. The understory is dominated by pawpaw, Virginia willow, spicebush, and beauty berry. In season, wildflowers add color throughout the forest; prominent species include Atamasco lily, Jack-in-the-pulpit, jewelweed, buttercup, and mist flower.

Individual trees of seven species have trunk diameters of 5.5 feet or more. Bald cypresses may measure up to 10 feet, and poplars may exceed 6 feet. Within the park are the state champion sugarberry, shagbark hickory, pawpaw, blackgum, and devil's walking stick.

An evergreen shrub community is present around the south shore of the lake in an area of bay bogs. Usually associated with Carolina bay lakes, the evergreen shrub community is typified by a canopy of pond or loblolly pine with a dense undergrowth of fetterbush, leatherwood, gallberry, pepper bush, and sweet, red, and loblolly bay. Marsh communities along the lakeshore include grasses and aquatic plants, such as pickerelweed, cattails, and yellow cow lily.

ANIMAL LIFE

The clear water of Lake Phelps is habitat for abundant and diverse fish populations, which attract large numbers of fishermen to the park. Important game species are largemouth bass, yellow perch, chain pickerel, channel and white catfish, and several sunfishes, including bluegill, shellcracker (redear), warmouth, and pumpkinseed. Many smaller species flourish and provide forage for larger fish; among the forage fish are golden shiners, tidewater silversides, and striped killifish. The shallow, sandy bottom along the lakeshore is habitat for the Waccamaw killifish, which is listed as endangered and is known only in Lake Phelps and Lake Waccamaw.

Eastern North Carolina has an abundant and diverse amphibian and reptilian fauna. The marshy perimeter of Lake Phelps and its associated canals and wetlands are home to large numbers of frogs and toads of several species. A chorus of sounds unfamiliar to many visitors may be heard on warm summer evenings, as bullfrogs, leopard frogs, several species of tree frogs, and various toads call to prospective mates. The wetlands are also home to various reptiles, including several species of snakes. Most visible, however, may be numerous turtles, referred to as sliders or cooters, which bask on stumps or logs on warm days.

The lake and its surrounding woodlands provide excellent bird-watching opportunities for visitors. Lake Phelps is one of several large, shallow, natural lakes of uncertain origin on the Pamlico-Albemarle peninsula. All lie within the primary North Carolina wintering ground for ducks, geese, and swans. Lake Mattamuskeet and Pungo Lake national wildlife refuges are the most important wintering areas for waterfowl, but Lake Phelps also provides refuge for significant numbers of birds. Lake Phelps serves primarily as a resting and roosting site for waterfowl that fly out to other sites in the surrounding region to feed. Canada geese and tundra swans often fly to surrounding agricultural fields, where they feed on waste grains. Ducks most often feed in wetlands and aquatic habitats that abound in the region.

The large, white tundra swans, the most conspicuous waterfowl at Lake Phelps, are becoming increasingly abundant. Canada geese are also large and easy to identify, but they are declining in numbers in northeastern North Carolina. Several species of dabbling and diving ducks are present. Scaup are usually the most abundant divers, but canvasback, redheads, and ruddy ducks are also present. Dabblers—species that tip up to reach for food on shallow bottoms—include mallards, black ducks, and pintails. Mergansers, which feed primarily on fish, also appear on the lake.

Most waterfowl arrive in northeastern North Carolina in October and November from their northern breeding grounds. December through February is the best period to see large numbers of waterfowl. The colorful wood duck is the only species that remains to nest in the region in significant numbers. A few hooded mergansers, mallards, and black ducks also raise their broods in the region, but most return to the western prairies and northern marshes for the summer.

The park is home to several species of birds of prey, including ospreys, great horned and barred owls, eastern screech-owls, American kestrels, red-tailed and red-shouldered hawks, and northern harriers; sightings of bald eagles have increased in recent years. The shoreline provides habitat for several of the most prominent avian residents of the park, including belted kingfishers, great egrets, great blue herons, green-backed herons, and spotted sandpipers, which seek small fish, insects, and other food at the water's edge. Bobwhite quail, mourning dove, and American woodcock occur in upland areas, and pileated woodpeckers may be seen throughout the park. Nesting songbirds include prothonotary and prairie warblers, northern parulas, and common yellowthroats.

Fortunate and observant individuals may discover several familiar mammals, even though most are secretive and avoid people. Densely wooded habitats such as bay bogs or pocosins may occasionally be visited by black bear. White-tailed deer, relatively common in the area, are often found in open woodlands. Other woodland species present in the park are eastern cottontail, gray squirrel, Virginia opossum, gray fox, and bobcat. Wooded areas along the lakeshore are a prime habitat for raccoon, mink, and muskrat, and river otters have been seen in the open water of the lake. Mammal-watchers should look for these animals at dawn or dusk, when all is quiet and still.

HIKING TRAIL

The Collins family and its guests enjoyed carriage rides on a road that passed Somerset Place and Bonarva along the north shore of Lake Phelps. Today, a portion of the original drive is known as **Carriage Trail**, a nature trail that provides a rewarding hiking experience for park visitors. Beginning at the park office parking lot, the first section of the trail, 1.4 miles in length, leads east past the campground, past Somerset Place and the Collins mansion at the 0.4-mile mark, and past Bonarva. The trail continues through a sweetgum forest to Bee Tree Canal and turns right along the canal to Bee Tree Canal Overlook, an elevated wooden platform with a beautiful view of Lake Phelps. A side trail that begins between Bonarva and Bee Tree Canal leads to the well-kept Pettigrew Cemetery; it is an easy walk of less than 1 mile.

The second section of Carriage Trail leads northwest from the park office for 2.7 miles through a narrow strip of parkland bordering the lake to the trail's terminus near Moccasin Canal, where another overlook was opened in July 1988; the overlook features a 300-foot boardwalk through the cypress forest. The wide, grassy trail passes through stands of bald cypress, sycamore, gum, and poplar trees, with impressive views of Lake Phelps at intervals along the route. Hikers must retrace their steps to the trailhead.

FACILITIES AND ACTIVITIES

The **park office** and parking lot are at the entry gate to the park, and major recreational facilities are nearby. Park personnel provide information, interpret the natural environment of the area, and assist in making a visit to the park an enjoyable experience.

A **picnic ground**, bordered by a split-rail fence and shaded by huge syca-more, sweet gum, and bald cypress trees, is adjacent to the parking lot and near the lakeshore. Picnickers are provided twenty tables, several grills, and drinking water. A playing field for visitor recreation is adjacent to the picnic area. Restrooms are at the park office.

The **family campground** is located between the park office and Somerset Place. A loop road provides access to thirteen tent and trailer spaces; some sites at the edge of a cypress/sweet-gum forest are well-shaded, but others are in an open, grassy area. Each site has a table and a grill; water and electric hookups for trailers are not provided. A centrally located washhouse has flush toilets, hot showers, and drinking water. Sites are available on a first-come basis, and a fee is charged.

A **youth group camp** with two tent pads, a hand pump for drinking water, a grill, and pit toilets is located east of Somerset Place in the vicinity of Bonarva; it is reached by way of Carriage Trail or by way of SR 1118, as shown on the map. The camp area accommodates up to twenty-five persons. Reser-vations are necessary, and a fee is charged; for additional information, contact the park office.

Fishing and **boating** are the most popular activities on Lake Phelps. The lake has been called an angler's paradise because large populations of many species of game fish are present. Spring and fall are the best times for catching largemouth bass. Yellow perch are numerous in summer. The best chance of catching channel catfish is in early spring; some specimens have weighed 20 pounds or more. Fishermen are welcome, but they must obey all North Carolina fishing regulations.

Fishing boats mingle with other private watercraft on the lake; powerboats, rowboats, canoes, kayaks, and sailboats all have ample room to enjoy the glistening, shallow water. Lake Phelps is especially well-suited for sailing, with an almost constant wind blowing across the water surface and no obsta-cles. Water-skiing is permitted.

A gravel road leads from the rear of the park office past the picnic ground and along an earthen roadbed that extends a short distance into Lake Phelps, providing the only public access to the lake. The road ends at a cul-de-sac with two **boat ramps** and two small piers for boarding or docking boats. Parking space for vehicles and boat trailers is limited, and the sides of the access road may become overcrowded during heavy-use periods.

An **information center**, a small building with educational displays, is located near the boat ramps; its displays include Indian dugout canoes found in Lake Phelps. Interpretive programs are scheduled on Friday evenings during the summer, and several special events are held annually. An Indian Heritage

Celebration in late September features exhibits of Lake Phelps artifacts, demonstrations of Indian crafts, and programs presented by special guests. An annual tree walk surveys the state-champion trees in the park. Information about these and other events may be obtained from the park office.

WAYNESBOROUGH STATE PARK

Address: Route 2, Box 50
             Seven Springs, N.C. 28578

Telephone: (919) 778-6234

Size: 142 acres

Established: 1979

Location: Wayne County, on the west side of Goldsboro off U.S. 117 bypass.

Principal Attractions: Neuse River; picnic and recreation facilities.

Visitor Activities: Picnicking; canoeing and fishing; hiking along the riverbank.

Season: Day-use park open each week from Wednesday through Sunday
except for holidays between Labor Day and Memorial Day.

Wayne County, formed in 1779, was without a county seat or an incorporated town until Dr. Andrew Bass provided 3 acres of land for a small frame
courthouse, a jail, and other county buildings in 1782. Bass deeded 60 additional acres to the newly organized town to be divided into one hundred lots to
be sold. The town of Waynesborough, named for Revolutionary War General
Anthony Wayne, had about 150 residents when it was incorporated in 1787. It
served as the county seat until 1847, when the courthouse building was moved
1.5 miles east to the new town of Goldsboro.

Waynesborough was built on the bank of the Neuse River near John Dixon's
Ferry and on the stagecoach road midway between New Bern, the colonial
capital, and Raleigh. Stagecoaches ran three times each week, and relay
stations—the places where horses were changed—were spaced 15 miles
apart. The trip from Waynesborough to New Bern, a distance of about 60
miles, lasted from 5:00 A.M. to 8:00 P.M. if there were no delays en route.
Steamboats also carried passengers and freight between New Bern and
Waynesborough, and sometimes as far west as Smithfield, along the Neuse
River. Because Waynesborough was at the midway point in the two-day
journey between New Bern and Raleigh, several taverns and hotels were built
to accommodate travelers.

Residents of Waynesborough migrated from the coast and from areas to the
north; estimates of the peak population range from two hundred to nearly five

hundred. Numerous businesses were established, including a harness and buggy manufacturing plant, sawmills and gristmills, a rosin still, warehouses, and dry-goods and grocery stores. The Neuse River was vital to commerce in the area. Steamboats and river barges plied the rivers, carrying cargos that included lumber, naval stores, cotton, and produce. The docks and the streets of the town bustled with activity.

Waynesborough went into decline following the completion of the Wilmington to Weldon Railroad in 1839. The railroad passed 1.5 miles from Waynesborough, and a new town, Goldsboro, rapidly developed around the depot and crossroads. A hotel for train passengers was built, and other buildings were located along the tracks. Many residents of Waynesborough moved their homes to the new town. In 1845, a vote to move the courthouse to Goldsboro failed; a second vote in 1847 was successful, however, and the decline of Waynesborough was accelerated. Goldsboro was incorporated in 1847 with 175 residents, and by 1865 only a few buildings and the boat docks remained in Waynesborough. The few surviving buildings were burned when Sherman's army marched through the area. A brick plant built in 1870 by H. L. Grant operated at Waynesborough until 1918, and for a time the docks received logs floated down the Neuse.

The old town site, which provided fill dirt during the construction of the U.S. 117 bypass, was purchased in 1960 by the city of Goldsboro for use as a landfill. In 1972, when the landfill was still in use, the Old Waynesborough Commission was formed for the purpose of determining the feasibility of creating a historic park at the site. In the 1970s, Goldsboro deeded 56 acres of land on the riverbank at what was once the center of Waynesborough to the commission, and an accompanying park proposal included limited restoration of several historic buildings. There was strong local support for the proposal; funds were provided by county and city governments and by the private sector. State appropriations were obtained, and in June 1979 the state was deeded 140 acres of land for the establishment of a state park. Present park development has been a joint effort by the local community and the state. Fill dirt to cover the landfill was provided by the North Carolina Department of Transportation. A boat basin was cleared and dredged by a unit of engineers from Seymour Johnson Air Force Base with the help of equipment loaned by a local construction firm. Although Waynesborough State Park does not currently meet some standards of acreage and resource quality established for state parks, the park master plan has been designed to address such problems.

FACILITIES AND ACTIVITIES

A colonial-style gate, park sign, and split-rail fence mark the entrance to the park, directly off U.S. 117 bypass. The paved entry road ends at a twenty-four-car parking lot with easy access to recreation facilities. Parkland is open except along the riverbank. Over a hundred trees, all native species, have been planted throughout the area. Paved walkways lead to three attractive brick structures—a modern restroom building, a picnic pavilion, and a gazebo. The restrooms are centrally located for all park users, and drinking water is provided. Twenty picnic tables are available to visitors; most are spaced about the park grounds near the access walkway, while others are sheltered within the pavilion. The octagonal gazebo is located on a bluff above the bank of the river; there are benches for relaxation, and the open sides provide an excellent view of the historic Neuse River. A short nature trail leads along the water's edge.

An attractive wooden ramp with side rails leads from the gazebo down the slope of the bluff to a floating dock on the Neuse River. Canoeing is a popular activity along the river, and sportsmen fish for channel catfish, bass, and bream either from the bank or from boats launched at a wildlife boat-access ramp located 2 miles downstream.

Waynesborough State Park offers excellent opportunities for daytime recreation. Families may picnic, play, and relax in open, unobstructed areas of the park and enjoy the serene beauty of the Neuse River. Visitors may also relive in their imaginations events that took place on this bit of land long ago—a stagecoach traveling a dusty road, a steamboat laboring against the currents of the Neuse, or a group of sturdy folk working to build a town.

NEARBY

Charles B. Aycock Birthplace State Historic Site commemorates the twelfth governor of North Carolina, elected in 1900, and his dedication to improving public education for all the children of the state. The site preserves a nineteenth-century family farm with its house, separate kitchen, and outbuildings. A one-room schoolhouse typical of the period has been moved to the birthplace as a reminder of Aycock's commitment to the teaching of children. Tours begin at the visitor center. The site is located 9 miles north of Goldsboro; from Fremont, proceed south 1 mile on U.S. 117, then turn east onto SR 1542 for 0.5 mile. For information, write: Site Manager, Charles B. Aycock Birthplace State Historic Site, P.O. Box 207, Fremont, N.C. 27830.

Bentonville Battleground State Historic Site preserves about 100 acres of the 6,000-acre battleground where sixty thousand Union and twenty thousand Confederate troops fought one of the last major engagements of the Civil War. Bentonville was the scene of the largest and bloodiest battle on North Carolina soil. The forces of General Joseph E. Johnston attempted to prevent Union General William T. Sherman from reaching Goldsboro, an important rail supply center. The battle lasted three days, from March 19 to March 21, 1865, with heavy casualties; Johnston retreated west, surrendering to Sherman on April 26 at Bennett Place, near Durham. The historic site is located in rural Johnston County; from Newton Grove, drive 3 miles north on U.S. 701, then turn east onto SR 1008 and follow the signs for 3 miles to the site. A visit should begin at the visitor center, which offers an audiovisual presentation and exhibits. Visitors may stroll about the battlefield, still dotted with earthworks, and to Harper House, an 1850s-style home that served as a field hospital for the wounded of both armies. The Harper family cemetery and the gravesites of casualties of the conflict are nearby. For information, write: Site Manager, Bentonville Battleground State Historic Site, Box 27, Newton Grove, N.C. 28366.

Piedmont

BOONE'S CAVE STATE PARK

Address: c/o North Carolina State Parks
West District Office
Route 2, Box 224M
Troutman, N.C. 28166

Telephone: (704) 528-6514

Size: 110 acres

Established: 1971

Location: Davidson County, 14 miles west of Lexington. From I-85, turn northwest onto N.C. 150 between Lexington and Salisbury and proceed 5 miles to Churchland; turn west onto Boone's Cave Road (SR 1165/1162/1167) for 4.5 miles to entry gate. Also, from U.S. 64, turn south onto N.C. 150 west of Lexington and proceed 6.5 miles to Churchland, then continue as above.

Principal Attractions: Yadkin River, with rock outcrops and entrance to Boone's Cave along its banks; reconstructed cabin; forest of hardwoods with rhododendron and mountain laurel; rest stop on the Yadkin River Canoe Trail.

Visitor Activities: Picnicking, hiking, fishing, and nature study.

Season: This is a day use park open year-round except weekdays from Christmas to mid-March.

Daniel Boone, folk hero and frontiersman best known for his explorations of wilderness lands west of the Appalachian Mountains, lived for twenty-one years in North Carolina, longer than he lived in any other part of the young and expanding nation. Squire Boone, Daniel's father, led his family down the Shenandoah Valley from Pennsylvania to the Yadkin region in 1752. Daniel, sixteen years of age, was one of nine children who made the journey. They were part of a migration of thousands of immigrant Scotch-Irish, English, and Welsh families lured to the foothills and the Piedmont of North Carolina by the promise of cheap or free land.

The Boones established homesteads at several locations in the state. According to tradition, the first was on the east bank of the Yadkin River in present-day Davidson County on land now included in Boone's Cave State

Park. The Daniel Boone Memorial Association, incorporated by the North Carolina General Assembly of 1909, sought to document the claim that the Boones lived at the current site of the park. The evidence included testimonials of old-time residents, records of family membership in nearby Boone's Ford Baptist Church, records in the Rowan County clerk's office, and the record of Daniel's 1756 marriage to Rebecca Bryan, whose home was only 4 miles from the site. Remnants of the walls and chimney of a cabin presumed to be that of the Boones existed on a high bluff overlooking the river until early this century; the rubble was removed gradually from the site by souvenir hunters. Large hearthstones remained, however, including one reportedly inscribed "D. Boone."

The claims of the association have been disputed, and both the authenticity of the site and its historical significance remain subjects of contention. If the Boone family did live there, it was only briefly; in 1753, Squire Boone acquired land on the west bank of the river and subsequently resided at a site near Mocksville in Davie County. For seventeen years following their marriage, Daniel and Rebecca established homesteads at different locations farther west along the Yadkin. The exploits of Daniel Boone in North Carolina, Kentucky, and elsewhere have been well-chronicled and are part of the lore of the country's westward expansion. Regardless of whether the site in Boone's Cave State Park was a Boone homestead in legend or in fact, the parkland serves as a treasured memorial to the "Long Hunter of the Yadkin."

In 1909, Phillip Sowers donated 3 acres of land on the east bank of the Yadkin River to the Daniel Boone Memorial Association. The land included the alleged homestead site of Squire Boone. A local park was established and administered by the association, which reconstructed a cabin on the site and provided facilities for picnicking. Additional land was acquired, enlarging the park to 110 acres. A proposal that the area be designated a state historic site was not approved by the North Carolina Division of Archives and History because its use by Daniel Boone was not clearly established. On November 12, 1970, however, the land was accepted as a gift to the state of North Carolina and became part of the state parks system. Efforts to enlarge the park to meet the minimum standard of 400 acres for state parks have been unsuccessful to date. At present, Boone's Cave State Park remains the smallest of the state's parks, a place of serene beauty on the bank of the storied Yadkin River.

PLANT AND ANIMAL LIFE

The park terrain is rugged, with high bluffs above the river and steep slopes to rock outcrops at the water's edge; knolls and ridges are small and narrow. An area of flat bottomland lies within the flood plain of the river. Timber has been cut from the area, but extensive secondary growth has developed. Hardwoods, including beech, elm, oaks, and hickories, cover the slopes and the higher ground, and rhododendron and mountain laurel are abundant on slopes along the river; ferns and more than thirty species of wildflowers grow on the forest floor. Pines predominate in lowland areas.

Vertebrate fauna in the park is characteristic of the North Carolina Piedmont and includes gray squirrels, white-tailed deer, foxes, raccoons, and many familiar songbirds. Fishermen may catch a variety of game fishes in the Yadkin, including catfish, sunfish, crappie, and largemouth and white bass. Applicable state fishing regulations are enforced.

FACILITIES AND ACTIVITIES

Boone's Cave Road leads past the entry gate and the park sign into a small parking lot and dead-ends at a bluff overlooking the Yadkin River. A **picnic shelter** on the bluff contains a table and a grill; five additional tables and a grill are in the shade of trees to the left. A restroom is nearby, and an exhibit board provides information about the life and exploits of Daniel Boone. To the left of the picnic shelter, a path curves downward to a wooden stairway with handrails that descends sharply to the bank of the river. Paths provide access to extensive outcrops of granite-gneiss rocks at the water's edge and, to the right, to the entrance to Boone's Cave.

Boone's Cave, also called Devil's Den, is the focal feature of the park. Its entrance, 2 to 3 feet in height, is adjacent to the riverbank in the rockface of the steep slope. The cave's tunnel is about 80 feet in length and varies in height from 4.5 feet near the entrance to less than 1 foot near its terminus; it

Boone's Cave

is narrow, and explorers must crawl along most of the passageway. The cave was formed by the action of floodwater and the splitting away of the walls and roof. Rocks and soil that fell to the floor of the cave were carried away by the river. According to tradition, Daniel Boone often slept in the cave and on at least one occasion hid from Indians there.

Daniel Boone Trail, 0.5 mile in length, leads from its trailhead on the left near the park entry gate through the hardwood forest to **Boone's cabin** and beyond. The reconstructed log cabin is on the site where the original structure considered to be that of Squire Boone once stood. The single-room cabin measures 18 by 36 feet and has a double fireplace, two windows, and three doors. It is situated in a clearing on a bluff above the Yadkin. The trail proceeds by a series of switchbacks down a steep slope to a flood plain and along the riverbank to Boone's Cave and the wooden stairway back to the parking lot.

The rock outcrop adjacent to Boone's Cave is a rest stop for canoeists along the **Yadkin River Canoe Trail**. The steepness of the wooden steps to the parking lot prohibits the launching and taking out of canoes. Canoeists seeking information about the trail and the locations of access points should write: Yadkin River Trail Association, 280 South Liberty Street, Winston-Salem, N.C. 27101.

NEARBY

Spencer Shops, located at 411 South Salisbury Avenue in Spencer and accessible from I-85 or U.S. 70, is a state historic site. The shops were once a staging and repair facility for locomotives of the Southern Railway; they are now restored as the North Carolina Transportation Museum. They feature exhibits and artifacts that trace the development of transportation in the state. Admission is free. For information, write: Spencer Shops State Historic Site, P.O. Box 165, Spencer, N.C. 28159 (704/636-2889).

INTERSTATE 85

SR 1122

Whiteside Road (SR 1122)

Linwood Road

Camp Rotary Road (SR 1131)

Freedom Mill Road (SR 1125)

N

Back-side Trail

CROWDERS MOUNTAIN

Tower Trail

Crowders Trail

Loop Trail

Group Camping

Family Camping

Crowders Trail

Park Office

SR 1106

Pinnacle Trail

Turn-back Trail

Lake Trail

PICNIC AREA

Lake Trail

KINGS PINNACLE

Fishing

Park Boundary

Sparrow Springs Road (SR 1125)

Pinnacle Road (SR 1104)

- - - - - Hiking Trails

━━━━━ Roads

Fishing Lake

. . . . . Bridle Trail

Major Ridge

CROWDERS MOUNTAIN STATE PARK

Address: Route 1, Box 159
             Kings Mountain, N.C. 28086

Telephone: (704) 867-1181

Size: 2,083 acres

Established: 1973

Location: Gaston County, 25 miles west of Charlotte and 6 miles southwest of
             Gastonia; exit I-85 at junction with U.S. 29/74, turn south onto SR 1125
             (Freedom Mill Road) to park entrance, and follow signs to park office.

Principal Attractions: Crowders Mountain, with sheer vertical cliffs and
             scenic overlooks, and Kings Pinnacle; excellent hiking trails; 9-acre
             lake; diverse plant and animal resources.

Visitor Activities: Hiking; rock climbing; primitive family and group camp-
             ing; fishing; nature study; picnicking.

Season: Open year-round.

The gently rolling landscape of
the North Carolina Piedmont near
Gastonia is punctuated by a pair of
rugged peaks that rise 800 feet
above the surrounding countryside.
Crowders Mountain (elevation
1,625 feet) and Kings Pinnacle (elevation 1,705 feet) are remnants of
an ancient mountain range, part of
the Appalachian chain, that formed
in the region 450 to 500 million
years ago. These surviving peaks,
classified geologically as kyanite-
quartzite monadnocks, were once
at the core of mighty mountains
that towered thousands of feet
above sea level. The rocks now exposed to view have thus far resisted the leveling forces of erosion
over vast periods of geological time.

*Rock climbers on cliffs
of Crowders Mountain*

Crowders Mountain, a registered North Carolina natural heritage area, is the dominant physical feature of the park. It features impressive rock formations and sheer vertical cliffs 100 to 150 feet in height; Kings Pinnacle, by contrast, has a more gently rounded profile. The two mountains and a connecting saddle are oriented in a northeast-to-southwest direction, their elongated slopes facing east and west. The views from the two summits are spectacular. In spite of extensive urban and industrial development in the area, belts of green stretch to the horizon in all directions. Rocky ledges and outcrops are "box seats" from which to view the panorama spread out below and to see eye to eye with hawks, vultures, and other birds as they soar effortlessly on the wind currents around the peaks.

Before the arrival of European settlers in the mid-eighteenth century, much of the land in the area was upland savanna or natural prairie grazed by herds of woodland buffalo. The peaks marked the boundary between the hunting lands of Catawba and Cherokee Indians, and a major trading route of the Cherokees crossed the northeast slope of Crowders Mountain. Settlers migrated to the region before 1750 from colonies to the north, and by 1775 approximately eighty thousand Scotch-Irish and Germans were established in the area. A treaty in 1777 allowed white settlers as far west as the Blue Ridge Mountains. The Catawbas retreated peacefully southward, but conflicts between settlers and Cherokees continued until after the Revolutionary War, often in the vicinity of Crowders and Kings mountains. During the revolution, a major victory for the colonists was won at nearby Kings Mountain in South Carolina in 1780.

An early settler, German merchant Ulrich Crowder, acquired land in the area and laid out the new town of Ulricksburg in 1789 before moving farther west. His landholdings included the mountain that now bears his name.

The discovery and mining of valuable minerals have had a major influence on the people and the land of the southern Piedmont, including Gaston, Mecklenburg, and Cabarrus counties. The most important mineral discovered was gold. A 17-pound nugget was found in Cabarrus County by twelve-year-old Conrad Reed in 1799; another found in 1803 weighed 28 pounds. Significant quantities of the coveted mineral were discovered in the area near Crowders Mountain in 1829. During

Rock formations on Crowders Mountain

the North Carolina gold rush, hundreds of mines and mining claims pockmarked at least ten counties. Until the famous discovery of gold in Sutter's Creek in California in 1849, North Carolina was the chief gold-producing state in the nation. Kyanite was also mined locally; Henrys Knob, near Crowders Mountain, was strip-mined, and the persistent scars of that operation provide mute testimony to the devastating effect such actions have upon the environment.

The threat that Crowders Mountain would be strip-mined motivated local citizens to seek its preservation. Exploratory drilling, excavation, and road grading began in August 1970. The Gaston County Conservation Society was organized in November of that year with the objectives of alerting people to the imminent danger of the loss of the landmark, attempting to block mining operations, and encouraging the state to acquire the mountain for a park. A proposal for the preservation of the area endorsed by the local Sierra Club, Centralina Council of Governments, and Gastonia City Council was presented to the state in January 1971 by the Gaston County Conservation Society. In July 1971, as a result of the efforts of the conservation society, the North Carolina Board of Conservation and Development accepted Crowders Mountain as a potential state park, and state funds were provided for land acquisition a year later. More than a hundred separate tracts of land needed for the proposed park were listed in the *Gastonia Gazette* on July 10, 1973; by July 1974, over 1,000 acres had been acquired by negotiation. The new state park was opened to the public in October 1974, but it was not until December 1977 that the 645 acres that included the summit of Crowders Mountain were purchased for a price of $2,148,320.

Dr. George Ball of Gaston College, an active member of the Gaston County Conservation Society, described the society's effort as a grass-roots project involving "one hundred or more people" operating on a very limited budget. He credited Richard Cone, first president of the society, with being "the one person who is most responsible for the park's existence." The people of North Carolina owe a debt of gratitude to the Gaston County Conservation Society for its leadership in adding this beautiful park to the state system.

Kings Pinnacle and a portion of the ridge connecting it to Crowders Mountain were added to the park in 1987 with the purchase of 182 acres of land from the Plonk family of Kings Mountain. The former owners had granted park visitors access to the summit of Kings Pinnacle since the establishment of the park, but the acquisition of this beautiful area has served to protect it from any possibility of future mining operations.

PLANT LIFE

Most Piedmont forest types are represented in the park. A mature climax forest consisting primarily of hardwoods is present throughout most of the park. Some areas, such as the south ridge of Crowders Mountain, have been disturbed by logging and fire; elsewhere, there were open fields thirty or more years ago. These areas are being restored by natural processes. Shrubby growth was followed by pines, like the Virginia pine, which in turn are gradually being replaced by hardwoods. Some of the forest trees one may encounter along the trails are red maple, American beech, black cherry, tag alder, black gum, flowering dogwood, and white, scarlet, blackjack, and chestnut oaks. Mountain laurel blooms in May and can be seen along Crowders Trail and Pinnacle Trail, among other places; rhododendron, though not abundant, grows at upper elevations. Blueberry and sparkleberry plants produce fruits that are eaten by many animals. Ferns are common in the park; bracken fern grows in sunny spots, and cinnamon, netted chain, and southern lady ferns can be seen along streams and in the mucky soil of bogs. Ferns over 6 feet tall grow on the north ridge of Crowders Mountain. Such rare species as bear oak, ground juniper, and Bradley's spleenwort are significant components of the park's flora. The ridge-top forest is unusual in that many species, especially Virginia pine, are dwarfs only 3 to 6 feet in height and in that a few specimens of the blighted American chestnut still persist.

ANIMAL LIFE

Park fauna is abundant and diverse but often unobserved. Clear, cold streams, such as the small creek along the self-guided nature trail, are home to crayfish, numerous minnows, and several species of frogs, including bullfrogs, pickerel frogs, and northern cricket frogs. Creek mud or boggy soil may reveal the footprints of muskrat, raccoon, or Virginia opossum. Such wet or moist areas are also habitat for dusky and two-lined salamanders, which are most often found under rotted logs, leaves, or rocks. Many species of turtles, such as mud, snapping, and spiny softshell turtles, are found in wetland habitats within the park.

Upland areas and mountain ridges support many other animals. Among resident amphibians and reptiles are Fowler's and American toads, slimy salamanders, eastern box turtles, and several species of snakes, including the poisonous copperhead. Hikers may glimpse a chipmunk, gray squirrel, or eastern cottontail scurrying across a trail; red and gray foxes are present but are rarely observed. The tunnels of eastern moles may be visible in the soft earth along hiking trails; the tunnels are formed as the insectivorous burrowers search for meals below ground. Small mammals such as shrews and white-footed mice inhabit the forest floor but rarely reveal their presence.

More than 160 species of birds, including waterfowl, wading birds, hawks, owls, woodpeckers, and many other groups, are listed as occurring in the park. Over 40 species of warblers have been found on the wooded hillsides of

Crowders Mountain and Kings Pinnacle as the birds migrate through the area. Black and turkey vultures roost on isolated rock outcrops near the peaks and fly daily into the surrounding countryside to search for carrion.

HIKING TRAILS

It is necessary to hike the well-marked trails to fully appreciate the beauty and diversity of Crowders Mountain State Park. Most of the trails lead along the ridges and to the summits of Kings Pinnacle and Crowders Mountain. The others are easy paths through quiet woods, along a gently flowing stream, or around a still lake.

Fern Nature Trail is an easy, forty-five-minute walk 0.9 mile in length that begins at the picnic ground parking lot. A guidebook available at the trailhead interprets much of the natural history of the area. Part of the trail is along a narrow creek that is home to aquatic plants and animals; the remainder leads through a quiet forest where the sounds are likely to be those of running water, the wind in the leaves, or the songs of birds among the shrubs. Forest trees that form a green canopy overhead are characteristic of the North Carolina Piedmont. Fern Nature Trail is a trail that nearly every park visitor can enjoy.

Lake Trail is an easy, graveled, 1-mile path that encircles the park's lake. The margin of the lake is beautifully wooded, and there is an excellent view of Kings Pinnacle from the trail. The trailhead is at the lake parking lot.

Pinnacle Trail, moderate in difficulty, begins at a trailhead near the park office and leads for 1.7 miles to the top of Kings Pinnacle. It follows a low, rocky ridge through an oak/hickory forest with scattered masses of mountain laurel to the base of Kings Pinnacle, then slopes gradually up its face to the top ridge and summit. There, the forest is dominated by conifers, especially Virginia pine, and there is a sweeping, 360-degree scenic view of the rolling Piedmont countryside. **Turnback Trail**, 1.2 miles in length, intersects Pinnacle Trail 0.8 mile below the summit of Kings Pinnacle and ends at the park office. It is a moderate to easy walk that provides an alternate return route from Kings Pinnacle or allows a hiker to turn back before ascending the slope to the summit. A late-afternoon hike along these trails is especially delightful when soft light filters through the green canopy overhead. The last segment of Turnback Trail passes through a disturbed area of woods where hikers can observe the ongoing process of natural restoration of the forest.

A complex of trails follows the ridges and leads to the summit of Crowders Mountain; this is the most rugged and spectacular portion of the park. The trails are moderately to strenuously difficult, but the effort is richly rewarded by the beauty of the mountain and by the views from the summit.

Crowders Trail is 3.2 miles in length and begins at the park office. The trail leads for 0.8 mile through a mature hardwood forest, crosses Freedom Mill Road (SR 1125), and skirts the west side of the ridge of the mountain to a junction with Backside Trail. The trailhead for **Backside Trail**, 1 mile in length, is on Linwood Road (SR 1131); the trail ascends the north end of the ridge and proceeds along the ridge top and up steep steps to the summit of Crowders Mountain, where it joins Rocktop Trail. **Rocktop Trail**, 2.25 miles in length, extends from its junction with Crowders Trail at Freedom Mill Road and ascends the south end of the ridge, where it proceeds along the crest of the ridge to the summit. Rocktop and Backside trails pass over rugged rock outcrops, and hikers look down from the tops of vertical cliffs up to 150 feet in height. **Tower Trail** begins with Backside Trail at Linwood Road, skirts the east side of the ridge, and ascends to the summit area; it extends for 2 miles along a service road to radio towers on the mountain.

FACILITIES AND ACTIVITIES

Climbing the cliffs of Crowders Mountain is one of the most popular and exciting activities for visitors to the park. Climbing is allowed at present without a permit, and numerous groups and individuals, many from nearby educational institutions, come to the park to learn or enhance mountaineering skills. Regulations governing climbing are posted in the park and are rigidly enforced; the most important rule is that all basic rock-climbing safety equipment and techniques must be used at all times. All climbing must be done with a safety rope, and, owing to the prevalence of loose rocks, use of a helmet is advised. Climbers must not employ pitons, bolts, or any similar devices that may damage the face of the cliffs. Violation of regulations is grounds for the revocation of the privilege to climb. Climbers as well as hikers must remember that plants, animals, and other park resources are protected and that every effort must be made to preserve the natural beauty of the park.

The **park office** is reached via a turnoff road from SR 1125. Follow the signs from the park entrance. Personnel at the office will provide information; several exhibits explain some of the natural history of the park. Most hiking trails lead from or return to the office.

Separate **family** and **group camping areas** are located 1 mile from the park office and are reached by trail; camping gear and supplies must be packed to campsites. Camping outside designated areas is prohibited. Hand-operated water pumps and pit toilets are provided at each area, and each numbered site has a grill. Group sites accommodate up to fifteen campers each and may be reserved by calling the park office; sites in the family area are available on a first-come basis. Campers must register at the office. A fee is charged. The park is open for camping year-round.

A beautiful **picnic ground** is located in a heavily wooded area. It has two shelters, twenty-eight outside tables, eight grills, drinking water, and a restroom. Ample parking space is nearby.

A 9-acre **lake** is near the park office and picnic ground; it is reached by way of a paved road and has a parking lot nearby. Boating and swimming are not permitted, but fishing from the bank for bass and bream is a peaceful, enjoyable experience. A scenic hiking trail loops around the lake.

NEARBY

Kings Mountain National Military Park, administered by the National Park Service, is located in South Carolina just across the state line from Crowders Mountain State Park. It preserves the battlefield where, on October 7, 1780, during a dark period of the Revolutionary War, nine hundred unsoldierly back-country men destroyed a British force of eleven hundred, a first step toward victory at Yorktown. A visitor center interprets the battle and its significance. For information, write: Superintendent, Kings Mountain National Military Park, P.O. Box 31, Kings Mountain, N.C. 28086.

Reed Gold Mine, south of Concord in Cabarrus County, is a North Carolina state historic site that marks the site where gold was discovered in 1799 by twelve-year-old Conrad Reed. Visitors can walk through mine tunnels, see a reconstructed ore-crushing mill, and pan for gold. The history of the area is interpreted at a visitor center. For information, write: Site Manager, Reed Gold Mine, Route 2, Box 101, Stanfield, N.C. 28163.

Excellent museums in the area focus on nature and provide exciting educational opportunities for the family. They are **Schiele Museum of Natural History**, 1500 East Garrison Boulevard, Gastonia, N.C. 28053; **Nature Museum**, 1658 Sterling Road, Charlotte, N.C. 28209; and **Discovery Place**, 301 North Tryon Street, Charlotte, N.C. 28202. Information about each can be obtained by mail.

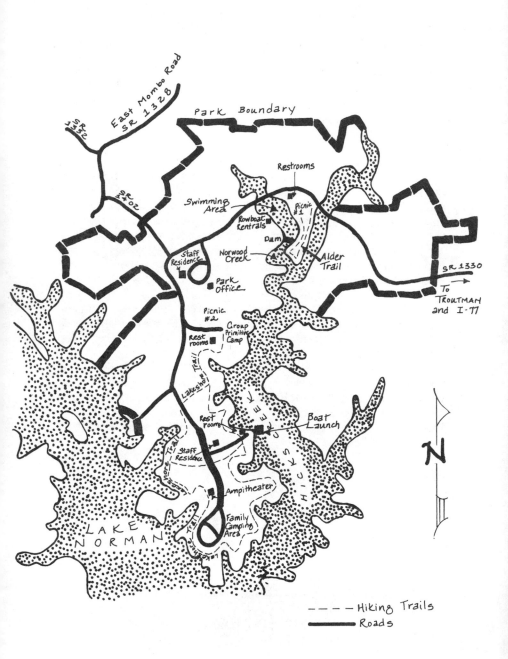

DUKE POWER STATE PARK

Address: Route 2, Box 224M
             Troutman, N.C. 28166

Telephone: (704) 528-6350

Size: 1,447 acres

Established: 1962

Location: Iredell County at Lake Norman, 10 miles south of Statesville and 32 miles north of Charlotte. Exit U.S. 21 in Troutman at the park sign and proceed west on SR 1321 (Wagner Road) and SR 1330 (State Park Road) for 4 miles to the main entrance of the park; from U.S. 21, visitors might also follow SR 1328 (East Monbo Road) and SR 1402 to an entrance on the northwest side of the park.

Principal Attractions: Thirteen miles of shoreline along Lake Norman, North Carolina's "Inland Sea"; a 33-acre lake within the park; water recreation.

Visitor Activities: Boating; fishing; swimming; water-skiing; hiking; picnicking; family and group camping; nature study.

Season: Open year-round.

Ospreys and nest

Lake Norman is the largest man-made lake in North Carolina. When filled to capacity, it has a surface area of 32,510 acres, a shoreline of 520 miles in four counties, and a main channel 34 miles in length. It was created between 1959 and 1964 by the construction of Cowans Ford Dam across the Catawba River by the Duke Power Company for the purpose of generating electrical energy. The lake and surrounding land have become a major recreational area for the people of the region, with opportunities for boating, fishing, swimming, and other water-based activities, as well as camping, picnicking, and hiking. In September 1962, Duke Power Company donated 1,362 acres of land on the northeastern shore of Lake Norman to the state for the establishment of a park. With 13 miles of shoreline, the park provides access to all the resources of the lake.

The western Piedmont surrounding the Catawba River has a rich historical heritage. Artifacts, including pottery shards, flint chips, and arrowheads, and several burial sites near the river are evidence that Indians were present long before European settlement. Early explorers John Lawson and John Lederer encountered Cherokees in the area, but by the eighteenth century the Cherokees were displaced by their enemies, the Catawbas, who were friendly to the settlers. In 1848, the native Americans were moved to a reservation in the west by an act of Congress.

Germans and Scotch-Irish from Virginia settled the area of the Catawba River in the mid-eighteenth century. Fort Dobbs was a frontier outpost built in 1756 to protect settlers during the French and Indian War. Daniel Boone was a defender of the fort against the Cherokees, and he departed the fort to enter Kentucky. The fort was abandoned after settlements were established farther west. A county capital, Fourth Creek Community, was located adjacent to the stockade of Fort Dobbs; it was incorporated as a town in 1847 and renamed Statesville. Kit Carson, a participant in the Indian wars in the West, was born near the present state park.

During the Revolutionary War, Lord Cornwallis set up camp near Charlotte, an anti-British stronghold that he referred to as a "damned hornet's nest." A skirmish was fought at Cowans Ford on the Catawba River, an area now covered by Lake Norman, as the British pursued a colonial force under General Nathanael Greene. Sherills Ford, at the Catawba-Iredell county line, was a crossing used by troops during the war. It, too, is now underwater.

The immediate area was not significant militarily during the Civil War, but Salisbury was a center for arms manufacture and the site of a prison camp. Statesville was the temporary state capital near the end of the war while Raleigh was occupied by Federal forces.

The counties surrounding the Catawba River were originally agricultural in character, with an abundance of grain mills and gristmills along the waterways, as exemplified by the old mill towns of Monbo and East Monbo, located northwest of the state park site. A dam across the river provided power for flour mills there; Monbo was flooded by Lake Norman, however, and little evidence of the towns' existence remains. The creation of the lake led to the industrialization of Mecklenburg County, helping to establish Charlotte as a major trade center.

PLANT LIFE

Most of the original hardwood forest that once covered what is now parkland was cleared by early settlers for farming. The land remained in agriculture for many years, but much of the area has recently been reforested by pines. Most of the forests are now in midsuccessional stages, with stands of Virginia pine dominant on dry ridges and slopes. Shortleaf pine is also native to the region, and loblolly pine has been planted widely in pine plantations. These forests are relatively open, with few understory species present.

Hardwood forests remain primarily as pockets in the more extensive stands of pine; hickories, sweet gum, flowering dogwood, and several species of oaks are most prevalent. Understories consist of small trees and shrubs, including mountain laurel, wild hydrangea, box elder, strawberry bush, and Christmas fern.

Moist lowland forests are usually limited to narrow streamside strips or small coves. Sweet gum, ironwood, and river birch dominate along the banks of streams, and beech may be present in coves. Alder and willow thickets occur along the lake's perimeter, and shallow marsh communities include a variety of grasses, rushes, and sedges.

ANIMAL LIFE

Fish populations in Lake Norman are among the best in the fresh waters of North Carolina. Important game fish include black crappie, bluegill, yellow perch, channel catfish, and striped, largemouth, and white bass. Sauger, a northern relative of the yellow perch, has been introduced. Carp and forage fish such as threadfin and gizzard shad also inhabit the lake. Many other species of small native fish are present but are seldom encountered.

Amphibians and reptiles are locally abundant and diverse; many varieties of frogs, turtles, and water snakes inhabit wetlands along the creeks and the perimeter of the lake. Copperheads, black racers, rough green snakes, skinks, and other reptilian species may be found in upland forests.

Bird life is typical of the Piedmont of the Carolinas. The uplands are home to such small land birds as pine warblers, Carolina chickadees, rufous-sided towhees, bobwhites, and mourning doves. Red-tailed hawks are common raptors, and ospreys may be seen fishing over the lake. Lake Norman is attractive to waterfowl; mallards, wood ducks, teal, and other species may be seen at appropriate seasons. A 3,000-acre waterfowl refuge is located on the lake south of Cowans Ford Dam. Wading birds such as great blue herons, green-backed herons, and great egrets may be encountered along the shallows in summer, and shorebirds may pause in these areas during spring and fall migrations.

At least thirty-five species of mammals, most rarely seen, have been found in the area. Possible inhabitants of upland communities are the raccoon, Virginia opossum, eastern cottontail, gray squirrel, red and gray foxes, and white-tailed deer, as well as eastern mole and several species of shrews and mice. Muskrats and raccoons may be seen in marshes along the creeks and lake.

HIKING TRAILS

Two trails in Duke Power State Park enable hikers to see many different plant species. Fortunate individuals may also encounter interesting wildlife.

Alder Trail is an easy loop 0.8 mile in length that begins at the parking lot next to the 33-acre park lake and swimming beach. The trail passes through picnic ground #1 and encircles the small peninsula between Norwood and Hicks creeks. A portion of the trail is along the edge of the lake, where openings in the vegetation allow fishing from the bank; a short side path leads to the dam across Norwood Creek and a view of the spillways and gates that control the water level in the lake. The remainder of the trail follows the banks of the creeks before returning to the trailhead.

Lakeshore Trail is 5.4 miles in total length, though hikers may elect a shortcut for a less taxing walk. The trailhead is at the parking lot of picnic ground #2 (the group camping area), but it may be entered elsewhere at several different points, as shown on the park map. At a junction 0.5 mile from the trailhead, hikers may proceed either right or left for a loop around the peninsula bordered by Lake Norman and Hicks Creek. The trail follows the shore, passes the family campground, and returns to the trailhead. A shortcut trail across the loop reduces the distance of the hike to 2.5 miles. Vegetation along the route includes pines and hardwoods such as red maple, hickory, and oaks; on the forest floor are wildflowers, ferns, and mushrooms, according to season.

FACILITIES AND ACTIVITIES

The main entry into the park is via SR 1330 from the southeast; an attractive sign is at the entry gate. The park road crosses the upper arm of Hicks Creek, passes the swimming and picnic area, and continues to the family campground at the tip of the peninsula. Short side roads lead to other park facilities. A second entrance, via SR 1402 from the northwest, connects with the main road midway through the park.

Swimming area/picnic ground #1 features a 33-acre constant-level lake that was created by the construction of an earthen dam across Norwood Creek upstream from its confluence with Hicks Creek. A sandy **beach** protected by lifeguards is open from June 1 to Labor Day for swimming and sunbathing; a diving platform is located in the swimming area. Fees may be paid and personal belongings checked at the center section of the **bathhouse**; changing rooms with showers and toilets are at either end of the building. A large **picnic shelter** overlooks the beach to the right of the bathhouse, and a similar shelter to the left is a **refreshment stand** with attached public toilets. Drinking water is provided nearby. Paved walks and ramps connect the three buildings, and steps lead down to the beach. The area is attractively landscaped. Nearby on the lake is a **boat dock** where rowboats can be rented. Private boats are not permitted on the lake. A large, paved parking lot provides access to the beach, dock, and picnic ground.

Picnic ground #1 is located in a beautifully wooded area a short distance east of the beach. Tables, grills, and drinking water are provided. Alder Trail passes through the area.

Past the swimming area, a short side road leads to the **park office**, where information may be obtained.

The **family campground** is at the terminus of the park road. It consists of thirty-three sites in a forest that is predominantly pine. Each site has a table and grill. Drinking water is provided at seven locations within the camping loop. There are no water or electrical hookups at individual sites, but a dump station for RVs is provided. A centrally located washhouse provides showers, toilets, and a laundry area with sinks. The bank of Lake Norman is nearby but is not accessible from the campground. A camping fee is charged; sites may be occupied on a first-come basis.

Two **group camping areas** are reached via a side road a short distance past the park office; from a paved parking lot, campers hike along gravel paths approximately 100 yards to open, wooded areas where tents may be pitched. The sites are available to nonprofit youth groups, and a fee is charged; advance reservations should be made by contacting the park office. Tables, a fire circle, and drinking water are provided at each site.

Picnic ground #2 consists of tables and grills scattered in a wooded area surrounding the parking lot that also serves the group camping areas. Restrooms are nearby. Picnic grounds #1 and #2 provide visitors a total of sixty-seven tables and seventeen grills.

A side road to the east between the group campground and the family campground leads to the **boat-launching area**, which consists of a large, paved parking lot and a boat ramp on the bank of Hicks Creek. The view of the tree-lined waterway is one of serene beauty but often of intense activity as well. Private motorboats, sailboats, and other types of watercraft may be launched for access to Lake Norman. A short pier/loading dock extends into the creek. Modern restrooms are located at the entry to the parking lot. Drinking water is provided.

Fishing for many species of game fish is a popular sport in the park lake and in Lake Norman. Most fishing is done by boaters outside the state park, but many visitors seek out choice spots along the bank of the small park lake. Appropriate licenses are required, and fishermen must comply with applicable state regulations. All boating and fishing activities are supervised by the North Carolina Wildlife Resources Commission.

NEARBY

A detailed map of Lake Norman and its environs is available from Duke Power Company. The map shows some forty-five recreational facilities on the lake in addition to Duke Power State Park. Ten of them are access areas provided by the company, while some others are commercial facilities. At least fourteen campgrounds, twelve picnic areas, and thirty-three boat ramps with parking areas are available to the public. To obtain a copy of the map and other information, write: Duke Power Company, Corporate Communications Department, P.O. Box 33189, Charlotte, N.C. 28242.

Fort Dobbs State Historic Site in Statesville preserves the excavated remains of portions of a frontier fort built in 1756 for the protection of settlers. Visitors can walk the grounds, relive the past through visitor-center exhibits related to the history of the fort, and enjoy recreational facilities that include a playground and a nature trail. The site is reached by exiting I-40 onto U.S. 21 north for 1 mile, then turning west on SR 1930 for 1.5 miles. For further information, write: Site Manager, Fort Dobbs State Historic Site, Route 9, Box A-415, Statesville, N.C. 28677.

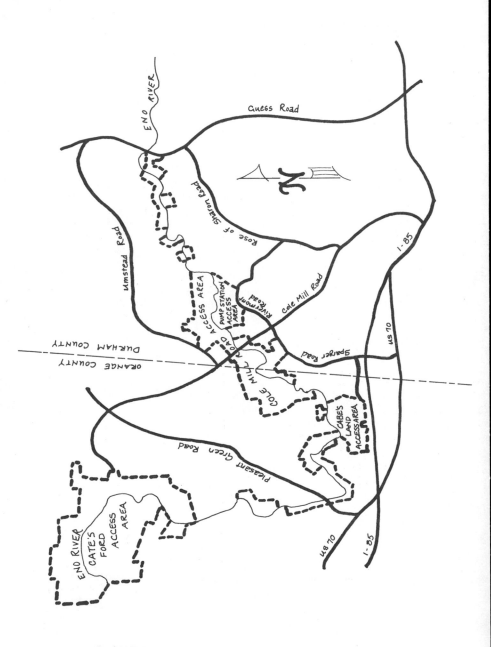

ENO RIVER STATE PARK

Address: Route 2, Box 436-C
              Durham, N.C. 27705

Telephone: (919) 383-1686

Size: 2,064 acres

Established: 1973

Location: Orange and Durham counties, along the Eno River northwest of
the city of Durham. Four noncontiguous access areas may be reached
from I-85 by exiting either onto Cole Mill Road (SR 1569) or Pleasant
Green Road (SR 1567), as indicated by the maps.
Cate's Ford Access Area. Two routes lead to the entrance of this focal
area of the park. Visitors may turn right onto U.S. 70 from I-85 at exit
170, follow Pleasant Green Road north for 3 miles, and turn left onto the
gravel extension of Cole Mill Road for 0.9 mile to entry gate; visitors may
also take the Cole Mill Road exit off I-85 and follow Cole Mill Road north
for approximately 6 miles to its intersection with Pleasant Green Road,
then continue on gravel extension to the entry gate, as above.
Cole Mill Road Access Area. The entrance is about 4.8 miles north
of I-85, off Cole Mill Road on the far side of the Eno River Bridge; the
entry road leads to a parking lot near the picnic ground.
Cabe's Land Access Area. Visitors may turn south off Cole Mill
Road onto Sparger Road 0.9 mile past the entrance to Cole Mill Road
Access Area, proceed 1.3 miles, turn right onto Howe Street, and drive
0.5 mile to a small parking area at the trailhead for Cabe's Land Trail.
Pump Station Access Area. Visitors may turn north off Cole Mill
Road onto Rivermont Road 0.9 mile past the entrance to Cole Mill Road
Access Area, proceed 0.8 mile to the bridge over Nancy Rhodes
Creek, and park on the roadside at the trailhead for Pump Station Trail.
Visitors must respect the rights of private landowners.

Principal Attractions: Scenic Eno River, with Class-II rapids, on its passage
through rolling or mountainlike terrain; extensive system of trails; diverse vegetation; historic sites.

Visitor Activities: Hiking; canoeing and rafting; fishing; nature study; primitive family and group camping; picnicking.

Season: Open year-round.

The Eno River begins inconspicuously in northwestern Orange County. It flows eastward for approximately 20 miles, then enters the Neuse with the Little and Flat rivers. A fragmented corridor of land along its banks east of Hillsborough constitutes Eno River State Park. At the park, the river valley is relatively narrow and steep-walled; frequent rock outcroppings lie along the banks, and rocky rapids occur at intervals in the streambed. The water flows through "Eno Wilderness," west of Cate's Ford, and past bluffs with mountain laurel and other flowering shrubs, storied swimming holes, historic mill sites, and fording places used by the early inhabitants of the area. The rolling terrain, sculptured by flowing water, is reminiscent of the rugged, mountainous landscapes farther west. Eno River State Park is located in a densely populated region of the state where urban development has increased in recent years; the park preserves a significant segment of the natural environment for those seeking sanctuary.

Indian farmers, hunters, and fishermen of the Eno and Shocco tribes lived along the river prior to European settlement. The tribes merged into a single nation in the late eighteenth century and established a village near present-day Durham. Exploration of the area in 1670 by John Lederer, a German physician, and in 1701 by John Lawson, an English surveyor, is documented by their journals, which provide information about the native cultures.

The Indians gradually dispersed from the area as white settlers from northern states moved in beginning about 1750. The settlers were farmers and millers, and the swift-flowing Eno provided abundant energy to operate their gristmills. More than thirty mills were once located along the river. The oldest in the Durham area is Synnott's Mill, which is located 1 mile downstream from

Eno River

Guess Road. William Few's Mill (c. 1758), John Cabe's Mill (1779), Holden's Mill (c. 1820), and others were all built on a short stretch of river within or near the present park boundaries. Area communities became influential in the political history of the state. The town of Hillsborough, established around a complex of mills owned by Revolutionary War hero Francis Nash, was an early state capital and social center. William Hooper, a signer of the Declaration of Independence, and two governors, Thomas Burks and William Holden, were from the area.

The establishment of Eno River State Park was marked by controversy and litigation. The Durham Department of Water Resources proposed in 1966 that a major reservoir be located in the Eno River Valley. Margaret and Holger Nygard led the efforts to save the river, and the Eno River Association was created to generate community support for its preservation. The association proposed that a state park be established along the river, and on May 17, 1972, the North Carolina Board of Conservation and Development endorsed the concept. The city of Durham abandoned its efforts to construct the impoundment in 1973, and by 1975 the state, with the assistance of the Eno River Association and the Nature Conservancy, had acquired 1,100 acres of land for the park. A series of lawsuits involving land acquisition delayed park development, but in 1978 a master plan for the park was completed.

The Eno River Association continues to actively support efforts to acquire additional parkland and to stand guard against adverse developments along the river. The association sponsors interpretive programs and guided hikes in the park and promotes Durham's annual Fourth of July Festival on the West Point of the Eno to raise funds for land purchases. For information about the association, write: Eno River Association, 4015 Cole Mill Road, Durham, N.C. 27712.

PLANT LIFE

The forests of the Eno River basin have been cut repeatedly for timber. The last stand of virgin trees was removed in 1941, but the ridges, slopes, and flood plains are once again heavily vegetated. Graceful branches overhang the cool waters of the river, a canopy of green produces shadows along the trails, and delicate ferns and wildflowers emerge through the duff on the forest floor. Visitors may find peaceful woodlands in spite of the dense urban development nearby.

Several distinct plant communities are present. Many abandoned fields along the Eno, once cultivated, are now reverting to forests typical of the Piedmont. Crabgrass and a mixture of pioneer herbaceous species are being replaced by trees as the characteristic pattern of old-field succession unfolds. These emerging forests are usually dominated by shortleaf and Virginia pines, red cedar, persimmon, and sassafras in upland areas; in moister lowland sites, the principal species are loblolly pine, sweet gum, tulip poplar, red maple, and winged elm. An understory of hardwoods has appeared at some sites and will eventually dominate the forest in such locations in the park.

A mature hardwood community dominates the Eno River Valley. The overstory is comprised of hickories, scattered pines, and white, post, southern red, and blackjack oaks. Common understory species include sourwood, dogwood, black gum, red maple, sassafras, poplar, sweet gum, and black and red oaks. Wildflowers are abundant in the spring beneath the trees, and shrubs and woody vines contribute to the diversity of the vegetation.

A hardwood forest dominated by beech, white and red oaks, sweet gum, poplar, and shagbark hickory is found on sites with deep, well-drained soil, like those on talus slopes below river bluffs or terraces above the extensive flood plains along the river. The understory is dominated by southern sugar maple, dogwood, holly, hornbeam, and hop hornbeam. Vines, including grape and poison ivy, are abundant, and mountain laurel and rhododendron occur on slopes and bluffs.

A bottomland hardwood community is associated with the flood plains along the river and its tributaries. The canopy layer is made up mainly of tulip poplar, sweet gum, ash, elm, red maple, river birch, and sycamore; willow oak, walnut, hackberry, and shagbark hickory are also present. Hornbeam, red mulberry, red cedar, and flowering dogwood contribute to the understory, along with woody vines such as greenbrier, spice bush, Virginia creeper, grape, and trumpet vine.

A mixed pine/hardwood community is seen at scattered upland locations in the park. It is comprised of pine and oak species, the ratio of which varies with soil type and amount of moisture. Drier upland sites contain shortleaf and loblolly pines and post and blackjack oaks, whereas lower and moister sites are more likely to contain loblolly pines and hardwoods characteristic of the bottomland hardwood community.

ANIMAL LIFE

The species diversity within the various plant communities along the Eno provides habitat for many animals. Each community has its own complement of animals adapted to the conditions present. Old fields are home to bobwhites, field sparrows, hispid cotton rats, black racers, and other species adapted to the open, weedy environments typical of the early stages of community succession in the Piedmont. The hardwood forests probably constitute the most significant wildlife habitat, producing in most years ample quantities of seeds, fruits, and browse to support such familiar mammals as white-tailed deer, gray squirrels, eastern cottontails, raccoons, and Virginia opossums. Gray foxes and long-tailed weasels are likely present. Although chipmunks are sometimes very bold, most small mammals, like shrews, moles, and mice, live unobtrusively on or beneath the ground and leaf litter. Furbearers such as mink, muskrat, and river otter are sometimes observed; beaver are abundant.

The hardwood forests support a population of wild turkeys as well as an abundance of songbirds, including titmice, chickadees, nuthatches, and several species of woodpeckers and warblers. The calls of barred owls, great horned owls, and red-tailed hawks may be heard. Wood ducks, great blue herons, and spotted sandpipers occur along the streams. Visitors may discover fence lizards, skinks, box turtles, and other forest reptiles.

Much of the river has a water-quality rating of A-2, which means that its water is suitable for drinking. The Eno is thus excellent habitat for many aquatic and semiaquatic organisms. Many common amphibians make their homes in wet areas of the park, and crayfish, freshwater mussels, and many game species of fish inhabit the Eno and its tributaries. The Roanoke bass is found only in the Eno and in the upper reaches of two nearby rivers, the Neuse and the Tar.

An animal of special interest along the Eno River is the beaver. This fascinating furbearer is the largest native North American rodent, with adults weighing as much as 60 pounds. Dark brown in color, it has large, webbed hind feet and a broad, horizontally flattened tail. The beaver is adapted for life in the water and has a very dense, soft, waterproof underfur overlaid by longer, coarse guard hairs.

The beaver lived throughout North Carolina at the time of European settlement. Because of its valuable fur, it was trapped extensively and extirpated from the state by the beginning of the nineteenth century. It has been reintroduced, however, and it again inhabits portions of its former range.

The semiaquatic beaver is usually found along small, wooded streams; it builds dams of sticks, small logs, and mud, forming shallow impoundments, or beaver ponds. Relatively large, dome-shaped lodges with underwater entrances are constructed in the impoundments; the family lives and the young are born within the lodges. Dens with underwater entry may be located in burrows in the banks of streams rather than in beaver ponds. Beaver along the Eno tend to live in bank dens rather than lodges.

Although the beaver themselves are seldom seen, there is ample evidence of their presence in the park in the form of gnawed stumps and trunks of small trees, the bark of which is consumed as food. A quiet walk along the river at dawn or dusk offers the best possibility of a glimpse of this large mammal.

FACILITIES AND ACTIVITIES

The focus of activity is the Eno River. Visitors may follow trails along its banks, test their canoeing skills in its swirling rapids, and try their luck fishing in its cool waters. The river and surrounding woodlands provide opportunities for enjoying the beauty of the park environment, for hiking and primitive camping, and for family picnicking. Hiking trails, campsites, and picnic grounds are described below for each park access area.

The best times for **canoeing** the Eno are normally in the winter and spring, when the water depth is between 1 and 3 feet. The Class-II rapids are extremely dangerous when the river is over 3 feet deep, and portaging is necessary at depths of less than 1 foot. Information on current conditions may be obtained from the park office; canoeists should always wear life jackets and exercise caution.

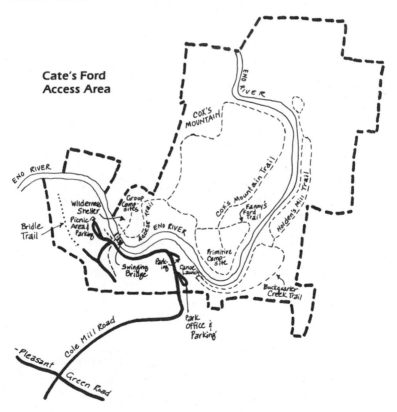

Canoe excursions may begin near Hillsborough, outside the park, at the Eno River Bridge on U.S. 70. Points at which canoes may be put in or taken out of the river are at Cate's Ford at the end of Cole Mill Road within the park, after 5.5 miles; at the bridge on Cole Mill Road, after 3.6 miles; at the bridge on Guess Road, after 3.2 miles; at the bridge on Pleasant Green Road, after 3 miles; and above the dam at West Point in Durham's Eno City Park on Roxboro Road, after 1.7 miles. There are no rapids downstream from Roxboro Road, and the river becomes placid and meandering.

The Eno is one of the best **fishing** streams in the Neuse River basin. The quality of its water is excellent, and many good fishing spots may be found along its banks. Game species present include largemouth bass, Roanoke bass, bluegill, crappie, chain pickerel, and bullheads. Fishing licenses are required, and state wildlife regulations are enforced.

Cate's Ford Access Area

Cate's Ford is the principal visitor-use access area of the park; most facilities and activities are concentrated there. The **park office** is near the entry gate; drinking water and modern restrooms are provided. A gravel road leads from the office to a parking area from which visitors may view the historic **Piper-Dixon house** and follow a short trail to the riverbank and the trailhead for Buckquarter Creek Trail and Holden's Mill Trail. Canoes may be launched into the river at that point. The site marks the former location of an early gristmill on the Eno River built by William Few in the 1750s, as well as the location of the center of a community that predated the city of Durham. The Piper-Dixon house is being restored and will serve as an interpretive center for the area. State-appropriated funds and money raised by the Eno River Association are being used to refurbish the structure and grounds and to prepare exhibits.

The road from the park office continues west to a parking lot at the **picnic ground**. Visitors may picnic either in the open or under a shelter; eighteen tables, six grills, and drinking water are provided. An access trail leads through the picnic area to a bluff overlooking the river. A short nature trail branches to the left; the main trail turns right, follows the bluff for about 100 yards, and descends steps to

*Swinging bridge
across Eno River*

the bank of the Eno. The trail crosses the river via a **swinging bridge**, ascends a slope on the opposite bank, and turns left to the **wilderness shelter**. The shelter is a five-room log structure on the riverbank about 0.25 mile from the parking lot. Picnic tables and grills are provided. A **group camp** is nearby on a shady, heavily wooded ridge. It has four tent pads and can accommodate twenty persons; benches, a fire pit, and pit toilets are provided. Group campers must provide their own wood, since wood gathering is prohibited in the park.

Eno Trace Self-guided Nature Trail is less than 1 mile in length and offers an easy to moderate walk. It leads down the bluff and across a small stream; numbered stations are along the trail.

After crossing the swinging bridge, the access trail turns right at the top of the slope and follows an old roadbed. Hikers should watch for a sign pointing to **Cox's Mountain Trail**, a 2.5-mile loop that proceeds north along old footpaths and roads through an upland hardwood forest to Cox's Mountain. As the musical sounds of the river recede, hikers are enveloped in quietness and the soft light of the woodlands. The first segment of the trail is strenuous, as it ascends nearly 700 feet to the highest point in the park; hikers can view the surrounding countryside for a distance of 30 miles. After descending to bottomlands along the river, the trail becomes an easy walk back to the trailhead. The remains of Holden's Mill and dam, which operated in the late eighteenth century, are located on the opposite bank of the river.

From the swinging bridge, hikers must proceed east past the sign for Cox's Mountain Trail to reach the trailhead for **Fanny's Ford Trail**, an easy 1-mile loop. The trail sign directs hikers to the left through a mixed pine/hardwood forest to a low bluff above the river. The trail follows the stream through the flood plain; Buckquarter Creek Trail is along the opposite bank, and the river between the two trails is often turbulent, as water rushes and swirls around rock outcrops in its path. Hikers may return to the trailhead and retrace their steps through the forest to the swinging bridge, or continue to follow the riverbank to the bridge. Fanny's Ford is a former river crossing near the home of Fanny Breeze, a black midwife during Reconstruction. She was the local medical authority and a friend to the children of the area.

The loop of Fanny's Ford Trail is transected by a secondary trail. The primitive **family campground** is located along the secondary trail approximately 1 mile from the parking lot. All supplies and equipment must be packed to the area; no water is available. There are five sites, each with a tent pad. A pit toilet is provided. There is no fire pit; fires are limited to camp stoves. A permit is required to camp. Sites are assigned on a first-come basis.

The trailhead for **Buckquarter Creek Trail** is at the ford near the Piper-

Dixon house. The trail is 1.5 miles long and follows the river to Buckquarter Creek; along the way, hikers must scramble over rocks at the water's edge. After continuing a short distance along the creek, the trail loops back to end near the trailhead, passing through abandoned farmland that now features growths of young pines and red cedars. **Holden's Mill Trail** begins after hikers cross a footbridge at Buckquarter Creek; the 2.6-mile loop leads to the Holden's Mill site and returns to the creek.

Horseback riding is allowed at Cate's Ford Access Area, but the **bridle trail** is limited to power-line easements. No horses are permitted on hiking trails, and horses must be transported into the park by trailer. A side road to the left between the office and the picnic ground leads to a trailer parking area.

Cole Mill Road Access Area

The entry road leads to a small parking lot; a **picnic ground**, with tables, grills, and a pit toilet, is nearby, as are the trailheads for four hiking trails. **Pea Creek Trail**, 1.25 miles in length, begins on the north (downstream) side of the parking lot. It descends to the bank of the Eno River, follows the flood plain northward to Pea Creek, and loops back to the trailhead. The trail passes beneath Cole Mill Road bridge, a launch point for canoes. Canoeists may park on the roadside near the bridge and descend steps to the stream. **Dunnagan Trail** is a 1.7-mile loop that begins across Pea Creek, near the river, and leads over a ridge to the Dunnagan grave site; it then continues down an old roadbed back to the river and along the riverbank to rejoin Pea Creek Trail. The trailhead for **Bobbit Hole Trail**, a 2.5-mile loop, is at the picnic ground. The trail leads to the right into a mixed pine/hardwood forest. After crossing the power-line easement, the trail traverses a succession of ridges forested by upland hardwoods and flood plains through which small creeks flow toward the Eno. At a junction in the trail, a sign directs hikers to **Cole Mill Trail**, which cuts across to the return segment of Bobbit Hole Trail for a shortcut back to the trailhead that totals only 1.25 miles. Beyond the junction, Bobbit Hole Trail crosses the power-line easement a second time and approaches the river. A side trail extends upstream to Bobbit Hole, one of the ten or more swimming holes that were popular in the past but are now closed to park visitors. Bobbit Hole is at a 90-degree bend in the stream and is one of the most scenic locations in the park; along the opposite bank, stone-lined bluffs are decorated by overhanging shrubs, and moving water rushes over and around rock outcrops. Bobbit Hole Trail follows the flood plain downstream alongside the river, which becomes silent and slow-moving, as though resting for its next turbulent encounter with barriers along its path. The trail terminates at the parking lot.

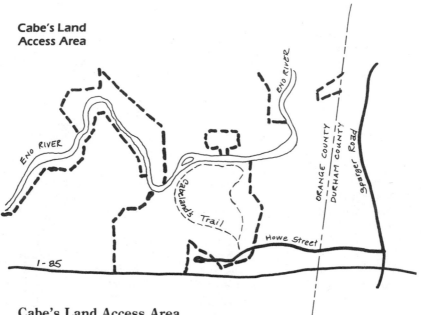

Cabe's Land
Access Area

Cabe's Land Access Area

There is parking space for three or four cars at the end of Howe Street at the trailhead for **Cabe's Land Trail**, an easy 1.5-mile loop. The trail begins along a service road, turns left onto a footpath down a gentle slope to the river, and follows the riverbank to remnants of the foundation of an old mill built in 1779. Hikers then turn right, cross a small stream, and ascend a relatively steep slope to the top of a ridge in an upland hardwood forest; the trail returns to the service road and the trailhead. Mountain laurel grows on the ridges, and wildflowers are abundant throughout the area.

Pump Station Access Area

The trailhead for **Pump Station Trail** is next to the bridge over Nancy Rhodes Creek on Rivermont Road. The trail is a 2.25-mile loop that passes the ruins of a water treatment plant that operated on the Eno River and served the city of Durham from 1887 to 1927. Much of the foundation and some of the lower walls of the brick building remain; hikers should exercise caution while exploring the crumbling structure.

From the trailhead, Pump Station Trail follows a bluff along Nancy Rhodes Creek to the river and reaches the site of the old water plant at 0.4 mile. Many

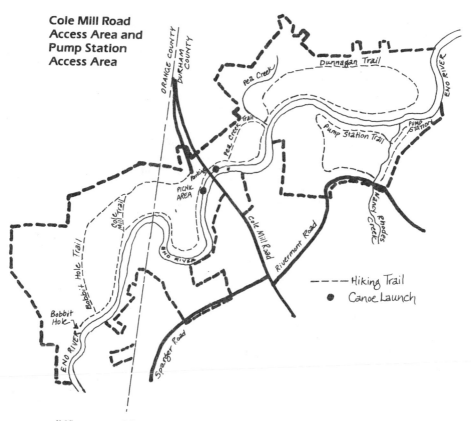

ORANGE COUNTY
DURHAM COUNTY
Pea Creek
Dunnagan Trail
ENO RIVER
Pea Creek Trail
Pea Creek
Pump Station Trail
PUMP STATION
Parking
PICNIC AREA
Cole Mill Trail
ENO RIVER
Cole Mill Road
Rivermont Road
Nancy Rhodes Creek
Bobbit Hole Trail
Bobbit Hole
ENO RIVER
Sparger Road

– – – – Hiking Trail
● Canoe Launch

wildflowers and ferns grow on the slope near the creek and elsewhere in the area. The trail turns left, crosses the creek, and continues along the bank of the river; after 1 mile, it loops back to the bridge and the trailhead.

NEARBY

Bennett Place, a North Carolina historic site, is where General Joseph E. Johnston and General William T. Sherman negotiated the surrender of Johnston's Confederate forces on April 26, 1865, ending the Civil War in the Carolinas, Georgia, and Florida. The restored home of James and Nancy Bennett, located east of Durham, is reached via exit 170 south from I-85. A visitor center provides exhibits and an audiovisual program to interpret the events that occurred at Bennett Place. For more information, write: Bennett Place, 4409 Bennett Memorial Road, Durham, N.C. 27705.

Duke Homestead, a North Carolina historic site, preserves the 1852 home, the factory, the curing barn, and the farm where the Duke family lived and where they grew and processed tobacco. The sons of Washington Duke founded the world's largest tobacco company, the American Tobacco Company. Exhibits in the Tobacco Museum trace the history of tobacco culture from the early Indians to modern times. The site is reached via Guess Road exit off I-85; visitors should drive north to Duke Homestead Road. For more information, write: Duke Homestead, 2828 Duke Homestead Road, Durham, N.C. 27705.

The **North Carolina Museum of Life and Science**, at 433 Murray Avenue in Durham, offers exhibits on topics in the physical and natural sciences as well as a trail and a small zoo. Special programs are available for school groups. An admission fee is charged, though children four years of age and under may visit free; special rates are available for groups. For information, write: Director, North Carolina Museum of Life and Science, P.O. Box 15190, Durham, N.C. 27704.

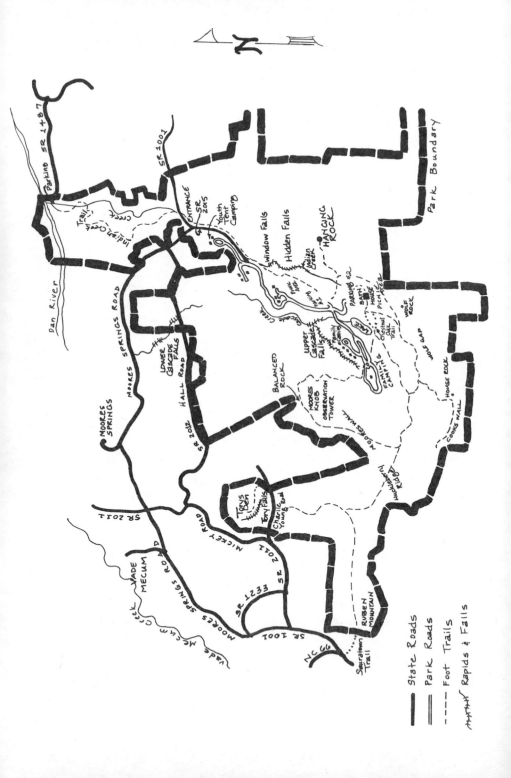

HANGING ROCK STATE PARK

Address: P.O. Box 186
           Danbury, N.C. 27016

Telephone: (919) 593-8480

Size: 5,852 acres

Established: 1936

Location: Stokes County, 4 miles west of Danbury. Park entrance is off
    Moore's Spring Road (SR 1001), which lies between N.C. 89 east of the
    park and N.C. 66 west of the park.

Principal Attractions: Quartzite formations, including Hanging Rock and
    Moore's Knob, and spectacular escarpments, such as Moore's Wall and
    Cook's Wall, all remnants of the ancient Sauratown Mountain range;
    scenic cascades and waterfalls along streams flowing through narrow
    ravines; diverse and colorful vegetation; hiking and bridle trails.

Visitor Activities: Hiking and nature study; scenic viewing; rock climbing;
    picnicking; fishing; swimming and boating in lake; family and group
    camping; cabin rentals.

Season: Open year-round.

Hanging Rock

The Sauratown Mountains are sometimes described as "the mountains away from the mountains" because they are separated from the Blue Ridge Mountains to the west. Prominent peaks in the Sauratown range rise from 1,700 to over 2,500 feet in elevation and dominate the landscape in Stokes and Surry counties. They stand in bold contrast to the surrounding countryside, which averages only 800 feet in elevation.

Hanging Rock State Park includes a portion of this ancient mountain range and preserves some of its most beautiful and dramatic scenery. The terrain of the park is rugged and features precipitous escarpments, among them Moore's Wall and Cook's Wall. Prominent rock outcrops overlook the Piedmont plateau and are identified by such fanciful names as Moore's Knob (the highest point in the park, at 2,579 feet), Hanging Rock, Wolf Rock, Devil's Chimney, and House Rock. These formations, known as quartzite monadnocks, consist of hard, resistant stone that remained after the forces of erosion and weathering wore away the remainder of the mountain range in the dim geologic past. In contrast to its sheer cliffs and peaks of bare rock, the parkland also includes quiet forests cloaking gently rolling hills in shades of green, sparkling streams flowing through narrow, rock-walled passageways, and water cascading over stony ledges into shallow pools.

The Saura Indians, for whom the Sauratown Mountains are named, were early inhabitants of the region, but few remained by the time European settlers arrived. Artifacts obtained along Town Fork Creek provide evidence that the main Indian village in the area was near the confluence of the creek with the Dan River. The earliest settlers in what is now Stokes County migrated south from Pennsylvania and Virginia to the rich bottomlands of the Twin Fork Creek area. They were established there prior to 1752, when Moravians passed that way. Although the Saura tribe had recently departed, pushed south by pressure from enemy tribes, settlers encountered hostile Cherokees to the west. There were occasional conflicts until after the French and Indian War. With the Cherokees pushed back to the Blue Ridge, the extensive Stokes-Surry region was fully open to settlement, but it remained sparsely populated.

During the Revolutionary War, British troops did not enter the region, but there were local conflicts between Whigs and Tories. Tory loyalists harassed settlers with nighttime raids and hid out in caves on Moore's Knob, in the Tory's Den area, and elsewhere in the present-day park.

In 1789, Stokes County was formed by the division of Surry County. A tobacco-based farming economy developed, and the area has remained essentially rural to the present. The mineral springs in the Sauratown Mountains attracted public attention after the Civil War, and resorts developed at Piedmont Springs and Moore's Springs on SR 1001; the resorts remained in operation until the early 1930s.

Establishment of the state park resulted from the donation of 3,096 acres of land to the state of North Carolina by the Stokes County Committee for Hanging Rock and the Winston-Salem Foundation; the deed to the land was executed on April 20, 1936. Additional land has been added to the park, some as recently as 1982, for both recreational development and resource preservation.

Many of the facilities in the park were constructed by a detachment of the Civilian Conservation Corps between 1935 and 1942. A concrete and earthen dam completed in 1938 impounded a 12-acre lake, and a stone bathhouse, a diving tower, and a sandy beach were built. The workers built a park road and a parking area, a picnic ground and a shelter, hiking and bridle trails, a sewage disposal system, and other facilities. After the departure of the Civilian Conservation Corps in March 1942, development in the park continued slowly; additions included access roads, campgrounds, trails, and more parking and picnic areas. A maintenance program to upgrade older facilities, including hiking trails, is under way. Fortunately, most visitor-use facilities in the park are concentrated in a basin bounded on three sides by Hanging Rock Ridge, Cook's Wall, and Moore's Wall; even though recreational activities are intense at times, most parkland remains in a relatively natural state.

PLANT LIFE

Plant communities in Hanging Rock State Park are typical of those at low elevations in the southern Appalachian Mountains. Most of the park is forested, predominantly by oaks and pines. More than three hundred species of plants have been recorded. In the mountains, direction and degree of the slope, altitude, and soil are factors that greatly influence the resulting plant communities.

Moist slopes and valleys are dominated by forests of chestnut, scarlet, and white oaks, with such species as red maple, tulip trees, and pignut hickory also present. Understories are often dominated by flowering dogwood, sassafras, and umbrella tree. Rhododendron thickets are common. Hemlock occurs as a canopy species in moist streamside forests and on steep, moist slopes like those near Moore's Wall.

On steeper, drier slopes, most of which face south, scrubby forests of chestnut oak and pines develop on poor, thin soils. Bear oak, a small tree or large shrub, occurs in the park near the southern limit of its distribution.

On the highest, steepest slopes and ridge tops, much bare rock is exposed. Mosses and lichens, however, may invade the bare rock; they slowly produce organic matter and accumulate windblown dust particles. As the underlying rock begins to weather, soil gradually fills small crevices in the rock, and a few flowering plants such as hypericum and saxifrage are able to gain a foothold. With time and continued soil accumulation, larger species invade and a succession of plant communities occurs. Where there is seepage of water, communities may become diverse; unless fire or some other catastrophe removes the soil, forests will creep uphill and ultimately cover the mountain. This long sequence of events, called primary succession by ecologists, may require thousands or even millions of years. By this process, most of the very old Appalachian Mountains have become covered by forests, and only the steepest slopes remain bare. On Hanging Rock, Moore's Knob, and elsewhere, visitors may see rocks still nearly bare after thousands or millions of years of exposure to the weather. Lichens still cling to rockfaces, and pockets of soil provide growing places for small plants, the pioneers of the mountain forests.

ANIMAL LIFE

The forests are home to many animals typical of the Piedmont and mountain foothills. Mammals are abundant and include such large species as white-tailed deer, raccoons, and gray foxes. Gray squirrels are often encountered, and eastern cottontails may be seen at dusk and dawn along roads and trails. White-footed mice are abundant in the forests, as are several other kinds of rodents and shrews that are seldom seen. On summer evenings, bats can be seen foraging high overhead for flying insects or dipping to the surface of a stream to drink.

Birds are abundant at all seasons, but they are most noticeable in spring and early summer, when they fill the woodlands with song as they migrate northward or set up breeding territories in the park. Several species of warblers and vireos nest in Hanging Rock State Park, along with wood thrushes, indigo buntings, and song sparrows. In the evening, whip-poor-wills, eastern screech owls, and barred owls may be heard.

The moist forests and streams of Hanging Rock State Park are home to a variety of salamanders. One species, Wehrle's salamander, is found in North Carolina only in this area. Other species, such as the slimy salamander and red salamander, may often be observed on warm, rainy summer nights, when they tend to leave their burrows and go walking along wet mountain roads. On an evening hike along one of the roads or trails after a summer rain, a flashlight may reveal the presence of an abundance of these seldom-seen vertebrates, which are more prevalent in the southern Appalachian Mountains than anywhere else on earth.

Frogs are also present, and spring peepers and chorus frogs may be heard on wet evenings from very early spring well into summer. Choruses of American toads, with their drawn-out, high-pitched trills, add a special effect to summer evenings.

Lizards and snakes are abundant and diverse. Fence lizards, which have a rough, scaly appearance and whose males have bright blue sides, may be encountered along trails or around campgrounds. Various small snakes, including the beautiful ring-necked snake, with its bright yellow belly and neck ring, are also present. Most snakes are small and harmless. They live beneath logs or under the bark of decaying trees, where insects are abundant. Hikers should remember, however, that there may be copperheads and timber rattlesnakes along the trails.

The streams of Hanging Rock State Park are home to many fishes. Colorful minnows of several species occur even in small feeder streams, and sunfishes and other larger species are present in the Dan River.

HIKING TRAILS

A complex network of more than 18 miles of trails leads to the major scenic locations in the park—high rock promontories and ridges with superb views, picturesque cascades and waterfalls, and a remote cave. Most trailheads are accessible from two parking areas reached via the park road (SR 2015).

Trails from Parking Area #1

The trailhead for **Hanging Rock Trail** is at the entrance to a large, paved parking lot. The trail leads east for 0.7 mile to the top of Hanging Rock and is moderately difficult. Hikers cross Indian Creek, ascend to the base of the ridge, and scramble upward over rock outcrops for 200 feet to the summit. The view from the high platform of bare quartzite is spectacular, especially in late afternoon as the sun sets behind Moore's Knob, which dominates the horizon to the west. The slopes and ridges surrounding Hanging Rock are covered with trees, and the parkland appears as an oasis of green, a sanctuary in the midst of land cleared for agricultural and residential uses.

Window Falls Trail begins at the north end of the parking lot, passes through the lower picnic ground, and continues downhill to Hidden Falls, at 0.4 mile via a side trail, and to Window Falls, at 0.6 mile. The trail is broad and easy, passing through woodlands featuring beds of rhododendron and a profusion of galax growing on the forest floor. The falls lie along Indian Creek. From near the top of Window Falls, hikers may follow a steep section of trail over a jumble of rocks to the pool and the stream below. Visitors may stand under and pass behind the veil of water cascading over the rock ledge above. The return to the picnic ground and parking lot is by the same route.

A sign on the west side of the park road at the intersection leading to parking area #1 indicates the trailhead for **Upper Cascades Trail**. This short trail, 0.2 mile in length, winds downhill over sand ridges and through a forest dominated by pines and featuring growths of rhododendron, mountain laurel, and blueberry. The trail leads to rock outcrops above Cascade Creek, the bank of which is overhung by giant hemlock trees. Water cascades 100 feet over a series of short drops into a shallow pool in a miniature amphitheater of stone; the water then flows through a narrow gap between rock walls.

Trails from Parking Area #2

A second large, paved parking lot serves the lake, bathhouse, and upper picnic ground. **Chestnut Oak Self-guided Nature Trail** is a 0.75-mile loop that begins south of the bathhouse, near the lake. A brochure available at the trailhead describes the plant life and the other natural features encountered along the trail. The first segment of the trail leads through a hardwood forest of chestnut oak, red maple, white oak, black gum, mockernut hickory, and flowering dogwood trees, with an understory containing sassafras, rhododendron, mountain laurel, witch hazel, and sourwood. On the forest floor are cinnamon and royal ferns, galax, and trailing arbutus. The return segment of the trail is along the lakeshore, where aquatic plants and numerous animals may be observed.

Moore's Knob Trail is a loop 4.2 miles in length of moderate difficulty. From the lower, or south, end of Chestnut Oak Trail, hikers may proceed right, through the family campground to an ascent of Moore's Knob, or left, along Cascade Creek and, subsequently, Moore's Wall; the latter option results in a descent, rather than an ascent, of the steepest portion of the trail. Hikers choosing to proceed to the left will follow a narrow trail, well-marked with red blazes, along a low ridge. At a junction in the trail, a sign points to **Cook's Wall Trail**, which leads to several scenic locations near the southern boundary of the park. To reach these locations, hikers turn left, cross Cascade Creek on a wooden bridge, pass through a rhododendron thicket, and ascend a ridge to another junction in the trail; to the right, the trail leads to Cook's Wall, and to the left, it leads to Wolf Rock. The trail to Wolf Rock is along the ridge and upward to an outcrop of rock with a view to the east. From there, hikers may choose to return to the parking area by way of trails that intersect Hanging Rock Trail or Chestnut Oak Trail, as indicated on the map; thus, three alternate routes may be followed to or from Wolf Rock. The trail to Cook's Wall leads upward past House Rock to the high, rocky cliff from which hikers can see Hanging Rock, the city of Winston-Salem, and much of the park and the surrounding countryside. The trail ends at Devil's Chimney, with its distant view of Pilot Mountain, which is part of the Sauratown Mountain range. Hikers must then backtrack to the junction with Moore's Knob Trail.

Moore's Knob Trail proceeds through hardwoods along the side of a low ridge above the creek, then curves sharply to the right to ascend Moore's Wall. At the curve, hikers may continue west across Huckleberry Ridge on **Tory's Den Trail** to Tory's Den and Falls, 3.9 miles from parking lot #2. The trail to Moore's Wall then becomes steep and rocky; it follows the cliff to the top of Moore's Knob, a windswept pinnacle with small conifers growing from thin soil in crevices between bare rocks. The spectacular, 360-degree view, which may be enhanced by making use of an observation tower on Moore's Knob, includes Hanging Rock to the east, the Dan River Valley, and the distant Blue Ridge Mountains. After passing Balanced Rock and Indian Face formations, the trail descends steeply for 1.4 miles to the family campground and the parking lot.

Trails in Peripheral Park Areas

The Indian Creek area encompasses 468 acres and is situated north of the entry gate and Moore's Springs Road (SR 1001); much of the Indian Creek land is a recent addition to the park, as it was purchased in 1982. **Indian Creek Trail** follows Indian Creek beyond Window Falls Trail, crosses SR 1001 at its intersection with the park road, and leads through the newly acquired parkland to the Dan River. The trail was constructed in 1987 by park staff and members of volunteer organizations. Plans for the trail include access to the **Dan River Canoe Trail**, which extends 27 miles along the river from the Jessup Mill access on SR 1432 to the Moratock Park access on SR 1652 east of Danbury. For information, write: Dan River Canoe Trail Club, P.O. Box 575, Winston-Salem, N.C. 27102.

The Lower Cascades area, encompassing 91 acres, lies between Hall Road (SR 2012) and Moore's Springs Road (SR 1001) at the northern boundary of the park and is best reached by car. Visitors should park at the sign on Hall Road near the trailhead for **Lower Cascades Trail**. The falls can be heard from the steep, rocky trail that leads to the edge of a deep gorge; below is a scene of exceptional beauty, as water cascades over a long series of drops, then disappears downstream between sheer rock walls. This is one of the highest falls in the park and a choice destination for visitors.

Rather than hiking the long trail from parking area #2 to Tory's Den, visitors may continue driving west on Hall Road, turn left on Mickey Road (SR 2011), and left onto Charlie Young Road (SR 2028). The Tory's Den area, encompassing approximately 86 acres, lies north of Charlie Young Road and includes the cave and a series of small falls on nearby Tory Creek. A short trail leads to these sites. A legend persists that during the revolution a group of Tories captured the daughter of a local member of the Whig party and held her in the 30-foot-deep cave in an effort to gain support for their cause. Historians, however, have discredited the story.

Some park trails, including those to Hanging Rock, Moore's Knob, and Lower Cascades, have been compacted by many years of use a .d are badly eroded. Each has a steep grade and downhill alignment without switchbacks. Surface soil has been lost, and bare rocks and tree roots are exposed. Such trails are rough and often difficult to hike. Plans have been developed for their realignment and restoration. Window Falls Trail was improved recently by the Young Adult Conservation Corps with the installation of water bars, timber steps, and other measures to minimize erosion.

FACILITIES AND ACTIVITIES

Major visitor-use facilities are accessible from a single entry gate by way of the paved park road (SR 2015), which leads to the group camping area and park office and to the family campground and two paved parking areas.

The **group campground** is 0.6 mile inside the entry gate; a gravel road leads to a parking area for cars and buses, and a loop trail gives access to eight sites for tent camping for organized youth groups. Water and pit toilets are provided, and each site has tables and a fire circle. A fee is charged. Approximately 0.8 mile past the group campground, a short road to the left leads to the **park office**. Visitors may stop for information and to use the public telephone located outside the building. At an intersection 0.4 mile past the turnoff to the park office, visitors may turn right to the family campground, left to parking area #1, or continue straight to parking area #2, the lake, and the bathhouse.

Parking area #1 provides space for 450 cars and access to the **lower picnic ground** and to trailheads for Hanging Rock, Window Falls, Indian Creek, and Upper Cascades trails. The large picnic area is at the north end of the parking lot in a hardwood forest. There are two stone-and-timber picnic shelters with tables and fireplaces and, in the shade of trees, approximately sixty tables and fifteen grills. Drinking water is provided, and restrooms are nearby.

Parking area #2 provides space for 350 cars and access to the lake and bathhouse, to the **upper picnic ground**, and to trails leading to Wolf Rock, Cook's Wall, Moore's Knob, and other destinations, as shown on the map. The picnic area is on a hillside that slopes upward from the parking lot; the hillside is well-shaded and terraced to reduce erosion. There is a large picnic shelter with ten tables, two fireplaces, restrooms, and drinking water; some sixty tables and fifteen grills are located beneath the trees. Nearby is a 12-acre **lake** created in 1938 with the construction of dams across Cascade Creek; the water's surface dramatically reflects the trees of the hardwood forest that extends to the shoreline from surrounding slopes and ridges. A large, attractive **bathhouse** of stone and timber on the lake's eastern shore includes restrooms, dressing rooms, a snack bar, and a lounge area with a beautiful view of the lake and of Moore's Knob in the distance. The bathhouse opens onto a sandy beach with a protected swimming area and a diving platform. A **boathouse** provides storage for twelve rental rowboats. The complex of facilities attracts large numbers of

Upper Cascade Falls

swimmers, boaters, fishermen, and sightseers during the summer months. Paths along the lakeshore lead to the dam, with excellent views of the lake and surrounding parkland.

The road to the **family campground** crosses Cascade Creek and leads up a long, forested ridge to two one-way loops with seventy-three spacious tent and trailer campsites. Centrally located within each loop is a washhouse with lavatories, hot showers, and a sink for laundry. Each site has a table and a grill, and drinking water is nearby; water and electrical hookups for trailers are not provided. Sites are available on a first-come basis, and a fee is charged. Moore's Knob Trail passes through the campground at site #36 and the visitor information display. A small amphitheater for outdoor interpretive programs is located near site #1.

A short road from the family campground leads to six rustic **rental cabins**. The cabins are for family use only and accommodate up to six persons. Each is completely furnished and equipped with modern conveniences. The cabins are available for rent from April 1 to November 1. Write the park superintendent for information about reservations and rental fees.

Boating and **fishing** are popular activities at Hanging Rock State Park. Rowboats, available for rent at the boathouse, may be used on the lake; private boats are not permitted. Fishing from either boat or lakeshore is permitted in accordance with state regulations. Bass and bream are the most abundant fishes.

Rock climbing on Hanging Rock began in the 1950s. A dozen or more routes have been established, the most popular of which is Preacher's Seat. The base of the promontory is reached from parking area #1 along Hanging Rock Trail. Moore's Wall also provides excellent opportunities for climbing. It is reached by trails from parking area #2, described above, or from Charlie Young Road. Moore's Wall is a series of cliffs up to 400 feet in height that extends for nearly 2 miles between Huckleberry Ridge and Upper Cascade Falls. Numerous routes that challenge experienced climbers have been established on the cliffs. Maps of routes on Hanging Rock and Moore's Wall are contained in *Southern Rock: A Climber's Guide* (Hall 1981) and other climber's guidebooks. Additional information, including local regulations, may be obtained from park personnel.

NEARBY

Sauratown Trail in Stokes and Surry counties was dedicated in October 1979. It is open to both hikers and equestrians. Citizens' groups obtained rights of way across private property and marked and cleared the route. The trail extends nearly 30 miles from the western boundary of Hanging Rock State Park past Sauratown Mountain and Pilot Mountain to the Yadkin River, thus linking two state parks. Within Hanging Rock State Park, a side trail intersecting Tory's Den Trail leads west past Ruben Mountain and across Huckleberry Ridge to connect the park's trail system to Sauratown Trail. Hikers may begin the trek from parking area #2. A bridle path begins at Trails Center, on Hall Road off SR 1001, and follows portions of Hall, Mickey, and Charlie Young roads to an intersection with the main trail. The route then leads through hardwood forests along mountain ridges and crosses rolling hills and flat farmland to Pilot Mountain and beyond. With the completion of Indian Creek Trail, hikers may now travel between the Dan and Yadkin rivers. The chapter on Pilot Mountain State Park provides further discussion of Sauratown Trail. For information, write: Sauratown Trail Committee, 280 South Liberty Street, Winston-Salem, N.C. 27101.

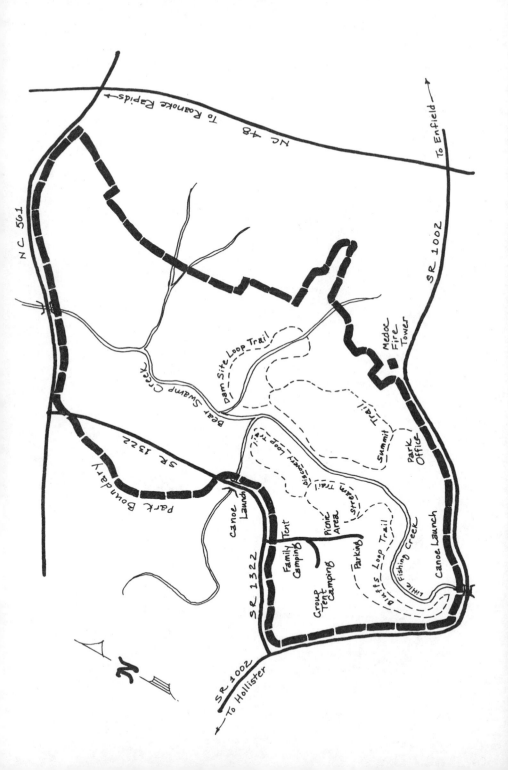

To Roanoke Rapids →

NC 48

To Enfield →

SR 1002

NC 561

Medoc
Fire
Tower

Dam Site Loop Trail

Bear Swamp Creek

SR 1322

Park Boundary

Summit
Trail

Park
Office

Canoe
Launch

Discovery Loop Trail

Family Tent
Camping

Picnic
Area

Street

Group
Tent Camping

Parking

Bluffs Loop Trail

Little
Fishing Creek

Canoe Launch

SR 1322

SR 1002

To Hollister ←

N

MEDOC MOUNTAIN STATE PARK

Address: Route 3, Box 219G
                Enfield, N.C. 27823

Telephone: (919) 445-2280

Size: 2,287 acres

Established: 1975

Location: Halifax County, 15 miles southwest of Roanoke Rapids and 23 miles north of Rocky Mount. From N.C. 48, turn west between Brinkleyville and Ringwood onto SR 1002 for 1.4 miles to the park office; from N.C. 561, turn east at Hollister onto SR 1002 for 4 miles to the park office, as shown on the map.

Principal Attractions: Medoc Mountain, a forest-covered ridge; Little Fishing Creek, a section of which follows bluffs 60 feet in height; excellent system of trails through diverse plant communities.

Visitor Activities: Hiking, nature study, canoeing, fishing, picnicking, family and group tent camping.

Season: Open year-round.

Medoc Mountain, the centerpiece of Medoc Mountain State Park, reaches only 325 feet in elevation. It is not really a mountain, but rather an elongated ridge of biotite granite, a product of time and of erosion that has worn away all but the core of an ancient range of mountains formed by volcanic action during the late Paleozoic age, about 350 million years ago. The persistent ridge is near the Fall Line separating the upper coastal plain and the Piedmont regions of the state. Ravines and steep slopes along the northern and western sides of the ridge and high bluffs along stream banks make the terrain more rugged than typical of the eastern Piedmont. There are no impressive, distant views of the "mountain" for approaching travelers, and the summit does not provide a scenic panorama of the surrounding countryside, since it is masked by forests. The beauty of Medoc Mountain State Park is intimate, and the woodlands must be entered and explored.

     The land around the park has long been farmed. In the nineteenth century, Sidney Weller grew grapes on a portion of his land located along present-day

Riffle on Little Fishing Creek
along Bluff Loop Trail

SR 1002 between N.C. 48 and Medoc Mountain. Weller developed the American system of grape culture and winemaking and produced a highly acclaimed wine known as Weller's Halifax. It was Weller who named the "mountain" Medoc, after a province in France well-known for its vineyards. Weller was an educator as well as a wine producer. He also assisted in organizing the first North Carolina State Fair in 1853.

After Weller's death in 1854, his land was sold to Charles and Mary Garrett and other local landowners. The vineyards continued to produce into the early twentieth century, but the land was subsequently subdivided, sold, and used for other agricultural crops; the vineyards disappeared gradually, and no trace of them remains. In the Medoc Mountain area, only the high ridge and the relatively steep slopes east of Little Fishing and Bear Swamp creeks have not been cultivated extensively.

Some of the land now included in Medoc Mountain State Park was used for purposes other than agriculture. Beginning in the 1930s, the mountain forest was cut for timber; recently, a tract west of the ridge was clear-cut. Such areas are undergoing regrowth, and the wilderness character of Medoc Mountain and the bottomlands near the creeks is being restored. A Boy Scout camp was built on the summit of the ridge in the 1920s, but little evidence of its existence remains. A deposit of molybdenum was identified near the summit; exploration of the site occurred in 1943 and 1944 and again in the late 1960s, leaving noticeable scars, though no significant mining operations have taken place. The Medoc Mountain area was used by local residents for many years for hunting, horseback riding, and hiking. Numerous old trails and roads pass through the woodlands.

A proposal was made in 1970 to locate a state park in the region. In February 1972, the North Carolina Division of State Parks agreed to survey a five-county area for a suitable site. A report published in May of that year recommended that Medoc Mountain and surrounding land be acquired for a park. The Halifax Development Commission obtained a one-year option to purchase timber on the mountain from Union Camp, allowing the state time to acquire 2,300 acres of land by March 1975 to establish the park.

PLANT LIFE

Much of the land surrounding Medoc Mountain is in various stages of reforestation. Many species of herbaceous plants, along with young pines, inhabit old fields. In time, these will become mature loblolly pine forests and, subsequently, hardwood forests. Few plants grow beneath the present dense stands of young pines, but blueberries, pipsissewa, and pink lady slipper are common in some pine forests.

Mixed forests occur in heavily logged areas of the park where stumps and understory vegetation were allowed to regenerate. Hardwoods, loblolly pines, and shrubs are found together there, and the forest will eventually return to an approximation of its original state.

Flood plain and lowland hardwood forests occur along the creeks, especially at the junction of Bear Swamp and Little Fishing creeks. Common species of trees found in these forests include sweet gum, river birch, ironwood, alder, and water, white, and swamp chestnut oaks. Rich soils near the creeks promote the growth of herbaceous plants, including jewelweed, poison ivy, numerous ferns, false Solomon's-seal, Mayapple, and many other wildflowers commonly associated with the Piedmont. Bluffs and ravines in the Medoc Mountain area are distinctive habitats, with tulip tree and sweet gum occurring in moist locales and with American beech and mountain laurel most prevalent on the steeper banks. Such large concentrations of mountain laurel, a highland species, are unusual as far east as Medoc Mountain.

A relatively mature upland hardwood forest with trees forty to seventy-five years old is found on the north side of Medoc Mountain. Many trees measure 18 inches or more in diameter. Chestnut oaks are numerous, as are other Piedmont species such as mockernut hickory, red maple, and white, northern red, and black oaks. A diverse understory includes fringe tree, blueberries, huckleberries, sparkleberries, and dangleberries.

ANIMAL LIFE

The creeks, small streams, and boggy areas throughout the park are habitat for many animals not often observed by visitors, including freshwater mussels, crayfish, numerous insects, several species of salamanders, frogs, turtles, and water snakes. The rare Carolina mudpuppy, a large aquatic salamander found only in the Neuse and Tar river systems, has been seen in Little Fishing Creek. Surveys indicate an abundance of game fish in the creeks, as discussed below. The waterways attract wood ducks, which breed in the area, and such fish-eating birds as green-backed herons, great blue herons, and belted kingfishers. The calls of the red-shouldered hawk and of great horned and barred owls may be heard in nearby forests. Several mammals that require homes near water, such as river otter, muskrat, and mink, may be present.

Old fields and young forests provide habitat and food for bobwhites, wild turkeys, and such nesting songbirds as brown thrashers, rufous-sided towhees, and prairie warblers. Relatively mature hardwood forests attract a rich diversity of birds, including wood thrushes, red-eyed vireos, and various woodpeckers. Medoc Mountain State Park is also home to many mammals; eastern cottontails, gray squirrels, raccoons, and Virginia opossums are common residents, and sign left by white-tailed deer, gray foxes, and eastern moles may be seen. The nocturnal southern flying squirrel nests in tree cavities within the forest.

HIKING TRAILS

Visitors must hike the trails or canoe the creeks to fully appreciate the beauty and diversity of Medoc Mountain State Park. Five trails totaling 8.6 miles in length wind along Little Fishing Creek, around the high ridge of Medoc Mountain, and through hardwood and pine forests. Hiking the trails is a rewarding experience at any season, but it is especially delightful on cool fall days when sounds are muted and the forest is a palette of vivid colors.

Summit Trail, a loop approximately 3 miles in length, reaches the top of Medoc Mountain. The trailhead is at the rear of the park office on SR 1002. The trail passes briefly through a dense growth of young pines, then turns left through an upland hardwood forest dominated by oaks and hickories. The broad, well-marked trail winds among the trees, crosses Rocky Spring Branch, and reaches the bank of Little Fishing Creek at 0.7 mile. In the bottomlands along the creek, the vegetation changes to water-tolerant species, and the presence of beech, ironwood, sycamore, and American holly may be noted. The trail follows the dark, slow-moving water of the creek northward and passes through a dense thicket of mountain laurel that grows along the bank and in the ravines of the high ridge. Mountain laurel blooms in May and early June and adds a profusion of white and pink to the green of the forest. To the right of the trail are granite outcroppings, the ancient rock core of the 325-foot "mountain" ridge formed about 350 million years ago, which is now exposed through the covering soil and vegetation. At a junction with Dam Site Trail, which continues northward, Summit Trail turns right to ascend to the highest point of the ridge. This is the only moderately strenuous section of trail in the park, as it climbs about 160 vertical feet in a distance of less than 0.25 mile. The summit of the ridge is an open area, formerly a Boy Scout campsite, surrounded by beautiful hardwood trees. The trail descends gently to the trailhead at the park office, completing the loop.

Dam Site Trail is accessible only from Summit Trail; from the junction, it leads around the north slope of the ridge before ascending to the summit. The total length of the two trails is 3.7 miles. There is much evidence of past human activity along Dam Site Trail. An artesian well exposed during mining operations is now free-flowing with clear, cool water. There is also evidence of a Boy Scout camp built in 1924; along the trail, hikers may find parts of the foundation of the camp mess hall and remains of a dam and spillway constructed to impound a small stream for swimming. There were once camp cabins in the clearing on the summit of Medoc Mountain. A second dam, on the former site of a cornmeal mill on the Wilcox plantation, is along the trail; it was last operated in the late nineteenth century. Among the vegetation passed on the trail are tall chestnut oak trees up to 100 feet in height, a large concentration of mountain laurel shrubs on the north slope, and a veritable paradise of ferns—Christmas, lady, cinnamon, and broad beech—growing in wet, low-lying areas. Dam Site Trail rejoins Summit Trail at the ridge top.

Trailheads for Bluff Loop Trail, Stream Trail, and Discovery Loop Trail are near the picnic ground and parking area. Hikers will find trail markers on the east side of the picnic shelter.

Bluff Loop Trail is 2.8 miles in length and an easy walk. En route to Little Fishing Creek, the trail passes along an old fence row and a field undergoing recovery. The trail turns right at the creek bank and follows the stream; the smooth surface of the water reflects the sky and countless overhanging limbs of trees. Growing in the flood plain along the creek are ironwood, witch hazel, and many lowland hardwood species that escaped early logging operations to reach enormous size. Among them are unusually large specimens of red maple, willow oak, and American beech. Also growing in the flood plain is one of the largest loblolly pines in the state; it is 12 feet, 9 inches in circumference and is estimated to be 275 years of age. Several natural springs are along the trail. At 0.7 mile, boardwalks cross streambeds that are usually dry.

The trail ascends to bluffs that overlook the creek, the highest of which is over 60 feet above the surface of the water. A formation of granite that has resisted the erosive forces of the creek underlies the bluffs and causes the water to curve sharply around it. The creek continues to cut away slowly at the steep bank, however, as is evident from silt and sand deposits along the low flood plain on the opposite bank. Hardwoods grow on the top and the slopes of the bluffs and color the area with bright yellow and brilliant red each fall. The trail descends to the creek bank at a spot where the water is shallow and the bottom rock-hard, a natural fording place for the horse-drawn carts and buggies of the past. An old road is visible through the woods on either side of the stream. This spot on the creek bank is a delightful place to rest from the trail, as water ripples over the miniature rapids, making woodland music, and soft light filters through the branches overhead. The trail continues a short distance to a point near the bridge over SR 1002, turns sharply west and north, and reaches the picnic area through an area of disturbed forest.

Stream Trail and **Discovery Loop Trail** are a combined 2.1 miles in length. Hikers may elect to take Stream Trail only, at a distance of less than 1 mile. Stream Trail leads from the picnic shelter to the bank of Little Fishing Creek, and it then follows the creek for a short distance to a junction with Discovery Loop; from the junction, hikers may circle back to the trailhead. Discovery Loop follows the creek through a flood-plain forest to the confluence of Little Fishing Creek and Bear Swamp Creek. It then loops through an area of old fields and returns to the picnic ground. The trail provides an opportunity to discover the beauty of the woodland stream and the flood-plain plant community; prominent plants along the trail are water oak, beech, shagbark hickory, American holly, bayberry, mountain laurel, and running cedar, which is a low-growing ground cover common in the park.

FACILITIES AND ACTIVITIES

The **park office** is on SR 1002, 1.4 miles from N.C. 48. Information may be obtained at the office, and parking space is provided for visitors hiking Summit Trail. Other park facilities are reached by following SR 1002 to the turnoff for SR 1322, a gravel road that connects to N.C. 561. A paved road enters the park from SR 1322 and provides access to picnic and camping areas and to trailheads for Bluff Loop Trail and Stream Trail. There are plans to relocate the office nearby.

The **picnic ground** and parking lot are at the end of the paved park road. A shelter is equipped with tables, a fireplace, a hand pump and drinking fountain, and modern washrooms and toilets. Outside areas in the shaded woods and in open pastureland provide thirty-two tables and eight grills. The open pastures are suitable for a variety of recreational pursuits.

Separate **family** and **group campgrounds** are located in a hardwood forest bordering open fields. There are six family campsites for tents, each equipped with a table, a grill, and a tent pad. The three group campsites can accommodate up to thirty people each. Serving both camp areas is a washhouse with showers, solar-heated water, flush toilets, and drinking water at a hand pump and a fountain. A fee is charged.

Canoeing is a pleasant experience on Little Fishing Creek. The creek flows for about 1.5 miles within the park and provides canoeists a distinctive perspective from which to see the area. The water flows slowly, and there are few obstacles along the stream. Shallow water near rock outcrops may make portaging necessary at isolated spots. The creek is accessible from a bridge on SR 1322, and canoes may be taken out of the creek at the bridge on SR 1002; the trip usually requires an hour and a half or two hours. No canoes are available for rent locally, so participants must supply their own equipment.

Fishing is a popular pastime in the park. Little Fishing Creek, considered to be one of the cleanest streams in the state, contains several species of game fish, including redbreast sunfish, bluegill, Roanoke bass, largemouth bass, and chain pickerel. Fishing is permitted in accordance with state regulations.

NEARBY

Historic Halifax, on the Roanoke River south of Roanoke Rapids, is a state historic site. An important political center during the American Revolution, it is the place where the Halifax Resolves' call for freedom from Britain and the state's first constitution were adopted. A guided walking tour includes four restored eighteenth- and nineteenth-century buildings. The outdoor drama *First for Freedom* is presented in the summer. A visitor center and a picnic area are provided. For information, write: Historic Halifax State Historic Site, P.O. Box 406, Halifax, N.C. 27839

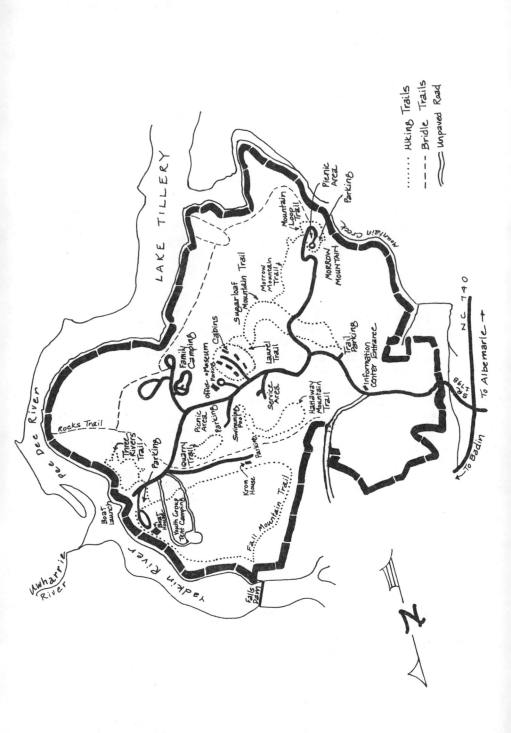

LAKE TILLERY

Pee Dee River

Uwharrie River

Yadkin River

Falls Dam

Rocks Trail

Three Rivers Trail

Parking

Boat Launch

Boat House

Youth Group Tent Camping

Quarry Trail

Picnic Area

Parking

Swimming Pool

Parking

Kron House

Fall Mountain Trail

Family Camping

Cabins

Parking

Old Museum

Laurel Trail

Service Area

Hattaway Mountain Trail

Sugarloaf Mountain Trail

Morrow Mountain Trail

MORROW MOUNTAIN

Mountain Loop Trail

Picnic Area

Parking

Mountain Creek

Trail Parking

Information Center Entrance

SR 1798

To Badin

To Albemarle →

NC 740

N

· · · · · · Hiking Trails

– – – Bridle Trails

═══ Unpaved Road

MORROW MOUNTAIN
STATE PARK

Address: Route 5, Box 430
Albemarle, N.C. 28001

Telephone: (704) 982-4402

Size: 4,693 acres

Established: 1935

Southern flying squirrel, a common but seldom-seen mammal

Location: Stanly County, between Albemarle and Badin. From the intersection of N.C. 24/27/73/740 at Albemarle, follow N.C. 740 (Badin Road) northeast 3.6 miles to SR 1798 (Morrow Mountain Road); turn right and proceed 3.5 miles to park boundary and an additional 0.7 mile to entry gate.

Principal Attractions: Remnants of the ancient Uwharrie Mountain range; extensive mixed hardwood forests and wildlife habitats; Yadkin River/Pee Dee River/Lake Tillery along the eastern boundary; historic Kron House; over 15 miles of hiking trails and 16 miles of bridle trails; natural history museum; vacation cabins.

Visitor Activities: Scenic viewing; hiking and horseback riding; boating and fishing; picnicking; family, primitive backpack, and youth group camping; swimming in pool; nature study.

Season: Open year-round, though some facilities close during the winter months.

Morrow Mountain State Park preserves a portion of the ancient Uwharrie Mountains, which extend north to south across much of Randolph, Montgomery, and Stanly counties in the lower Piedmont of North Carolina. Now worn down to rounded ridges that average less than 1,000 feet in elevation, they are the remnants of one of the oldest mountain ranges in the eastern United States. The dramatically beautiful landscape of the Uwharries has resulted from powerful geological forces that began their action some 500 million years ago.

The initial event in the building of the Uwharries was the spewing forth of molten lava from fissures in the floor of a shallow sea that once covered the area. Deposits of lava gradually rose above the sea, forming volcanic islands, and deposits of volcanic ash were consolidated under pressure into layers of shale and slate, which were then folded and uplifted. The subsequent cataclysmic eruption of volcanoes released lava over the uplifted land, depositing basalt, tuff, and rhyolite on the surface of lofty peaks. These high mountains no longer exist; they were eroded over immense periods of time by the action of wind, water, and other forces. As quantities of the softer surrounding rocks were slowly carried away to the valleys below, the harder, resistant rhyolite and basalt formed protective caps for the ridges, or monadnocks, that survived. Prominent among these ridges are Morrow Mountain—the highest peak in the park, at 936 feet—and Sugarloaf, Hattaway, and Fall mountains, the skeletal remains of a once-mighty range of peaks.

Archaeological research has provided abundant evidence that Indians were present in the Uwharries and the vicinity of the park for at least ten thousand years before settlement by Europeans. The excavation of village and burial sites and the discovery of numerous artifacts tell of their occupation of the area into the early eighteenth century. Indians traveled the Yadkin/Pee Dee River, rested and camped in the flood plains, and later built villages. They caught fish, hunted game, and farmed the lowlands. Rhyolite on ridge tops

View of Yadkin River from Fall Mountain Trail

was quarried for making projectile points and tools; fragments of stone left from toolmaking are present in many areas of Morrow Mountain State Park. Explorers encountered Sapona, Saura, and Catawba Indians in the region. The last group abandoned their camp beneath Great Falls on the Yadkin River in 1720. The native tribes eventually became victims of disease and conflicts with competing Indians from the north and with European traders and settlers.

The earliest recorded explorations in the region around Morrow Mountain were in 1673 by John Lederer, a German trader and doctor; in 1701 by John Lawson, a colonial surveyor; and by various traders who ventured south from Virginia. The journals of Lederer and Lawson reported on the life and customs of the Indians they encountered, and one of the explorers described the Uwharries as "a beautiful land of giant trees, broad open savannahs, and plentiful game, including elk, buffalo, bear, and cougar," as quoted in the park brochure.

Settlement of the area was primarily along Mountain Creek and the bank of the Yadkin/Pee Dee River. As early as 1760, families of English, Welsh, Scotch-Irish, and German origin established the town of Tindalsville on the west bank of the river opposite its junction with the Uwharrie River. The town flourished briefly and was the county seat for several years, but it was abandoned by 1815 following an epidemic of typhoid fever and a damaging tornado. The locations of many former dwellings, fields, and roads remain dimly discernible.

A public ferry across the Pee Dee River was established in the vicinity of Tindalsville in the 1780s by John Kirk, a Scotch-Irish settler who also built a sixteen-room inn nearby. The road between Fayetteville and Salisbury passed through the area, and the ferry was an important link along the route. Local legends recount the passage of such notables as Henry Ford, Thomas Edison, and Jefferson Davis, as well as Confederate soldiers returning from the war, on Kirk's ferry. George Kirk inherited the ferry and the inn from his father, then sold both to Dave Lowder in 1883. The inn was destroyed by a tornado in 1884, but the ferry continued in operation until the construction of a bridge downstream in the 1920s. In addition to destroying the Lowder Inn, the 1884 tornado denuded the summit of the highest ridge in the present-day state park; the peak was known as Naked Mountain until the establishment of the park in 1935, when it became Morrow Mountain.

Dr. Francis J. Kron, born in Prussia in 1798, emigrated with his wife to America and bought a homesite and farmland on the Fayetteville-to-Salisbury road a mile west of the ferry landing on the Pee Dee in 1834. Dr. Kron remained until his death in 1883. He often traveled long distances to provide medical care to the people of the region, and he continued his practice until after the age of eighty, by which time his own health was failing. He also carried out significant horticultural experiments and was active in public affairs. By 1912, Dr. Kron's land had been sold. His homesite was eventually acquired by James McKnight Morrow, the donor of land for the park and the person for whom the mountain and the park are named.

A committee of local citizens was formed around 1930 to promote interest in a state park. Through the efforts of the committee, the Stanly County Board of Commissioners was authorized to issue twenty thousand dollars in bonds for the purchase of land in 1935. In February of that year, more than 1,800 acres were donated to the state. The donated land, which included Morrow Mountain, formed the nucleus of the new park, and the process of development began. By 1937, more than 3,000 acres had been acquired, and in subsequent years additional acres were added, including land leased from the Carolina Power and Light Company along the shore of Lake Tillery. The park was opened for public use on August 17, 1939, and a daylong dedication ceremony and celebration were held in Albemarle on June 29, 1940.

The early development of the park between 1937 and 1942 was a cooperative effort by the state and federal governments. Work crews of the Work Projects Administration and the Civilian Conservation Corps constructed many of the facilities now present in the park. Other facilities were added with state funds through the 1960s. Development of the park has continued, and through further acquisition of land it now encompasses 4,693 acres of the Uwharrie landscape.

Lake Tillery and the Yadkin/Pee Dee River border the park to the east and northeast. The river was an avenue for travel and commerce for both Indians and European settlers. The river is known as the Yadkin for the 203 miles from its source at Blowing Rock to the mouth of the Uwharrie River; beyond that point, for the 230 miles to the Atlantic Ocean near Georgetown, South Carolina, it is known as the Pee Dee, which was the name of a tribe of Indians that entered the area between 1450 and 1500. Two hydroelectric dams were constructed across the Yadkin River—Falls Dam, adjacent to the park, formed Falls Reservoir, and Norwood Dam, to the south, formed Lake Tillery. The dams served to flood "the Narrows," a steep-sided gorge where the river narrowed from 1,800 to 60 feet and dropped nearly 70 feet in a distance of 4 miles before plunging over Great Falls, a ledge 25 feet in height. The Narrows was impassable to canoes and other small boats, forcing portage around the barrier. Dr. Kron wrote that the sound of Great Falls could be heard across the mountain from his porch, over a mile away. Today, the sounds of the Yadkin River are muted; Falls Dam stands at the approximate site of Great Falls.

PLANT LIFE

The plant life at Morrow Mountain State Park resembles that of the western Piedmont and the mountain foothills. A continuum of communities exists, ranging from old fields just beginning the process of forest regeneration to well-developed, second-growth deciduous forests.

Vegetation varies with topography and direction of slope, with substrate, and with the degree and kind of disturbance prior to establishment of the park. On flat, poorly drained soils along the flood plain of Mountain Creek and the area adjacent to Lake Tillery, forests of sweet gum, tulip tree, river birch, sycamore, and red maple occur. Silverbell, a small understory tree with showy, bell-shaped white flowers that bloom in early spring, may also be found; silverbell is uncommon outside the mountains and upper Piedmont.

Most of the upland flats and lower slopes of the park were farmed in earlier times, and their communities range from old fields with many species of herbaceous plants to well-developed forests dominated by Virginia and shortleaf pines. Some stands support deciduous species such as sweet gum, black gum, and flowering dogwood in the understory. Old homesites are made conspicuous by the lingering presence of cultivated species of flowering plants or by the thick tangle of shrubs and vines that follows human occupancy.

Most mountain slopes are covered with mixed pine/hardwood forests. Virginia and shortleaf pines share dominance with deciduous species such as sweet gum, yellow poplar, red maple, and various oaks and hickories. Flowering dogwood is an important understory species.

On higher slopes and peaks, an oak forest dominates the landscape. Chestnut oak is most abundant, but several other species are also in evidence, including white oak, black oak, post oak, scarlet oak, and red oak. Mountain laurel is an important component of the shrub layer, and sourwood adds brilliant reds to the fall color of the understory.

ANIMAL LIFE

Because Lake Tillery and the Yadkin/Pee Dee River provide corridors of riverside forests stretching toward both the coastal plain and the mountains, many animals travel through and make their homes in Morrow Mountain State Park.

The fish fauna is varied and plentiful. Fishing is a popular activity both on Lake Tillery and from the banks of the river. The principal game fishes in the area are largemouth bass, striped bass, white bass, crappie, perch, bluegill, and catfish.

Frogs and salamanders live in and near small streams, pools, and marshes. The mating calls of spring peepers and chorus frogs begin with the first warm rains of late winter, and the resounding calls of bullfrogs can be heard along lakeshore marshes throughout the summer. Salamanders are much more difficult to observe, but a few minutes of searching through the leaf litter that chokes most small streamlets that drain into larger streams will almost always reveal the presence of dusky salamanders; two-lined and mud salamanders may also be found.

Turtles and water snakes may be found along lake and stream edges, and several kinds of lizards and snakes occupy the uplands. No cottonmouths are present in the park. The observant watcher may see one of North Carolina's most colorful snakes, the scarlet kingsnake, in upland forests.

Birds are abundant at all seasons. Waterfowl may often be observed on Lake Tillery or the rivers in winter, and resident wood ducks nest in tree hollows along stream banks. In summer, red-eyed vireos, great crested flycatchers, several species of woodpeckers, and a host of other insect-eating species take advantage of the multitude of defoliating insects that feed on the leaves of deciduous forest plants. Among the nesting songbirds present is the black-throated green warbler, a species associated with cypress swamps and with the moist evergreen forests of the mountains; in the central part of the state, it is confined mostly to the Uwharrie Mountains. Raptors, such as red-tailed and Cooper's hawks, reside in the park and may be seen occasionally.

A quiet walk along the lakeshore or the stream bank may provide a glimpse of a mink, muskrat, or raccoon. Hikers along woodland trails often encounter, if only briefly, white-tailed deer, which are present in many areas of the park. Gray squirrels are abundant, and their nocturnal cousins, southern flying squirrels, live in the park as well, occupying hollows in old hardwood trees. Chipmunks, which are typical of forests farther west in the state, dig their burrows in the forest floor. Winged mammals such as red and silver-haired bats fly silently at dusk over clearings and water surfaces seeking meals of insects. Many other mammal species are present but seldom seen, due largely to their nocturnal and secretive habits.

HIKING AND BRIDLE TRAILS

More than 15 miles of trails are available to hikers, up mountain slopes, through hardwood forests, and along gentle streams. Hikers may choose short loops less than 1 mile in length or more extensive excursions through the park. Each trail provides an informative and rewarding experience.

Laurel Self-guided Trail, 0.6 mile in length, loops around six rustic vacation cabins from its beginning near the nature museum. The trail passes through a woodland that includes oaks and hickories, flowering dogwood, sweet gum, tulip tree, river birch, American holly, and Virginia and loblolly pines. Wild azalea, also known as pinxter-flower, blooms in spring, and mountain laurel adds its color in early summer. Part of the trail passes near Sugarloaf Branch, a refreshing stream where crayfish, insect larvae, snails, and various aquatic animals live and where the tracks of larger animals may appear in soft streamside mud. A printed trail guide is available at the park.

Sugarloaf Mountain Trail, 2.75 miles in length, begins at an unpaved parking area a short distance past the park entry gate. The trail ascends the second highest mountain in the park before looping back to the trailhead. A grassy field near the trailhead is habitat for many songbirds and is an ideal place to see white-tailed deer. Hikers follow trail signs and yellow blazes into woodlands, cross the park road, and ascend the ridge line to the summit. The slopes and the ridge top are heavily forested, and a view of the surrounding countryside is possible only in winter, when the trees are bare. Outcrops of erosion-resistant rhyolite are encountered along the trail in the summit area. The descent is steep, often through thickets of mountain laurel; there are views of the Pee Dee River and Tater Top, a rounded hill at the base of Morrow Mountain, on the descent. The return segment of the trail passes a junction with Morrow Mountain Trail, crosses the park road, and ends at the parking lot.

Morrow Mountain Trail begins at the parking lot that serves the park office and museum and follows segments of Laurel and Sugarloaf Mountain trails for a total distance of 3 miles to the mountaintop; the trail may be entered at several points along its route for a shorter hike, however, as shown on the map. Hikers may experience solitude as the trail winds through forests of hardwoods, follows small streams, and crosses gentle slopes. Its final quarter mile steeply ascends the side of Morrow Mountain to join **Morrow Mountain Loop Trail**, 0.8 mile in length. Morrow Mountain Loop Trail is cut into the slopes of the mountain. It encircles the summit area and picnic ground, passes through a beautiful woodland, and crosses several wooden bridges over narrow ravines. The trailhead and terminus are near the observation deck at the east end of the summit parking lot.

Big Rocks Trail may be entered at a trailhead between the B and C loops of the campground for a one-way distance of 2.5 miles. Marked by red blazes, it is also a bridle trail. At the end of the trail is a dense thicket of mountain laurel and a rock outcrop 35 feet in height overlooking the Pee Dee River. Hikers may return by the same route or by alternate routes along bridle trails.

Hattaway Mountain, the third highest of the remnant Uwharrie peaks in the park, may be viewed from the area of the swimming pool and picnic ground as an elongated, gently rounded ridge. **Hattaway Mountain Trail**, a loop trail 2 miles in length, ascends the slope of the mountain from its trailhead and terminus near the bathhouse. The trail is marked with yellow blazes and follows a series of switchbacks to the crest of the long ridge at the summit.

Extensive outcrops of stone mottled by growths of lichens are relics of the volcanic origin of the mountain. The dense forests are dominated by chestnut oak and sourwood trees typical of such dry, rocky ridges. Portions of the descending loop of the trail follow streambeds where ferns and mountain laurel grow in abundance.

Quarry Trail, a 0.6-mile loop, begins and ends at the picnic ground near the swimming pool. A portion of the trail passes through a man-made gorge, the result of the quarrying of stone used in the construction of the bathhouse, museum, and other park buildings until 1957. Hikers may observe folded beds of slate that have been exposed at the quarry site. The folded bedrock is evidence of the violent volcanic action that formed this ancient range of mountains. The floor of the old quarry is now undergoing successional plant growth; ferns, grasses, and wildflowers are present beneath young trees.

Three Rivers Self-guided Trail, a 0.6-mile loop, passes through a diversity of habitats and is an easy walk suitable for most park visitors. The trailhead is near the boat-launch parking lot. After crossing the park road, the trail turns left and parallels a small creek that flows into the Pee Dee River. It passes through a thicket of vines, including trumpet vine, Virginia creeper, and muscadine grapes, and then enters a bottomland hardwood forest with sycamores, river birches, sweet gums, tulip trees, and alders. The area is swampy, with a thick mat of grasses and ferns; in wet seasons, it is often filled with water and is home to frogs and other aquatic animals. At the riverbank, the trail turns right and skirts an open marsh; hikers may view the confluence of the Yadkin and Uwharrie rivers to the left and the Pee Dee River and Lake Tillery to the right. The shallow cove along the bank is an excellent place to see wildlife, including turtles, muskrats, belted kingfishers, great blue herons, and green herons, which often feed in the shallow water. The trail then loops away from the river through an abandoned field and ascends a steep ridge. This high point on the trail, cloaked with hardwoods and featuring prominent outcrops of rhyolite, provides a view of Lake Tillery. The trail then descends to the trailhead. Along its route, it passes the sites of the ferry landing and the inn built by John Kirk, as well as the ruts of old roads cut by the hooves of horses and the wheels of wagons and other vehicles. A trail guide available in the park provides detailed information on the natural and human history of the area.

The longest and most rugged trail in Morrow Mountain State Park is **Fall Mountain Trail**, 3.75 miles in length, which provides energetic hikers a rewarding wilderness experience. The trailhead and terminus are at the parking lot for the boat launch and boathouse; hikers may follow the loop trail in either direction. To the left of the boathouse, the trail follows the bank of the Yadkin River, enters a forest of hardwoods, and passes near the youth group camping area. After approximately 1.5 miles, Falls Dam comes into view, one of the two hydroelectric dams on this stretch of the Yadkin. A sharp left turn in the trail leads up a steep, rocky slope to an outcrop of rhyolite and other volcanic rocks with a view of the river, its maze of small islands, and the dam. The outcrop is part of a dike formed by lava that spewed upward from a crack in the earth; extending across the Yadkin, the dike created Great Falls, a waterfall destroyed by the construction of Falls Dam. The trail passes from the outcrop through thickets of laurel and other shrubs to the long ridge top of the mountain. The summit of Fall Mountain is a beautiful, peaceful place where soft sunlight filters through the leaves and branches of the abundant hardwoods of the forest, a place for relaxation and contemplation. The trail gradually descends the slope and passes near Kron House en route to its terminus.

Approximately 16 miles of bridle trails provide equestrian access to many areas of the park. Trailheads and parking for trailers are located a short distance past the entry gate. Trails meander through forests, loop around the base of Morrow Mountain, follow a portion of beautiful Mountain Creek, which flows for about 2 miles along the southwestern boundary of the park, and lead to "the Rocks" on the Pee Dee River. Various combinations of trails may be followed back to the trailhead without the necessity of backtracking. Trails are marked by red blazes.

FACILITIES AND ACTIVITIES

The park road provides access to most areas and facilities of Morrow Mountain State Park. Near the entry gate, an **information center** features exhibits that describe park resources and attractions. Beyond the information center, the road passes the turnoff to an unpaved parking area for the use of hikers on Sugarloaf Mountain Trail and the bridle trails, then continues to a prominent junction.

The right-hand turn at the junction is a winding road up Morrow Mountain. Near the top, the road is steep, with sharp curves. A parking area cut into the slope of the mountain allows cars to park facing overlooks into the valley. An observation deck offers a beautiful view of Lake Tillery and the surrounding countryside to the east. A **picnic ground** is on the summit. Tables are distributed beneath the trees, and a picnic shelter contains additional tables and a fireplace. Drinking water is available, and restrooms are nearby. A plaque at the summit memorializes James McKnight Morrow, who lived from 1864 to 1941 and "whose generosity made possible Morrow Mountain State Park, a place of natural beauty created by God for the enjoyment of all who come here." The trailhead for Mountain Loop Trail is nearby.

The left-hand turn at the junction leads past turnoffs to major visitor-use facilities, as described below in sequence. Its terminus is at the boat launch and boathouse on the Pee Dee River.

Six rustic **vacation cabins** are available for rent to families; each can accommodate up to six persons. The cabins are in a beautifully wooded section of the park near the museum and swimming pool. During summer months, cabins are rented only by the week; in spring and fall, daily rentals are accepted. Reservations are limited to a maximum of one week each summer. For reservations and information about rental fees and other details, call or write the park superintendent.

A side road to the **park office** leads to a large, paved parking lot. Information may be obtained at the office. Within the building are exhibits, restrooms, a telephone, and a meeting room. In the 1950s, the building was a restaurant operated by a concessionaire and was known as Uwharrie Lodge. The large meeting room, with its high ceilings with exposed beams, fireplace, and flagstone patio, was used for dining; it may now be used for public gatherings such as interpretive programs. The **nature museum**, located at the far end of the parking lot, is open from June 1 to Labor Day. Exhibits describe the geology of the Uwharrie Mountains, the forests and wildlife of the area, and the Indians of Morrow Mountain. The trailhead for Laurel Trail is nearby.

A **swimming pool** is beyond and to the left of the park office near a large, paved parking lot. The pool at Morrow Mountain State Park is the only such facility in a state park. It is open from June 1 to Labor Day. A stone **bathhouse** provides restrooms, changing rooms, and showers; a fee is charged. A refreshment stand is near the pool. The trailhead for Hattaway Mountain Trail is to the left of the bathhouse.

A **picnic ground** in a forest of hardwoods is adjacent to the parking lot. Tables and grills are beneath the trees. A picnic shelter contains eight tables and a fireplace. Drinking water is provided, and restrooms are nearby. The trailhead for Quarry Trail is located at the picnic ground.

A **family campground** for both tents and RVs consists of three camping loops and a total of 106 sites. The area is beautifully forested, and the campsites are well-shaded. Each site has a table and a grill; there are no hookups for RVs, but sources of drinking water are available, and a dump station is provided. Modern washhouses contain toilets, showers, and laundry tubs. A fee is charged. Sites are assigned on a first-come basis. An **amphitheater** for interpretive programs and the trailhead for Big Rocks Trail are near the entrance to the campground.

Backpack camping is permitted at sites that may be reached by hiking approximately 2 miles from the park office parking lot. A pit toilet is provided at the camping area; drinking water and all other supplies must be carried to the site. All garbage and trash must be packed out. A back-country camping permit is required and may be obtained from the park office during summer months or from the ranger on duty at other times of the year.

A gravel loop road provides access to a **youth group tent camping area** near the Yadkin River. The area includes six sites, each with tables and a fire circle. Drinking water and pit toilets are provided. A reservation is required, preferably one month in advance, and a fee is charged. For additional information, contact the park office.

Past the family campground, a paved road leads to **Kron House**. Local residents were instrumental in initiating the restoration of the homesite of Dr. Francis J. Kron, which is located within the park at the foot of Fall Mountain. The original buildings had fallen into ruin, but the Kron home, the doctor's office and infirmary, and the greenhouse were reconstructed in the late 1960s. They appear today much as they did in 1870, when Dr. Kron was actively engaged in his medical practice and other pursuits. A brochure with a map of the site and a brief biographical sketch of Dr. Kron is available at the park.

The park road ends at a paved **boat launch**, which provides public access to the Pee Dee River and Lake Tillery. A paved parking lot is to the left of the launch, alongside the river. Several picnic tables are provided, and a wooden deck offers a view of the waterway. A **boathouse** at the far end of the parking area is open from June 1 to Labor Day; rowboats and canoes are available for rent. The trailheads for Fall Mountain Trail and Three Rivers Trail are nearby.

NEARBY

Uwharrie National Forest, established in 1961, covers more than 46,000 acres in Montgomery, Randolph, and Davidson counties. It consists of many separate parcels of federal land surrounded by tracts that are privately owned. The national forest lies east of Lake Tillery and Badin Lake Recreation Area, across the Yadkin/Pee Dee River from Morrow Mountain State Park. The **Uwharrie Wildlife Management Area**, more than 13,000 acres in size, is located 10 miles northwest of Troy off N.C. 109. Facilities for public recreation include hiking and bridle trails, campgrounds, and access for boating, fishing, and hunting. For information and maps, write: District Ranger, United States Forest Service, Route 3, Box 237, Troy, N.C. 27371.

The **Uwharrie Trail** extends along the crests and ridges of the Uwharrie Mountains for 33.6 miles between a trailhead on SR 1142 in Randolph County, 6 miles southwest of Asheboro, and a trailhead on N.C. 24/27 in Montgomery County, 10 miles southwest of Troy and 6 miles east of Albemarle. The northern section of the trail, in Randolph County, was pioneered by Joseph T. Moffitt and the Boy Scout troops of Asheboro in 1968. Because much of the northern section of the trail crosses private rather than national forest land, it is not officially open to the public. The southern section of the trail, in Montgomery County, was established between 1972 and 1975 by the United States Forest Service, Boy Scout troops, and the Uwharrie Trail Club. In 1980, the southern part of the trail, 20.5 miles in length, was designated a national recreation trail. It is accessible to the public from trailheads and parking lots on N.C. 24/27, N.C. 109 (6 miles northwest of Troy), and SR 1306 (1.8 miles east of Ophir). Several primitive campsites are located along or near the trail. For further information, write: Uwharrie Trail Club, P.O. Box 2073, Asheboro, N.C. 27206. Hikers may also consult Nicholas Hancock's *Guide to the Uwharrie Trail,* published in 1982 by Menasha Ridge Press.

Town Creek Indian Mound State Historic Site is on SR 1160 between N.C. 73 and N.C. 731 near Morrow Mountain State Park, 9 miles southeast of Mount Gilead. Located on a bluff overlooking the Little River, the site was a tribal ceremonial center built by Pee Dee (Creek) Indians who migrated to the area prior to 1500. Excavations that began in 1936 have led to the reconstruction of a sacred earthen mound and temple, a burial house, a priest's dwelling, and a palisade of logs that enclosed the center. Various celebrations and religious ceremonies were held at the site. A visitor center provides exhibits and a slide program on Indian culture and archaeological techniques. There is also a picnic ground. For further information, write: Historic Site Manager, Town Creek Indian Mound, Route 3, Box 50, Mount Gilead, N.C. 27306.

North Carolina Zoological Park is 6 miles southeast of Asheboro on N.C. 159 between U.S. 64 and U.S. 220; prominent signs are posted along the route. Located on Purgatory Mountain in the Uwharrie range and near the geographic center of the state, this magnificent zoo was designed to allow most of its animals to roam freely in a nearly natural environment behind moats, cliffs, or other inconspicuous barriers. Construction at the 1,372-acre site began in 1971 and is continuing. Presently, visitors can explore a 300-acre representation of Africa. Six habitats are provided for elephants, rhinos, zebras, giraffes, lions, ostriches, and primates such as baboons and chimpanzees; the 40-acre Africa Plains area is home to herds of hoofed mammals such as impalas and gazelles. Indoor-outdoor exhibits of other species of animals and plants are contained in the African Pavilion and the R. J. Reynolds Forest Aviary. Next to be developed is an area for the animals of North America. Visitors may view exhibits during a leisurely stroll along 2 miles of paved trails, or they may ride a tram between exhibits. In addition to a large parking area, the zoo grounds provide a 12-acre lakeside picnic ground, an amphitheater, lunch and refreshment stands, gift shops, and restrooms. An admission fee is charged. Individual or family membership in the Friends of the

Zoo organization includes free admission and other privileges. Continued development of the park and further acquisition of animals depend upon public donation of funds; donations are matched by state appropriations. For further information, write: North Carolina Zoological Park, Route 4, Box 83, Asheboro, N.C. 27203 (919/879-5606).

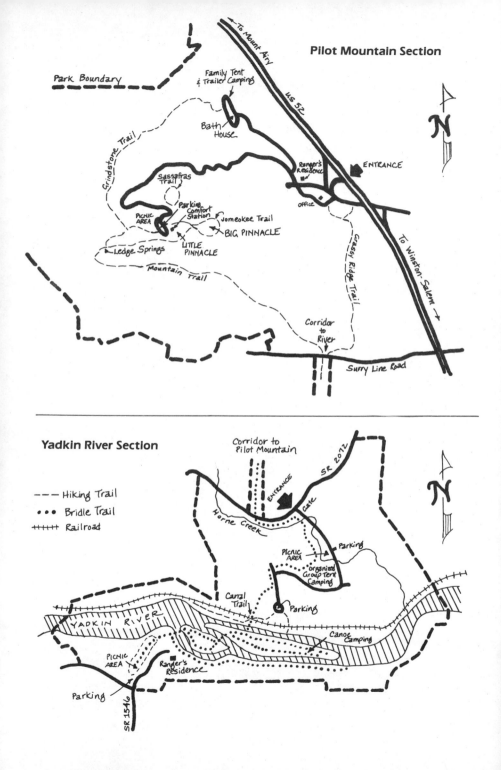

Pilot Mountain Section

To Mount Airy

Park Boundary

Family Tent & Trailer Camping

US 52

Bath House

ENTRANCE

Grindstone Trail

Ranger's Residence

Sassafras Trail

office

Parking Comfort Station

Jomeokee Trail

PICNIC AREA

BIG PINNACLE

Ledge Springs

LITTLE PINNACLE

Grassy Ridge Trail

Mountain Trail

To Winston-Salem

Corridor to River

Surry Line Road

Yadkin River Section

Corridor to Pilot Mountain

SR 2072

– – – Hiking Trail

••• Bridle Trail

++++++ Railroad

ENTRANCE

Gate

Horne Creek

PICNIC AREA

Parking

Organized Group Tent Camping

Canal Trail

Parking

YADKIN RIVER

Canoe Camping

PICNIC AREA

Ranger's Residence

Parking

SR 1546

PILOT MOUNTAIN STATE PARK

Address: Route 1, Box 21
             Pinnacle, N.C. 27043

Telephone: (919) 325-2355

Size: 3,703 acres

Established: 1968

Location: Surry and Yadkin counties, 24 miles north of Winston-Salem and 14 miles south of Mount Airy. The **Pilot Mountain Section** of the park lies midway between the towns of Pinnacle and Pilot Mountain along U.S. 52; exit onto SR 2053 to the main park entry gate and office. The **Yadkin River Section** of the park is reached from the north side of the Yadkin River by turning south from U.S. 52 onto SR 2065 at the Pinnacle exit, as indicated by the park sign, and by traveling 8.2 miles via SR 2065 and SR 2072 to the entry gate; the Yadkin River Section may be reached from the south side of the river from N.C. 67 via SR 1546 in East Bend, east of Elkin, as indicated by the park sign.

Principal Attractions: Pilot Mountain, a national natural landmark, whose pinnacle stands 2,420 feet above sea level; overlooks with spectacular distant views; a scenic 2-mile section of the Yadkin River; extensive system of hiking and bridle trails; a diverse and distinctive flora.

Visitor Activities: Hiking and horseback riding; nature study; scenic viewing; canoeing and fishing in the Yadkin River; climbing on Little Pinnacle; picnicking; family and primitive group camping.

Season: Open year-round; family campground may be closed from December 15 to March 15.

Pilot Mountain, a distinctive landmark of the region, rises more than 1,400 feet above the gently rolling countryside of the upper Piedmont in southeastern Surry County. The solitary peak is visible from great distances. To the native Saura Indians, the mountain was known as Jomeokee, the Great Guide (or Pilot). It guided both Indians and early European hunters and traders along a well-worn north-south trace through the area, and it today continues to guide travelers along U.S. 52, which roughly parallels the old

Big Pinnacle, Pilot Mountain

trace. The dramatically beautiful mountain is now part of Pilot Mountain State Park and is the dominant natural feature of its landscape.

Pilot Mountain, like the rocky escarpments in nearby Hanging Rock State Park, is a remnant of the ancient Sauratown Mountain range. It is a quartzite monadnock shaped by the forces of erosion that wore away surrounding peaks of softer, less resistant rock over the course of millions of years. Its base, generally conical in shape, slopes gradually upward from the valley floor and is capped by prominent pinnacles, the exposed dome of the dense inner core of the mountain. Big Pinnacle, with vertical walls of bare rock and a top that is rounded and cloaked by vegetation, rises 200 feet above its base. It is connected to less imposing Little Pinnacle by a narrow saddle. The peak of Pilot Mountain is sometimes enveloped in the gray mist of low-lying clouds and fog, but it usually stands clear against the sky. Visitors have easy access to the top of Little Pinnacle, from which a breathtaking view encompasses hundreds of square miles of the Piedmont and the mountains of North Carolina and Virginia.

The earliest known inhabitants of the land around Pilot Mountain were the Saura Indians. They were driven southward by the more aggressive Cherokees, who subsequently occupied the area and established a village near present-day Mount Airy. European explorers entered the region from Virginia; they included, in 1670, John Lederer, a German trader. The first land grant in the area was in 1744 to absentee owner Andrew Bailie. Movement into the Surry area was led by Moravian settlers, but the population remained sparse during colonial times because of frontier turbulence created by an alliance between the Cherokees and the British.

The mountain was mapped in 1751 by a team of geographers that included Joshua Frye and Peter Jefferson, the father of Thomas Jefferson. Pilot Mountain was measured by Joseph Caldwell, the first president of the University of North Carolina. It was called Mount Ararat or Stonehead Mountain by early settlers before it began to appear as Pilot Mountain on maps drawn after 1808.

Pilot Mountain was owned until 1857 by André Mathieu, a French soldier who fought in the American Revolution. After it was inherited by William Gilliam, Mathieu's son-in-law, the mountain had several owners before it was bought in 1915 by W. L. Spoon, an engineer-geologist who built a road to the summit and a stairway to the top of Big Pinnacle. The property was acquired in 1944 by J. W. Beasley, who paved the summit road and maintained the wooden ladders that ascended the pinnacle. Pilot Mountain was purchased from the Beasley family in 1968 for the state of North Carolina and became the centerpiece of the fourteenth state park.

Until 1968, Pilot Mountain was a commercial attraction and a recreation area for tourists. A fee was charged for admission. In late 1966, local citizens proposed the establishment of Pilot Mountain State Park as a means of protecting the mountain and surrounding area from further commercial development. At the request of the Northwest Economic Development Commission, state officials investigated the feasibility of a park in the area, and in August 1967 the North Carolina Board of Conservation and Development adopted a resolution concurring with the proposal.

The Pilot Mountain Preservation and Park Committee played a major role in the creation of the park. The group secured options on tracts of land within proposed park boundaries and raised matching funds that made it possible to obtain federal grants for the purchase of land. A total of $1,321,225 was expended for 2,143 acres on and around Pilot Mountain. Deeds were transferred to the state of North Carolina on July 24, 1968, and the establishment of the park was officially declared; the superintendent of state parks cancelled the $1 admission fee that had been charged by private owners. Continuing its support of the park, the Pilot Mountain Preservation and Park Committee took the lead in the acquisition of 1,202 acres of land along the Yadkin River, which were added to the park in 1970. Additional acreage was subsequently acquired, bringing the park to its present size.

The park is divided into two sections connected by a corridor 5 miles in length and 300 feet in width. The Pilot Mountain Section, entirely within Surry County, includes the mountain and major visitor-use facilities. The Yadkin River Section of approximately 1,400 acres is traversed by the scenic, fast-flowing river; parkland south of the river lies in Yadkin County. Corridor Trail connects the two sections of the park through pine and hardwood forests. Each section has an extensive system of trails. Corridor Trail is used by both hikers and equestrians. It may be entered at the north end from SR 2061 or the south end from SR 2072. An area for loading and unloading horses and parking trailers is located at each terminus of the corridor.

PLANT LIFE

Much of the vegetation on Pilot Mountain is similar to that associated with mountain habitats farther west, like those in the Blue Ridge Mountains. Dominant trees and shrubs more common in the mountains than in the Piedmont are chestnut oak, pitch and table mountain pines, rosebay and Catawba rhododendrons, mountain laurel, fetterbush, and sweetfern. At Pilot Mountain, such trees and shrubs mingle with other species that have a stronger affinity with the Piedmont.

Members of over seventy families of vascular plants may be seen on or around the mountain, and several distinct plant communities are present. A chestnut oak/pine community occurs on the western slopes of the mountain as well as on south-facing slopes from the base of the pinnacles downward to an altitude of 1,800 feet. The canopy is dominated by chestnut oak and pitch pine, with scarlet oak and table mountain and Virginia pines; the understory includes blackjack oak, sourwood, and black gum. Mountain laurel and huckleberry are in the shrub layer. The canopy is relatively open, and trees growing in the shallow, rocky soil show stunted growth.

A chestnut oak/heath community occupies slopes facing north and east just below the pinnacles. It is characterized by dwarf chestnut oaks and pines and a dense underlayer of evergreen shrubs, primarily mountain laurel and rhododendron, with clumps of bear oak and blueberry. Though separated from the Appalachian Mountains, this community contains few Piedmont species.

An oak/hickory forest more typical of the Piedmont occurs in most ravines and on slopes midway down the mountain, especially on the east side. Compared with the two communities previously described, there is a greater diversity of species in the canopy layer, which includes black locust, tulip tree, hickories, and chestnut, white, and red oaks. Important in the understory are flowering dogwood, sourwood, mulberry, and redbud; evergreen heaths, prevalent at higher elevations, are absent. Much of the base of the mountain is covered by a mixed forest similar in composition to the oak/hickory community, and with a close affinity to forests on dry, open slopes of the upper Piedmont.

The tops of the pinnacles are well-vegetated. Chestnut oak, dominant at the center of the pinnacles, is replaced by table mountain pine near cliff edges; also present are mountain laurel, Catawba rhododendron, fetterbush, and blueberry. Within crevices in the cliff walls of the pinnacles are mountain spleenwort, alumroot, silverling, and other species rarely found elsewhere on the mountain.

Typical Piedmont vegetation grows in the river section of the park and along the corridor connecting the mountain and the river. Pines in various stages of succession grow on abandoned farmland. Upland sites near the river are covered with various species of hickories and oaks, along with red maple, black gum, sourwood, and dogwood. Vegetation typical of flood plains occurs along the river. Overhanging the rushing waters of the Yadkin are enormous river birch and sycamore trees; they are joined by sweet gum, tulip tree, ash, and various oak species where the flood plain is sufficiently wide. Much of the river section has been cut over, burned, or cultivated; mixed stands of pine and upland hardwoods are now restoring the woodlands.

ANIMAL LIFE

Park fauna is typical of that found in the western Piedmont and the foothills of North Carolina. Life along the lower slopes and valleys is similar to that associated with the Piedmont, while that of the higher slopes resembles the fauna of the Blue Ridge Mountains to the west. The uplands are home to a wide variety of amphibians, including slimy, dusky, and two-lined salamanders. Each spring, American toads, chorus frogs, and spring peepers call from roadside pools. The forests are home to various lizards and small non-poisonous snakes; visitors should be alert for the presence of the poisonous copperhead and timber rattlesnake.

Birds are abundant throughout Pilot Mountain State Park even in winter, but they are especially evident in spring, summer, and fall. The brilliant scarlet tanager, woodpeckers, and other perching birds occur in the deciduous woodlands in summer. A special feature of the upland wildlife of Pilot Mountain is the presence of nesting common ravens. These large relatives of the American crow are generally found in North Carolina only in the western mountains, and they are uncommon even there. They generally nest on steep cliffs in high, remote mountain areas, and Pilot Mountain represents their easternmost nesting site in the state. Ravens are easily separated from the familiar

Northern flicker, female

crow by their larger size, their wedge-shaped tail that is distinct from the square tail of crows, and their frequent hoarse, guttural calls. Ravens are most often seen as they soar high over the peaks; hikers on the trails to Big and Little pinnacles should watch and listen for them.

Most of the larger mammals in the park are seen only by careful and patient observers. Among the mammals present are red and gray foxes, raccoon, Virginia opossum, and an occasional white-tailed deer. Hikers may encounter the burrows of woodchucks or chipmunks or glimpse a cottontail along a trail. Numerous species of mice, such as the white-footed mouse, and insectivores, including tiny shrews, move about beneath the leaf litter on the forest floor. They are usually unobserved.

The passage of the Yadkin River through the park provides a diversity of habitats for aquatic life. One of the longest river systems in North Carolina, the Yadkin extends from its cold headwaters in the Blue Ridge Mountains to a junction with the Rocky River near Ansonville and a meeting with the Atlantic Ocean at Georgetown, South Carolina. En route, the Yadkin becomes known as the Pee Dee River for the latter part of its journey. By the time the Yadkin reaches the park, it has already begun the gradual process of slowing and warming and accumulating a load of silt from the adjacent uplands, which gives the Pee Dee its perennially muddy appearance downstream. At Pilot Mountain, however, the Yadkin is still relatively clear and cool, and its movement is moderate. It is no longer home to populations of mountain trout but does provide habitat for largemouth bass and several other sunfishes, crappie, and white and striped bass. Channel, white, blue, and flathead catfish are present, as are brown bullheads. Smaller fishes, including shiners, darters, and chubs, are present but seldom seen.

Animal life in the corridor along the river is diverse. Several species of frogs and toads occupy quiet wetlands adjacent to the river, and their calls are frequently heard. Especially noticeable is the twang of the green frog as it picks sporadically on its one-stringed banjo. Although there are no cottonmouths this far west, nonpoisonous water snakes may be seen in sunny spots along the riverbank. Ducks are not abundant, but mallards, wood ducks, and other species may occasionally be flushed by canoeists. Belted kingfishers may be heard giving their rattling calls as they patrol chosen sections of the river.

Forests along the riverbanks are important corridors for wildlife, allowing them to avoid cleared areas and reach isolated blocks of forest. Many birds and mammals may be seen adjacent to the river, and glimpses of raccoon, river otter, or mink are a possibility.

PILOT MOUNTAIN SECTION

Travelers along U.S. 52 have an excellent view of Pilot Mountain and easy access to the entry gate. A well-graded, paved road leads from the park entrance to a large parking lot near the summit of the mountain. Downhill from the parking lot is the picnic ground; uphill is a visitor-use area with benches, drinking water, restrooms, and an exhibit board with a map of the park's trail system. Most trailheads are located nearby.

Hiking and Bridle Trails

Little Pinnacle Trail leads for 100 yards up a gentle grade from the parking lot, through pitch pine and chestnut oaks, to rock outcrops on Little Pinnacle overlook. Visitors have an unsurpassed close-up view of nearby Big Pinnacle as well as superb distant views of the Dan River Valley below. Rappelling on the rock cliffs of Little Pinnacle is permitted. Regulations require that climbers be experienced and well-equipped.

Visitors are not permitted to ascend to the top of Big Pinnacle. The old wooden steps built by W. L. Spoon were removed in 1970, and rock climbing and rappelling are prohibited. **Jomeokee Trail**, a 0.75-mile loop, circles the base of Big Pinnacle and allows hikers ground-level access to its vertical walls. The trailhead is on the north side of Little Pinnacle, at the rear of the restrooms. The narrow trail, moderate in difficulty, passes shallow caves and alcoves, protruding rock formations often covered by lichens, numerous flowering plants, and, high above, nesting sites for ravens. This impressive sentinel of stone, a monument to geologic time and the forces of nature, commemorates the past glory of the Sauratown Mountain range.

Sassafras Nature Trail is a 0.5-mile loop along a hillside that overlooks the Piedmont landscape to the east. Ravens, hawks, and vultures may be seen soaring in the area, and warblers, Carolina chickadees, and various woodpeckers may be heard among the trees. Mountain laurel, Catawba rhododendron, black huckleberry, and sassafras are common shrubs along the trail, and sweetfern, trailing arbutus, galax, and pipsissewa are wildflowers and herbs found on the forest floor. Numerous lichens and mosses adorn rock surfaces and crevices. Pitch and table mountain pines are adapted to such dry mountain ridges, and common hardwoods along the trail are chestnut, scarlet, and southern red oaks. On clear days, the persistent peaks of the Sauratown range can be seen from an overlook; in succession from near to far are Big Pinnacle of Pilot Mountain, Sauratown Mountain, and Cook's Wall and Moore's Knob in Hanging Rock State Park. A printed guide is available at the trailhead.

Ledge Springs Trail is a strenuous 1.6-mile loop that is suitable for energetic hikers. The trailhead and terminus are at the summit parking lot; hikers proceed either east past Little Pinnacle or west past the picnic ground, following trail signs with yellow blazes. To the west, the trail passes close to high cliffs and overlooks with distant panoramic views. Past its junction with Grindstone Trail, Ledge Springs Trail veers left and descends steeply over rocky ledges to a sharp, nearly 180-degree turn to the east; nearby, at 0.6 mile, is the junction with Mountain Trail. Near the junction, Ledge Springs produces a flow of gurgling water from a fissure in the rocks; mosses and ferns grow profusely at the springs, and mountain laurel is abundant in the area. The trail proceeds eastward along the base of the ledges, climbing over rock outcrops and around trees and thickets of rhododendron and other shrubs. Hikers may scramble over bare rocks to the Little Pinnacle overlook or continue to the junction with Jomeokee Trail for the return to the parking lot.

Grindstone Trail begins at the family campground between campsites #16 and #17 and ascends the mountain through a hardwood forest with mountain laurel and other shrubs for 1.8 miles to a junction with Ledge Springs Trail. Grindstone Trail then continues to the summit parking lot for a total distance of 2.1 miles. The trail is rocky and moderate in difficulty.

The northern terminus of **Mountain Trail** is its junction with Ledge Springs Trail; from that point, it descends the mountain for 2.5 miles to its southern terminus at SR 2061 (Surry County Line Road) and the north end of the corridor that leads to the Yadkin River Section of the park. Hikers may enter the trail at either end.

Grassy Ridge Trail, approximately 1 mile in length, is shared by hikers and equestrians. From the trailhead near the park entry gate on SR 2053 and the park office, it circles the base of the mountain on the east and extends to the northern terminus of the corridor on SR 2061. Grass Ridge Trail connects **Sauratown Trail**, which is outside the park, with **Corridor Trail** and the Yadkin River Section of the park.

Facilities and Activities

A solar-powered **park office** completed in 1981 is located immediately past the entry gate. Visitors may stop for information provided by park personnel and by the small exhibit area.

A short distance past the office, a side road leads to the **family campground** on the lower slopes of Pilot Mountain. There are forty-nine spacious campsites for tents and trailers in the deep shade of a hardwood forest. Each site has a tent pad, table, and grill, and drinking water is provided by vacuum pumps; electrical and water hookups for campers are not available. Two modern washhouses with showers are conveniently located within the camping loop. Campers may select sites on a first-come basis. A fee is charged.

A large **picnic ground** is located approximately 100 yards downhill from the summit parking lot; paved access for handicapped persons is provided. Picnic tables, grills, and a small covered shelter are located in the shade of pines and hardwoods. Drinking water is available.

YADKIN RIVER SECTION

From the entry gate on SR 2072, a dirt and gravel road winds through beautiful woodlands to a cul-de-sac that overlooks the Yadkin River. Vehicles must ford Horne Creek three times as it meanders through the area; visitors should inquire about the condition of the stream before making the trip. The 2-mile stretch of the river that flows through the park is perhaps the most scenic along its course. The river is broad and shallow, with many riffles; two islands, 45 and 15 acres in size, lie in its channel and may be reached on foot or horseback or by canoe.

Hiking, Bridle, and Canoe Trails

Canal Trail, on the north shore, is 0.5 mile in length. It begins at the cul-de-sac parking area, descends to the river's edge after crossing railroad tracks that parallel the river, and follows the riverbank westward. Rock outcrops, the Yadkin Islands, and the south shore are part of the view between overhanging limbs of river birch and sycamore trees at the water's edge. The trail passes the remains of Bean Shoals Canal Wall, part of an ambitious project undertaken between 1820 and 1825 to build a 3 mile-long canal around Bean Shoals. The project was abandoned before construction was completed.

Yadkin River Bridle Trail connects with the southern terminus of Corridor Trail at SR 2072, crosses Horne Creek, and leads to the north shore of the Yadkin. It then extends through the shallows of the river, encircles each island, and continues east along the south shore in Yadkin County. Altogether, the system of bridle trails in Pilot Mountain State Park—Grassy Ridge Trail, Corridor Trail, and Yadkin River Bridle Trail—provides a 12-mile route for equestrians.

The 2-mile section of the river that flows through Pilot Mountain State Park is part of the **Yadkin River Trail** for canoeists. The trail is 165 miles in length, following the course of the river and traversing five reservoirs created by dams from Ferguson in Wilkes County to the confluence of the Yadkin and Uwharrie rivers. There are thirty-eight access sites for canoes on the trail, eighteen of which are within the reservoirs. Shoals Access Site, on the east side of the river, is reached via SR 1546 near East Bend in Yadkin County; parking, picnic areas, and pit toilets are provided. The site is 0.5 mile upstream from the Yadkin Islands, which are within the state park; canoeists may camp on the larger of the two islands. Information about the trail and the trail access system may be obtained from the Yadkin River Trail Association, 280 South Liberty Street, Winston-Salem, N.C. 27101.

Facilities and Activities

A **picnic ground** near the north shore of the Yadkin River is in an open, grassy area along Horne Creek; tables, grills, drinking water, and pit toilets are provided. A similar facility on the south shore is accessible from SR 1546.

A **tent camping area** for youth group organizations is near the picnic area on the north side of the river; tables, a fire circle, drinking water, and a pit toilet are provided. Reservations are required, and a fee is charged; visitors should inquire at the park office. Two **wilderness campsites** for canoeists are on the larger of the two islands in the Yadkin River.

Visitors may fish in the river for sunfish and catfish species, as well as largemouth, white, and striped bass. A state fishing license is required, and anglers must obey regulations established by the North Carolina Wildlife Resources Commission.

NEARBY

Sauratown Trail extends from the western boundary of Hanging Rock State Park, passes Sauratown Mountain, and connects with Grassy Ridge Trail at the eastern boundary of Pilot Mountain State Park. For a more detailed treatment of Sauratown Trail, consult the chapter on Hanging Rock State Park in this volume. For further information, write: Sauratown Trail Committee, 280 South Liberty Street, Winston-Salem, N.C. 27101.

Several science centers/museums/zoos are located in the northern central region of the state; each charges an admission fee. **Natural Science Center of Greensboro** (4301 Lawndale Drive, Greensboro, N.C. 27408) includes a museum with exhibits on the natural and physical sciences, the Edward R. Zane Planetarium, and a 30-acre zoo with representative animals of North and South America. The **Nature Science Center** (Museum Drive, Winston-Salem, N.C. 27105) provides exhibits and demonstrations on astronomy, meteorology, and the natural sciences. The **Museum of Man** (114 Reynolda Village, Winston-Salem, N.C. 27106) is a small anthropology museum with artifacts from American Indian cultures and from other cultures around the world. It is operated by the Anthropology Department of Wake Forest University. The **High Point Environmental Center** (Route 1, Box 401, High

Point, N.C. 27260) is a 200-acre tract of land with 4 miles of trails, an interpretive center, a small zoo, and various outdoor exhibits.

Old Salem, a town founded by a Moravian congregation in 1766, has been faithfully restored and is one of the nation's most authentic colonial sites. Located within the city of Winston-Salem, the historic district, with its more than eighty structures and its beautiful landscape, is a living museum. It offers restored private homes as well as nine exhibit buildings, including Winkler Bakery, Shultz Shoemaker Shop, Salem Tavern, Miksch Tobacco Shop, and the Single Brother's House. For information about schedules and admission fees, write: Old Salem, Inc., Drawer F, Salem Station, Winston-Salem, N.C. 27108.

Guilford Courthouse National Military Park near Greensboro was the site of a March 1781 battle between the British forces of Lord Cornwallis and the poorly equipped colonials led by General Nathanael Greene. Even though the British won the battle, Cornwallis lost 25 percent of his troops and went on to ultimate defeat at Yorktown, Virginia. For additional information, write: Superintendent, Guilford Courthouse National Military Park, P.O. Box 9806, Plaza Station, Greensboro, N.C. 27429.

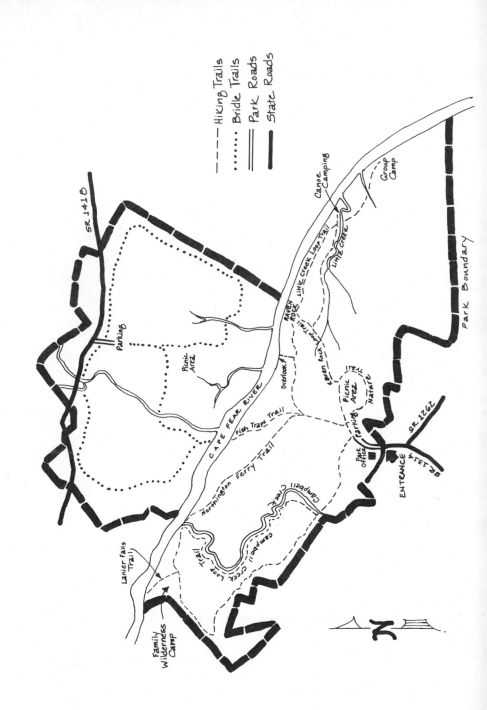

Hiking Trails
Bridle Trails
Park Roads
State Roads

SR 1418

Parking

Picnic Area

CAPE FEAR RIVER

Fish Trap Trail

Overlook

RAVEN ROCK

Little Creek Loop Trail

Little Creek

Canoe Camping

Group Camp

Park Boundary

Raven Rock

Loop Trail

Picnic Area

Nature Trail

Parking

Picnic Area

Park Office

ENTRANCE

SR 1314

SR 1262

Worthington Ferry Trail

Campbell Creek

Campbell Creek Loop Trail

Lanier Falls Trail

Family Wilderness Camp

N

RAVEN ROCK STATE PARK

Address: Route 3, Box 1005
             Lillington, N.C. 27546

Telephone: (919) 893-4888

Size: 2,847 acres

Established: 1970

Raven Rock

Location: Harnett County, 9 miles west of Lillington and 20 miles east of
            Sanford. Turn off U.S. 421 and follow SR 1314 for 3 miles to the park
            entrance. The more remote northern section of the park is reached via
            SR 1412 and SR 1418; turn off U.S. 401 between Lillington and Kipling.

Principal Attractions: Quartzite cliffs, 120 to 150 feet in height, carved by
            the Cape Fear River; diverse flora and fauna, including a profusion of
            spring wildflowers; 15 miles of hiking trails and 7 miles of bridle trails.

Visitor Activities: Hiking; nature study; fishing in Cape Fear River; canoe-
            ing on the river and canoe camping; primitive family and group camping;
            picnicking.

Season: Open year-round.

At Raven Rock State Park, there is a welcome silence and an opportunity to
observe and contemplate the forces and processes of nature that have shaped
and restored the land. The forest prevails at the park, healing old scars left by
man and continuing the timeless annual cycle of growth and renewal. Flowing
water, too, has been at work through the ages, slowly and inexorably wearing
away and sculpturing the land; the Cape Fear River has exposed a monument
in stone, Raven Rock, which stands high above the water's surface, and small,
clear streams have cut their beds through soil and rock in their rush to join the
river in its passage toward the sea.

The Cape Fear River divides Raven Rock State Park into two sections. High cliffs along the south side of the river overlook broad, flat flood plains, which are most evident on the lower, north-side bank. The park is located on the Fall Line, where the hard, resistant rocks of the Piedmont are separated from the softer rocks and sediments of the coastal plain. In the park, the Fall Line is characterized by rock outcroppings that have formed rapids in the river that are barriers to navigation and also by quartzite rock formations approximately 450 million years old that have been laid bare and eroded. Starkly beautiful Raven Rock is such a formation. It rises about 100 feet along more than 1 mile of the river's south bank. Immediately overlying the quartzite is a layer of volcanic rocks, and above that, at the surface, are gravel terraces of sediments transported downstream and deposited by swiftly flowing river currents, probably during Pleistocene interglacial periods.

During the 1740s, the principal rock formation along the river was named Patterson's Rock for its alleged discoverer, who found refuge there after his canoe capsized nearby. The name was changed to Raven Rock in 1854, when locks and dams were built on the river and ravens were observed roosting on the rock ledges. The locks and dams made navigation along the river between Haywood and Fayetteville possible, and Raven Rock was an important landmark for pilots of river steamers. A hurricane in 1859 destroyed the system of locks and dams in the river basin. They were not replaced, chiefly because the construction of railroads in 1886 eliminated the need for river navigation.

The park area was a hunting ground for Siouan and Tuscarora Indian tribes before the first European settlers pushed up the river in the mid-eighteenth century. The settlers were mostly hunters and trappers searching for hill country that reminded them of their native Scotland. From 1777 to 1838, the Northington family owned up to 6,000 acres of land in the area and built stores, mills, quarries, and roads. Northington Road, which stretched from Raleigh to Fayetteville, crossed the Cape Fear River via a ferry and was a major transportation route at the time. Many of the woodland bottoms now in the park were farmed early this century, but the forest was later allowed to return. Until the establishment of the park, the chief use of the land was growing timber.

With the closing of Northington's ferry and the building of new roads elsewhere, the Raven Rock area was visited mainly by local people for recreation. Walter Johnson of Goldsboro suggested in 1965 that a state park be established in the area, and in 1968 the acquisition of Raven Rock was endorsed by state authorities; however, it was primarily due to the efforts of Robert F. Soots, then a faculty member at nearby Campbell College (now University), that the concept became a reality. Aware of the possibility that the land might be sold to a mining company or a lumber company, Dr. Soots organized local support for the proposed park, obtained the backing of the Harnett County Board of Commissioners, and represented the county in presentations to the North Carolina Board of Conservation and Development. The Raven Rock Preservation and Park Committee was incorporated on July 16, 1969, and a bill to establish the park was introduced that year in the North Carolina General Assembly. Passage of the bill was accompanied by a state appropriation of $120,000; additional funds were provided by other agencies. The first tract of land, some 221.7 acres, was purchased and deeded to the state on March 23, 1970; subsequently, Burlington Industries donated 170 acres and additional tracts were purchased. The park presently encompasses 2,847 acres.

PLANT LIFE

The highly diverse topography of the park is rough and broken. Along the river are both low flood plains and high bluffs. Numerous swift-flowing streams have cut into bedrock, forming steep-sided ravines between which are divides with rather smooth, rounded profiles. The uplands tend to be flat and dry. The resulting biological environments are characterized by distinctive plant communities.

The flood-plain forest community along the river contains some of the largest trees in the park. The most common species are sycamore, sugarberry, black willow, beech, and river birch; also present are American holly, hop hornbeam, black gum, and American elm. The understory includes ironwood, yellow buckeye, and pawpaw.

Some of the same species grow on the face of the bluffs and in cool, moist ravines throughout the park; in addition, such sites contain red maple, winged

Dutchman's breeches

elm, and loblolly pine. In the understory are storax, strawberry bush, and flowering dogwood, as well as mountain laurel and rhododendron, which are more commonly associated with the western part of the state.

An oak/hickory forest characterizes the upland forest community on the relatively dry ridge crests; dominant species are the mockernut hickory and chestnut, black, post, blackjack, and southern red oaks. In the understory are sourwood, dogwood, gooseberry, sparkleberry, and blueberry. The driest of the upland communities are vegetated by post oaks and a mixture of pines, including loblolly, shortleaf, and Virginia.

Portions of the park were cleared for agriculture in earlier days. Such areas are now undergoing the typical succession of community types that will culminate in forests appropriate to the environmental conditions at each site. Visitors may find several stages of forest succession. Changes occur rapidly, as new plant species invade and successfully compete against established species. Successional communities often provide habitat for animals different from those in mature forests, and they should not be overlooked.

One of the real joys of a spring visit to Raven Rock State Park is the abundance of wildflowers. Moist deciduous forests are often characterized by the presence of many species of small flowering plants that begin growth very early, bloom, and complete their annual cycle prior to the closing of the forest canopy. In essence, they take advantage of the sheltered warmth and sunshine available before the leafing out of the canopy plunges them into heavy shade for the summer. This phenomenon occurs throughout Piedmont and mountain forests. Appropriate conditions are seldom found in the coastal plain.

The rich, moist soils of the ravines and flood plains at Raven Rock State Park provide ideal conditions for small, delicate flowering plants. Their growth is also enhanced by the Cape Fear River, which may provide a route of access for seeds of species more common in the foothills and mountains, and which regularly adds nutrients to the flood-plain soils at each flooding. Thus, at Raven Rock State Park in early spring, visitors may find extensive stands of Dutchman's breeches, bloodroot, saxifrage, spring beauty, trailing arbutus, Solomon's seal, bellwort, and many other plants usually associated with moist mountain coves. The wildflowers are often mixed with maidenhair ferns, lichens, liverworts, and mosses. Later in spring, thickets of mountain laurel and rhododendron bloom along bluffs overlooking the river. The drier oak/pine forests and other plant communities can also be spectacular in the spring, with understories of flowering dogwood and carpets of bird-foot violets.

To enjoy these wildflowers at their peak of bloom, visitors should travel to the park in early April, when the forest canopy leaves are just breaking dormancy and beginning to color the deciduous forest with the haze of pale greens and yellows that rivals the fall season for overall beauty. Visitors may then discover a world of beauty that can provide a lifetime of fascination and enjoyment.

ANIMAL LIFE

Park fauna is abundant, with a diversity of species from each of the vertebrate groups. The best game-fish habitat is in the Cape Fear River at the mouths of major creeks, especially Campbell's and Fishing creeks. Visitors fishing in these waters may catch largemouth bass, warmouth, bluegill, catfish, and redear and green sunfishes; other interesting species include longnose gar, American eel, chub, shiners, suckers, and pirate perch. Anglers must have a valid state fishing license.

The many springs and streams create ideal habitat for salamanders. Large populations of these amphibians are present, particularly in the vicinity of the high bluffs; the most common species are dusky, two-lined, and slimy salamanders. Streams and riverbanks are also ideal places to find frogs, including the familiar bullfrog, the southern leopard frog, and the green frog, plus several species of chorus frogs and treefrogs. Choruses of frogs add immeasurably to the enjoyment of a walk in the woods, especially during their breeding seasons. Toads occur throughout the park; the most common is Fowler's toad.

Piedmont forests are home to many reptiles, especially where there is considerable habitat diversity, as in Raven Rock State Park. Visitors may look for several species of terrapins in the river and for spotted turtles in the small streams; other turtles present are the eastern box turtle and the common snapping turtle. Common lizards are Carolina anoles, fence lizards, and several kinds of skinks. Snakes are secretive animals that usually avoid people. Most snakes in the park are harmless. Banded water snakes, black rat snakes, rough green snakes, eastern garter snakes, and eastern hognose snakes are among those present. The poisonous copperhead occurs in the park but is rarely encountered.

Bird life is diverse at all seasons, but it is especially interesting in spring, when the newly emerging leaves of deciduous plants attract large numbers of defoliating insects at the time when many species of birds are migrating northward through North Carolina. It may be possible to see twenty or more species of warblers in a single day in the park at the peak of the migratory passage. Many species remain to raise their broods, and visitors may find an abundance of small land birds all summer. The park also has a population of wild turkeys, and wood ducks nest in hollow trees along the river. Hawks and owls of several species are present. In winter, waterfowl on the river show an increase in both number and diversity; mallards, black ducks, and other species may be seen. The winter woodlands have flocks of mixed species, including chickadees, titmice, woodpeckers, and other birds typical of the region. During some years, northern finches, including bold and colorful evening grosbeaks, invade the park and provide additional excitement for visitors.

Mammals of the woodlands in and around the park usually remain well-hidden in the abundant protective cover. White-tailed deer are present but are observed infrequently. The small, familiar mammals a visitor is most likely to see are eastern cottontails, Virginia opossums, raccoons, and gray squirrels. The southern flying squirrel lives in the park but emerges from its nesting site in tree hollows only at night, and fox squirrels are occasionally seen in the pine forests. Other mammals that fortunate visitors may glimpse are long-tailed weasels, gray foxes, and muskrats. Various mice and small insectivorous mammals such as shrews and moles commonly inhabit such woodlands. They are rarely seen, though elevated mounds indicating the passage of burrowing eastern moles often appear in the soft earth. Several species of bats, such as eastern pipistrel, brown bat, and evening bat, may be seen in flight as they forage for insects at dusk.

HIKING, BRIDLE, AND CANOE TRAILS

The section of the park on the south side of the Cape Fear River, where most visitor activities are concentrated, is a mecca for hikers. With over 15 miles of foot trails, Raven Rock State Park offers a trail for every hiker, regardless of age or physical condition. Ranging from the short nature trail that circles the picnic ground to Campbell's Creek Loop Trail, which is 5.3 miles in length, the trails are easy to moderately strenuous. Trails provide the only access to the interior of the park.

Raven Rock Loop Trail is a scenic hike through a hardwood forest. The trail begins at the parking lot, passes the picnic ground, and leads after 1 mile to the park's main feature, Raven Rock. Wooden stairs down the face of the high bluff lead to the base of Raven Rock, where hikers may walk along the river's edge and explore the area beneath the overhang. Before the arrival of European settlers, Indians are believed to have camped there while hunting in the surrounding wilderness. On the return segment of the trail, a short spur leads to a stone balcony located above Raven Rock. The balcony overlooks the river and its forested north bank; rock outcroppings that extend across the river may be seen a short distance upstream. These outcroppings may be reached via Fish Traps Trail. Raven Rock Loop Trail continues to its terminus at the parking lot, for a total distance of 2.1 miles.

American Beech Nature Trail is a walk of less than 1 mile that begins and ends at points along Raven Rock Loop Trail and circles the picnic ground. A brochure available at the park office interprets the natural history of this portion of the park. Hikers will see such plants as sparkleberry, muscadine grape, sweet bay, several kinds of ferns, and mushrooms in season. Mountain laurel grows on the cool, moist, north-facing slopes. Among the trees seen from the trail are tulip tree, sweet gum, red maple, and beech. Decaying stumps are a reminder of logging operations that preceded the establishment of the park. Such animals as Virginia opossums, raccoons, gray squirrels, and owls make their homes in such woods. Hikers should not miss this easy and interesting trail.

To take **Little Creek Loop Trail**, 1.4 miles in length, turn right off Raven Rock Loop Trail between the picnic ground and the river. A portion of the trail is over varied terrain along Little Creek; the return segment is a wide, even trail through beautiful hardwoods parallel to the river. The terminus is near the stairs that lead beneath Raven Rock. A short spur trail leads to the canoe camp and the canoe launching and take-out point on the river. A second spur trail, 0.5 mile in length, begins at Little Creek bridge and leads to the group wilderness camp.

Both Fish Traps Trail and Northington's Ferry Trail begin at the parking lot and follow the western (return) segment of Raven Rock Loop Trail for 0.4 mile. At the place where the two trails separate, Fish Traps Trail proceeds to the right and Northington's Ferry Trail to the left, as shown on the map.

Fish Traps Trail proceeds one-way for a total distance of 1.1 miles, descending a moderate slope to a rock outcropping that extends across the Cape Fear River. The outcropping is an idyllic spot where a hiker may find solitude and hear the musical sounds of the wind in the trees and the water flowing swiftly over and around the smooth-surfaced rocks. The scene is enhanced by the reflections of great trees on the water and by the sights and sounds of the many birds that move about the river. This place was well-known to early Indian inhabitants of the area, who placed baskets below the rocks to trap fish migrating upstream.

Northington's Ferry Trail is an easy walk to the mouth of Campbell's Creek, which is an excellent spot for fishing. As early as 1770, a road led to the same location, and Northington's ferry provided a means of crossing the river for travelers between Raleigh and Fayetteville. The return to the parking lot is by the same route for a round-trip distance of 4.4 miles.

Campbell's Creek Loop Trail begins and ends at the parking lot. It is a moderately strenuous trail that provides a view of a diversity of habitats and natural features within the park. The first segment of the trail follows Campbell's Creek to where its waters enter the Cape Fear River. Many smaller streams and laurel thickets are encountered along the way. Access to the family wilderness camp is on the return segment of the trail. At the 2.3-mile mark, Campbell's Creek Loop Trail passes the trailhead for **Lanier's**

Falls Trail, a spur trail that extends for 0.4 mile round-trip to a rock outcropping on the river. The beautiful area around the outcropping is an excellent place to see many birds and other kinds of animals as well as a variety of wildflowers. The total distance of Campbell's Creek Loop Trail and Lanier's Falls Trail is 5.7 miles.

The section of the park on the north side of the river contains 7 miles of bridle trails through undeveloped woodlands. Areas for parking and picnicking are provided.

The **Cape Fear Canoe Trail** extends along 56 miles of the Cape Fear River from an access point at U.S. 1 bridge over Deep River to Pope Park in Fayetteville. The trail includes the section of the river that flows through Raven Rock State Park. A brochure and a map with details about the trail are available from the park office or from the Carolina Canoe Club at P.O. Box 9011, Greensboro, N.C. 27408. A buoy signals the location of the canoe camping area in the park. Lanier's Falls and "the Fishtraps" are small rapids that canoeists must negotiate; each was formerly the site of a lock and dam on the river.

FACILITIES AND ACTIVITIES

SR 1314 dead-ends at the park entry gate; a gravel road continues past the **park office** to two large parking lots that provide access to the picnic ground and trailheads. Visitors may stop at the office for information, and campers must register there. The parking lots are separated by a strip of pine forest within which are located a source of drinking water, benches for relaxation, and a refreshment stand with cold-drink and snack machines.

Modern restrooms opened in 1987 are near the parking lots and the picnic ground; paved access for handicapped persons is provided, and drinking water is available.

The **picnic ground**, approximately 150 yards beyond the parking lots, is easily accessible by way of a wide trail. Thirty tables and six grills are located in the shade of the oak/hickory forest and are widely spaced to avoid crowding. The trail continues through the area to Raven Rock and other places in the park.

A campground to accommodate trailers and other RVs is not yet available, though there are three primitive camping areas for tents only. All equipment and supplies, including water, must be backpacked or brought by canoe to these back-country sites. A **family wilderness camp** 2.5 miles from the office is reached via Campbell's Creek Loop Trail; there are five campsites, each accommodating up to four persons. A **group wilderness camp** is located in a low flood plain east of Raven Rock some 2.2 miles from the office;

it is reached via Little Creek Loop Trail. The camp has a capacity of two hundred persons; advance reservation is advised. A **canoe camp** is in a low-lying pasture beside the Cape Fear River 1.7 miles from the office. Five campsites are available for canoeists on the Cape Fear Canoe Trail; campers should register at the park office.

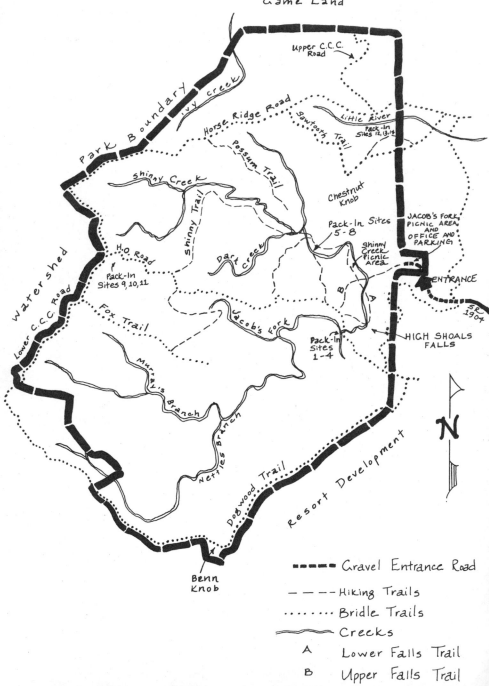

Game Land

Upper C.C.C. Road

Park Boundary

Ivy Creek

Horse Ridge Road

Sawtooth Trail

Little River

Pack-In Sites 12, 13, 14

Possum Trail

Shinny Creek

Shinny Trail

Chestnut Knob

Pack-In Sites 5-8

JACOB'S FORK PICNIC AREA AND OFFICE AND PARKING

Watershed

H.O. Road

Dart Creek

Shinny Creek Picnic Area

ENTRANCE

Lower C.C.C. Road

Pack-In Sites 9, 10, 11

B

A

SR 1904

Fox Trail

Jacob's Fork

HIGH SHOALS FALLS

Murray's Branch

Pack-In Sites 1-4

N

Nettles Branch

Dogwood Trail

Resort Development

Benn Knob

- - - - - Gravel Entrance Road

- - - - Hiking Trails

. . . . Bridle Trails

~~~~~ Creeks

A   Lower Falls Trail

B   Upper Falls Trail

SOUTH MOUNTAINS
STATE PARK

Address: Route 1, Box 206-C
          Connelly Springs, N.C. 28612

Telephone: (704) 433-4772

Size: 6,586 acres

Established: 1975   *High Shoals Falls*

Location: Burke County, on the boundary with Cleveland County. From
    Morganton, 18 miles north of the park, take exit 105 off I-40 onto N.C.
    18 south for approximately 10 miles; turn right onto SR 1913 for 3.5
    miles; turn left onto SR 1924 (old N.C. 18) for 2 miles; turn right onto
    SR 1901 for 1.5 miles; and turn right onto SR 1904 for 3.6 miles to the
    park entrance. From Shelby, 24 miles south of the park on U.S. 74,
    turn onto N.C. 226 to Polksville, then onto N.C. 10 past Casar; exit
    onto SR 1545 at Pisgah Baptist Church, then follow SR 1905, SR 1901,
    and SR 1904 to the park entrance.

Principal Attractions: The rugged terrain of the South Mountains, which
    reach nearly 3,000 feet in elevation; High Shoals Falls and boulder-
    strewn, picturesque mountain streams with numerous cascades; dense
    deciduous forests with abundant wildlife; spectacular view from Benn
    Knob; wilderness experience.

Visitor Activities: Hiking and horseback riding; nature study; scenic view-
    ing; picnicking; primitive backpack camping; fishing in mountain
    streams.

Season: Open from the first Saturday in April to the end of February; closed
    in March.

_____

    The Catawba River Valley is a corridor of the Piedmont plateau that ex-
tends westward through Burke County between the Blue Ridge Mountains

and the South Mountains. The South Mountains, eroded outliers of the Blue Ridge, are a broad belt of peaks and knobs that rise abruptly from the valley floor and encompass approximately 100,000 acres in Burke, Cleveland, and Rutherford counties. The peaks are steep and rugged, averaging about 2,000 feet in elevation, with narrow ridge tops and valleys; the highest point, at Buzzard Roost, reaches 3,110 feet. A portion of this beautiful, densely forested range of mountains is preserved within South Mountains State Park in southern Burke County.

Within the park, elevations range from less than 1,200 feet at points along Jacob's Fork River to 2,894 feet on Benn Knob on the park's southern boundary. The rugged terrain has resulted primarily from the erosive action of flowing water. Jacob's Fork River, Shinny Creek (a name derived from the moonshine stills of an earlier era), and their tributaries drain eastward through the park into the watershed of the Catawba River. They have cut steep slopes, some of which exceed 60 degrees, and produced narrow, boulder-strewn streambeds. Numerous cascades and massive outcrops of rock occur along the waterways. The most spectacular geological feature in the park is High Shoals Falls on Jacob's Fork; its torrent of water streams over a cliff face of bare rock onto the massive boulders 80 feet below and then continues downstream through a series of quiet pools and turbulent cascades. By contrast, Benn Knob offers a restful stillness and a view of peaks and ridges extending, row upon row, to the distant horizon.

The Catawba Valley and the gaps across the mountain ranges to the west were major avenues of travel for Indians, explorers, and settlers, and they have long been a focus of human history in the area. The South Mountains separated Cherokee and Catawba Indian tribes. The Cherokees traveled through the valley to fight the Catawbas. Early Indians in the area apparently established villages and cultivated land near the rivers, setting up temporary camps in the mountains for the purpose of hunting and gathering food. There is no definitive archaeological evidence that they inhabited present-day parkland.

Explorers and the first permanent settlers were in the area as early as 1752. Daniel Boone and John Sevier passed through the region, as did patriots in the revolution on their way to the battle at Kings Mountain. German, Scotch-Irish, Welsh, and English settlers from Pennsylvania, Virginia, eastern North Carolina, and elsewhere farmed fertile river bottomlands, and by 1790 the Burke County area contained 1,257 families. Early settlers included the grandfather of Zebulon Vance and Waightsville Avery, the first attorney general of North Carolina, who acquired hundreds of thousands of acres of land for speculation.

Gold was discovered at Brindle Creek Ford in 1828. Sam Martin, a wanderer who had prospected for gold in South and Central America, is credited with the discovery. Given temporary lodging at the home of cobbler Bob Anderson, Martin observed gold flakes in the mud used to chink the cracks of the log cabin, and he subsequently panned gold in a nearby stream. Martin and Anderson mined over $40,000 worth of the yellow metal within a year. The ensuing gold rush attracted immigrants, wealthy slave owners, and mining companies to the area. Boom towns developed, such as Brindleton, Brackettown, Huntsville, and Jamestown. Gold valued at well over $1 million was mined in the area. The productivity of the mines gradually declined, though some mining continued into the early twentieth century.

A few early settlers entered the fringes of the South Mountains, and immigrants from the gold rush added to their numbers. Among the inhabitants of what is now part of South Mountains State Park was Dave Bibby, whose homesite was on Jacob's Fork near High Shoals Falls. Bibby built and operated a corn mill at the top of the falls. Only the foundation and chimney of the house remain. A second homesite, that of Johnny Smith, was built near the park office where the ranger residence now stands; family graves remain at the site. Within the mountains, pioneer life persisted and residents depended upon hunting and subsistence farming for survival. The lives of such self-sufficient people changed little until the twentieth century.

The opening of the undeveloped land in the park area was begun in the 1930s by youths of the Civilian Conservation Corps (CCC) encamped at Enola. They constructed service roads through forests, built an observation tower on Horse Ridge, and cleared streambeds. Upper and Lower CCC roads remain in use, but the tower has been replaced by a similar structure on Benn Knob.

The land in the area of the park has long been in private ownership. More than 26,000 acres owned by timber companies were cut extensively, resulting in the second- and third-growth forests now vegetating the mountains. The city of Morganton and other agencies own and maintain over 8,000 acres in the Henry Creek/River watershed as a water supply. The North Carolina Wildlife Resources Commission leased from private owners the more than 11,500 acres of land on which it established the South Mountains Wildlife Management Area. Programs for the management of populations of trout, wild turkeys, white-tailed deer, and other game species were carried out from the early 1950s until the late 1960s.

Most of the timberland in the area other than that in the Morganton watershed was acquired by Champion International Company and Liberty Life Insurance Company. Champion International Company currently leases more than 4,600 acres east of the park to the North Carolina Wildlife Resources Commission for the South Mountains Game Land. Liberty Life Insurance Company leases approximately 2,600 acres bordering the park on the southeast to a development firm for the construction of houses and recreational facilities.

Recommendations for the establishment of a state park in the South Mountains were made in 1940, 1961, and 1970; in each case, the state failed to take positive action. In 1973, however, the North Carolina General Assembly appropriated funds for land acquisition for state parks, and $1.5 million was allocated for the South Mountains. The state purchased 5,779 acres from Liberty Life Insurance Company, and the park was established. Additional land has been acquired. The park remains relatively undeveloped and retains its wilderness quality.

PLANT LIFE

South Mountains State Park is primarily a forested park. At low elevations, there has been some clearing of land in the past, and natural succession is in the process of recreating forests. On such sites, Virginia pine is usually the dominant species, and plant diversity is relatively low. Other disturbed areas associated with roadsides and buildings provide an opportunity for pioneer grasses and forbs, but these are a minor element in the park.

Narrow flood-plain communities border the streams. Steep slopes mean very narrow zones of flooding, and the forests dominated by river birch, sycamore, sweet gum, and yellow poplar are usually only a few feet in width. Rhododendron thickets are abundant on the steepest slopes.

North-facing coves offer the best soils and the most moisture. Yellow birch, red maple, beech, yellow poplar, basswood, umbrella tree, red oak, and other deciduous species occur, as does hemlock, a conifer. Such coves often develop magnificent forests if logging does not remove the mature trees. Logging has occurred on all but the steepest sites among the coves, and most trees are second- or third-growth. Coves are often excellent sites for wildflowers, and visits in May should offer opportunities to enjoy the many small species that flower in spring.

The slopes of the South Mountains are relatively steep, and variations of slope, soil, and exposure to the sun result in varied forest communities. North-facing slopes that retain good moisture are forested by mixed stands of hickories, oaks, black locust, white pine, and many of the same species found in coves. A shrub layer is usually well-developed and often includes mountain laurel and rhododendron.

South-facing slopes, more exposed to the sun, and areas of thin, excessively drained soils are often covered with forests of oaks and pines. Rock chestnut oak, scarlet oak, pitch pine, and Virginia pine are most abundant in such areas. The shrub layer often consists of an almost complete cover of blueberries.

ANIMAL LIFE

Park wildlife is abundant, but it may sometimes be difficult to observe, as is often the case in forested areas. Because South Mountains State Park is relatively new, studies of its fauna are incomplete.

The clear, cold, highly oxygenated, and turbulent streams are good habitat for trout and other cold-water fishes. Introduced rainbow and brown trout thrive along with smallmouth bass. Minnows, darters, and other small fishes also occur, but they are seldom seen except as darting shadows when disturbed by passing hikers.

The moist forests, stream margins, and wet seep areas are home to several species of salamanders, and frogs and toads may be heard calling from pools in spring. Reptiles living within the forests include eastern fence lizards, skinks, many small, secretive snakes, and several larger species, such as the eastern garter snake, black rat snake, and copperhead.

Bird life is abundant, especially in spring and summer, when the deciduous forests are fed upon by hordes of insect larvae, which in turn are food for insectivorous birds. More than sixty species of birds have been reported to nest in the South Mountains. While most species are typical of the western Piedmont, ruffed grouse, black-throated green warblers, and rose-breasted grosbeaks are usually considered more typical of mountain forests. Other common species include Acadian flycatchers, common crows, Carolina chickadees, American robins, wood thrushes, red-eyed vireos, ovenbirds, hooded warblers, indigo buntings, and rufous-sided towhees. Park rangers have reported the presence of a small nesting population of common ravens on rock ledges near High Shoals Falls.

White-tailed deer are abundant in the South Mountains, and many smaller mammals also live in the area. Woodchucks may be seen along grassy roadsides, and chipmunks inhabit the forests along with their larger cousin, the gray squirrel. Raccoons and Virginia opossums may be seen foraging along streams, and several species of small rodents, shrews, and eastern moles are important forest inhabitants seldom encountered by visitors.

ROADS AND HIKING AND BRIDLE TRAILS

The roads in the park were constructed either by the CCC in the 1930s or by timber companies during logging operations. They have only one lane, and most are steep and rough; only the CCC roads are graded periodically by the North Carolina Forest Service. The roads provide access to the interior of the park and to remote areas of the South Mountains. Upper CCC Road crosses the northeast corner of the park and South Mountains Game Land, but it is not available for public use and is gated. Lower CCC Road passes along the west and southwest boundaries of the park and continues north to Enola and west to N.C. 64.

Two old logging roads cross the park; their use is limited to park vehicles. Headquarters (High Shoals) Road meanders across the center of the park from the office and parking area to Lower CCC Road at the west boundary. Horse Ridge Road, on the north side of the park, connects Upper and Lower CCC roads. Many dead-end side roads extend along ridges into the woodlands.

Many miles of these park roads are used by hikers and equestrians. Several foot trails have been constructed and others are planned. An extensive system of hiking trails will eventually be available to visitors; at present, various combinations of roadbeds, foot trails, and bridle trails lead to attractions throughout the park.

Hemlock Nature Trail, 0.25 mile in length, leads from the parking lot along Jacob's Fork River and joins Headquarters Road; it is an easy walk that provides an opportunity to see much of the abundant plant and animal life along the rocky mountain stream. Hikers may proceed along Headquarters Road past Shinny Creek picnic ground to a pair of trails that lead left, as indicated by the trail sign, to the focal attraction of the park, High Shoals Falls. The site is 1.5 miles from the park office.

Lower Falls Trail leads 0.5 mile from the trail sign to the bottom of the falls. The rocky trail leads along the edge of a high ridge, down wooden steps to the bank of Jacob's Fork, and along the stream. Hemlock, elm, beech, and sycamore trees line the pathway; ferns and mosses grow luxuriantly from the moist soil. The river flows through a deep ravine, and masses of rosebay rhododendron cloak the steep slopes on either side. The musical sound of the flowing water increases in intensity near the falls, and the large rocks at the water's edge may be dangerously slick. The trail, marked by yellow blazes, crosses the stream over boulders that create a rushing cascade. On the opposite bank, the trail is steep and strenuous; hikers must scramble over huge boulders to the base of the falls. The view from the base of the falls is spectacular, as Jacob's Fork River plunges 80 feet to cascade over boulders into a quiet pool 6 to 8 feet deep before flowing onward through the narrow ravine. The shoulders of the cliff face over which the waters fall are steep and fragile and should not be ascended. Trail improvements are planned in order to give access to the top of the falls; until then, hikers should return to the trail sign at the trailhead and Headquarters Road.

Upper Falls Trail leads for 0.9 mile from the trail sign to the top of the falls. It is an excellent trail along an old logging road that follows the ridge line to the river. Above the falls is an area of flat rocks from which to observe the exceptional beauty of the area. From upstream, the water flows along its boulder-strewn, tree-lined course into a shallow pool before making its sheer drop over the high cliff.

Other trails are more distant from the park office and require a greater investment of time and energy. The trailhead for **Shinny Trail** is off Headquarters Road a short distance past pack-in campsites #5 through #8, as shown on the park map; Shinny Trail rejoins the road after a distance of about 1.5 miles. Along the way, hikers cross Shinny Creek at three points on rustic bridges built in 1987 as a project of the South Mountains and Broad River Sierra Club groups. **Fox Trail** leads east from Lower CCC Road; it connects to Headquarters Road via **Jacob Ridge Bridle Trail**. Pack-in campsites #9 through #11 lie along Fox Trail, as does the gravestone of William Crotts, a man identified as a member of Company F of the Thirty-fourth North Carolina Infantry in the Confederate army. In the northern section of the park, **Possum Trail** is along a dead-end roadbed off Horse Ridge Road, and **Sawtooth Trail** is a loop between Upper CCC Road and Horse Ridge Road.

An unloading area for horses is located along SR 1904 near the park office. Equestrian access to bridle trails is via **Dogwood Trail**, which leads along the southeast boundary of the park to Benn Knob and beyond, or via an unnamed trail that leads along the northeast boundary to Horse Ridge and beyond. These routes connect to form an extensive loop around the park. There are more than 13 miles of bridle trails, many of them, like Dogwood Trail, shared with hikers.

FACILITIES AND ACTIVITIES

Park access is by way of SR 1904, a gravel road that is dusty but in good condition. Much of the road is near or alongside the meandering Jacob's Fork River, which is crossed three times by narrow bridges. The **park office** and ranger residence are located approximately 1 mile past the entry gate. Information about camping, hiking, and fishing in the park is available at the office, and campers must register there. The road leads into a gravel parking lot adjacent to the office and along the bank of the river. Vehicles may not proceed beyond the parking lot. Headquarters Road continues past the ranger residence and picnic ground into the interior of the park; its use is restricted to hikers and park personnel.

The park is a delightful and restful place for picnicking and experiencing the South Mountains environment. Two picnic areas are available to visitors. **Jacob's Fork picnic ground** is adjacent to the parking lot, next to the beautiful, fast-flowing stream. Twelve tables and nine grills are spaced beneath the trees. A newly constructed, modern restroom is located in the picnic area; its rustic design blends well with the surrounding woodlands. Drinking water is available outside the building. Large display cases with exhibits about plant and animal life and a relief map of the park are nearby. **Shinny Creek picnic ground**, a smaller, primitive facility, is reached after a stroll of less than 0.5 mile along Headquarters Road. There are four tables and three charcoal grills around an open, grassy meadow; a pit toilet is provided.

The park provides four primitive **backpack camping areas**; there is no family campground for trailers and RVs. All camping equipment and supplies, including drinking water, must be carried to campsites, and all trash and garbage must be packed out. Each area is a grassy meadow cleared and used by the North Carolina Wildlife Resources Commission at an earlier time for the feeding and management of deer. Fire circles, firewood, and pit toilets are provided. Visitors must register at the park office; a fee is charged. **Pack-in sites #1 through #4**, accessible by woodland trail, are located a short distance west of High Shoals Falls and about 1 mile from the park office. Campers may pitch their tents beneath tall hemlocks and white pines near Jacob's Fork River. **Pack-in sites #5 through #8** are along Shinny Creek; hikers should turn right at the trail sign about 100 yards past Shinny Creek picnic ground and proceed 0.9 mile to the camping area. **Pack-in sites #9 through #11** are located approximately 5 miles from the park office, off Fox Trail near the western boundary of the park. They are reached by a combination of trails, including Headquarters Road, Jacob Ridge Bridle Trail, and Fox Trail; visitors should refer to the park map or ask directions from park personnel. **Pack-in sites #12 through #14** are at the north side of the park off Horse Ridge Road and Sawtooth Trail; visitors should inquire about access to this area.

Approximately 12 miles of streams flow through South Mountains State Park and feature an abundant population of trout; **angling** for this favorite game fish is a popular recreation for visitors. Jacob's Fork, Shinny Creek, and their tributaries are the principal waterways of the park. Most local streams are classified as native trout waters, which means that they provide good habitat suitable for reproduction. Because the streams are not stocked, only artificial lures may be used, and fish less than 10 inches in length must be released. Below its confluence with Shinny Creek, Jacob's Fork is classified as general trout waters, and it is stocked with legal-size fish; there are no lure restrictions or size limits. The fishing season is closed from March 1 to the first Saturday in April. The streams are stocked and administered by the North Carolina Wildlife Resources Commission; a valid license is required, and all applicable regulations are enforced.

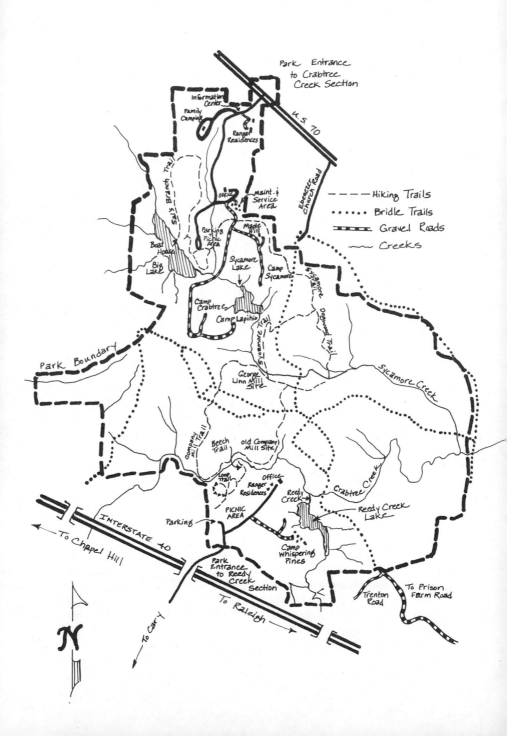

Park Entrance
to Crabtree
Creek Section

U.S. 70

Information
Center

Family Camping

Ranger Residences

Ebenezer Church Road

Sal's Branch Trail

Office

Maint. & Service Area

- - - Hiking Trails
· · · · · Bridle Trails
▭▭▭ Gravel Roads
∿∿∿ Creeks

Parking Picnic Area

Maple Mill

Boat House

Big Lake

Sycamore Lake

Camp Sycamore

Sycamore Trail

Dogwood Trail

Camp Crabtree

Camp Lapihio

Sycamore Trail

Park Boundary

George Linn Mill Site

Sycamore Creek

Company Mill Trail

Beech Trail

Old Company Mill Site

Crabtree Creek

Loop Trail

Office

Ranger Residences

PICNIC AREA

Reedy Creek

Reedy Creek Lake

To Chapel Hill

INTERSTATE 40

Parking

Park Entrance to Reedy Creek Section

Camp Whispering Pines

To Prison Farm Road

Trenton Road

To Raleigh

To Cary

N

WILLIAM B. UMSTEAD STATE PARK

Address: Route 8, Box 130
             Raleigh, N.C. 27612

Telephone: (919) 787-3033

Size: 5,334 acres
             Crabtree Creek Section - 3,979 acres
             Reedy Creek Section - 1,355 acres

Established: 1943

Location: Wake County. The entrance to the **Crabtree Creek Section** is 6 miles northwest of Raleigh on U.S. 70; the **Reedy Creek Section**, 11 miles west of Raleigh, is reached from I-40 by taking exit 287 onto Harrison Avenue and turning north to the entry gate.

Principal Attractions: Pine, hardwood, and mixed forests that demonstrate the process of old-field succession; diverse flora and wildlife; three man-made lakes; extensive system of hiking and bridle trails.

Visitor Activities: Hiking and horseback riding; nature study; picnicking; family and group camping; fishing and boating.

Season: Open year-round, though some facilities close during the winter months.

William B. Umstead State Park lies between the cities of Raleigh and Durham in the rapidly developing Research Triangle region of the state. As the region becomes more urbanized and populous, the significance of the park as an oasis of green where the resources of nature are preserved for the enjoyment of the people is increasingly evident. The park epitomizes the purpose and mission of the entire North Carolina system of parks.

Unlike most other state parks, William B. Umstead State Park has no dominant feature or landmark. There is no lofty peak, dazzling waterfall, or grand scenic vista. Instead, there are occasional small and unexpected threads of beauty woven into the fabric of the park waiting to be discovered by those attentive visitors with the time to observe—a rockface supporting a small patch of maidenhair fern, wild teaberry along a laurel-covered slope, a quiet pool where multicolored leaves float in early fall, a beaver's lodge and dam, a flood plain with a stand of giant sweet gums, or the crumbling remains of an old gristmill with hints of the life of a bygone era. A major attribute of the park is the ongoing process of ecological succession that is much in evidence. Exhausted and eroded farmland and forests stripped of most of their timber are experiencing restoration. Old wounds are being healed, new forests typical of the Carolina Piedmont are being established, and diverse plant and animal communities are returning. The parkland is a natural laboratory where visitors may observe and come to understand the basic processes of recovery and restoration.

Prior to its occupation by settlers, the present-day parkland was a wilderness with magnificent forests of oaks, hickories, beech, and other species of deciduous trees. American bison, American elk, bobcat, beaver, and many other animals roamed the area. Indians inhabited the land, and two important traces, or avenues for trade, were nearby, the Occoneeche Trail to the north and the Pee Dee Trail to the south. As early as 1774, land grants in present-day Wake County opened the area to settlement; trees were felled, and the virgin soil was cleared to make way for fields of grain, tobacco, cotton, potatoes, and other crops. Early tillers of the soil were successful, but poor cultivation practices and the one-crop production of cotton after the Civil War led to the depletion and erosion of topsoil and a submarginal existence for much of the farming community. By 1930, many houses, fields, and mills were abandoned. Second-growth timber was stripped from most upland areas, accelerating erosion.

In 1935, during the Great Depression, the land within present-day William B. Umstead State Park was purchased from farmers by the Resettlement Administration as a demonstration project designed to show the recreational potential of such submarginal lands. Until 1943, the development of Crabtree Creek Recreation Demonstration Area was financed by federal money and supervised jointly by the National Park Service and the North Carolina Department of Conservation and Development. In 1938, a work force of the Civilian Conservation Corps (CCC) was based in the area, and projects for the revitalization of the land were initiated. The CCC built group camps, temporary roadways, trails, picnic shelters, a lake, and other facilities; the workers also planted trees and constructed check dams to retard erosion. Perhaps most significantly, the natural processes of restoration of land and forests were permitted to proceed without further human interference.

The work of the CCC and the participation of the federal government in the project ended when World War II began. On April 6, 1943, for the sum of one dollar, 5,088 acres of land were deeded to the state to serve "public park, recreation, and conservation purposes," and Crabtree Creek State Park was officially established. The name of the park was changed in 1955 to William B.

Umstead State Park in honor of a former governor with strong conservation ideals and interest in state parks. Crabtree Creek State Park was subdivided in 1950; 1,234 acres were set aside for the establishment of Reedy Creek State Park for black citizens. Racial segregation of the parks ended in 1966 when the two sections were integrated as William B. Umstead State Park.

Much of the topography of the parkland has resulted from the actions of the picturesque streams that course through the region. Crabtree Creek flows from west to east through the park, its waters ultimately reaching the Neuse River. Sycamore Creek from the north and Reedy Creek from the south drain into Crabtree Creek. Steep slopes along stream banks contribute to the difficulty of access to some areas. Three man-made lakes lie along the creeks. The largest is Big Lake, 55 acres in size, on Sycamore Creek. Farther downstream, Sycamore Lake covers about 25 acres. Reedy Creek Lake, near the confluence of Crabtree and Reedy creeks, is also 25 acres in size.

Today, after many years of restoration, the parkland is well-forested, though the process continues. A rich diversity of animal life inhabits woodlands, streams, and lakes. William B. Umstead State Park is one of the most frequently visited parks in the state, with abundant opportunities for recreation and for the enjoyment and appreciation of natural beauty.

PLANT LIFE

The park contains a diverse flora characteristic of the eastern edge of the Carolina Piedmont; it is estimated that over eleven hundred species of plants occur in the parkland. Much of the land is vegetated by second- or third-growth forests that have developed since the land was abandoned as active farmland. Some portions, especially flood plains and very steep slopes overlooking creeks, may not have been cleared, but most such areas were probably logged in the past.

A mosaic of forest communities now occurs as natural succession continues and forests mature under the protection provided by the park. Uplands that were the last sites abandoned by farmers are vegetated by pine forests; loblolly and shortleaf pines dominate, but an understory of hardwoods presages the future. In older forests, tulip trees, oaks, and hickories have already invaded the canopy to share dominance with the pines. Flowering dogwood is an important tree in the understory.

Steep slopes overlooking the creeks, especially those that face north, are vegetated primarily by hardwoods. In some areas, dense thickets of mountain laurel occur, and rhododendron, more common in mountain habitats, is present. Moist coves are dominated by a mixed deciduous forest in which yellow poplar, beech, red maple, and sweet gum are prevalent; yellow lady's slippers add a dramatic touch in late spring. A 50-acre remnant stand of large—

possibly virgin—beech trees and southern sugar maples along Crabtree Creek has been included in the National Registry of Natural Landmarks by the United States Department of the Interior; the area is known as the Piedmont Beech Natural Area.

Forests dominated by sweet gum, river birch, and American elm occur on flood plains adjacent to the creeks. Such forests are excellent places to enjoy wildflowers, including bloodroot, spring beauties, trout lilies, and Mayapple, all of which bloom in early spring before the forest canopy leafs out.

Although most of the parkland is forested, small areas of other types of habitats add to the diversity of plant life. Pond edges are occupied by small, diverse marsh communities or by willow and alder thickets. A power line right of way that crosses the park provides an avenue of open land reminiscent of old-field habitats. The right of way provides habitat for many species of grasses and herbaceous flowering plants that require full sun.

ANIMAL LIFE

The animal life of William B. Umstead State Park has been well-studied. The park is located near major universities, and it provides excellent opportunities to study animals in their natural habitats.

The park's creeks have a diverse fish fauna, with robins, green sunfish, and largemouth bass most commonly seen; other sunfishes, darters, and minnows are also present. Lakes within the park are stocked with largemouth bass and bluegills, and other common species are natural inhabitants.

An abundant amphibian fauna may be observed by visitors willing to seek out these usually secretive animals. Spring peepers, toads, and southern leopard frogs can easily be distinguished by voice as they call from pond edges and temporary pools in spring. Careful observers will also be able to distinguish chorus frogs and several species of treefrogs. Small, leaf-choked drainages provide habitat for dusky and two-lined salamanders; mud, marbled, and spotted salamanders are found occasionally.

The reptilian fauna includes turtles that live in the ponds and along the creeks as well as the terrestrial eastern box turtle, which occurs in the uplands. Skinks and eastern fence lizards are present in the uplands, as are numerous snakes. Banded water snakes occur along pond margins and streams; they are often mistaken for cottonmouths, which are not present in the park. Black racers and several small, secretive species occur in appropriate habitats. Copperheads are present but are seldom encountered.

Bird life is varied and abundant. Deciduous forests in the Piedmont offer both resident and transient species a bounty of food in spring, when defoliating insects attack the new crop of leaves. Coniferous forests, on the other hand, offer living conditions for some insects year-round, thus providing birds a

Wild Turkey

steady source of food. Seeds and fruits are abundant in the forests in the park, and many forms of wildlife depend on this bounty. One study identified fifty species of birds nesting within the park. Most abundant and widespread are pine warblers, wood thrushes, and red-eyed vireos. A total of nine species of nesting warblers, including the Kentucky warbler and the Louisiana water-thrush, occur in the park. Wild turkeys have become established, and though turkeys are secretive and difficult to see, the loud gobbling of the males during the spring provides evidence of their courtship. In spring, the deciduous forests of the flood plains provide an excellent opportunity to witness the passage of hordes of birds as they migrate from wintering grounds farther south toward their nesting habitats to the north. In winter, the park is a good place to see evening grosbeaks and other northern finches.

Numerous species of mammals make their homes in the park. One of the most widespread and abundant is the gray squirrel, whose life history has been studied extensively within the parkland. The preferred habitats of these familiar animals are forests of hardwoods mixed with conifers, whether along river bluffs or wooded bottomlands, in places where there is an abundance of nesting sites and of food, mainly seeds and nuts. Gray squirrels are adept climbers that nest in trees, either in cavities or in masses of leaves and twigs on branches high above the ground. They are active in the daytime and can often be seen in early morning or late afternoon foraging on the forest floor. The gray squirrel is an important game animal that generally succeeds in maintaining large, stable populations in suitable habitats.

Other resident mammals of the forest are the raccoon, Virginia opossum, eastern cottontail, red and gray foxes, and southern flying squirrel. Long-tailed weasel, mink, and muskrat may occur, and evidence of the presence of beaver, reintroduced into the area in 1956, may be found along streams. An abundance of seldom-seen small rodents, such as white-footed mice, shrews, and eastern moles, live under cover on the forest floor. White-tailed deer are also important members of the forest community.

HIKING AND BRIDLE TRAILS

Approximately 17 miles of hiking trails provide access to most areas of the park. The trails lead across forested ridges and slopes and along meandering, rock-strewn streams. The beauty and the diversity of the park are best witnessed from one of its trails. Visitors may choose a short, leisurely walk along a nature trail or a more extensive hike into the heart of the woodlands. Several trails interconnect; a park map should therefore be consulted in preparation for an excursion far from visitor-use areas.

Trailheads in both sections of the park are near parking and picnic areas accessible by park roads. Short, self-guided nature trails are located at both Crabtree Creek and Reedy Creek. **Crabtree Creek Self-guided Trail** is a 1-mile loop with nineteen markers keyed to a descriptive booklet available at the park office. **Reedy Creek Self-guided Trail** is a 1.2-mile loop with twenty-five trailside plaques that describe major features along the trail.

Loop Trail, 0.5 mile in length, begins near the picnic shelter in the Reedy Creek Section. It provides an introduction to some of the small, colorful plants of the park. In moist areas, royal, Christmas, southern lady, rattlesnake, and broad beech ferns thrive as lush natural gardens. Mushrooms may grow in profusion when rain is abundant, and pipissewa, Jack-in-the-pulpit, and wild ginger are common.

Sal's Branch Trail, 2.4 miles in length, is a loop in the Crabtree Creek Section. The trailhead is to the right off the broad gravel path from the parking lot to Big Lake. The trail passes through mixed pines and hardwoods beside Big Lake, continues along the creek, and returns. Club moss and Christmas fern are common along the trail, which leads hikers through overgrown, abandoned fields where furrows remain visible. Several check dams built by the CCC in the 1930s are evident; the check dams are piles of quartz rocks placed in gullies and ravines to help prevent the erosion of topsoil.

Other trails in the park interconnect; various segments of trails or combinations of trails may be taken to make a hike as long as time and energy permit. Visitors may hike between the picnic areas of the Crabtree Creek and Reedy Creek sections by way of Sycamore, Company Mill, Dogwood, and Beech trails; several different routes may be followed, as shown on the map. Hikers must either return via the trails or arrange transportation from the opposite park entrance.

Sycamore Trail, marked with yellow blazes on tree trunks, begins at the Crabtree Creek picnic ground. It crosses gravel roads at 0.5 and 1.6 miles and proceeds through a mixed pine/hardwood forest to a junction at 1.9 miles with the northern terminus of **Dogwood Trail**. Sycamore Trail continues to the right across a hardwood ridge and down a steep slope to the bank of Sycamore Creek. The creek is cut deeply into the face of the slope, exposing rock outcrops; numerous colorful herbaceous plants grow along the moist bank, and the creek is habitat for small fish, salamanders, crayfish, and freshwater mussels. The trail continues along the creek and ends at its connection with Company Mill Trail near the former site of George Linn Mill, 2.9 miles from the trailhead. The large rocks visible in the creek were once part of the mill's dam. To return to the trailhead, hikers may retrace their steps for a round-trip distance of 6 miles or cross the creek and follow Company Mill Trail eastward for 0.2 mile to its junction with the southern terminus of Dogwood Trail. Part of this short segment of Company Mill Trail passes along a deep slough that carried water back to the creek after turning the mill's large paddle wheel. After 1.1 miles, Dogwood Trail rejoins Sycamore Trail for a round-trip distance back to the trailhead of 6.2 miles.

Company Mill Trail, marked with blue blazes, is a 3.5-mile loop. It may be entered from Sycamore or Dogwood trails, as described above, or from Beech Trail in the Reedy Creek Section. **Beech Trail** provides the most direct access for visitors who do not desire to hike the length of the park. It begins near the midway point of Loop Trail and winds for 0.5 mile through beautiful hardwoods to the bank of Crabtree Creek and its junction with Company Mill Trail. Large outcrops of granite formed during the Paleozoic era, approximately 300 million years ago, mark the site of Old Company Mill, once one of the largest gristmills in the area. Built early this century, the mill served farmers who paddled their grain-laden boats downstream to have their corn ground into meal. Today, only remnants of the mill's dam remain. Sycamore and birch trees line the banks of the creek. The prevailing sound is that of water rushing over and around rocks lining the streambed.

Hikers must cross Crabtree Creek to join Company Mill Trail; the crossing must be made carefully, for the rocks are round and slick and the stream is often swift. On the opposite side of the creek, the loop trail may be followed to the right or left. In either direction, the route passes near the creek for a short distance, then turns northward across ridges, moist ravines, and tributary streams to the side of Sycamore Creek. The scenery along the sparkling streams is picturesque; mountain laurel and rhododendron grow on rocky slopes, and frogs splash in the shallow water. Numerous animal tracks may be visible in the soft mud. Company Mill Trail can be an adventure of discovery for those who will look and listen with care and patience.

Approximately 16 miles of bridle trails provide access for equestrians to the park's remote woodlands. Marked by white-capped posts, the trails pass along gravel roads as well as narrow pathways. Entry to the trails is from Ebenezer Church Road or from Trenton Road and Old Reedy Creek Road. Horses are restricted to the bridle trails; they are not permitted into other areas of the park.

FACILITIES AND ACTIVITIES

Crabtree Creek Section

Visitor-use facilities are accessible from the entry gate off U.S. 70 by way of a paved park road that leads past turnoffs to the family campground, the group camps, and the park office and terminates at an extensive parking and picnic area. An **information center** a short distance past the entry gate contains exhibits describing park resources.

A side road to the right at the information center leads to the **family campground**. The campground is open Thursday through Sunday from March 15 to November 15. There are twenty-eight campsites, each with a table and grill; water and electrical hookups are not provided at the sites, but drinking water is accessible throughout the camping area. A centrally located washhouse provides toilets and showers. The campground is well-shaded by a beautiful hardwood forest. A fee is charged; sites are available on a first-come basis.

The **picnic ground**, open year-round, is in a mixed pine/hardwood forest. Ample parking is provided nearby. The picnic ground is a popular facility that is often crowded, especially on summer weekends. There are forty tables with grills spaced beneath the trees; two picnic shelters provide fireplaces and additional tables. Drinking water is available, and modern restrooms are nearby.

From the parking lot, a broad gravel path leads to **Big Lake** and to a **boathouse** where rowboats and canoes may be rented. The boathouse is open every day from June 1 until Labor Day and on weekends from March 15 to June 1 and from Labor Day through the fall. Private boats are not permitted on the lake, and swimming is not allowed. **Fishing** for bass, bluegill, and crappie from lakeshore or boat is a popular activity on the lakes of the park.

Three **group camps** (Camp Sycamore, Camp Crabtree, and Camp Lapihio) are located in the Crabtree Creek Section near Sycamore Lake. They are accessible by gravel roads from the park office. The group camps are available to nonprofit organizations, both youth and adult. Each camp includes a well-equipped mess hall, camper and counselor cabins, and washhouses. **Maple Hill Lodge** is also available to youth groups for a camping experience with a taste of the wilderness; its facilities include a fireplace, drinking water, and pit toilets. For reservations and for information about fees and other details, write the park superintendent.

Reedy Creek Section

From the entry gate off I-40, the park road leads to a large parking area adjacent to the **picnic ground**, which is located in a forest of pine trees. There are twenty-five tables with grills scattered beneath the trees; a picnic shelter with an attached wooden deck provides additional tables and fireplaces. Drinking water is available, and modern restrooms are nearby. Trailheads are at the rear of the shelter.

A side road leads to the **park office**, to maintenance facilities, and to Camp Whispering Pines, near Reedy Creek Lake. **Camp Whispering Pines** is a group camp similar to those described for the Crabtree Creek Section. For information, write the park superintendent.

NEARBY

The **North Carolina Museum of Natural Sciences** is open from 9:00 A.M. to 5:00 P.M. Monday through Saturday and from 1:00 P.M. to 5:00 P.M. on Sunday except on state government holidays. There is no charge for admission. The state museum houses excellent exhibits on the natural history of North Carolina and extensive collections of specimens from the region and around the world. Major exhibits include birds in typical habitat settings, mounted game mammals from many areas of the earth, and whales and whaling implements. The skeletons of four whales and of several other marine mammals are on display. The Brimley Room is a replica of the office and workspace of H. H. Brimley, the first director of the museum. The museum's outstanding educational programs include scientific and popular publications, public lectures and audiovisual presentations, field trips, and special services for schoolteachers and school groups. Registration is required for some classes and programs. The museum is located in downtown Raleigh between the Legislative Building and the North Carolina State Capitol, which is a state historic site. For information, write: Director, North Carolina Museum of Natural Sciences, P.O. Box 27647, Raleigh, N.C. 27611 (919/733-7450).

Falls Lake and Jordan Lake state recreation areas and Eno River State Park are located close to Raleigh and William B. Umstead State Park. For further information, consult the discussions of those park units elsewhere in this volume.

Mountains

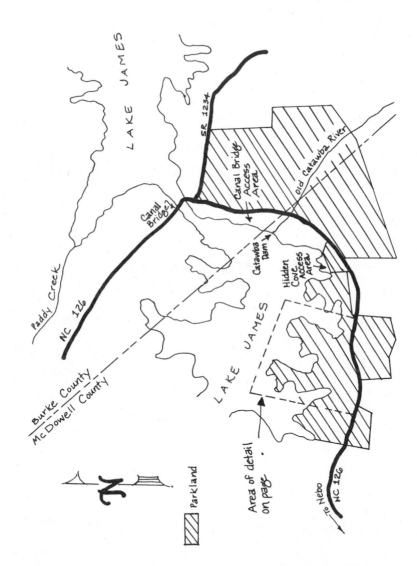

LAKE JAMES

SR 1234

Canal Bridge Access Area

old Catawba River

Canal Bridge

Catawba Dam

Hidden Cove Access Area

Paddy Creek

NC 126

Burke County
McDowell County

LAKE JAMES

Parkland

Area of detail on page

To Nebo

NC 126

N

LAKE JAMES
STATE PARK

Lake James

Address: P.O. Box 340
           Nebo, N.C. 28761

Telephone: (704) 652-5047

Size: 564 acres

Established: 1987; opened June 1989

Location: McDowell and Burke counties, between Marion and Morganton; exit I-40 onto U.S. 70 and proceed 5 miles to Nebo, then follow N.C. 126 east for 2.8 miles to the park entrance. Travelers on the Blue Ridge Parkway may reach the park either by way of U.S. 221 from Linville Falls to U.S. 70 and Marion, a distance of 23 miles, or by way of N.C. 80 from Buck Creek Gap, southeast of Crabtree Meadows, to U.S. 70 and Marion, a distance of 16 miles; from Marion, visitors should proceed as above.

Principal Attractions: Lake James, a 6,510-acre impoundment on the Catawba and Linville rivers; forestland with an abundance of wildflowers and wildlife; proximity to the Blue Ridge Mountains and Linville Gorge in Pisgah National Forest.

Visitor Activities: When the construction of facilities is complete, visitors will have access to a swimming beach, picnic ground, tent camping area, hiking trails, and opportunities for boating, fishing, and other water-related activities on Lake James.

Season: Open year-round.

Lake James is one of nine man-made lakes constructed as hydroelectric impoundments along the Catawba River by Duke Power Company and its predecessors since 1904. The sequence of lakes extends 238 miles through

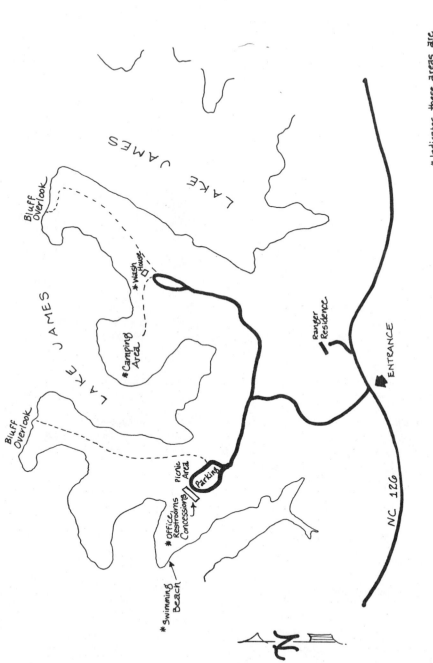

* Indicates these areas are scheduled to open Summer, 1990

LAKE JAMES

LAKE JAMES

Bluff Overlook

Bluff Overlook

* Wash House

* Camping Area

Ranger Residence

ENTRANCE

NC 126

* Office, Restrooms Concessions

Picnic Area

Parking

* Swimming Beach

the Catawba Valley from Lake James, which is near the river's headwaters on the eastern slope of the Blue Ridge Mountains, to Lake Wateree in the central Piedmont of South Carolina near Camden. The Catawba lakes vary in size from the smallest, at barely 1,000 acres, to Lake Norman, North Carolina's 34,000-acre "inland sea." Lakes and watershed lands owned by Duke Power Company are used for a variety of purposes, including production of electricity, growth and logging of timber, public recreation, and game management programs administered by state agencies. The Catawba Valley is a land of beautiful forests with an abundance of wildflowers and wildlife.

Lake James, with 150 miles of meandering shoreline, lies within the upper reaches of the Catawba Valley. Peaks of the nearby mountain range are visible against the horizon to the north, and the waters of Lake James, among the most pristine in the state, reflect the green foliage of forest trees growing down to its edge. The lake, named for James B. Duke, the founder of Duke Power Company, was created between 1916 and 1923 by the construction of three dams across the Catawba River and two tributary streams, Paddy Creek and Linville River. The Catawba River and Paddy Creek/Linville River impoundments were connected by a broad canal, forming a body of water 6,510 acres in size. Located at the base of the Blue Ridge Mountains between the towns of Marion and Morganton, Lake James lies 1,200 feet above mean sea level.

The establishment of Lake James State Park by the North Carolina General Assembly in 1987 was the result of strong local support for the proposal and the efforts of area legislative delegations. Funds were appropriated for the purchase of land from the Crescent Land and Timber Corporation—a subsidiary of Duke Power Company—for the initial phases of facilities development, and for park operations. The parkland lies approximately 3 miles east of Nebo along N.C. 126. The portion of the park west of Hidden Cove includes three small peninsulas that extend into the lake, providing access for water-related activities. The parkland includes portions of the river and flood plain downstream of the impoundment and the Catawba River Dam, as shown on the map.

FACILITIES AND ACTIVITIES

From the park entrance on N.C. 126, a paved road leads north to a junction; to the left, it continues to a parking area near the lakeshore and to visitor-use facilities. A picnic ground is nearby; a picnic shelter is provided, and outdoor tables are beneath the trees. A multipurpose building provides space for the park office, a concession stand, and restrooms. Rinse-off showers are available. A section of the lakeshore at the rear of the building will be developed as a protected beach for swimming. The beach and concession stand were not in use when the park opened to the public in June 1989, but they will be available by the summer of 1990. The beach offers an excellent view of Lake James, with its densely forested shore, and the distant mountains. The peninsula of land extends north beyond the parking area; trails lead to a bluff above the lake.

The park road to the right at the junction leads along a second peninsula of parkland to the place where a tent camping area will be constructed in phase two of the park's development. Construction of camping facilities is scheduled for completion in 1990. An extensive system of hiking trails is also planned. Beyond the proposed camping area is a high bluff overlooking Lake James with a view of forested parkland and distant mountain peaks near the Linville Falls area of the Blue Ridge Mountains. Lake James State Park will be a delightful place for hiking and enjoying the beauty of the Catawba Valley.

NEARBY

Four access areas for boaters on Lake James have been provided by Duke Power Company in cooperation with the North Carolina Wildlife Resources Commission. Each has space for parking and a ramp for launching boats. Scenic **Hidden Cove Access Area** is located near the southwest end of the Catawba River Dam, while **Canal Bridge Access Area** is near the northeast end of the dam; each is on N.C. 126 adjacent to parkland, and in the future they may be added to the park. **North Fork Access Area** is 0.5 mile north of the intersection of U.S. 221 and U.S. 70 west of Marion and is reached by SR 1501 and SR 1552. **Linville River Access Area** is 1 mile east of the Linville River bridge on N.C. 126, at the north side of the lake.

There are ten additional public recreational facilities on Lake James, seven of which provide ramps and parking for boaters. Some facilities provide gasoline, fishing supplies, food, and boat rentals and storage, as well as picnicking and camping sites. For additional information and a map of the area, write: Duke Power Company, Corporate Communications Department, P.O. Box 33189, Charlotte, N.C. 28242.

The **Blue Ridge Parkway**, a unit of the national park system, lies 16 miles northwest of Lake James via N.C. 80. Additional information about the Blue Ridge Parkway is contained in the chapters on Mount Jefferson and Mount Mitchell state parks in this volume. Linville Falls Recreation Area and the Museum of North Carolina Minerals, both located along the parkway, are nearby.

Linville Falls Recreation Area is located at milepost 316.3. It is a 440-acre preserve that features white pine, a magnificent virgin stand of hemlocks, and a profusion of rhododendrons. Linville River flows placidly through the forest to Linville Falls, where it drops 102 feet through a series of clefts in the bare rock to the bottom of Linville Gorge. Linville Falls has two levels; at the upper level, water cascades into a quiet pool, then plunges dramatically over a high ledge into the gorge. Linville Falls Trail, 2 miles in length, leads from the parking lot across Linville River bridge and through the hemlock forest to three overlooks, each with excellent views of the falls. A visitor center with restrooms and drinking water is a source of information about the area and about other short trails with views of the falls and gorge. Linville Falls Recreation Area is open year-round and has an excellent campground with fifty-five sites for tents and twenty sites for RVs; electrical hookups and a dump station are not provided. Interpretive programs are presented by park personnel at the campground amphitheater in the evenings. A picnic ground provides a hundred tables to accommodate Blue Ridge Parkway visitors.

Below the falls, Linville River, designated a state natural and scenic river in 1976, flows through **Linville Gorge Wilderness Area** into Lake James. The gorge, 18 miles long and 2,000 feet deep, is one of the wildest and most rugged areas in the eastern United States. Linville Gorge is rimmed by Table Rock and Hawksbill mountains and Jonas Ridge on the east and by Linville Mountain on the west. The peaks of these mountains reach up to 4,000 feet. Because most of the inaccessible chasm was bypassed by loggers, signs of human activities are minimal. In 1951, 7,600 acres of the gorge were designated a wilderness area by Congress; the area is now part of the Pisgah National Forest and is administered by the United States Forest Service. Much of the land that is now preserved in the Linville area was purchased and donated to the government by John D. Rockefeller. Approximately 25 miles of trails lead into and through the gorge; they are rugged, steep, and challenging. The Linville Gorge Wilderness Area offers some of the best opportunities for rock climbing in the eastern United States. An entry permit is required; permits are obtainable up to thirty days in advance from the District Ranger, United States Forest Service, P.O. Box 519, Marion, N.C. 28752.

The **Museum of North Carolina Minerals** is located at milepost 331. It is open from 9:00 A.M. to 5:00 P.M. Easter through Thanksgiving. There is no admission charge. Located in the mine-rich Spruce Pine District, the museum features commercially important minerals found in North Carolina, such as mica, feldspar, tungsten, spodumene, kaolin, and pyrophyllite; gemstones, such as ruby, emerald, garnet, quartz, amethyst, and sapphire; and a variety of fluorescent minerals. The building also serves as a Blue Ridge Parkway visitor center, and it includes a small bookstore.

Mount Mitchell State Park and South Mountains State Park are nearby and are easily accessible from Lake James State Park.

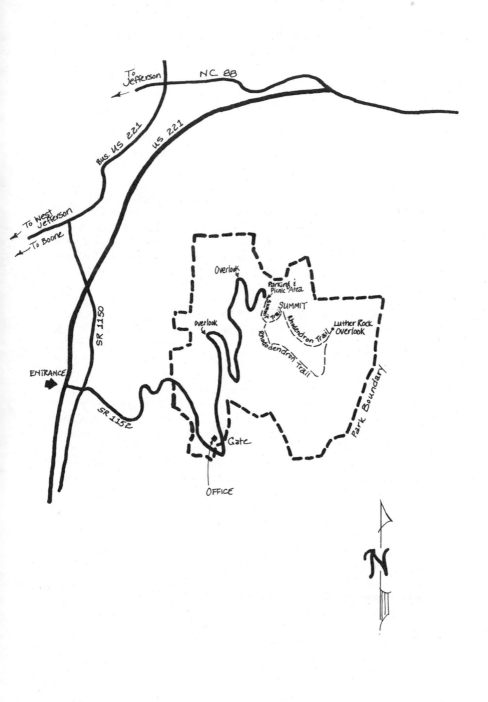

MOUNT JEFFERSON STATE PARK

Address: P.O. Box 48
            Jefferson, N.C. 28640

Telephone: (919) 246-9653

Size: 555 acres

Established: 1956

Location: Ashe County. Turn east at the park sign on U.S. 221 midway between the towns of Jefferson and West Jefferson. Proceed on SR 1152 for 1.5 miles to the gate at the park boundary; the road continues for 2 miles to the summit parking lot. The Blue Ridge Parkway is approximately 15 miles east of Mount Jefferson, by way of either N.C. 16 or N.C. 163.

Principal Attractions: Mount Jefferson, 4,683 feet in elevation, with its panoramic views; a magnificent oak/hickory forest, the basis for the designation of the park as a national natural landmark.

Visitor Activities: Scenic viewing; nature study; hiking; picnicking.

Season: Open year-round.

This small park located near the center of Ashe County in the state's rugged northwest corner includes the peak and steep slopes of Mount Jefferson. The mountain rises abruptly more than 1,600 feet above the surrounding valley and dominates the landscape to the east for travelers along U.S. 221. On a clear day, the views from overlooks along the park road and at the summit are spectacular. The overlooks are windows in the forest that provide distant vistas of mountain peaks that seem to extend into infinity. The panorama includes part of the Blue Ridge Mountains; on the horizon from northeast to southwest can be seen Mount Rogers and Whitetop Mountain in Virginia, Snake Mountain in east Tennessee, and Grandfather Mountain and Mount Mitchell in North Carolina. The near view of the valley below is one of green pastures, forests, and farmland, but also of residential and commercial developments that reach toward the mountain from neighboring towns. The proximity of man-made structures bears witness to the foresight and wisdom of those who led the way in preserving such beautiful areas as Mount Jefferson as state parklands.

Mount Jefferson and other nearby peaks are remnants of a lofty, broad plateau that existed throughout much of western North Carolina in the remote geological past. The weathering action of streams—tributaries of the North Fork and the South Fork of New River—and of other erosive forces wore away the relatively soft rocks and sedimentary layers of the plateau. The present landscape bears witness to the presence of harder, more resistant rocks that have thus far survived the slow, inexorable wearing away and leveling of the land. Mount Jefferson lies along the drainage divide between the forks of New River, which is the oldest river in North America and the second oldest in the world.

The first settlers in the area were Virginians; few North Carolinians other than such adventurous individuals as Daniel Boone and his fellow travelers along the Cumberland Trail into Kentucky had ventured westward beyond the Blue Ridge Mountains. Prior to the revolution, Mount Jefferson was known as Panther Mountain, perhaps because of a legend that tells of a panther that attacked and killed a child there. Other names were applied to the mountain by inhabitants of the area until Mount Jefferson became the official name in 1952 in honor of Thomas Jefferson and his father, Peter Jefferson, who surveyed the nearby North Carolina–Virginia state line in 1749 and owned land in the area.

A road 2.1 miles in length was constructed to the summit of the mountain in the 1930s by the federal Work Projects Administration. The establishment of a park resulted from a 1939 effort by local officials to have the road improved. Because state funds could not be expended on a road leading to private property, H. C. Tucker and J. B. Hash, two prominent local citizens, donated 26 acres of land for a public park; the needed funds for the road were then obtained.

An effort to have the local park accepted as a state park failed in 1941, though the area was subsequently designated a state forest wayside park in 1952. Continued efforts to attain state park status were unsuccessful because standards for state parks adopted in 1955 required a minimum size of 400 acres. A group of local citizens succeeded in raising funds and acquiring the necessary

View of Mount Jefferson from U.S. 221

land; as a result, 164 acres were purchased for the park, and an additional 300 acres were donated to the state. Mount Jefferson State Park was established on October 8, 1956, by action of the North Carolina Board of Conservation and Development. An additional 79 acres have since been purchased for the park.

A North Carolina Forest Service tower was built on the peak of the mountain in the early 1950s, while the summit area was still a wayside park; the tower remains in operation. Several communications antennas and small buildings are used by commercial and governmental agencies. The master plan for the park proposes that Mount Jefferson be designated a state natural area and that the unattractive and incompatible structures be removed.

PLANT LIFE

The slopes and summit of Mount Jefferson are a botanical paradise with a diversified aggregation of forest trees, shrubs, and wildflowers; the mature forests at the top of the mountain have never been logged. The great variety of interesting and unusual plants qualified the area for designation as a national natural landmark by the National Park Service of the United States Department of the Interior in 1975.

Composition of the forests varies with altitude and direction of the slope. Above 4,000 feet, a superb oak/chestnut forest dominates slopes that face south, east, and west; it is considered to be one of the finest examples of this forest type remaining in the southeastern United States. Its prominent species are northern red oak and white oak. In openings beneath the canopy layer of oak trees is an understory of Catawba rhododendron, mountain laurel, flame azalea, and dogwood. Wildflowers on the forest floor include trilliums, pink lady's slipper, and false lily of the valley.

Until the early twentieth century, American chestnut trees grew in the area. Throughout its range in the eastern United States, the chestnut's rot-resistant wood was immensely valuable to early settlers for the construction of buildings and fences, and its large, sweet nuts were food for both humans and wild animals. Tragically, the chestnut blight, a disease introduced from Europe in 1910, destroyed the species here and elsewhere. In the summit area of Mount Jefferson, ghostly trunks still stand; sprouts arise from the diseased roots and thrive until reaching maturity and becoming susceptible to the blight.

A northern cove forest is present on north-facing slopes above 4,000 feet. It includes red maple, yellow birch, tulip tree, and basswood; within the understory are mountain ash, prairie willow, black huckleberry, and mountain pepperbush, with hobblebush, Mayapple, bluebeard lily, and other shrubs and

Trillium, a common flower of moist mountain slopes

herbs covering the forest floor. On the ridge and slopes below Luther's Rock is a stand of large-toothed aspen trees in combination with red maple and other species. Large-toothed aspen is primarily a northern plant, known in North Carolina only in Ashe and Haywood counties. Other plants growing on Luther's Rock and similar outcrops include such northern species of perennial herbs as lettuce saxifrage, stonecrop, and rusty woodsia, a rare fern.

Trees growing on summit ridges and north-facing slopes tend to be gnarled in appearance and dwarfed in stature, averaging only about 20 feet. They have been stunted by exposure to the strong northerly winds that often blow across the summit and by heavy loads of ice in winter.

Forests below an elevation of 4,000 feet are dominated by chestnut oaks, along with black locust, hickories, poplars, red maple, and white oak. Wildflowers grow in profusion there and throughout the entire park, blooming from spring until fall.

ANIMAL LIFE

Although little work has been done on the animal life at Mount Jefferson, the park is inhabited by animals typical of the mountains of western North Carolina. Red squirrels (called "boomers" locally) may be seen in forests near the peak, and several species of small mice, such as deer mice and southern red-backed voles, are common. Bird life in these high-altitude forests includes several species not encountered at elevations below 4,000 feet. Visitors may see nesting chestnut-sided warblers, Canada warblers, and black-throated blue warblers, as well as rose-breasted grosbeaks, dark-eyed juncos, and white-breasted nuthatches. The veery's flutelike song may be heard at dusk or dawn. Reptiles and amphibians are less common in the high mountain forests than they are farther down the slope, but several species of woodland salamanders are restricted to cool, moist woodlands. They are encountered most frequently on wet evenings, when they emerge from their burrows to forage for insects and other invertebrates on the forest floor.

The mature deciduous forests of the middle altitudes are home to many common mammals—gray squirrels, southern flying squirrels, eastern chipmunks, red foxes, raccoons, Virginia opossums, and such small, secretive animals as shrews, moles, and white-footed and golden mice. Woodchucks may be seen along forest edges, and a few white-tailed deer occur in the area. The rich hardwood forests are a summer home to many species of songbirds, such as least flycatchers, rose-breasted grosbeaks, American redstarts, hooded warblers, black-and-white warblers, wood thrushes, and scarlet and summer tanagers. Winter wrens are heard mainly in April and May, and a resident pair of red-tailed hawks often soars between the first and second overlooks along the park road. Reptiles are fairly abundant at the middle altitudes; skinks and small snakes may be found in and around rotting logs and other places that offer food and hiding places, and garter snakes and black racers are frequently seen on the park trails.

Forests at low elevations are inhabited by wildlife typical of the western Piedmont and mountain valley communities.

HIKING TRAILS

Hiking trails at the summit of Mount Jefferson total 1.4 miles in length. In return for an investment of little more than an hour of hiking time, visitors are rewarded with exciting distant views of the surrounding countryside as well as an intimate look at the varied plant life and other features that make Mount Jefferson State Park distinctive.

Summit Trail begins at the parking area, passes through the picnic ground, and gently ascends 0.3 mile to the highest point on Mount Jefferson, 4,683 feet above sea level. This short gravel trail also serves as an access road to the North Carolina Forest Service tower and communications facilities. The panoramic views at the summit are partially obstructed, and the visual experience for visitors is less than satisfactory. Fortunately, nearby overlooks provide magnificent, unobstructed vistas that make a hike to the summit memorable.

Rhododendron Trail is an easy 1.1-mile hike. Its trailhead is to the right near the terminus of Summit Trail. A printed guide is available that provides descriptive information keyed to numbered markers along the trail.

Rhododendron Trail follows a ridge southeast along the crest of the mountain from the summit area to Luther's Rock Overlook; hikers may look back along the horseshoe-shaped ridge to the summit and tower. Catawba rhododendrons are abundant on the ridge, and they produce a profusion of pink blooms during the month of June. This is a virgin forest of northern red oaks with yellow birch and specimens of sugar, mountain, striped, and red maples. Rock ledges or bluffs extend along the ridge below the trail; outcrops of black mica gneiss are visible from below in the winter, when the trees are bare of leaves. The "caves" eroded beneath the ledges served as hideouts for escaped slaves traveling northward to freedom on the Underground Railroad, according to legend. On the slope of the mountain is Luther's Rock, an impressive formation of mica gneiss that provides an unexcelled view of the valleys and peaks beyond Mount Jefferson. On clear days, New River is visible to the east; this ancient river with bedrocks more than a billion years old was traveled by early Indians entering the area from the Ohio Valley more than ten thousand years ago, and it is reputed to have carried escaped slaves northward by night.

Near Luther's Rock, the return segment of the trail descends the south slope of the mountain; this area is less exposed to the frigid winds of winter than is the ridge, and trees tend to be of larger size. Additions to the flora on the south slope are white ash, basswood, and dogwood; mountain laurel, rhododendron, and other shrubs are abundant. The trail's terminus is at the picnic ground and parking area.

FACILITIES AND ACTIVITIES

The **park office** is just inside the entry gate on the lower slope of the mountain. The paved park road (SR 1152) winds upward through beautiful woodlands, past two scenic overlooks with superlative views, to a parking area near the summit. A **picnic ground** at the end of the park road provides thirty-two tables and nine grills scattered among the trees on the side of the mountain. Drinking water is available and restrooms are nearby, along Summit Trail. There are no camping facilities in the park, though campgrounds may be found nearby. The trailheads for Summit Trail and Rhododendron Trail are at the picnic area.

Park personnel present a year-round series of interpretive programs on the natural and cultural history of Mount Jefferson State Park and the surrounding area. The series includes guided walks, talks, demonstrations, and displays. For a program calendar and additional information, contact the park office.

NEARBY

Commercial campgrounds are located in the area. The nearest is Greenfield Campground, which offers full-service facilities; it is located 1 mile east of West Jefferson on SR 1549.

The **Blue Ridge Parkway**, the longest scenic road in the world and a choice unit of the national park system, is 15 miles east of Mount Jefferson. The Blue Ridge Parkway extends for 469 miles along the crest of the Blue Ridge and other mountain ranges between Shenandoah National Park in Virginia and Great Smoky Mountains National Park on the state line between North Carolina and Tennessee; 252 miles of this magnificent roadway are in North Carolina. It is unsurpassed in the natural beauty and the diversity it offers to those who travel its length. Numerous paved overlooks from 2,000 to 6,000 feet in elevation allow travelers to stop and enjoy magnificent views of mountains extending into the distance, range upon range, and of deep, narrow coves and valleys. Elsewhere, the road tunnels through solid rock, curves sharply down precipitous slopes, and passes through peaceful, grassy meadows with grazing cattle. A new vista and a fresh experience await travelers around each curve or over each ridge of the mountains.

Small parks and recreation areas are located at intervals along the Blue Ridge Parkway, strung like priceless jewels along the narrow ribbon of asphalt. Each is distinctive, but in combination they provide visitors opportunities to camp, hike, fish, and enjoy the beauty and peace of the mountains. They also offer lodging, food, gasoline, and other services; visitor centers provide interpretive programs and exhibits. Two of these park/recreation areas are near Mount Jefferson; they are Doughton Park and E. B. Jeffress Park.

Doughton Park lies between mileposts 238.5 and 244.7, approximately 22 miles north of the turnoff to Mount Jefferson. It is about 6,000 acres in size, and it is an ideal place for a leisurely hike. One of its trails leads to Wildcat Rocks on Bluff Mountain, where sheer cliffs and a shelter constructed of logs overlook the valley and the ridges below. Much of Doughton Park is open meadowlands where white-tailed deer, woodchucks, and other animals may be seen. Brinegar Cabin, the home of an early settler, is now a crafts shop where weaving demonstrations are presented. An excellent campground, open from May through October, has eighty-one sites for tents and twenty-six sites for RVs. Bluffs Lodge has a restaurant and twenty-four rooms for rent, as well as a gasoline station and a camp store. Evening interpretive programs are often scheduled at Bluffs Lodge.

E. B. Jeffress Park is located at milepost 272, approximately 12 miles south of the turnoff to Mount Jefferson. It offers restrooms and a delightful picnic ground. A self-guided nature trail leads through a hardwood forest to "the Cascades," where water flows over the sloping, bare rock of a cliff face.

For information about other areas along the parkway, write: Superintendent, Blue Ridge Parkway, 700 Northwestern Bank Building, Asheville, N.C. 28801. There are further discussions of sections of the Blue Ridge

Parkway in the chapters on Lake James and Mount Mitchell state parks in this volume.

New River State Park is located near Mount Jefferson, and Stone Mountain State Park is only 23 miles away. A discussion of each park is included in this volume.

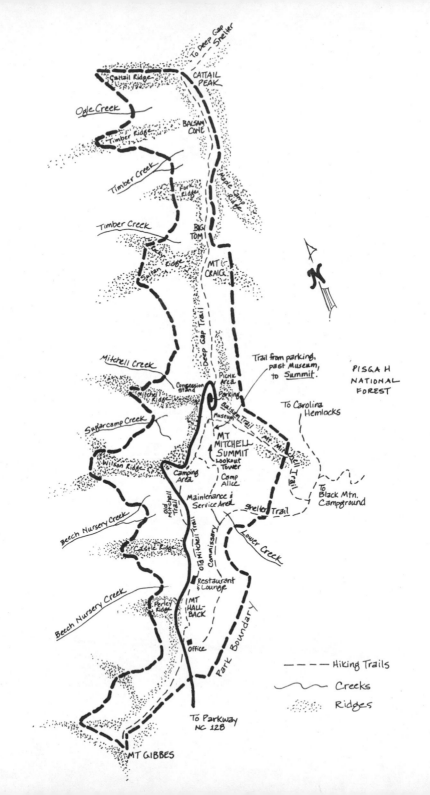

To Deep Gap Shelter

Cattail Ridge

CATTAIL PEAK

Ogle Creek

BALSAM CONE

Timber Ridge

Timber Creek

Fork Ridge

Maple Camp Ridge

Timber Creek

BIG TOM

Sultan Ridge

MT CRAIG

N

Deep Gap Trail

Mitchell Creek

Trail from parking, past Museum, to Summit.

PISGAH NATIONAL FOREST

Concession Stand

Picnic Area

Parking

Mitchell Ridge

Museum Balsam Trail

To Carolina Hemlocks

Sugarcamp Creek

MT MITCHELL SUMMIT

Mt. Mitchell Trail

Wilson Ridge

Lookout Tower

Camping Area

Camp Alice

To Black Mtn. Campground

Beech Nursery Creek

Old Mitchell Trail

Maintenance & Service Area

Shelter Trail

Castle Ridge

Old Mitchell Trail

Commissary

Lower Creek

Restaurant & Lounge

Beech Nursery Creek

Perley Ridge

MT HALLBACK

Park Boundary

Office

To Parkway NC 128

MT GIBBES

- - - - Hiking Trails

～～～ Creeks

⋰⋰⋰ Ridges

MOUNT MITCHELL STATE PARK

Address: Route 5, Box 700
             Burnsville, N.C. 28714

Telephone: (704) 675-4611

Size: 1,677 acres

Established: 1916

Location: Yancey County, in the Black Mountains 33 miles northeast of Asheville; turn off the Blue Ridge Parkway at milepost 355.4 onto N.C. 128, which continues for 5 miles to the parking lot near the summit of Mount Mitchell.

Principal Attractions: The Black Mountains, with six peaks over 6,000 feet in elevation; spruce/fir forest; magnificent scenery; 18 miles of hiking trails; observation tower and interpretive center on Mount Mitchell.

Visitor Activities: Viewing mountain scenery; hiking; nature study; family tent camping; picnicking.

Season: Open year-round, except when heavy snows make the roads impassable.

View of peaks of Blue Ridge from the park

Mount Mitchell State Park lies along the crest of the Black Mountains. Most travelers first view the park and the mountains from scenic overlooks on the Blue Ridge Parkway. The verdant slopes and peaks of the Black Mountains are often clothed by the mists of low-hanging clouds, and they dominate the horizon. Six peaks within this magnificent park are among the highest in the Appalachian chain: Mount Hallback (6,391), Mount Mitchell (6,684), Mount Craig (6,645), Balsam Cone (6,611), Cattail Peak (6,583), and Big Tom (6,558). Each is accessible to energetic and adventurous visitors by way of several moderately or strenuously difficult hiking trails. The summit of Mount Mitchell is reached by most visitors along a short path from a parking lot; hardier individuals may follow longer, more demanding trails. On clear days, visitors will be rewarded for their efforts with unsurpassed views of lesser peaks and rolling ridges extending to the horizon, for visitors who stand upon the summit of Mount Mitchell have ascended the highest point of land east of the Black Hills of South Dakota.

These are ancient mountains, much older than the higher, rugged Rockies of the western United States. The area where Mount Mitchell and her sister peaks now stand was once covered by an extensive inland sea that contained countless marine organisms. An earlier range of mountains had slowly eroded into the shallow seabed, and over a long period of time immense pressures in the earth's crust transformed the buried sand and mud into layers of gneiss and schist. About 250 million years ago, the rock formations were thrust upward to form the present Appalachians. The processes of erosion and weathering have since been at work, wearing down the once-lofty peaks to the rounded, worn mountains visible now. The mountains survive because of

Black Mountains north from Mount Craig

the erosion resistance of their rocks, but the slow process of leveling continues.

These southern peaks contrast sharply with others in the Appalachians farther north. The southern mountains escaped the scouring and tearing action of the bulldozing glaciers, and no boulders were strewn in the paths of the retreating ice sheets as in New England and eastern Canada. The contours of the peaks are muted by vegetation, and the effect is gentle and pleasing to the senses; there is no timberline in this section of the Appalachians. The extreme cold of the Pleistocene profoundly affected the life on the mountains, however. The plants and animals of more northern latitudes were able to extend their ranges to the south; subsequently, as warmer climates returned, the immigrant cold-adapted species became restricted to the tops of the highest peaks. Therefore, many of the plants and animals on Mount Mitchell and the adjacent peaks are much like those native to alpine environments.

Winters in the area are characterized by subfreezing temperatures, high winds, and heavy snow. The average annual snowfall is 104 inches, and snow flurries have occurred in every month of the year, though there usually is no snow on the ground after early May. In the summer, temperatures are moderate, averaging about 60 degrees Fahrenheit, sometimes accompanied by rain and fog but more often by brilliant sunshine and clear vistas.

Established in 1916, Mount Mitchell State Park was the first state park in North Carolina and one of the first in the South. Most of the land for the park was acquired with twenty thousand dollars appropriated by the state legislature, primarily as a result of the altruistic efforts of Governor Locke Craig and other early conservationists. The action was taken to stop the destruction of boreal forests caused by logging and frequent fires on the mountains and to make the area available "for the use of the people of the entire state seeking health and recreation."

During a collecting trip in 1789, French botanist André Michaux became the first European to climb in the Black Mountains. Michaux predicted that the highest peak in the eastern United States would be found within the range. Subsequently, Dr. Elisha Mitchell, a professor of chemistry, geology, and minerology at the University of North Carolina, made barometric and other scientific measurements in the area. In 1835, he determined that the highest peak was 6,476 feet in elevation; after further work in 1838 and 1844, he corrected his figure to 6,672 feet, a remarkable estimate only 12 feet in error. *Smith's Geography and Atlas of 1839* listed Mount Mitchell as the highest peak in the east.

Dr. Mitchell's claim that he was the first man to measure the peak was disputed by North Carolina Senator Thomas L. Clingman, who set the elevation at 6,941 feet in 1855. Clingman insisted that Mitchell had measured another peak in Buncombe County. In June 1857, the sixty-four-year-old Mitchell returned to verify his earlier measurement and support his claim. While hiking alone across the mountains, presumably on his way to visit his friend Big Tom Wilson, a well-known hunter and mountaineer, Mitchell fell to his death from a cliff above the 40-foot waterfall that is now known as Mitchell Falls, which lies outside the present park boundaries. Mitchell's body is buried next to the observation tower on the summit of the peak that bears his name.

PLANT LIFE

In the days when Michaux and Mitchell explored the Black Mountains, the forests possessed an unparalleled concentration of plant species. A dense forest of red spruce that covered the slopes above 4,500 feet gradually gave way to an almost pure stand of Fraser fir above 6,000 feet on the peaks. The understory was predominantly a tangle of rhododendron, along with such northern hardwood species as yellow birch, mountain ash, and beech. Below 4,500 feet, the coniferous forest was replaced by southern hardwoods.

Though the southern Appalachians remain, in the words of Freeman Tilden, a "display window of botany," the scene on Mount Mitchell and environs has changed. Repeated fires and clear-cut logging on the slopes prior to the establishment of the park greatly reduced the coniferous forest. Today, relic stands of the original climax forest remain; carpeted by a profusion of ferns, they form a dark green canopy on the highest peaks. Several northern hardwood species also survive. Secondary successional communities have become established where fir and spruce were disrupted; these include fire cherry, mountain maple, silky willow, oaks, and hickory, as well as such shrubs as rhododendron, blueberry, mountain cranberry, hobblebush, red elder, and bush honeysuckle, many of which produce flowers in the spring and berries in the fall. The garden of wildflowers produces a pageant of color on the mountains from June through early September; common species include bluets, St. John's wort, mountain aster, ox-eye daisy, mountain goldenrod, purple turtlehead, common yarrow, and white snakeroot. Mountain lettuce produces hanging gardens of delicate white flowers around exposed rocks, mountain wood sorrel carpets the forest floor in many places, and filmy angelica attracts hordes of bees to its intoxicating nectar.

Sadly, the spruce/fir forests of the Appalachians are in trouble. Trees at elevations above 6,350 feet on Mount Mitchell and other peaks in the park are dropping their needles and gradually dying. Their annual growth rate has declined dramatically since about 1960. Much of the forest seen along park hiking trails or from the observation tower contains dead trees; fallen and shattered trunks lie among healthy trees and young seedlings emerging from the dark soil. While there is cause for concern for the future of the forests, young trees are thriving and researchers are studying the problem. The cause of the "great dying" of the spruce and fir trees is not certain, but studies suggest an interaction of several factors. The trees exist in an extreme winter environment of high winds, cold temperatures, and other adverse climatic conditions. Since the late 1950s, a tiny insect, the balsam wooly aphid, has been on Mount Mitchell and has attacked and apparently killed many fir trees; the red spruce is immune to the effects of the insect, however, and it too is dying. Obviously, some additional agent is contributing to the problem. Recent research by Dr. Robert I. Bruck, a plant pathologist at North Carolina State University, and others has focused on pollutants borne through the air by moisture-laden clouds. The pollutants accumulate on tree branches and soil. Researchers have found massive amounts of pollutants at study sites. The research also suggests that trees stressed and weakened by pollutants are vulnerable to insect attack, and that death may result. If the studies are correct, the survival of the forests may depend on the imposition of stringent controls on emissions into the air. In addition, ways must be found to aid the natural regeneration of the forests. Despite the recent decline, portions of the forests have endured, still beautiful, for the enjoyment of all visitors.

ANIMAL LIFE

Animal life in Mount Mitchell State Park is abundant, though many species are seldom seen. Among the mammals, the vociferous red squirrel is at home in the coniferous forests at the highest altitudes and may be seen looking for handouts at the picnic ground. Woodchucks and their burrows may be observed along the road to the summit of Mount Mitchell; they prefer to dig their burrows in relatively open areas, such as those near the park office and the summit parking lot. A visitor may also glimpse white-tailed deer, black bears, striped skunks, or even a bobcat or a gray fox. Casual observers are likely to remain unaware of the numerous small and unobtrusive species that scurry about under the cover of vegetation, rocks, or fallen logs; among these are northern short-tailed shrews, deer mice, and southern red-backed voles. Several mammal species native to the area, such as the mountain lion, have been extirpated; our lives are impoverished by their loss.

The park is an excellent place to see birds; ninety-one species have been recorded. At high elevations may be found nesting red-breasted nuthatches, brown creepers, winter wrens, and golden-crowned kinglets, birds more characteristic of the coniferous forests of New England and Canada. Lucky campers who listen carefully may hear the call of the diminutive northern saw-whet owl, another species that has extended its range southward into the high mountain forests of western North Carolina.

Near the peak, visitors are able to see and hear common ravens. In spring and early summer almost anywhere in the park, visitors may hear the distant drumming of the ruffed grouse or be startled by its explosive departure when flushed. Several species of brightly colored warblers occur in the park; nesting black-throated green and Blackburnian warblers may be found in the spruce/fir communities, while Canada, black-throated blue, and chestnut-sided warblers may be found in the second-growth forests.

Though most bird-watching is done during the summer season, the park is a great place to see birds in spring and fall as well. Springtime brings a host of migrants moving from their southern wintering areas to their northern breeding grounds. In late April and May, vast numbers of warblers and other small birds pass through the park, feeding on the abundant insect population that is emerging to feast on the new growth of leaves. In the fall, northwesterly winds create favorable conditions for the migration of several species of hawks southward through the mountains of western North Carolina. Tall peaks such as those in the park provide excellent places for hawk watching.

Only in winter are bird numbers and diversity diminished. Winter is severe on the elevated peaks, and only about twenty species are known to spend the winter in the park. Year-round residents include ravens and ruffed grouse, while several species such as evening grosbeaks and purple finches spend the summer farther north and winter in the high mountains of North Carolina.

The cool, moist mountain forests of the southern Appalachian Mountains provide habitat for the world's most diverse population of salamanders, close relatives of the more familiar frogs and toads. Members of the family Plethodontidae, called woodland or lungless salamanders, are especially abundant. They have neither gills nor lungs and obtain oxygen through their skin. During daylight hours, visitors may see several species in or around wet, rocky seeps or along the edges of small, rocky streams. Salamanders are most active at night, however, and they are best discovered by taking an evening walk through the moist forest or to a seep. A quiet walk with a good flashlight may reveal the presence of a whole community of animals a visitor may not have realized existed. Salamanders can be rather difficult to identify, and a good field guide is necessary for accuracy. Some species, such as the pigmy salamander, are restricted to the spruce/fir forests at the top of these peaks of the southern Appalachian Mountains and occur nowhere else in the world. All animals are protected within state parks; visitors may enjoy their presence but may not remove them from their habitats. Once removed from their natural habitats, many species will soon die.

HIKING TRAILS

Except for N.C. 128 from the Blue Ridge Parkway to the summit of Mount

Mitchell, access to Mount Mitchell State Park is by foot along a network of trails.

Old Mitchell Trail originates outside the park along the North Fork of the Swannanoa River and extends along the crests of the mountains, terminating at the summit of Mount Mitchell. It was used by explorers as early as the mid-nineteenth century and was the primary trail to Mount Mitchell into the early part of this century. Today, most hikers join Old Mitchell Trail at the park office and follow it to the summit, passing the restaurant and the campground en route. The trail is moderately difficult and requires about one hour.

Mount Mitchell Trail connects the summit of Mount Mitchell to Black Mountain and Carolina Hemlocks Campground in Pisgah National Forest, which surrounds the park. It is the main trail used by hikers to climb the mountain. The 6-mile trail to Black Mountain Campground drops a vertical distance of 3,684 feet and is strenuous; the descent requires about three and a half hours and the more difficult ascent about four and a half hours. The United States Forest Service has provided two sleeping shelters with water, a pit toilet, and a fireplace at Commissary Ridge, about 1.5 miles from the summit. A 7-mile trail from Carolina Hemlocks Campground joins Mount Mitchell Trail at the Commissary Ridge trail shelters.

Balsam Trail is a short, 0.75-mile, self-guided nature trail that provides an opportunity for an easy walk for most park visitors. It begins at the lower summit parking lot and joins Mount Mitchell Trail, along which hikers may return to the summit and the parking area.

Camp Alice was a logging camp used in the early part of this century and was served by a railroad. With the establishment of the park, Camp Alice served tourists who arrived on excursion trains and later by a one-way toll road for automobiles. Visitors took lunch at a dining hall at Camp Alice, then walked to the summit of Mount Mitchell; cottages and tents were available for those who stayed overnight. The camp and the road have been removed, and no camping is permitted on the site now. Strenuous **Camp Alice Trail** intersects Old Mitchell Trail 0.25 mile below the summit and descends the south side of Mount Mitchell to the former site of Camp Alice. A less strenuous route is via the abandoned railroad bed from the park office.

Deep Gap Trail begins at the picnic ground near the summit of Mount Mitchell and extends for about 3 miles to the northern boundary of the park. It follows the crests of the mountains, crossing Mount Craig (named for Governor Locke Craig), Big Tom (named for Thomas D. Wilson, the mountain man who was a friend of Dr. Mitchell's), Balsam Cone, and Cattail Peak. Beyond the park boundary, the trail continues to the Deep Gap shelter. The trail is moderately to strenuously difficult, but it offers spectacular views on clear days as well as the opportunity for a wilderness experience.

The section of Deep Gap Trail between the summits of Mount Mitchell and Mount Craig is 1.25 miles long. It is an excellent choice for a short, moderately strenuous hike for visitors with limited time who want to get away from the crowded areas of the park. The windswept rocks on top of Mount Craig provide a vantage point from which to view both Mount Mitchell and the long ridge of peaks of the Black Mountains to the north. The air is cool and refreshing, the views are magnificent, and the sounds are those of the wind blowing and birds calling.

FACILITIES AND ACTIVITIES

Most park facilities are accessible from N.C. 128. The **park office** is just inside the entry gate; a parking area is provided for hikers who join Old Mitchell Trail, which passes nearby.

The **restaurant/lounge** is about 0.5 mile from the office. It is open from May 1 through October 31; the hours are from 11:00 A.M. on weekdays and 8:00 A.M. on weekends until one hour before the park gate closes. The restaurant offers a menu of specialty meals and sandwiches served in a pleasant atmosphere enhanced by an excellent view of the mountain range to the east. A large parking area is nearby.

The park **campground** is in a beautiful section of a coniferous forest 0.75 mile beyond the restaurant. There are nine campsites for tents only. Each site has a table, a fire pit, and a gravel pad for pitching a tent. Modern toilet facilities are provided, but not hot water or showers. The campground is open from mid-May through mid-October on a first-come basis.

The summit of Mount Mitchell is 0.75 mile beyond the campground; the summit parking lot provides access to other facilities. A short trail leads to the stone **observation tower**, from which visitors may look out over the Black Mountains and Pisgah National Forest. The body of Dr. Elisha Mitchell is buried next to the tower, and a stone marker describes his work on the mountain.

The **interpretive center** is located midway on the trail to the summit. It is open from 8:30 A.M. until 5:30 P.M. from April 1 through December. Exhibits interpret the geology, forests, and wildlife of the mountains as well as the story of Elisha Mitchell. Interpretive programs are presented in the summer by park personnel.

A **concession stand** with restrooms is located next to the parking lot. It is open from 10:00 A.M. until 5:30 P.M. from June 1 through Labor Day and on weekends until the end of October. Light snacks, crafts, and books are for sale. Park rangers are on duty.

A delightful **picnic ground**, shaded by conifers, is at the north end of the summit parking lot. It has forty tables, stone fire grills, drinking water, and two shelters with tables and fireplaces. The site is home to a large population of red squirrels.

NEARBY

Because **camping facilities** within the state park are only for tenters, most visitors who wish to camp must locate nearby. Excellent campgrounds on the Blue Ridge Parkway operated by the National Park Service are at Crabtree Meadows (milepost 339) and Linville Falls (milepost 316). There are two campgrounds located on the South Toe River in the Pisgah National Forest; both are operated by the National Forest Service. Carolina Hemlocks Campground is on N.C. 80 north from the Blue Ridge Parkway, while Black Mountain Campground is reached via N.C. 80 by turning onto forest road 472. All four campgrounds can accommodate trailers as well as tents. There are no electrical or water hookups at campsites, and showers are not provided. Toilet facilities and a source of water are available. Bear Den Campground, privately owned and operated, has all conveniences; it is on Bear Den Mountain Road off the Blue Ridge Parkway at milepost 324.8.

A visit to Mount Mitchell State Park should be combined with travel along the **Blue Ridge Parkway,** a part of the national park system. Further discussion of the Blue Ridge Parkway is contained in the chapters on Lake James and Mount Jefferson state parks. The two park/recreation areas on the Blue Ridge Parkway nearest Mount Mitchell are at Crabtree Meadows and Craggy Gardens.

Crabtree Meadows (milepost 339) is a 250-acre park with a gift shop, a camp store, a service station, and a small restaurant. It is a rest stop where visitors may stroll among large hardwood trees, see the blooms of rhododendrons and flame azaleas, and watch chipmunks scurry about the forest floor. The nearby campground is a beautiful place to camp; it has seventy-one sites for tents and twenty-two sites for RVs. Interpretive programs are provided by park personnel in the evenings at the amphitheater. An excellent picnic ground with tables, grills, drinking water, and restrooms is at milepost 340. The campground and the restaurant are open from May through October. Beautiful, 80-foot-high **Crabtree Falls** is reached by a pleasant, 1.6-mile wooded trail that begins at a parking lot next to the campground. The trail is moderately difficult, but the effort is generously rewarded by the music of the falls, the vision of soft light filtering through a canopy of green, and the refreshment of cool water flowing over bare feet.

South of Mount Mitchell, the highway passes through the Great Craggy Mountains. At **Craggy Gardens Recreation Area** (mileposts 363.4 to 369.6), there is an extensive heath bald with a dense tangle of Catawba rhododendrons that blankets the area with a profusion of purple and pink blooms in mid-June. Otherwise, the Craggy Mountains are well-forested; most of the forest is an oak/hickory/maple mix, but the trees present also include beech, birch, and yellow buckeye. A visitor center at milepost 364.6 provides exhibits on the vegetation of the high Craggy Mountains and other information about the Blue Ridge Parkway. Craggy Pinnacle Trail begins at the Craggy Gardens parking overlook (milepost 364.1) and leads 0.8 mile to the summit of "the Pinnacle" via several switchbacks through the garden of rhododendrons. Visitors can enjoy magnificent 360-degree views from an elevation of 5,840 feet. A picnic ground with tables, grills, drinking water, and restrooms may be reached either via the Blue Ridge Parkway by turning off at milepost 367.6 or via the Craggy Gardens Self-guided Trail, which begins at the visitor center and leads through the forest for 0.8 mile. Bear Pen Gap Trail extends for 0.2 mile through the picnic area.

Other areas along the Blue Ridge Parkway within easy reach of Mount Mitchell State Park are Linville Falls (milepost 316) and the Museum of North Carolina Minerals (milepost 331) to the north and the Folk Art Center (milepost 382) to the south. For information about these and other facilities, write: Superintendent, Blue Ridge Parkway, 700 Northwestern Bank Building, Asheville, N.C. 28801.

Wagoner Road Access Area

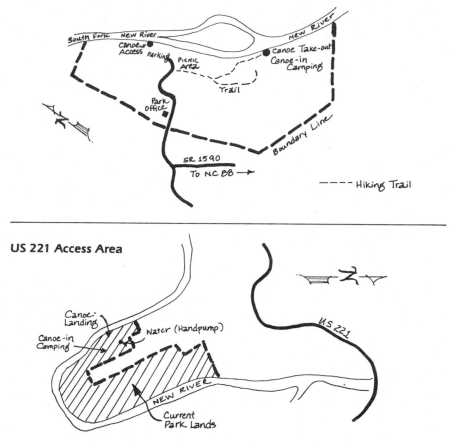

South Fork New River

New River

Canoe Access Parking

PICNIC Area

Canoe Take-out
Canoe-in Camping

Trail

Park Office

Boundary Line

SR 1590
To NC 88 →

‑‑‑‑ Hiking Trail

US 221 Access Area

Canoe Landing

Canoe-in Camping

Water (Handpump)

US 221

NEW RIVER

Current Park Lands

Alleghany County Access Area

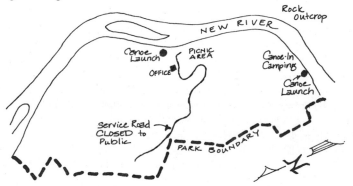

Rock Outcrop

NEW RIVER

Canoe Launch

PICNIC AREA

OFFICE

Canoe-In Camping

Canoe Launch

Service Road CLOSED to Public

PARK BOUNDARY

NEW RIVER STATE PARK/SCENIC RIVER

Address: P.O. Box 48
           Jefferson, N.C. 28640

Telephone: (919) 982-2587

Size: 498 acres of parkland; 33 acres (4.5 miles) of river-front easement
        land; and a 26.5-mile stretch of the New River and the South Fork of
        the New River

Established: 1977

Location: Ashe and Alleghany counties. The portion of the New River desig-
            nated a state scenic river extends 26.5 miles north from Dog Creek in
            the Wagoner Road Access Area to the North Carolina–Virginia line.
            Wagoner Road Access Area encompasses 104 acres at river mile
            26. It is reached by way of SR 1590 off N.C. 88, 8 miles southeast of
            Jefferson; from the turnoff at Wagoner Baptist Church, visitors should
            proceed 1 mile to the entry gate. **U.S. 221 Access Area** encompasses
            83 acres at river mile 15, and **Alleghany County Access Area** en-
            compasses 285.6 acres at river mile 1; they may be reached by canoe
            from several points along the river. At present, there is no drive-in
            access to these areas of the park.

Visitor Activities: Canoeing or rafting on the New River; canoe-in primitive
        camping at three access areas; picnicking; fishing; scenic viewing; na-
        ture study.

Season: Open year-round.

Ashe and Alleghany counties, in the northwestern corner of the state, are
the heart of New River country. The North Fork and the South Fork of the
New River flow from headwaters in the Blue Ridge Mountains to their confluence a few miles south of the North Carolina–Virginia line. The New River
continues its passage through southwestern Virginia and West Virginia into
the Kanawha and Ohio rivers, its waters eventually reaching the Gulf of
Mexico by way of the mighty Mississippi River.

New River is the oldest river in North America. Of the rivers now flowing
on the planet, it is second in age only to the Nile of Egypt. New River existed
before the mountains through which it presently journeys were uplifted, and it

has followed essentially the same course for millions of years. A natural resource of infinite value, it has geological, archaeological, and biological significance. A view of New River is a look back in time to primeval eras before humans existed, to the days of the American Indians who used the waterway as an avenue for migration and trade, and to the earliest European settlers who came to farm and mine the land and cut the forests.

Preliminary archaeological investigations in the New River Valley have suggested human habitation of the region for at least ten thousand years. The Canawhay Indian tribe occupied the valley during the precolonial period. Some of the artifacts discovered include arrowheads, pottery shards, and stone axes. Numerous sites have been identified for future excavation, and they are expected to yield valuable information on prehistoric cultures. The valley was a hunting ground for bands of Creek, Shawnee, and Cherokee Indians. Indian hunting trails later used by European settlers led north along the New River to the Ohio River. Several rock shelters discovered near the confluence of the forks of New River were probably used by hunters who entered the area and camped in the broad bottomlands. The river served as a major route of travel for transient hunters, but there were no permanent Indian settlements, due perhaps to the proximity of the valley to the lands of more aggressive northern tribes.

The earliest Europeans to enter New River country discovered a land of wild beauty with dense forests, open meadows, and an abundance of wildlife, including bison, elk, white-tailed deer, black bear, and beaver. The first white man to see New River was probably Colonel Abraham Wood, who sought to trade with the Indians in 1654; the river was first known to Europeans as Wood's River. Other than Indians, the only regular visitors to the region before the 1770s were white hunters and trappers, men such as Daniel Boone and Nathaniel Gist, who had settled along the Yadkin River near present-day Wilkesboro to the south.

Bishop Augustus Spangenberg, head of the Moravian church in America, passed through the New River area in 1752 when he came from Pennsylvania to locate a site for a permanent settlement. Spangenberg and his group were impressed with the land, but its remoteness and difficult access convinced them to move on to the North Carolina Piedmont, where they built the town of Salem. Peter Jefferson, the father of Thomas Jefferson, was also an early visitor; in 1749, he surveyed the North Carolina–Virginia boundary through New River country. He is credited with changing the name of Wood's River to New River.

Settlers of English, German, and Scottish descent began to move into the New River Valley in the late eighteenth century, traveling south through Shenandoah Valley. They were attracted by the fertile land and the abundant water and timber. In spite of the remoteness and ruggedness of the land, they persevered in clearing farmland and developing an agricultural economy. The river and other waterways in the region and the Blue Ridge escarpment to the southeast were barriers to east-west movement, and New River country remained isolated from the east until early this century; the region came to be known as the "lost provinces" of North Carolina. Northwestern North Carolina and southwestern Virginia were included with much of present-day Tennessee in the short-lived state of Franklin formed in 1785 by John Sevier and his followers. Sevier was declared an outlaw for his actions, and his new state was dissolved, paving the way for the formation of the state of Tennessee. The New River region, however, remained a part of North Carolina.

Ashe County was established in 1799, and the town of Jefferson became its seat in 1800. Ore Knob, with six hundred people, was incorporated in 1875. The area was rich in minerals, including iron, copper, lead, gold, and silver, and Ore Knob was the location of the richest copper mine in the country in the post–Civil War period. The mine continued to operate into the 1960s but has now virtually disappeared.

Transportation in the region was improved by the arrival of the Norfolk and Western Railroad (known as the Pea Vine or Virginia Creeper) early this century. Commerce, including mining and farming, and the growth of towns and new industries increased, and the logging of old-growth timber became an important business. The Virginia Creeper was the principal means of transporting products to market. Its route to Bristol was the highest of any railroad east of the Rockies, and the train remained a tourist attraction until operations ceased in the mid-1970s.

The region is still largely agricultural in character, though it now has improved roads and larger towns. In most respects, New River country remains much as it was at the beginning of the present century. The landscape is one of exceptional natural beauty, with rugged, wooded hillsides and gently flowing streams. The land is rich in history, and it is an inviting and fascinating place to visit.

A lengthy struggle to keep the New River flowing wild and free and to preserve the scenic qualities of the surrounding landscape was initiated in 1965, when the Appalachian Power Company applied for a license to dam the river and build reservoirs for water storage in Virginia and North Carolina. Over time, opposition to the proposal arose from citizens' groups, federal agencies, and the states of North Carolina and West Virginia; hearings, litigation, and legislative action followed. On May 26, 1975, the North Carolina General Assembly declared the 26.5-mile stretch of the river from its confluence with Dog Creek to the Virginia state line a state scenic river. In April 1976, the secretary of the interior designated the same portion of the New

River a part of the national wild and scenic river system; that action was reaffirmed and construction of the dam and reservoirs prohibited by an act of the Congress passed that August and subsequently signed by President Gerald Ford in September. The responsibility for developing and administering the scenic river area was assigned to the North Carolina Division of Parks and Recreation. Included in the plans for the area was the establishment of a state park on lands along the river, thus creating New River State Park.

PLANT LIFE

Dense forests once blanketed the land in the New River Valley. Most of the virgin forest has been cut for timber or cleared for farms and pastures, and woodlands now consist of second- or third-growth trees. Nevertheless, there is an abundance of forest cover, the preponderance of which grows on ridges and on the steep slopes of the valley wall. The soil is fertile, and much of it is moist; it supports many species of hardwoods, pines, shrubs, and wildflowers.

Approximately 60 percent of the forest cover is an oak/hickory hardwood community. Stands of oaks, hickories, maples, elms, eastern red cedar, and pines grow on slopes and ridges where the soil is relatively shallow and dry. The moist soils of coves and valleys along tributary streams of New River support a more diverse flora that also includes oaks and hickories as well as American beech, black gum, yellow poplar, black locust, and yellow birch; hemlocks and pines occur at high elevations. The understory includes flowering dogwood, sourwood, sassafras, huckleberries, alders, and hydrangeas; in addition, dense thickets of mountain laurel and rhododendron grow on north-facing slopes and enrich the woodlands with their colorful and beautiful blooms in the spring.

A mixed pine/hardwood community is present on ridges where clear-cutting and heavy logging have removed the oak/hickory forest. The woodland is being regenerated in such areas through the process of succession, and the forest is recovering its scenic beauty.

The moist alluvial soils of the flood plain of the river and its tributaries support a bottomland hardwood community that includes sycamore, red maple, American beech, and willows. Because much of the flood plain is now used for agriculture, this forest community is not extensive.

At least fourteen species of plants considered by state agencies to be rare, endangered, or threatened occur in the New River Valley and are of special interest. They include rattlesnake root, Carolina saxifrage, Carey's saxifrage, spreading avens, and purple sedge.

ANIMAL LIFE

The New River Valley provides habitat for a diversity of animal species.

Large mammals such as white-tailed deer occur in moderate numbers, and black bear are seen occasionally. Mink, muskrat, river otter, and raccoon may be encountered along the river, and beaver have been reintroduced to the area. Gray squirrels and eastern cottontails are common, as are many seldom-seen small rodents and shrews.

Bird life is abundant and varied, and the valley is home to several nesting species uncommon in other parts of the state. A small population of wild turkeys is present in lowland forests, and ruffed grouse may be seen at higher elevations. Sightings of ospreys along the river have increased in recent years. Red-tailed hawks nest on cliffs above the river. Scarlet tanagers, American goldfinches, and indigo buntings provide brilliant flashes of color, and serious bird watchers should look for such uncommon nesting species as black-billed cuckoo, willow and least flycatchers, tree swallow, warbling vireo, golden-winged warbler, and northern (Baltimore) oriole. Spotted sandpipers, belted kingfishers, and wood ducks may be encountered occasionally along the waterways.

Amphibians are common, especially in the wetlands adjacent to streams. Choruses of frogs may be heard on wet summer evenings. Salamanders of many species occur in the shallow, rocky tributaries and in the moist upland habitats. Nonpoisonous water snakes can be seen along the river's edge, and a variety of lizards, turtles, and snakes occupy the region. Several species of animals considered to be rare are found in New River State Park; as in all other parks, collecting is not permitted.

New River and its tributaries are generally clear, with little silt, and contain an abundance of aquatic organisms. Many kinds of fishes are present, including muskellunge, smallmouth and redeye bass, and brook, rainbow, and brown trout. Many species of colorful minnows and other small fishes are present but seldom noticed.

FACILITIES AND ACTIVITIES
State Parklands

New River State Park includes three access areas that total 472.6 acres in area and a rest stop for canoeists of 16.5 acres. Each area provides a canoe-in primitive campground, a picnic ground, and other facilities for park visitors. Much of the park remains undeveloped.

Wagoner Road Access Area (104 acres) is the only area in the park that can be reached by automobile at present. It is located at river mile 26, as measured from the North Carolina–Virginia state line, at the end of SR 1590 off N.C. 88. The park office is a short distance beyond the entry gate; information about the park and the scenic river may be obtained there. The road continues to a central parking area for day visitors and for canoeists who wish to leave their vehicles. The gravel parking area overlooks New River; to the left, or northwest, are access steps to the waterway for canoeists. A pit toilet and a source of drinking water are nearby. To the right, or southeast, across a grassy meadow is a pleasant picnic ground in a grove of old apple trees; fifteen tables and two grills are provided. A small campground with eight campsites is located beyond the picnic area, approximately 800 yards from the parking lot. Campers may either carry their equipment and supplies along a service road to their sites or canoe downstream to a takeout ramp at the campground. The campsites and a pit toilet are in a wooded area. Each campsite has a table and a grill. Water is available from a hand pump located near the parking lot. The river flows placidly past the campground, and campers may fish from its bank. A short trail follows the edge of the river.

New River at Wagoner Road Access Area

U.S. 221 Access Area (83 acres) is located at river mile 15, approximately 1 mile upstream from the U.S. 221 bridge at Scottville. At present, it is accessible only by canoe. The area lies within a sweeping oxbow of the river and includes high, wooded ridges with beautiful views of the stream and the surrounding landscape. The canoe landing is on a grassy beach with a gentle slope adjacent to a primitive campground with three campsites. Each campsite has a table and a grill; a pit toilet and a hand pump for drinking water are provided. Campers must record their visit at a registration box near the landing. A fee is charged.

An additional 114 acres of land must be acquired to complete the development of U.S. 221 Access Area. The main park office will be located at this access area, and plans include the construction of a park road from U.S. 221, a visitor center, a family campground that will accommodate both tents and trailers, and a family picnic ground on the grassy slopes of a high ridge at the center of the area. It will become a choice destination for state park visitors. New River General Store and New River Outfitters are located nearby at Scottville.

Alleghany County Access Area (285.6 acres) is located at river mile 1 near the North Carolina–Virginia state line and the confluence of the North and South forks of New River. At present, it is accessible only by canoe. The area consists of both grassy meadows and wooded ridges and is bordered by approximately 1 mile of river front. Access steps for canoeists are adjacent to a primitive campground near the upstream boundary of the access area. Each campsite has a table and a grill; a pit toilet and a pump for drinking water are provided. Campers must register at a registration box. A second ramp for launching and landing canoes is located several hundred yards downstream, adjacent to a picnic ground in an open meadow. There are twelve tables at the picnic ground. This is a beautiful area on a wild, scenic stretch of the river. A high cliff with rock outcrops stands above the river on the bank opposite the campground. The cliff is a nesting area for ravens, vultures, hawks, and other birds. An access road and other facilities are planned for Alleghany County Access Area.

Plans for park development include two rest stops along the New River. Land for **rest stop #1** has not yet been acquired; the rest stop will be located between the Wagoner Road and U.S. 221 access areas. **Rest stop #2**, with 16.5 acres, has been established between the U.S. 221 and Alleghany County access areas at river mile 7.5, next to RiverCamp USA, a private campground at Piney Creek bridge on SR 1308. Rest stop #2 will eventually provide a picnic ground and a primitive camping area with eight campsites. Easements, which would allow the land to remain in its natural state, are being sought along the corridor of the scenic river; at present, 33 acres totaling 4.5 miles scattered along the river front have been donated by landowners and are protected. Funds have been appropriated for additional acquisitions.

Scenic River

The state scenic river, 26.5 miles in total length, includes 22 miles of the South Fork of New River downstream to its confluence with the North Fork and 4.5 miles of the main stem of New River north to the North Carolina–Virginia line. Most stretches of the river flow through remote countryside not readily accessible by roads or trails. Several roadways and bridges do cross the river, providing access points for launching canoes. The beautiful and tranquil stream and the corridor of green along many miles of its banks are best seen from the seat of a canoe during its silent passage over the slow-moving waters. Canoeists may experience a feeling of peaceful isolation. The view is one of wooded hillsides, pastoral meadows and farmland, and an occasional farmhouse and settlement. Along the way, small tributary streams merge with New River, minor rapids and riffles stir the water's surface and add excitement as canoes are maneuvered downstream, and rock outcrops in cliff walls along the waterway add variety to the scenic beauty. Silent and

CANOEIST'S GUIDE TO THE STATE SCENIC RIVER

Wagoner Road Access Area to US 221 Access Area

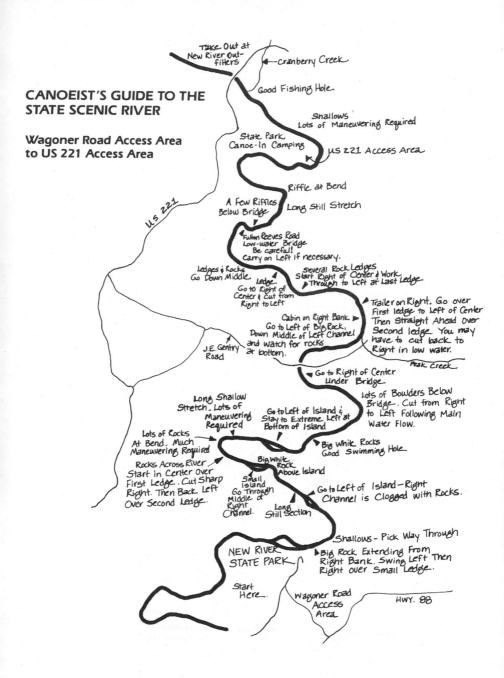

From AN AREA GUIDE TO NEW RIVER COUNTRY, New River Country Travel Association. Used by permission.

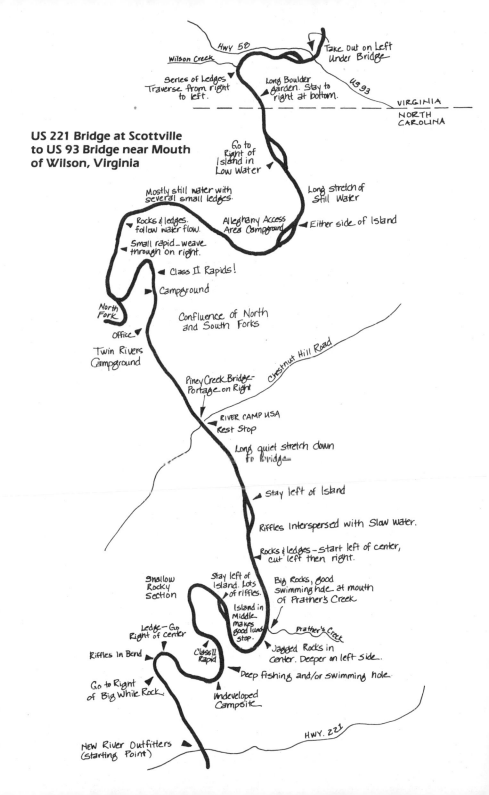

US 221 Bridge at Scottville to US 93 Bridge near Mouth of Wilson, Virginia

Hwy 58

Wilson Creek

Take Out on Left Under Bridge

Series of Ledges Traverse from right to left.

Long Boulder garden. Stay to right at bottom.

US 93

VIRGINIA
NORTH CAROLINA

Go to Right of Island in Low Water

Long stretch of Still Water

Mostly still water with several small ledges.

Rocks & ledges. follow water flow.

Alleghany Access Area Campground

Either side of Island

Small rapid - weave through on right.

Class II Rapids!

Campground

North Fork

Confluence of North and South Forks

Office

Twin Rivers Campground

Chestnut Hill Road

Piney Creek Bridge - Portage on Right

RIVER CAMP USA
Rest Stop

Long quiet stretch down to Bridge

Stay left of Island

Riffles Interspersed with Slow Water.

Rocks & ledges - start left of center, cut left then right.

Shallow Rocky Section

Stay left of Island. Lots of riffles.

Big Rocks, good swimming hole at mouth of Prather's Creek

Island in Middle makes good lunch stop.

Prather's Creek

Ledge - Go Right of center

Jagged Rocks in center. Deeper on left side.

Riffles In Bend

Class II Rapid

Deep fishing and/or swimming hole

Go to Right of Big White Rock.

Undeveloped Campsite

HWY. 221

New River Outfitters (Starting Point)

observant visitors on the river may see a variety of wildlife along the banks and in the forests of the river corridor.

The maps on pages 256 and 257 are a guide for canoeists on New River. A journey along the full length of the canoe trail may be divided into two day trips, or it may be divided into shorter segments that require briefer periods of time. Overnight camping areas and launch and take-out points are at several locations along the trail.

Day trip #1 is from the Wagoner Road Access Area to the U.S. 221 bridge at Scottville. It is 11.5 miles in length and requires a minimum of four hours of paddling; canoeists should allow additional time for floating the current, snacking, or recreational activities along the way. There is easy access to the river at the beginning point of the trip, as well as at the end point, New River Outfitters at U.S. 221 bridge. Cars may be parked at either access point. A fee is charged at New River Outfitters, and canoes may be rented there; supplies may be purchased next door at New River General Store. Canoeists may camp on parkland at the U.S. 221 Access Area. Alternative launch and take-out sites are at bridges on J. E. Gentry Road and Fulton Reeves Road, as shown on the map.

Day trip #2 is from U.S. 221 bridge to U.S. 93 bridge near Mouth of Wilson, Virginia. It is 16 miles in length, and it requires six to eight hours of paddling. The first portion of the trip is on the South Fork to its confluence with the North Fork. The route then continues for 6 miles on New River through perhaps the most beautiful section of the scenic-river area. Along the way are two Class-II rapids, the most difficult rapids on New River in North Carolina. Canoeists may elect to extend their trip by camping overnight at the

Primitive campground at Wagoner Road Access Area

park's rest stop or at RiverCamp USA, adjacent to SR 1308 at the Piney Creek bridge; at Twin Rivers Campground, at river mile 6; or at Alleghany County Access Area, at river mile 1. Shorter trips may be taken by exiting the river at the Piney Creek bridge, 7 miles from New River Outfitters, or by exiting the river at Twin Rivers Campground, 8.5 miles from New River Outfitters. The two commercial campgrounds—RiverCamp USA and Twin Rivers Campground—charge a fee for the use of their facilities; each provides a variety of visitor services, and provisions may be purchased at RiverCamp USA.

Fishing is a popular activity on New River and its tributary streams. The South and North forks of the river provide some of the best smallmouth bass and redeye bass fishing in the region. Catfish are also abundant, and the South Fork downstream from the U.S. 221 bridge has been stocked with muskellunge. Trout fishing is excellent in the smaller, faster tributaries, most of which are designated general trout waters and are stocked regularly with brook, rainbow, and brown trout. Creeks upstream from the SR 1361 bridge are designated native trout waters; they are not stocked, and special restrictions apply. A state fishing license is required; fishermen should check current local regulations before trying their luck.

NEARBY

For information about the region, write: New River Country Travel Association, Route 1, Box 13, Scottville, N.C. 28672 (919/982-9414). Persons planning to visit New River State Park should obtain a copy of *An Area Guide to New River Country* for information about family camping in the area, river outfitters, lodging and eating places, mountain crafts, and scheduled events.

Mount Jefferson State Park and Stone Mountain State Park are nearby. **Doughton Park**, which has excellent camping facilities, is on the Blue Ridge Parkway. All three areas are discussed in this volume.

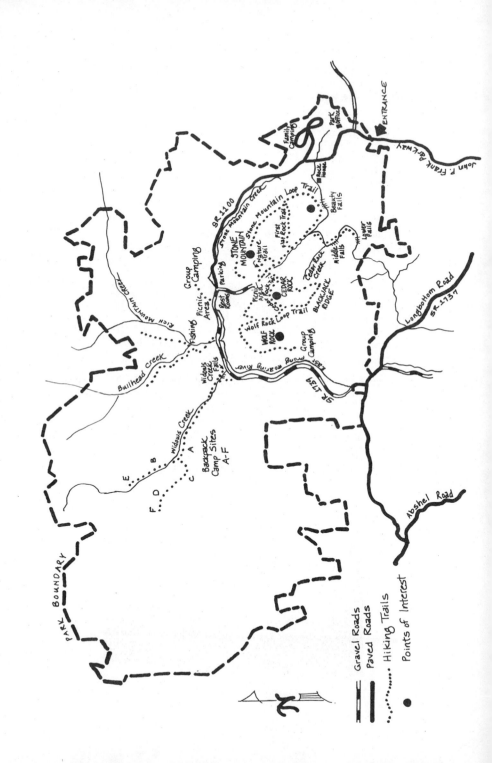

ENTRANCE

John P. Frank Parkway

Park Office

Family Camping

SR 1100

Rock House

Stone Mountain Creek

Beauty Falls

Stone Mountain Loop Trail

First Flat Rock Trail

STONE MOUNTAIN

Lower Falls

Middle Falls

Cedar Rock Trail

Nature Trail

BLACKJACK RIDGE

CEDAR ROCK

Group Camping

Picnic Area

Flat Rock Trail

Best Parking

Wolf Rock Loop Trail

WOLF ROCK

Group Camping

East Roaring River

Longbottom Road

SR 1737

SR 1739

Rich Mountain Creek

Fishing

Bullhead Creek

Widows Creek Falls

Widows Creek

Backpack Camp Sites A–F

E

F

D

B

C

A

Abshel Road

PARK BOUNDARY

Gravel Roads

Paved Roads

Hiking Trails

Points of Interest

STONE MOUNTAIN STATE PARK

Address: Star Route 1, Box 17
             Roaring Gap, N.C. 28668

Telephone: (919) 957-8185

Size: 13,378 acres

Established: 1969

Location: Wilkes and Alleghany counties, approximately midway between Elkin and Sparta. From U.S. 21, turn west onto SR 1002 at the park sign between Thurmond and Doughton and proceed 4.3 miles to Traphill; turn south onto John P. Frank Parkway (SR 1784) and continue 2.5 miles to park entrance.

Principal Attractions: Stone Mountain, a dome-shaped granite mass that rises 600 feet above its base and is a national natural landmark; lesser granite faces including Wolf Rock and Cedar Rock; 17 miles of trout streams; waterfalls and cascades along Big Sandy Creek and other streams; mountain scenery of exceptional beauty; extensive system of hiking trails; opportunity for a wilderness experience.

Visitor Activities: Scenic viewing; rock climbing on Stone Mountain; hiking and backpacking; fishing for trout in mountain streams; picnicking; family camping; primitive back-country group camping and backpack camping.

Season: Open year-round.

View of Stone Mountain from Cedar Rock

Travelers who stop at the scenic overlook at milepost 232 on the Blue Ridge Parkway enjoy a sweeping view southeastward down the steep escarpment of the Blue Ridge Mountains to the valleys and ridges that extend to the horizon. The dominant feature of the landscape, approximately 8 miles distant, is the bare, granite north face of Stone Mountain, which, in stark contrast to the dark green of the surrounding forest, reflects the glow of the late-afternoon sun. The oval-shaped mass of stone, the largest plutonic monadnock in the state, rises 600 feet above its base and 2,305 feet above sea level. Its massive base, with a circumference of approximately 4 miles, is bordered by the woodlands of the valley floor, and its broad, sloping shoulders and peak are crowned by a sparse community of trees and shrubs growing from the thin veneer of soil that clings to the otherwise exfoliated surface. Travelers at the scenic overlook are looking out upon the landscape of Stone Mountain State Park, an area of rugged, low ridges and narrow valleys, with rushing streams, picturesque waterfalls, sylvan trails, and the great stone faces of Stone Mountain, Wolf Rock, and Cedar Rock.

The rock exposures within the park are part of a 25-square-mile pluton of biotite granite formed approximately 300 million years ago from molten lava that flowed into the original bedrock. Geological disturbances and erosion have exposed the prominent outcrops visible today. The softer layers of rock and soils that overlay the immense granite block were gradually carried away by wind, water, and other forces, denuding portions of the mass. This process began in the dim geological past and is continuing.

Little is known of the early human history of the area; archaeological data are lacking, though it is known that Catawba Indians were present before settlers arrived. Farmers established scattered homesteads, and a few log cabins, chimneys, foundations, and old roadbeds remain. The best-preserved structures are Hutchinson House at Stone Mountain View and rustic Garden Creek Baptist Church on the bank of the East Prong of Roaring River, which was built around 1779 and which continues to hold Sunday services.

Efforts to establish a state park that would include Stone Mountain were under way in the early 1960s, primarily due to the work of three persons who recognized the scenic values and the recreational potential of the area: Doris B. Potter of the Northwest North Carolina Development Association; Claude Billings, a native of Traphill and a state legislator; and Alfred Houston, director of the Blue Ridge Planning and Development Commission. Potter, Billings, and Houston sought to generate interest in the creation of a park and to find means of acquiring land. Much of the acreage needed for a park was owned by the North Carolina Granite Corporation of Mount Airy. John Frank and Frank Smith, two officers of the corporation, were impressed with the proposal and offered on behalf of their board of directors to donate a 418.5-

acre tract that included Stone Mountain. The North Carolina Granite Corporation subsequently agreed to sell an additional 1,069 acres to the state.

In August 1967, the North Carolina Board of Conservation and Development approved a resolution that the Stone Mountain area be included in the state parks system, and in April 1968 the Stone Mountain Park and Preservation Commission was incorporated to coordinate efforts to establish a park. Grants were obtained from several federal agencies for land acquisition, and on February 4, 1969, the governor and the council of state approved the gift and purchase of 1,463.7 acres from the North Carolina Granite Corporation, thereby establishing the park. By early 1970, 413.7 additional acres had been purchased, and a 59.8-acre tract had been donated by Philip Hanes, Jr., of Winston-Salem. Land acquisition has continued, and parkland now includes more than 13,000 acres of woodlands, streams, and granite domes.

PLANT LIFE

Piedmont and mountain vegetative communities merge within Stone Mountain State Park, which lies below the escarpment of the Blue Ridge Mountains. As a result of extensive lumbering and agriculture in the past, most woodlands in the area are composed of second- or third-growth trees. Most parkland is well-forested, though some evidence of human disturbance remains.

Forests along streams, in coves, and on other moist sites include tulip tree, beech, northern red oak, hickory, birch, Fraser magnolia, and hemlock. The understory along streams is usually dominated by rosebay rhododendron; elsewhere, shrubs are generally absent, and the forest floor is carpeted by spring and summer flowers.

On the relatively dry, open slopes, oaks dominate the woodlands. At elevations below 2,500 feet, white, northern red, and black oaks occur along with hickories, black gum, and red maple; flowering dogwood and sourwood dominate the understory. At middle elevations, chestnut and scarlet oaks are prevalent. The shrub layer is more pronounced, though species are few in number; bearberry, blueberry, and mountain laurel are abundant in suitable habitat.

Dry ridges are dominated by pitch and table mountain pines, with shortleaf and Virginia pines occurring in some locations; these give way abruptly to the oak-dominated forests below the crests. Mountain laurel and other shrubs in the heath family dominate the understory. Few wildflowers grow on the forest floor. Old fields in the process of reforestation are characterized by almost pure stands of shortleaf, Virginia, and table mountain pines. In most areas, the pines will eventually be replaced by hardwood species.

The slopes around the rockfaces of Stone Mountain, Wolf Rock, and Cedar

Rock are covered by forests dominated by chestnut oak, though scarlet and black oaks, red maple, mockernut hickory, white pine, and dogwood are also present. In the understory are blueberry, rhododendron, and mountain laurel. The transition between forests and rock surfaces is abrupt. Small, slow-growing pines and red cedar fringe the rock. Mats of vegetation grow from thin soil on areas of open, exposed granite, especially at the edges of the forest on the less precipitous upper slopes. The mats are composed of lichens, mosses, club mosses, small ferns, and various flowering species. Through the process of succession, these areas may in time be invaded by small shrubs and trees. Farther down the slopes, mats of vegetation live a precarious existence, as patches of soil are often dislodged and carried down the rockfaces by heavy rains, ice, or snow.

ANIMAL LIFE

The fauna of Stone Mountain State Park has not been well-studied, though many species familiar to most visitors are known to occur in the area. Brown, brook, and rainbow trout are the most important game fish in park streams; while native trout occur in these waters, most fish present were stocked from state hatcheries. Moist streamsides provide habitat for frogs and salamanders, and some reptile species, including box turtles and the poisonous copperhead, are present in the woodlands. Many species of birds inhabit the area, among them the scarlet tanager, whip-poor-will, American woodcock, ruffed grouse, pileated woodpecker, eastern screech owl, and wood duck. Wild turkeys are probably present. There is an abundance of mammals, many of which are small insectivores and mice that are largely unseen by most observers. Larger animals include white-tailed deer, which often appear along hiking trails, gray and red foxes, red and gray squirrels, bobcats, raccoons, and Virginia opossums. Beaver have created small ponds near East Prong of Roaring River. Black bear are seen in the area on occasion.

HIKING TRAILS

Trailheads for the most popular hiking trails in the park are concentrated at the south side of Stone Mountain. The area is reached by following SR 1100, a well-graded, paved road, for approximately 2 miles from the entry gate to its terminus at a large, paved parking lot surrounded by woodlands. Modern restrooms, drinking water, and shaded benches are available to visitors. A single-lane gravel road 0.6 mile in length leads from the parking lot to a place near the base of the mountain. Visitors who can walk the short distance to reach the trailheads and the small picnic ground at road's end should do so, as only limited parking space is available and the area is often congested.

The picnic ground is a delightful site alongside dense woodlands and a small, bubbling stream; seven tables and two grills are provided. A broad gravel path 0.2 mile in length leads from the picnic area to **Stone Mountain View**, a restful area in an open, grassy meadow that slopes downward to the base of Stone Mountain. A marker beside the path commemorates the National Park Service's designation of the 345 acres that include the granite dome as a national natural landmark in 1975. Trailside benches allow hikers to stop and enjoy a magnificent view of the south face of Stone Mountain and the dramatic interplay of sunlight and shadows across the broad tapestry of stone. A border of trees grows along the base of the south face, where rock climbers begin their ascents; visitors may watch the climbers' progress from the meadow. On occasion, wild goats may be seen walking confidently across the bare, sloping face of the dome. Those who come to this beautiful place in early morning or late afternoon may see white-tailed deer emerging from the security of the forest to graze on meadow grasses. Beside the meadow stands the old cabin that was the home of the Hutchinson family. The cabin is typical of such structures built during the early settlement of the area. The path continues into the forest and leads to trails from the top of Stone Mountain, along Blackjack Ridge, to Cedar Rock, and beyond. From the climbers' access area, a nature trail less than 1 mile in length passes along the base of Stone Mountain to the lower end of the meadow before it returns to Stone Mountain View.

Hiking trails interconnect and form loops with trailheads at or near Stone Mountain View. The discussion that follows focuses upon Stone Mountain Loop Trail, a loop trail that crosses the top of Stone Mountain and descends to waterfalls on Big Sandy Creek, and Wolf Rock Loop Trail, a loop trail that leads to Wolf Rock and Cedar Rock and descends Blackjack Ridge. Several side trails and shortcut trails between the loops allow hikers to select various alternate routes and segments of trails, as shown on the map. Information about trail distances is incomplete, but data will be provided wherever possible.

The trailhead for **Stone Mountain Loop Trail** is at the wooden stairs that ascend into the woodlands across the gravel road from the picnic ground. The steep, strenuous trail ascends the west shoulder of the mountain through the forest to the top of the massive dome. Portions of the summit section of the trail are over bare rock; elsewhere, the trail passes through sparse woodlands highlighted by such colorful shrubs as mountain laurel and rhododendron. On Stone Mountain, as well as on Wolf Rock and Cedar Rock, mats of lichens, mosses, and ferns cling to the rock surfaces along the margins of the woodlands. The rockface here and elsewhere in the park, created by the weathering action of water, ice, and wind, appears as a miniature moonscape; small, water-filled craters and potholes dot the surface, and long crevices carved in the rock carry rivulets of water down the sloping face. Hikers may venture from the trail onto the bare brow of the dome for magnificent views of the green ridges and valleys of the Blue Ridge Mountains to the north and of the Piedmont to the southeast. On the crest, hikers may stand in silence and look out upon the work of time and the eternal forces of nature.

Stone Mountain (or Beauty) Falls

The trail descends the east shoulder of the mountain to a junction; to the right, **First Flat Rock Trail** leads back to Stone Mountain View and the picnic ground. Small rock outcrops are in the area— Hitching Rock, First Flat Rock, and Indian Den Rock. The main trail continues downhill past a tall stone chimney, a remnant of an old homestead and a mute reminder that farming was once widespread in the area. The sound of flowing water is soon audible, and the head of Stone Mountain Falls (known locally as Beauty Falls) comes into view as the trail emerges onto rock outcrops. A sheet of water rushes over the rock surface and drops approximately 200 feet down a precipitous slope into a pool. The waterfall is approximately 1.2 miles from the trailhead. The trail descends steeply on a course parallel to the cascading falls to the base, then follows the bank downstream through thickets of rhododendron. The sound of the water is loud and musical as it flows over boulders and between narrow walls of stone. At a junction, a side trail follows the creek and leads to impressive views of Middle Falls, which is a series of low cascades, and Lower Falls, which drops about 25 feet into a shallow pool. The main trail is joined by Wolf Rock Trail before entering the meadow at Stone Mountain View.

Wolf Rock Loop Trail is approximately 2.7 miles in length. Its trailhead is to the right beyond the picnic ground, off the gravel path that leads to Stone Mountain View. Since the return arm of the loop terminates at the picnic ground, hikers may elect to follow the trail in the direction opposite that described. The loop is transected by **Cedar Rock Trail**; a one-way hike from the trailhead to Cedar Rock is about 0.7 mile.

From the trailhead, Wolf Rock Loop Trail passes through rhododendron thickets into a forest of hardwoods, then ascends a moderately strenuous slope along an old roadbed to the ridge top, where the walking is level and easy. After 0.5 mile, there is a junction with a side trail to the right; the side trail descends the ridge to a primitive group camp located near East Prong of

Roaring River. (The camping area is also accessible from SR 1739.) The main trail continues on the old road. A crumbling rock wall follows the left side of the trail, and beyond the wall an abandoned field overgrown with pines is undergoing reforestation. To the right of the trail is Wolf Rock (as indicated by the trail marker), at an elevation of 2,041 feet. It is an immense area of bare granite that slopes downward toward the densely forested valley. The rockface is bordered by woodlands and mats of tiny plants in shallow soil. The scenic view to the northwest is of ridges and slopes that are richly carpeted in shades of green during the summer.

A short distance past Wolf Rock, the upper end of Cedar Rock Trail forms a junction with Wolf Rock Loop Trail. Hikers may elect to turn left and follow Cedar Rock Trail toward Stone Mountain View and pass Cedar Rock on this shortcut back to the trailhead. From the junction, Wolf Rock Trail continues uphill past the dome of Buzzard Rock at 1.2 miles and descends the long, gentle slope of Blackjack Ridge. After a sharp left turn, the trail crosses a small stream and ascends steeply to a junction with the lower end of Cedar Rock Trail, as shown on the map. Wolf Rock Trail eventually merges with Stone Mountain Loop Trail and exits the forest at the meadow at Stone Mountain View.

Like Wolf Rock and the summit of Stone Mountain, Cedar Rock is a broad expanse of bare granite that provides scenic views of the surrounding landscape. An overlook facing northeast provides what is perhaps the most spectacular view of Stone Mountain in the park. From a grandstand seat high above the meadow of Stone Mountain View, hikers may relax and look out upon the beautiful, sunlit face of the mountain. Cedar Rock is a choice spot that all park visitors should enjoy.

Other more strenuous, less well-known trails are within the park. **Garden Creek Trail** is approximately 7 miles in length. It follows Garden Creek north to the park boundary, then across private property up the escarpment to the vicinity of Doughton Park on the Blue Ridge Parkway. Hikers interested in exploring remote areas of the park should seek additional information from park rangers.

FACILITIES AND ACTIVITIES

John P. Frank Parkway (SR 1784) provides visitors access to the main entrance, on the east side of the park. Information is available at the **park office**, located a short distance past the entry gate. A paved road (SR 1100) leads to the interior of the park. A turnoff to the right 1 mile past the office building leads to the **family campground**. This excellent camping facility accommodates both tents and RVs; its design blends well with the natural features of the area. Thirty-seven spacious campsites are located along two loop roads. The loop to the right is through a forest of hardwoods, and each of its campsites is well-shaded. The loop to the left passes along the edge of a forest adjacent to an old field that is undergoing reforestation; its campsites are in deep woodlands and in the open field. All sites are equipped with a tent pad, a table, and a grill. Sources of drinking water are provided nearby. A centrally located washhouse has toilets, hot-water showers, and laundry tubs. There is a dump station for RVs. A fee is charged, and campsites are occupied on a first-come basis.

SR 1100 continues for 1 mile along Stone Mountain Creek past the campground turnoff to the large parking lot near Stone Mountain. A gravel road continues as SR 1739; it follows East Prong of Roaring River for 3.1 miles to the southern entrance to the park on Longbottom Road (SR 1737), which leads to Traphill to the east. Fishermen may park at several locations on the side of SR 1739 for access to the stream.

A small **picnic area** with five tables and a grill is located a short distance past the parking lot beside SR 1739 on the bank of the river. It is a pleasant, shaded spot ideal for relaxation. Nearby, a trail into the woodlands leads to a primitive **group camp**. A second group camp is reached either by way of a side trail off Wolf Rock Trail or from SR 1739 between Widow's Creek and Longbottom Road. The group camps provide a total of fifteen primitive campsites with tables, fireplaces, and pit toilets. Sites are available to groups by advance reservation. A fee is charged. For additional information, contact the park office.

Six **backpack campsites** designated A through F are located on or near Widow's Creek at distances ranging from 1.5 to 3 miles from a trailhead on SR 1739 that is 1 mile past the parking lot. All equipment and supplies must be packed to the camping area. Water is available near sites A through E and approximately 0.5 mile downhill from site F. Each site accommodates up to four persons. A fee is charged, and a permit is required; permits are issued on a first-come basis. Campers should seek additional information at the park office. A short stroll along the trail from SR 1739 leads to picturesque **Widow's Creek Falls**, where the stream cascades over an outcrop of bare stone into a shallow pool before flowing into East Prong of Roaring River.

Rock climbing on the south face of Stone Mountain is one of the most popular activities in the park. The face of the mountain challenges even experienced climbers. The granite dome was first climbed in 1965, and thirteen routes to the summit have subsequently been established, with such fanciful names as Fantastic, Grand Funk Railroad, Taken for Granite, Electric Boobs, and the Great White Way. Climbing bolts and hangers have been placed in the rock along each route, and climbers are secured by ropes during ascents. The bare granite surface is considered to provide some of the best and purest friction climbing in the South. Friction climbers use cracks and crevices in the rock for footholds and handholds and for balancing their weight as they ascend the steep, sloping surface.

Access to the base of the mountain is by way of paths through the meadow from Stone Mountain View. Climbing is prohibited when the rock is wet. Established routes must be followed, and beginners must be accompanied by an experienced climber. The privilege to climb will be denied individuals lacking proper equipment or not following standard safety procedures. All climbers must complete their ascents and leave the park before the gate is closed for the day. A map of climbing routes is posted at the base of the mountain; climbers may also consult *Southern Rock: A Climber's Guide* (Hall 1981). Climbing in the park is permitted on a trial basis; the continuation of the practice depends upon climbers' compliance with regulations and a good safety record. Climbing of the north face is discouraged.

Trout fishing is also a popular activity in the park. More than 17 miles of streams in the park have been designated trout waters. Brook trout are caught in cool sections of the streams at high elevations; rainbow and brown trout occur at lower elevations. The heavily fished East Prong of Roaring River is classified as general trout water; it is stocked regularly during the fishing season by the North Carolina Wildlife Resources Commission. Bait of any type is allowed, and the daily limit is seven fish of any size. Widow's Creek, Garden Creek, and the section of Big Sandy Creek within the park are native trout waters; artificial lures with a single hook are required. The daily limit is four fish at least 7 inches in length, only one of which may be over 10 inches.

Bullhead Creek and Rich Mountain Creek are "fish-for-fun" streams in which fishermen may seek to perfect their angling technique rather than to take fish for their frying pans. The program is administered from an office located on SR 1739 near the head of Bullhead Creek, 0.6 mile past the parking lot. Fishermen must register at this office and pay a fee. Each fisherman is assigned one of the eight "sections" of the streams, where he or she must remain. Only fly rods and flies with barbless hooks may be used, and all trout must be released; other rules are posted at the "fish-for-fun" office. Persons fishing in any park stream must possess a valid license. All applicable state regulations are enforced.

NEARBY

Visitors to Stone Mountain State Park may also wish to plan stops at New River State Park and Mount Jefferson State Park, which are discussed elsewhere in this volume. The **Blue Ridge Parkway**, a beautifully scenic unit of the national park system, is reached by way of U.S. 21; Doughton Park provides excellent camping and picnicking facilities and other recreational opportunities. Sections of the Blue Ridge Parkway are discussed in the chapters on Mount Jefferson, Mount Mitchell, and Lake James state parks.

STATE NATURAL AREAS/
NATURE PRESERVE

THEODORE ROOSEVELT STATE NATURAL AREA

Address: P.O. Box 127
             Atlantic Beach, N.C. 28512

Telephone: (919) 726-3775

Size: 265 acres

Established: 1971

Location: Carteret County, at Salter Path on Bogue Banks, 7 miles west of
Atlantic Beach. Visitors should turn off N.C. 58 onto SR 1201 and follow
the signs. The North Carolina Aquarium at Pine Knoll Shores is within
the natural area.

Principal Attraction: Barrier island ecosystem.

Visitor Activities: Nature study; hiking.

Season: Open year-round.

Theodore Roosevelt State Natural Area is a small but ecologically significant tract of land that preserves a segment of the barrier island ecosystem
that is rapidly being lost to commercial and residential development. It is one

Brackish wetlands in old dune swales

of the few places on Bogue Banks where natural vegetation and wildlife habitats remain undisturbed.

Alice Roosevelt Hoffman acquired the land where the natural area is now located in 1917. The land had long been occupied by squatters, residents of Salter Path and Bogue Banks who fished the local waters for their living. Mrs. Hoffman's attempts to evict the squatters led to confrontation and controversy and contributed to the colorful history of the area. Mrs. Hoffman willed the land to Mrs. T. R. Roosevelt, Jr. The grandchildren of our twenty-sixth president subsequently donated the land to the state of North Carolina in 1972, and Theodore Roosevelt State Natural Area survives as a living memorial to a man who contributed significantly to raising the nation's awareness of the need to conserve natural resources.

The primary community in the Theodore Roosevelt State Natural Area is a dense maritime forest dominated by laurel oak, loblolly pine, red cedar, and live oak. Shaped by salt spray, the forest is only about 15 feet tall along the ocean side of the island but almost 60 feet tall on the sound side. In dune swales within the forest, water may accumulate, and open ponds, shrub swamps, and forested swamps occur. The maritime forest is bordered on the sound side by shrub thickets dominated by wax myrtle, silverling, bay trees, and American olive. An irregularly flooded, brackish marsh dominated by black needlerush, saltmeadow cordgrass, and salt grass extends into the forest and may be viewed from a wooden observation deck behind the aquarium building. Beyond the brackish marsh, in areas regularly flooded by incoming tides, smooth cordgrass dominates the salt marsh. Shallow, open bays that often contain beds of aquatic eelgrass and slough grass extend to the Atlantic Intracoastal Waterway.

These varied communities provide good habitat for a number of animals. Eelgrass beds often contain scallops, and the regularly flooded salt marshes and tidal creeks are home to blue crabs, oysters, clams, mussels, sea squirts, and a host of other interesting animals. Fiddler crabs and marine snails inhabit the muddy margins of the marsh. Raccoons and clapper rails feed upon the fiddler crabs. Bird life is abundant throughout the natural area. The maritime forest provides nesting sites for such uncommon species as black-throated green and Swainson's warblers. Wading birds, including great and snowy egrets, stalk for meals at the edges of ponds and marshes, and many other coastal birds may be observed in the wetland habitats. Ospreys hunt and nest in the area.

The 0.4-mile **Hoffman Nature Trail** begins at the southeast corner of the aquarium and extends through a portion of the maritime forest and along the edge of the salt marsh. It provides an opportunity to watch the wildlife that inhabits the area.

The **North Carolina Aquarium at Pine Knoll Shores** is one of three aquaria located on the North Carolina seacoast; the others are at Fort Fisher to the south and on Roanoke Island to the north. The North Carolina Aquarium at Pine Knoll Shores serves as a center for information, education, and research on the coastal resources of the state and provides marine aquaria, exhibits, educational programs, a bookstore, and a nature trail. A seasonal calendar of events is available. Admission is free.

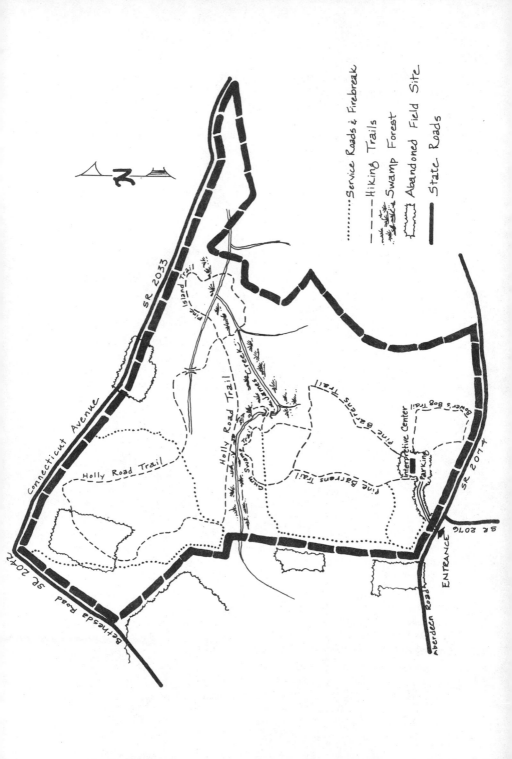

WEYMOUTH WOODS/SANDHILLS NATURE PRESERVE

Address: 400 North Fort Bragg Road
              Southern Pines, N.C. 28387

Telephone: (919) 692-2167

Size: 676 acres

Established: 1963

Location: Moore County, one mile southeast of Southern Pines on Fort Bragg Road (SR 2074); signs on U.S. 1 in Southern Pines and Aberdeen and on N.C. 211 east of Aberdeen give directions to the nature preserve.

Principal Attractions: Sandhills longleaf pine forest community; hiking trails; natural history museum.

Visitor Activities: Nature study; hiking.

Season: Open year-round. The gate is closed at 5:00 P.M. on Sunday and at 6:00 P.M. Monday through Saturday from November through March. Closing time is 7:00 P.M. Monday through Saturday from April through October.

The famed Sandhills region of the state, which includes Weymouth Woods, is an area of nearly 1 million acres on the western boundary of the coastal plain. The Weymouth Woods/Sandhills Nature Preserve features a remnant of the plant and animal communities peculiar to the "pine barrens," a term used by early settlers when the region was covered by extensive climax forests dominated by longleaf pine. Most of the preserve was donated to the state in 1963 by the widow of James Boyd, a well-known author who wrote about North Carolina. Additional land has subsequently been added, including a satellite area of 167.5 acres near Southern Pines known as the Boyd Estate Tract, which was acquired in 1977; the tract contains a sizeable stand of old-growth longleaf pines that are from 250 to 400 years old. The land that now makes up the nature preserve was purchased by Boyd's grandfather early this century in an effort to save longleaf pine trees from being logged. The estate was named Weymouth Woods apparently because the pines reminded their owner of trees he had seen at Weymouth, England.

The Sandhills region is characterized by a series of flat-topped, sandy ridges alternated with relatively broad, flat valleys. The landscape apparently resulted from the transport of great quantities of clay, sand, and gravel by streams and rivers flowing eastward from the Piedmont; the materials were deposited as sediment along the margin of an ancient sea that covered much of the present coastal plain millions of years ago. After the sea retreated eastward, the processes of weathering and erosion shaped the sediment into the ridges and valleys that now exist. Evidence of the ancient sea is provided by sedimentary deposits with fossil shells and other remains of marine organisms.

PLANT LIFE

Longleaf pines dominate many plant communities of the Sandhills. They have massive, straight trunks and produce a forest canopy of sparkling green with their shiny needles, which may measure up to 18 inches in length. In spring, small, reddish, male cones appear in clusters at the ends of branches and dust the countryside with yellow pollen before dropping to the ground. The female cones measure 6 to 10 inches in length and remain on the trees for two years before releasing seeds from between their bracts and dropping to the ground to become part of the accumulated duff on the sandy soil.

When Scotch Highlanders settled in the region around 1740, the vast forests consisted of original-growth longleaf pines that reached heights of 100 to 120 feet. The forests were cut for timber, and choice stands were set aside and cultivated for use as masts for the ships of the Royal Navy. Elongated, inverted V-shaped cuts in the trunks of many of the remaining trees collected

Longleaf pine forest

sap that was distilled into rosin—for such uses as sealing the hulls, decks, and masts of sailing vessels—and into turpentine; by 1800, North Carolina's pine forests were producing one-third of the world's supply of turpentine. Many surviving trees bear the prominent scars that resulted from sap collecting. Most of the virgin growth of longleaf pines was gone from the Sandhills by 1900 as a result of lumbering, naval stores operations, and other human activities.

Longleaf pine forests are communities adapted to periodic burning; they depend upon fire for survival. The original forests were maintained by summer fires that were usually begun by lightning and that served to remove competing hardwood and loblolly or pond-pine seedlings and provided open areas where longleaf seedlings could germinate and grow. The fires also added nutrients to the soil. When firefighting practices prohibit fires from running their course, competing plant species thrive, inhibiting longleaf regeneration. The small old-growth forest on the Boyd Estate Tract and forests elsewhere at Weymouth Woods are a vestige of the vast forests that once covered the region. Even there, hardwoods 40 feet in height have encroached beneath the pines and threaten their survival.

Nearly five hundred species and varieties of plants are present in Weymouth Woods. On sandy slopes and ridges, turkey and blackjack oaks grow along with the longleaf pines. These give way in the bottomlands and swamp thickets to various hardwoods, including dogwood, red and white oaks, American holly, sourwood, black gum, sweet gum, hickory, yellow poplar, persimmon, and red maple, and to conifers such as loblolly and pond pines. Present beneath the forest understory is a rich diversity of small plants ranging from lichens, mosses, and ferns to wildflowers and woody shrubs; species include cinnamon ferns, Indian pipe, wild ginger, trailing arbutus, wild grapes, blueberries, wild azaleas, dwarf iris, fall gentian, and wild orchids. A pamphlet available at the natural history museum lists a hundred species of common wildflowers in the approximate order of their annual bloom in the preserve.

James Creek flows through the preserve, cutting a narrow path that is green with aquatic vegetation. It gives rise to a small hardwood swamp like those common in the flat valleys throughout the Sandhills. Insectivorous pitcher plants grow in moist areas along the creek.

ANIMAL LIFE

There is an abundant fauna in the preserve. Among the amphibians are slimy salamanders and many species of frogs and toads, including the rare pine barrens treefrog. Because of its very specific habitat requirements, this rare treefrog occurs only in the pine barrens of southern New Jersey, in southeastern North Carolina, and in a nearby portion of the South Carolina coastal plain. Weymouth Woods is home to many reptiles characteristic of Sandhills habitats, including such species as scarlet and hognose snakes, skinks and glass lizards, box turtles, and several species of pond turtles. More than 260 species of birds have been observed in the Sandhills region. Species associated with mature longleaf pine forests are abundant in the preserve at all seasons. Visitors may expect to see red-cockaded woodpeckers, brown-headed nuthatches, pine warblers, and many other species associated with pine forests.

The red-cockaded woodpecker, which was declared an endangered species in 1970, is a permanent resident of the Sandhills and a species of special importance. Unlike other woodpeckers, it excavates cavities for roosting and nesting in the heartwood of living, mature pine trees rather than in the softer wood of dead trees. Red-cockaded woodpeckers are social birds that live in groups or clans of from two to nine individuals. A clan consists of a single breeding pair and its associates, or "helpers," which are usually nonbreeding, adult males that assist in incubating eggs, searching for food, defending the clan's territory, and excavating new cavities. A group of from two to twelve trees with cavities constitutes a colony, within which the clan roosts and rears its young. Within a colony, cavities are in various stages of use, with some under construction, others completed and occupied, and still others abandoned. Cavities are usually located 20 to 50 feet above the ground and beneath the lowest live branches of the trees. The excavation of a cavity requires months and often years. A completed cavity is used for several years. Excavation begins with a shallow hole that is extended as an upwardly sloped tunnel for 6 or more inches through sapwood. Rosin drains from the opening as well as from secondary rosin wells chipped through the bark near the cavity entrance. After reaching heartwood, which lacks flowing rosin, the birds excavate downward to form a roosting chamber, which is typically 6 to 10 inches deep and 3 to 5 inches wide. The entrance to an active cavity is maintained by chipping the bark around both the opening and the rosin wells to induce the flow of clear, sticky rosin. Each cavity is occupied by a single bird except when nestlings are present. Numerous other animals compete for use of the completed cavities, among them southern flying squirrels, eastern bluebirds, and red-bellied, red-headed, and pileated woodpeckers.

Both the range and the population of red-cockaded woodpeckers have been reduced in recent years, primarily through the loss of habitat. Mature pine trees eighty-five years of age or older are required for cavities. Outside the preserve, many suitable trees have been cut, and stands of large, mature trees are rare. The growth of the hardwood understory above 15 feet can inhibit the excavation of cavities at otherwise suitable sites, and colonies may

Fox squirrel

be abandoned when this occurs. An important management practice that helps to maintain suitable habitat for the red-cockaded woodpecker is controlled burning, which removes ground litter and undesirable shrubby undergrowth. This management technique is currently being employed at Weymouth Woods.

Many mammal species live in the preserve, but most are secretive or nocturnal and are not often seen by casual observers. Perhaps most visible are two species of tree squirrels. The more common is the gray squirrel, which is distributed throughout North Carolina. Its larger relative, the fox squirrel, is usually gray in color also, but it has black on its head, feet, and tail. The fox squirrel has a more restricted range. Within North Carolina, it occurs mostly in the southeastern counties; the mature longleaf pine forests of the Sandhills are one of its strongholds. Other familiar mammals present are white-tailed deer, red and gray foxes, Virginia opossum, raccoon, and eastern cottontail. Small, unobtrusive mammals include long-tailed weasels, eastern moles, several species of shrews, and such small rodents as the hispid cotton rat. Mink, river otter, and beaver may also be present around aquatic habitats.

HIKING TRAILS

Approximately 4 miles of trails provide access to most areas of the preserve and to vantage points for observing plant and animal life. Trails are well-marked and easy to hike.

Bower's Bog Trail, a short, self-guided nature trail, loops through a bog with abundant ferns and shrubs; it begins and ends at the right side of the natural history museum building. South of James Creek are two trails, Pine Barrens Trail and Gum Swamp Trail. **Pine Barrens Trail** is a 1-mile loop through longleaf pines and turkey oaks; its trailhead is at the visitor center. **Gum Swamp Trail** is a 0.4-mile loop that branches off Pine Barrens Trail and passes through a stand of hardwoods and alongside James Creek. **Holly Road Trail**, 1.9 miles in length, connects with Gum Swamp Trail, crosses James Creek, and loops through the northern half of the preserve. **Pine Island Trail**, 0.4 mile in length, loops off Holly Road Trail and passes through swampland, crossing 300 feet of boardwalk en route.

FACILITIES

The **visitor center** has facilities for greeting visitors, an auditorium for interpretive programs, and a **natural history museum**. The museum features excellent exhibits on both the human and natural history of the Sandhills, including material on the Indian cultures of the Sandhills, the early Sandhills settlers, the evolution of the Sandhills, lumbering and the decline of the longleaf pine forests, the plant communities of the Sandhills, blackwater pond life, and the sounds of the night. A park naturalist provides illustrated lectures for groups and guided hiking tours for visitors. The museum is open from 9:00 A.M. until 6:00 P.M. Monday through Saturday and from noon until 5:00 P.M. on Sunday.

There are no facilities for picnicking, camping, or other recreational activities. The nature preserve is dedicated to the study, interpretation, and protection of its natural ecosystem.

UNDEVELOPED STATE NATURAL AREAS

Eight undeveloped natural areas are units of the state parks system. Each preserves an outstanding and unique natural environment. Most are too small or too environmentally sensitive to permit unlimited visitation.

Baldhead Island State Natural Area

Baldhead Island State Natural Area is a complex of barrier islands, salt marshes, shallow bays, tidal creeks, and estuarine islands that lies between Baldhead Island and Fort Fisher State Recreation Area. Portions of the natural area are managed by the North Carolina Division of Parks and Recreation, the North Carolina Division of Coastal Management, the North Carolina Wildlife Resources Commission, and the National Audubon Society. The Baldhead complex is an excellent example of a coastal river-mouth estuary. It is important as an area of high natural primary productivity. It is a nursery for many marine animals, including shrimp and commercially valuable fishes. Research on estuarine ecosystems is an important activity at Baldhead Island and Masonboro Island state natural areas. Battery Island, a part of the Baldhead Island State Natural Area that is managed by the National Audubon Society, is a nesting site for herons and egrets. Zeke's Island, along the northern edge of the area, is a national estuarine sanctuary managed by the North Carolina Division of Coastal Management.

Bay Tree Lake State Natural Area

One of several state-owned Carolina bay lakes, Bay Tree Lake, formerly known as Black Lake, is 1,418 acres in size with a maximum depth of only 7 feet. The state also owns 609 acres of the lakeshore. Off N.C. 41, a corridor of land is maintained from the highway to the northwest side of the lake. The lake is difficult to reach, however, and access is restricted. There are long-range plans to develop and operate Bay Tree Lake State Natural Area as a state park.

Bushy Lake State Natural Area

Bushy Lake State Natural Area, 1,341 acres in size, is located southeast of Fayetteville in Cumberland County. Its principal feature is a Carolina bay wetland dominated by dense shrub-thicket communities, called pocosins. Bushy Lake is not a lake in the typical sense, as it has very little open water. Rather, the dense vegetation at Bushy Lake covers a layer of peat that acts as a sponge, holding water throughout most of the year. Carolina bays are unique to the coastal plain of the southeastern states, and the communities that occupy these characteristically elliptical depressions often contain rare and unusual plants and animals. Bushy Lake features a variety of insectivorous plants as well as the rough-leaf loosestrife, a federally listed endangered species. Bushy Lake State Natural Area protects an excellent example of a community type that is rapidly being lost to drainage and clearing.

Chowan Swamp State Natural Area

Located in Gates County, Chowan Swamp State Natural Area encompasses 11,200 acres along 12 miles of the north shore of the Chowan River. It averages 3 miles in width. Portions of the area are managed by the North Carolina Division of Parks and Recreation and the Wildlife Resources Commission; 3,800 acres are owned by the Forestry Foundation of North Carolina State University. Chowan Swamp consists primarily of a second-growth swamp-hardwood forest dominated by black gum, red maple, loblolly pine, and bald cypress. Older cypress and tupelo occur along the river. Small ridges, or "islands," are covered by upland forests, which include beech and oaks, as well as loblolly pines in some instances. Freshwater marshes are at the mouths of Sarem, Bennett's, and Catherine creeks, which pass through the property. These beautiful blackwater streams are excellent for canoeing and boating. The area's complex of freshwater wetlands and upland communities provides habitat for river otter, muskrat, beaver, mink, bobcat, black bear, and an abundance of birds.

Dismal Swamp State Natural Area

The state of North Carolina, with the assistance of the Nature Conservancy, acquired 14,343 acres of the Great Dismal Swamp on the northeast border with Virginia. An additional 102,000 acres of the adjacent swamp comprise the Great Dismal Swamp National Wildlife Refuge, which is managed by the United States Fish and Wildlife Service. The state-owned land will remain a natural area for environmental protection and scientific study; public access points are not provided.

None of the magnificent original forest that was first surveyed by George Washington remains, but second-growth swamp forests, shrub pocosins, pockets of upland forest, and a 75-acre remnant of the once-extensive Atlantic white cedar forest are protected by the Dismal Swamp State Natural Area. This remote natural area preserves a segment of one of the largest swamps in eastern North America. Although much of it has been ditched, drained, logged, and converted to agricultural uses, the undrained portions that remain are still wild and mysterious. Wildlife is abundant and diverse in this huge wetland, and several rare plants and animals are present.

Hemlock Bluffs State Natural Area

Hemlock Bluffs State Natural Area is a small, 150-acre tract south of Cary in Wake County. It protects a disjunct population of hemlock trees that grows along a north-facing bluff overlooking Swift Creek. This relict community contains elements that are typical of western North Carolina forests, though it is more than 200 miles east of the mountain communities where hemlocks usually occur. The 80-foot bluff, which provides conditions similar to those farther west, has enabled hemlock and other mountain-adapted species, present since the time when the region was cooler and more moist, to survive near the eastern edge of the Piedmont. The site also includes small units of other habitats typical of alluvial Piedmont areas. Situated in a region undergoing rapid urbanization, the natural area is protected by a combination of state, municipal, and public-school ownership. The town of Cary is helping to develop visitor access, trails, and interpretive facilities.

Masonboro Island State Natural Area

Masonboro Island, a low, narrow, 9-mile-long barrier island, and its estuarine system lie between Wrightsville and Carolina beaches in New Hanover County. Although much of the island remains in private ownership, the state has begun to purchase sections of land, and portions of the marshes have been declared a national estuarine sanctuary. Masonboro Island is an excellent example of the barrier island/estuarine system that protects much of the North Carolina coastline from the direct erosive forces of the ocean. The primary objectives for the natural area are the maintenance of the high rate of productivity associated with barrier island/estuarine systems, the protection of nesting habitat for the endangered loggerhead sea turtle, and research on important natural processes.

Mitchell's Millpond/Rolesville Outcrop State Natural Area

Mitchell's Millpond/Rolesville Outcrop State Natural Area encompasses 67 acres. It includes an old stone dam and millpond as well as natural granite flatrock outcrops. Little River flows through the area, which is located in eastern Wake County off N.C. 96 east of Rolesville.

The millpond is partly covered by an emergent swamp forest. Swamp-dwelling birds like prothonotary warblers and wood ducks are present, and a variety of fishes, amphibians, and reptiles occurs, including an unusual endemic salamander, the Carolina mudpuppy.

Mitchell's Mill Outcrop, the most extensive of many such flat rocks in North Carolina, is part of the Rolesville pluton, a layer of granite lying just beneath the earth's surface over an area approximately 50 miles long and 10 to 12 miles wide in Wake and Franklin counties. In places like Mitchell's Mill, the granite has been exposed by the erosive forces of nature.

Much of the outcrop is bare, but a succession of plant species may occur in pockets of thin soil that have collected in hollows and crevices scattered over the rock surface. The sequence of species is precisely ordered, each successional stage giving way to the next over an extended period of time. The pioneers in the process are lichens and mosses, which cling to the granite and trap particles of soil borne by wind and water. Lichens and mosses are followed at the edges of growing mats of soil and vegetation by such hardy annuals as sedum, sandwort, and false croton, and, as the soil layer thickens, by haircap moss, reindeer lichens, and perennial herbs. Wind-borne seeds take root where the depth of soil and degree of wetness are optimal. Broomsedge and other grasses appear, along with small shrubs and tree seedlings. In time, large areas of the outcrop become covered by more advanced plants, and forest communities of pines and hardwoods typical of the later stages of plant succession develop. The process is ongoing at Mitchell's Millpond/ Rolesville Outcrop. The natural area is a treasured resource that is fragile and easily damaged; unguided visitation should not be undertaken.

STATE RECREATION AREAS

FALLS LAKE STATE RECREATION AREA

Address: 12700 Bay Leaf Church Road
             Raleigh, N.C. 27614

Telephone: (919) 846-9991

Size: 1,026 acres

Established: 1983

Location: Wake and Durham counties. The temporary office is 7 miles north
of Raleigh; from the U.S. 1/64 belt line, turn onto Six Forks Road (SR
1005) to Bay Leaf and proceed on Bay Leaf Church Road (SR 2003) to
Yorkshire Center at the terminus of the road. Four access areas may be
reached from N.C. 50 and N.C. 98.

Highway 50 Access Area encompasses 50 acres. Exit N.C. 50 at
the sign immediately north of the bridge over Falls Lake and proceed to
the entry gate.

Sandling Beach Access Area encompasses 330 acres. Exit N.C. 50
at the sign north of Highway 50 Access Area, 3.5 miles from the
intersection of N.C. 50 and N.C. 98; the entrance is 5 miles south of
Creedmoor.

Rollingview Access Area encompasses 356 acres, and
Rollingview Marina encompasses 290 acres. Exit N.C. 98 west of
its intersection with N.C. 50 onto either SR 1803 or SR 1807 and
proceed to the entry gates.

Principal Attractions: An 11,000-acre lake on the Neuse River with access
for water-related activities; commercial marina.

Visitor Activities: Boating, fishing, swimming, and other water-based activities; picnicking; nature study. Camping facilities are scheduled for
construction.

Season: Open year-round.

Falls Lake Dam, an earth and rock structure 1,915 feet in length and 92.5
feet in height, was constructed by the United States Army Corps of Engineers
across the Neuse River in Wake County near the village of Falls, north of
Raleigh. The water impounded behind the dam created Falls Lake, a reservoir
that extends 22 miles upstream to a point above the confluence of the Eno and

Falls Lake

Flat rivers in Durham County. The lake is maintained at a level of about 250 feet above mean sea level; it covers an area of 11,310 acres and has a shoreline of 230 miles. The total Falls Lake project, including the lake and surrounding land, encompasses 38,000 acres in Wake, Durham, and Granville counties. The land is being managed for recreation and conservation purposes by the North Carolina Division of Parks and Recreation and the Wildlife Resources Commission, in cooperation with the United States Army Corps of Engineers. At present, four access areas with a total of 1,026 acres constitute Falls Lake State Recreation Area. Other access areas are planned for this unit of the state parks system.

Construction of the dam and reservoir was authorized by the Flood Control Act of 1965. Work on the dam began in mid-1978 and was completed in February 1981; full impoundment was achieved in January 1983. The objectives of the project were to provide a water supply for Raleigh and nearby communities, to control flooding in the region, to control water quality downstream by regulating flow releases from the lake, to provide a variety of recreational opportunities for the public, and to manage fish and wildlife habitats.

Continuous human habitation of the Falls Lake area for at least nine thousand years is evident from archaeological studies. The earliest known inhabitants were hunters and gatherers; later, villages appeared as the people became more settled and began to farm the land. Indians were present when the first Europeans entered the area. John Lawson, colonial surveyor and explorer, visited the region in 1701; he reported on the village of Adschusheer, which is believed to have been located on what is now project land.

Also located in the Falls Lake area were the home of General James Mangum, a politician and a leader of local militia; portions of the large, pre–Civil War Bennehan-Cameron Plantation; and numerous mills that stood along the Neuse in the early nineteenth century. A wooden dam built about 1830 as part of a paper manufacturing company was located near the site of present-day Falls Lake Dam.

Prior to the construction of Falls Lake Dam, the Neuse was about 75 feet at its widest point along the 22-mile stretch now covered by the impoundment. It meandered through its tree-lined channel past sites where Indians built rock shelters on their hunting forays in the prehistoric past. Today, Falls Lake covers what were once the first falls on the Neuse, a series of rock outcrops and shallow pools where the river dropped 30 feet in a distance of less than a mile. The falls area had been a popular swimming place for local youngsters. Ziegle's Rock, a geological landmark formed of biotite gneiss and quartz, once towered 55 feet above the river's surface, but it has now been partly inundated. Changes have brought new and different recreational opportunities and scenic values to the Falls Lake area.

PLANT LIFE

Plant communities within the recreation area range from upland pine and hardwood forests to wetlands adjacent to the lake. The topography is generally rolling, and forests are second-growth, having been logged or perhaps cleared and farmed in earlier times. Present-day forests are dominated by loblolly and Virginia pines, southern red oak, chestnut oak, hickories, sweet gum, yellow poplar, and other species typical of the Piedmont. American beech may be present on moist slopes, and willows have invaded the perimeter of the lake. Flowering dogwood is an important and showy component of the understory of most forests.

ANIMAL LIFE

Wildlife is abundant and diverse both in the uplands and in the lake. White-tailed deer are seen occasionally, and other forest mammals such as gray squirrels are abundant. Cottontails may be seen feeding along roadsides, and raccoons and Virginia opossums may be encountered during their nocturnal forays along the lakeshore.

Birds are abundant at all seasons. Most species typical of the Piedmont may be seen. The presence of wild turkeys is of special interest; though seldom seen, these secretive birds are often heard gobbling in the distance early on spring mornings. Falls Lake and nearby Jordan Lake are two of the best places in North Carolina to observe our majestic national symbol, the bald eagle.

Amphibians and reptiles typical of the eastern Piedmont occur at Falls Lake.

Lizards of several species are often encountered in upland habitats. Fence lizards are distinguished by their rough scales and blue flanks, while skinks are easily identified by their shiny, smooth scales and the bright blue tails of young individuals. They are harmless animals.

Falls Reservoir and its shoreline provide habitat for many animals, among them river otter, muskrats, wood ducks, double-crested cormorants, and various turtles. There is an abundance of fishes of many species. When Falls Lake was created, resident populations of fish in the Neuse and its tributaries moved into the lake, and many such species have thrived. Largemouth bass, bluegills, crappie, and several kinds of catfishes are present, as are many small, seldom-seen species that are an important food source for large game fish and for fish-eating birds and mammals.

FACILITIES AND ACTIVITIES

Falls Lake is open to **fishing** all year. Largemouth bass, bluegills, and crappie are highly sought-after by fishermen, but several other species of sunfishes as well as catfishes also provide a challenge to sportsmen. Most fishing is from boats launched from one of the several public ramps around the lake, but bank fishing, which requires less equipment and preparation, is also possible. North Carolina fishing licenses are required, and state regulations are enforced.

A recreation area office will be constructed near the entrance to Highway 50 Access Area; a temporary office is located at Loblolly Point at the end of Bay Leaf Church Road. Visitors may seek information at the office. **Yorkshire Center** houses part of the administrative staff of the North Carolina Division of Parks and Recreation. Situated at a scenic overlook on the shore of Falls Lake, this attractive building is the remodeled Yorkshire House, a popular restaurant prior to the damming of Neuse River.

The North Carolina Division of Parks and Recreation operates facilities for public use at four access areas within Falls Lake State Recreation Area. Visitor-use fees are charged at each access area; for more specific information, contact the recreation area office.

Highway 50 Access Area

The entrance to the Highway 50 Access Area is a short distance north of the N.C. 50 bridge across Falls Lake. The entry road forks beyond the park sign; to the left are a paved parking lot and a picnic area and to the right a six-lane boat ramp on the lake. No camping facilities are provided.

A paved walk leads from the parking lot through a beautifully forested family **picnic ground** along the bank of the tranquil lake. Twenty tables and grills are spaced along the path in the shade of numerous trees. Drinking water is provided. It is a delightful and peaceful place for a family outing. The paved trail leads south from the picnic area along the lakeshore, passing en route modern restrooms and more than twenty additional picnic sites bordering the lake, many with scenic views of the water and the far shore. Trail markers identify nearly twenty species of trees native to the area.

The trail continues down a high slope above the shoreline to Beaver Dam, constructed across a tributary of the Neuse River. The dam separates Beaverdam Lake to the left from Falls Lake to the right. Completed prior to Falls Lake Dam, Beaver Dam Reservoir provided Raleigh with water. Fishermen are attracted to the banks of Beaverdam Lake, but boats with gasoline engines are not permitted on the lake.

A large, paved parking lot for boaters and a six-lane **boat ramp** may be reached either by road or hiking trail. Boats may be launched into Falls Lake. Modern restrooms and drinking water are provided.

Sandling Beach Access Area

The entry road to Sandling Beach Access Area turns west off N. C. 50 at the park sign and leads to Sandling Beach and picnic areas along the lakeshore. The facilities are for day-use only. A campground is not provided.

The road enters a large parking lot adjacent to Sandling Beach on Falls Lake. Visitors may sunbathe on the long, sandy strand or swim in the protected waters of the lake. A large, modern restroom with changing rooms is located at each end of the beach; rinse-off showers and drinking water are provided. Playground equipment is located near each building, and several picnic tables and grills are available beneath trees bordering the beach.

The recreation area road extends along the lakeshore both north and south from Sandling Beach to a series of **picnic sites** and **shelters**. To the north are five sites with four shelters, and to the south are four sites with three shelters. There is ample parking space at each site. The shelters are large, attractive structures with tables, grills, and fireplaces; some have restrooms. Additional tables beneath the trees are usually available at each site. The picnic sites and shelters are at pleasant locations with scenic views of the lake. Five of the shelters are available by reservation, while the remaining two may be used on a first-come basis. For reservations or additional information, write or call the office.

Rollingview Access Area and Rollingview Marina

Rollingview Access Area is under construction and is scheduled to be in operation before the end of the 1989 summer season. It will add significant new facilities to the recreation area.

A **family campground** with 131 campsites and full hookups for RVs will be available to visitors. Restrooms and washhouses will be centrally located within three loop roads. A pier is planned, and opportunities for pier and lakeshore fishing will be available. A **group camping area** with five group camps and a central washhouse will also be provided.

A **swimming and picnicking area** on the northwest side of the property will include a swimming beach, a building with restrooms and changing rooms, five picnic shelters, and a fishing pier. A **sailing center** located at the northern tip of a peninsula will include a boat beach, a four-lane boat ramp, a group assembly building with a kitchen, picnic shelters, and restrooms. Sail-boating and windsurfing will be popular activities.

The concessionaire-operated Rollingview Marina is reached by way of SR 1807. It includes a pair of two-lane boat ramps, two hundred uncovered boatslips, and dry storage facilities; fuel and boating supplies are available. For information, write: Rollingview Marina, Route 6, Box 172-A, Durham, N.C. 27703 (919/596-2194).

Additional Access Areas and Natural Areas

Other access areas for public recreation at Falls Lake will be developed by the North Carolina Division of Parks and Recreation in the future. An access area at Holly Point will provide major facilities similar to those at Rollingview.

The North Carolina Wildlife Resources Commission manages several public access areas on Falls Lake. They include **Upper Barton Creek**, which may be reached by SR 1005 off N.C. 98; **Hickory Hill**, which may be reached by SR 1637 off I-85; and **Ledge Rock**, which may be reached by SR 1727/1903/1900 off U.S. 15. Each access area has a four-lane boat ramp. **Eno River Portage Area**, with a one-lane ramp for canoes and small boats, may be reached by SR 1632 north from I-85.

Twelve natural areas totaling about 1,290 acres have been designated around Falls Lake; most have been recommended for inclusion in the North Carolina Registry of Natural Heritage Areas. Thirteen plant species that occur within these areas are recognized as rare in North Carolina. One area, **B. W. Wells Interpretive Center**, is managed by the North Carolina Division of Parks and Recreation, while the others are managed by the North Carolina Wildlife Resources Commission. The 44-acre center is located on an ingrown meander, or "Big Bend," of the Neuse River. It includes Rockcliff Farm, formerly owned by Dr. and Mrs. B. W. Wells. Dr. Wells was an eminent botanist and ecologist at North Carolina State University who published significant research on the vegetation and geology of the state. He extolled the variety and the value of the natural communities and resources of North Carolina and worked for the preservation of the state's natural heritage. Wells maintained Rockcliff Farm in a natural state and documented the flora there;

vegetation on the lower slopes above the river is now inundated. The Wells home is maintained as an interpretive center, and the area will continue to be a focus of botanical studies. Access to the area is regulated.

NEARBY

Jordan Lake State Recreation Area is southwest of Raleigh, 45 miles from Falls Lake. William B. Umstead State Park is west of Raleigh and is also nearby. Both park units are discussed elsewhere in this volume.

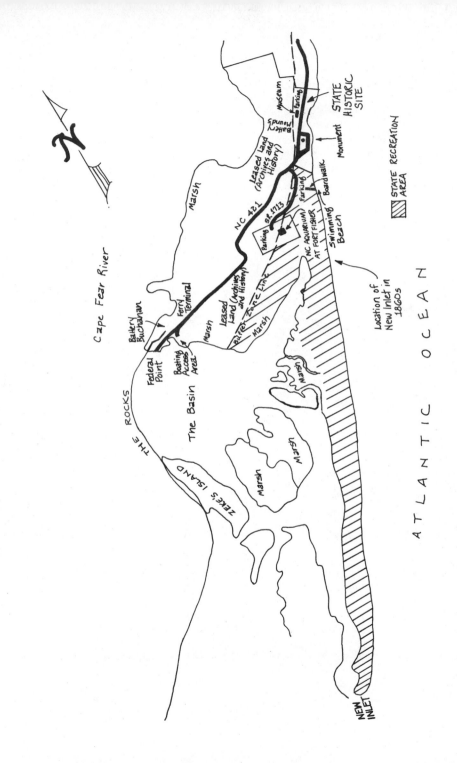

N

Cape Fear River

THE ROCKS

ZEKE'S ISLAND

The Basin

Marsh

Marsh

Marsh

Marsh

Federal Point

Boating Access Area

Battery Buchanan

Ferry Terminal

Marsh

Leased Land (Archives and History)

Buffer Zone Line

Marsh

Marsh

Marsh

NC 421

SR 1713

Parking

NC AQUARIUM AT FORT FISHER

Swimming Beach

Parking

Boardwalk

Location of New Inlet in 1860s

ATLANTIC OCEAN

NEW INLET

Leased Land (Archives and History)

Museum

Parking

Baker's Mounds

Monument

STATE HISTORIC SITE

STATE RECREATION AREA

FORT FISHER STATE RECREATION AREA

Address: c/o Carolina Beach State Park
              P.O. Box 475
              Carolina Beach, N.C. 28428

Telephone: (919) 458-8206

Size: 287 acres

Established: 1986

Location: New Hanover County, 5 miles south of Carolina Beach off U.S. 421; the recreation area may also be reached from Brunswick County by way of the Southport–Fort Fisher ferry, which crosses the Cape Fear River near its mouth.

Principal Attractions: Approximately 4 miles of undeveloped beach on the Atlantic Ocean, bounded to the west by extensive salt marshes, shallow creeks and bays, and the Cape Fear River; proximity to Fort Fisher State Historic Site, the North Carolina Aquarium at Fort Fisher, and area beaches.

Visitor Activities: Swimming and fishing in the surf; beachcombing and hiking along the seashore; bird-watching and studying marine life; visiting historic sites in the area. No camping is permitted.

Season: Open year-round.

Remains of Fort Fisher at state historic site

Fort Fisher State Recreation Area lies at the southern end of New Hanover County. It occupies a portion of an elongated triangle of uplands that extends southward between the Atlantic Ocean to the east and the Cape Fear River, extensive salt marshes, and shallow estuaries to the west. The slender tip of the peninsula points south across New Inlet toward Brunswick County, Baldhead Island, and Cape Fear.

The land within and adjoining Fort Fisher State Recreation Area was the scene of events of historic significance during the Civil War. A battle was fought that helped to determine the outcome of the long and bitter struggle between the Union and the Confederacy.

As a consequence of its predominantly agricultural economy, the Confederacy was forced to import supplies, munitions, and other goods necessary to equip and maintain its armies. Southern ports were blockaded by Union naval forces in an effort to prevent provisions from being received. Wilmington, on the Cape Fear River, was an important port of entry for the Confederacy, and by late 1864 it was the last port remaining open to trade. Sleek, fast, steam-powered blockade runners had considerable success in evading Union ships and returning from abroad with vital materiel. Shipments from the port on the Wilmington and Weldon Railroad eventually reached General Lee's Army of Northern Virginia.

Numerous fortifications served to secure the Cape Fear River from attack, to protect blockade runners as they entered or departed, and to keep Union ships offshore. These included Fort Johnson at Smithville (or Southport); Fort Caswell on the west side of the river's mouth; Fort Holmes on Baldhead Island; and Fort Anderson, an earthwork structure at the site of Brunswick Town. The largest fortification in the South, as well as one of the most important, was Fort Fisher, located to the north of New Inlet. (It should be noted that the New Inlet of the 1860s passed from the Atlantic Ocean to the Cape Fear River at Federal Point, a channel that is now closed; Battery Buchanan and Mound Battery were nearby on the sea face of Fort Fisher. Today, the name New Inlet designates a channel between the southern tip of the state recreation area and Baldhead Island.)

The construction of Fort Fisher was begun in April 1861. In July 1862, when Colonel William Lamb took command, the fort consisted of several batteries with fewer than two dozen cannons. When completed, the L-shaped fort was a massive structure of sand and sod. The side of the fort facing land to the north (the land face) stretched 0.5 mile across the peninsula from the river to near the seashore; it consisted of fifteen mounds, each 32 feet in height, with a total of twenty-five guns. Interior rooms connected by passageways served as barracks, bombproof shelter, headquarters, hospital, and telegraph office. A palisade fence of wooden posts 9 feet in height extended the length of the land side of the fort. From a corner bastion, the side of the fort facing the sea (the sea face) ran southward for approximately 1 mile; most of its length was made up of a series of batteries 12 feet in height, with a total of twenty-two guns. At the south end was the 60-foot-high Mound Battery, which overlooked the ocean entry into New Inlet. Battery Buchanan was separate from the fort and was located 0.5 mile from the end of the sea face at Federal Point.

By the summer of 1862, three cordons of Union ships were positioned off the two inlets at the mouth of the Cape Fear River. Approximately a hundred blockade runners were in operation. As other ports were closed, Wilmington became increasingly important to the survival of the Confederacy, and Fort Fisher was of strategic concern to both North and South. The first of two attacks on the fort began on December 24, 1864; after heavy naval bombardment and the landing of a large force of Union troops, the fort proved to be too strong, and the Union forces withdrew. The second attack began on January 13, 1865; a Union fleet of fifty-six ships with approximately six hundred guns bombarded the fort prior to a land assault by a force of more than thirty-three hundred infantry. On January 15, after six hours of fierce combat, the fort was overrun and captured, and the Confederate supply line was broken. The naval bombardment and the land-sea battle at Fort Fisher were the largest in any war to that time. Other fortifications along the river were subsequently taken, and Union forces entered Wilmington. The war ended on April 19, 1865, approximately three months after the fall of Fort Fisher.

Efforts to acquire and preserve the Fort Fisher site began in the early 1930s, without success. The area again became an active military post during World War II, then was abandoned by the army. Much of the old fort had by then been destroyed. The sea had eroded the corner bastion and most of the sea face, and the construction of a landing strip during World War II and of U.S. 421 down the peninsula had claimed part of the land face. Nevertheless, some battery mounds remained. Interest in preserving the area was revived, and in 1960 the state purchased a 15-acre tract of land at the site of the fort. An additional 187 acres that included the surviving earthen mounds of the fort's land face were leased from the federal government; this land lies west of the boundary line of a buffer zone around the army facilities at Sunny Point. Fort Fisher State Historic Site, administered by the Division of Archives and History of the North Carolina Department of Cultural Affairs, was established in the early 1960s; 9.7 acres were added to the site in 1967. Portions of Fort Fisher have been restored, and visitor-use facilities have been developed.

In 1969, in response to a threat of commercial development of land south of the historic site, the state purchased 287 acres located east of the army buffer zone. Initially the responsibility of the North Carolina Department of Cultural Affairs, the land was jointly administered from 1982 to 1986 by personnel of the state parks system and New Hanover County. On March 5, 1986, administrative responsibility for the area was transferred to the Division of Parks and Recreation of the North Carolina Department of Natural Resources and Community Development, and Fort Fisher State Recreation Area was established.

The state began the establishment of three marine resources centers along the coast in the late 1960s. The most southern of these facilities, now known as the North Carolina Aquarium at Fort Fisher, was completed in 1976. The aquarium is operated by the Office of Marine Affairs of the North Carolina Department of Administration. Also adjoining the recreation area are a boating access area, provided by the North Carolina Wildlife Resources Commission at the terminus of U.S. 421, and a terminal for a North Carolina Department of Transportation toll ferry across the Cape Fear River between the Fort Fisher peninsula and the Brunswick County mainland.

The Fort Fisher area provides a unique combination of opportunities for visitors. They can enjoy an undeveloped series of coastal communities including a stretch of wide, sandy beach. They may also gain boating access to coastal waters, visit Fort Fisher and a museum that interprets the history of the area, visit a public aquarium with exhibits of local marine life, and take a ferry trip across a major coastal river.

PLANT LIFE ·

Visitors arriving at Fort Fisher first experience the uplands of the peninsula. The northern portion of the recreation area is the oldest geologically, and the uplands there are occupied by forests of live oak and loblolly pine. On the oceanfront, salt-tolerant live oaks shaped by wind and spray grow no more than 20 to 30 feet in height. Sheltered conditions west of U.S. 421 have given rise to taller forests, and the less salt-tolerant loblolly pine is prevalent. Farther south, substrates are younger and uplands are dominated by developing forests and dense shrub thickets. Live oaks and pines are present, but wax myrtle, yaupon, and other shrubs dominate. Dense tangles of greenbrier and poison ivy make many thickets almost impenetrable.

Most visitors spend their time enjoying the beach and dunes habitats. East and south of the recreation area parking lot, dunes covered with sea oats extend from the high-tide line westward across the primary dune system and southward about 4 miles to New Inlet at the southern end of the peninsula. Sea oats can tolerate the constant wind and frequent salt spray; they are invaluable for their abilities to grow in this inhospitable environment and to stabilize dunes against the erosive force of the wind. Driving on the dunes is prohibited, and visitors driving off-road vehicles down the peninsula must follow established and marked trails.

Bordering the west side of the peninsula are extensive salt marshes. The upper, less frequently flooded perimeter is occupied mostly by saltmeadow cordgrass, while the regularly flooded marshes are vegetated by smooth cordgrass. Both habitats are considered to be among the most productive on earth and are extremely important to life in nearby creeks, bays, and inshore ocean waters. The seafood served at local restaurants very likely grew on the nutrients derived from this "salt hay."

ANIMAL LIFE

The Fort Fisher area is an excellent place to study coastal animal life. The inshore ocean provides good fishing during the warm months of the year, with bluefish, Virginia mullet, spot, and puppy drum the most common catches in the surf. The shallow bay adjacent to the recreation area is good habitat for flounder, crabs, and clams. As is almost always the case in estuarine and ocean waters, however, part of the enjoyment of fishing is never being quite sure what will bite next.

The beach at Fort Fisher provides nesting habitat for the loggerhead, a large sea turtle that is a threatened species. At night in June and July, female loggerheads crawl onto the beach to lay eggs just above high tide. In August and September, the hatchlings emerge from their nests, crawl down the beach to the ocean, and begin the cycle that may bring them back to the same location when they mature in fifteen to eighteen years.

The complex of habitats, including ocean, beach, dunes, marshes, and open estuarine waters, is an excellent place to see an abundance of coastal birds. Waterbirds, shorebirds, and land birds all migrate along the coast in spring and fall, passing by or through the recreation area. Waterfowl winter on the bays and the lower portions of the Cape Fear River. Many species of shorebirds feed on exposed mud and sand flats, while herons, egrets, and ibises feed along the water margins. In summer, willets, American oystercatchers, least terns, and black skimmers nest in the dunes, and such local specialties as painted buntings nest in upland thickets. Birding is especially good in September and October, when weather patterns and local geography result in a concentration of migrants at the southern end of the peninsula.

The area is also a good location to see marine mammals. Bottle-nosed dolphins are present offshore and in the river at all seasons, and larger whales are sometimes seen as they swim near shore. Land mammals such as gray foxes, Virginia opossums, gray squirrels, and several species of rodents may be observed occasionally.

FACILITIES AND ACTIVITIES

Because the state recreation area is closely related physically and historically to other, adjoining administrative areas, each is described briefly; refer to the map.

Fort Fisher State Historic Site

The 24.7-acre Fort Fisher State Historic Site is the first of the administrative areas reached by visitors traveling south on U.S. 421. To the left, between the highway and the seashore, is a forest of live oaks that have been shaped by the effects of wind and salt spray. Visitors may explore the forest area and the edge of the ocean; the unprotected **beach** is an excellent place to relax in the sun, though swimming is not recommended. A natural rock outcrop is exposed at low tide in the intertidal zone at the north end of the beach. The coquina rocks were formed in the distant geological past by natural processes that cemented together oyster shells and clamshells, sand, and other materials. It is the only natural rocky shore in the state; it is a registered state natural heritage area from which plants, animals, and rocks must not be removed.

A large, paved parking lot to the right of the highway is adjacent to a **visitor center and museum** that offers excellent exhibits and an audiovisual program that interprets the history of Fort Fisher and the surrounding area; artifacts recovered from the fort are displayed. A trail begins at the rear of the museum and loops around a series of earthen mounds that are the remains of the land face of the fort. The trail follows a restored palisade fence similar to those of the 1860s. The trail provides views of the mounds and the beautiful live oaks growing from them. It crosses a footbridge over a salt marsh near the Cape Fear River and leads past restorations of a bombproof entryway and Shephard's Battery. On top of the battery is an observation platform from which visitors may view the area. The trail then returns to the museum building. Narrated guided tours on the trail are scheduled four times a day throughout the year. A small picnic area with five tables is located on the west side of the parking lot.

A laboratory for underwater archaeological research is located on the property; numerous ships that sank offshore have been investigated, and salvaged artifacts may be seen in the museum. Nearby, U.S. 421 loops around Battle Acre and a monument memorializing the Confederate casualties at Fort Fisher. For additional information, write: Fort Fisher State Historic Site, P.O. Box 68, Kure Beach, N.C. 28449 (919/458-5538).

Fort Fisher State Recreation Area

The 287-acre Fort Fisher State Recreation Area extends south from its boundary with the state historic site for 3.7 miles to New Inlet. The recreation area consists of open beach, dunes, shrub thickets, and salt marshes, and it is bordered to the west by estuarine waters.

The entry is to the left at the park sign, a short distance past Battle Acre; a paved road (SR 1713) leads past a gravel parking lot for visitors to the recreation area. From the parking lot, an elevated boardwalk through shrub thickets and frontal dunes provides access to the beach. A building on the boardwalk contains a refreshment stand and modern restrooms/changing rooms; a cold-water shower is outside. A sheltered deck near the beach is a beautiful spot for relaxing and viewing the surf. Steps lead to a protected section of the beach for swimming and sunbathing; outside this area, visitors may fish in the ocean, stroll along the water's edge, and enjoy other activities. The long stretch of undeveloped beach to the south provides an opportunity to experience the ocean environment in relative isolation, away from the crowds often present at other area beaches.

Immediately past the parking lot, a sandy side road provides access to the beach for off-road vehicles. Drivers must follow designated routes to the south, and they must not drive on the dunes.

North Carolina Aquarium at Fort Fisher

SR 1713 continues past the recreation area parking lot for 0.3 mile to a gravel parking area adjacent to the aquarium. An elevated ramp gives access to the building. The stated purpose of the aquarium is "to promote an awareness, understanding, and appreciation of coastal North Carolina's natural resources." The facility contains research laboratories, aquaria, exhibits, class-

Surf fishing in the Atlantic Ocean

rooms, an auditorium for special programs, and a bookstore. It is open from 9:00 A.M. to 5:00 P.M. Monday through Saturday and from 1:00 P.M. to 5:00 P.M. on Sunday; admission is free. Aquarium exhibits include habitat tanks for saltwater fishes (including sharks), a saltwater touch tank, displays about whales, and a river otter habitat. Special family adventure programs and field trips are scheduled; some activities require preregistration and a fee. For additional information and a schedule of events, write: North Carolina Aquarium, P.O. Box 130, Kure Beach, N.C. 28449 (919/458-8257).

A short nature trail begins at the aquarium, loops through upland shrub-thicket habitats, crosses a section of salt marsh on an elevated walkway, and leads to the open beach. Hikers then have access to several miles of beach, dunes, and soundside marshes. The trail returns to the aquarium parking lot.

Southport—Fort Fisher Ferry Terminal

The 8 acres of ferry terminal property are located 1.3 miles past the entry gate to the recreation area, near the terminus of U.S. 421. Toll ferries transport vehicles and passengers on the Cape Fear River between Fort Fisher and Brunswick County near the town of Southport. During the summer, vessels depart at intervals of an hour and forty minutes; the crossing time is about thirty minutes. Schedules and fees are posted along area roads. The capacity of the ferries is twenty cars; waits are often necessary during busy summer months.

Fort Fisher Boating Access Area

A 4.7-acre boating access area provided by the North Carolina Wildlife Resources Commission is at the terminus of U.S. 421 at Federal Point, a short distance past the ferry terminal. The area includes a gravel parking lot and two boat ramps. It opens into a broad, shallow bay and, by way of a series of narrow channels, into New Inlet. Visitors should be aware that the bay is very shallow and that considerable knowledge of coastal tidal waters is necessary for boating in the area.

NEARBY

Carolina Beach State Park is 5 miles to the north of the recreation area. A campground with eighty-three campsites and a marina with access to the Cape Fear River are within the park. A chapter on Carolina Beach State Park is included in this volume.

"**The Rocks**" is a dam constructed of large boulders. It extends from the end of Federal Point, near Battery Buchanan and the Fort Fisher Boating Access Area, past Zeke's Island and south to the marshes of Baldhead Island. A major engineering feat completed in 1881, the dam closed New Inlet at the south end of the sea face of Fort Fisher, created a shallow estuarine bay known as "the Basin," and increased the rate of water flow through Old Inlet at the river's mouth. The Rocks is a popular spot for fishermen, bird watchers, hikers, and others interested in the coastal environment. A walk on the Rocks should begin on a falling tide and be timed for a return to land before high tide wets or covers the boulders.

JORDAN LAKE STATE RECREATION AREA

Address: Route 2, Box 159
             Apex, N.C. 27502

Telephone: (919) 362-0586

Size: 1,925 total acres

Established: 1982

Location: Chatham County; Raleigh, Cary, and Apex are to the east, Durham and Chapel Hill are to the north, Pittsboro is to the west, and Moncure is to the south. Five access areas may be reached from U.S. 64 between Apex and Cary.

Crosswinds Boat Ramp Access Area encompasses 50 acres; exit U.S. 64 north to the entry gate at the east end of B. Everett Jordan Bridge.

Crosswinds Marina encompasses 175 acres adjacent to Crosswinds Boat Ramp; exit U.S. 64 on the east side of Jordan Lake at Wilsonville and proceed north on SR 1008 (Beaver Creek Road) to the entrance.

Parkers Creek Access Area encompasses 656 acres; exit U.S. 64 north to the entry gate on the peninsula near the west end of Jordan Bridge.

Ebenezer Church Access Area encompasses 200 acres; exit U.S. 64 on the east side of Jordan Lake at Wilsonville, turn south onto SR 1008 (Beaver Creek Road), and proceed 2.2 miles to the entry gate.

Vista Point Access Area encompasses 499 acres; exit U.S. 64 west of Jordan Lake at Griffins Crossroads, turn south onto SR 1700 (North Pea Ridge Road), and proceed 3 miles to the entry gate.

Principal Attractions: 13,900-acre Jordan Lake on the New Hope and Haw rivers, with access for water-related activities; commercial marina; three hundred campsites on or near the lakeshore.

Visitor Activities: Boating, fishing, swimming, and other water-based sports; camping; picnicking; nature study.

Season: Open year-round; the campgrounds are closed from December 13 to the end of March.

B. Everett Jordan Dam, an earth and rock structure 1,330 feet in length, was constructed by the United States Army Corps of Engineers across the

Haw River just downstream of its confluence with New Hope River in Chatham County. The waters from the two rivers impounded behind the dam have created B. Everett Jordan Lake, a reservoir that encompasses 13,900 acres and that has 150 miles of shoreline. The lake extends for 17 miles along New Hope River and for 5 miles along Haw River. It is a permanent body of water that provides flood control for the Cape Fear River basin downstream from the dam and that also provides a water supply to nearby cities. A total of 32,868 acres of the surrounding land is managed for recreation and wildlife conservation by the North Carolina Division of Parks and Recreation and the Wildlife Resources Commission, in cooperation with the Corps of Engineers. Five access areas with more than 1,900 acres constitute Jordan Lake State Recreation Area; three additional access areas will soon be added to this unit of the state parks system.

Construction of the dam and the lake was authorized by Congress in 1963, partly in response to a 1945 hurricane that caused extensive flooding in the Cape Fear River basin. The dam was begun in 1967 and completed in 1974. In 1973, Congress changed the project name from New Hope Lake to B. Everett Jordan Dam and Lake in honor of a former North Carolina senator. The project was highly controversial, and litigation was initiated by the Conservation Council of North Carolina and other parties in an effort to prevent its completion. In 1974, the Corps of Engineers was enjoined from stripping the area, and the dry dam functioned solely for flood control downstream. The injunction was lifted in July 1977, allowing the clearing of land and the creation of the lake.

Prior to the creation of Jordan Lake, the lower Haw River and most of the New Hope were prime whitewater stretches for canoeing and rafting. Much of the area stripped for the lake, especially that in the alluvial bottomlands along the waterways, was excellent habitat for a rich diversity of plants and animals. Conservationists objected to the loss of these resources and were concerned that the lake would become polluted by discharges from nearby towns and cities. Nevertheless, the lake was completed and one set of recreational opportunities and environmental habitats was replaced by another. Judgment of whether the change was for better or worse is a matter of personal philosophy, but the resources of Jordan Lake State Recreation Area are now available to the people of North Carolina.

PLANT LIFE

The plant communities surrounding Jordan Lake are those characteristic of the eastern Piedmont. Forests of pines and hardwoods occur, and old fields in the process of reverting to forests are common. Willows are invading shallow coves, and dense stands of such wetland pioneers are becoming established around the shallow lake margins.

ANIMAL LIFE

The animals of the upland portions of the recreation area are typical of Piedmont habitats. There is an abundance of such species as bobwhites and eastern cottontails, which often occupy areas in the early stages of old-field succession. Jordan Lake itself is a special place for several groups of animals adapted for life in and around large freshwater lakes. Fish populations are large, with largemouth bass and other sunfish most abundant. Waterfowl use the lake in winter, and duck hunting is permitted on portions of the lake.

The most spectacular aspect of the wildlife at Jordan Lake is the unexpected presence of a year-round population of bald eagles. The eagles roost on the peninsula east of Morgan Creek. In 1987, more than fifty eagles were in residence throughout the summer months. This concentration represents a nonbreeding gathering and is by far the largest population of eagles ever recorded in North Carolina. The New Hope Audubon Society, in cooperation with the North Carolina Wildlife Resources Commission, has constructed an eagle-viewing platform on the lakeshore adjacent to Indian Creek. Between May and August, viewers have an excellent chance of seeing bald eagles from the observation platform. The platform may be reached by turning north off U.S. 64 onto N.C. 751 and proceeding 6.7 miles to SR 1733 (New Hope Church Road). An obscure dirt road to the left past SR 1733 leads to a gravel parking area; a 0.7-mile trail that leads past old fields and through woodlands ends at the lakeshore and the observation deck.

Bald eagles require five years to mature. Immature birds are easily distinguished from adults. They lack the white heads and the tails of mature birds and look more like large, dark hawks. Bald eagles are easily identified in flight by their large size and their very straight wings; by contrast, most hawks have a bend in the wing while in flight. Bald eagles, our national symbol, are strictly protected by law and should not be harassed in any way.

Jordan Lake also provides habitat for nesting ospreys and double-crested cormorants. The cormorants were not known to breed so far inland before their discovery at Jordan Lake.

FACILITIES AND ACTIVITIES

As of 1989, the North Carolina Division of Parks and Recreation operates facilities for public use at five established access areas. Facilities at three additional access areas are under construction but will not be available until 1990 or later; the new areas are Poplar Point Access Area, Seaforth Access Area, and Crosswinds Campground. Poplar Point will include a family campground with 580 campsites, washhouses, picnic grounds, a swimming beach, and a boat ramp. Seaforth will be a day-use access area with a swimming beach, picnic ground, and boat ramp. Crosswinds Campground will provide 190 campsites and related facilities; it will neighbor Crosswinds Boat Ramp and Marina. Information about the opening dates for these access areas may be obtained from the recreation area office, which is located at Crosswinds Boat Ramp adjacent to a spacious, paved parking area.

From Memorial Day through Labor Day, daily and weekend fees are charged for entrance to the access areas. In April, May, and September, a fee is charged only on weekends.

Campgrounds are located at Parkers Creek and Vista Point access areas. Other access areas are for day-use only.

At Parkers Creek, the family campground has 250 campsites in five loops near the lakeshore. The spacious sites are shaded by woodlands; each campsite is equipped with a table and a grill. Drinking water is provided. Electrical hookups are not available at waterside campsites due to potential problems in times of high water, but hookups are provided at 120 sites more distant from the lake. Washhouses with showers and toilets are located within each loop. A dump station for RVs is near the entry to camping loop #1. Many campsites are on the lakeshore, and boats launched at the nearby boat ramp can be moored at those sites. A group campground is located near the terminus of the Parkers Creek park road. There are 6 campsites, each of which can accommodate thirty persons. Each site has tables, grills, a fire circle with benches, and a source of drinking water. A washhouse with showers and toilets is located nearby.

At Vista Point, both a group campground and a family campground for RVs are located near the access area entrance; an information booth and a washhouse are nearby. The washhouse serves all campers and has showers and toilets. There are five wooded campsites, similar to those at Parkers Creek, for groups of twenty to thirty persons. The unusual family campground provides fifty parallel spaces for RVs and other campers. Each site has water and electrical hookups.

Campsites at Parkers Creek and Vista Point may be reserved for a minimum stay of seven consecutive days; they should be requested at least fourteen days in advance. Campers are limited to stays of fourteen days in a thirty-day period. Unreserved campsites are assigned on a first-come basis. A fee is charged. For information or reservations, telephone or write the recreation area office.

Picnic grounds are located at Parkers Creek, Vista Point, and Ebenezer Church access areas. Group shelters may be reserved at all three access areas by contacting the office. A fee is charged.

At Parkers Creek, a road to the right past the entry gate leads to a single group picnic shelter with twelve tables that can accommodate up to seventy-five persons. A road to the left past the entry gate leads to a large visitor-use area with a picnic ground and a sandy beach for swimming. From the parking lot, there is paved access to facilities. Tables and grills are scattered among the trees near the lakeshore. There are two group picnic shelters, each with eight tables; each shelter can accommodate thirty-five persons. A third shelter with two tables can accommodate fifteen persons. Drinking water is provided. A large washhouse with changing rooms and toilets is centrally located; rinse-off showers are outside. A playground for children is near the beach. Parkers Creek Access Area is a pleasant place for relaxation and enjoyment of the beauty of Jordan Lake.

At Vista Point, the park road continues past the campgrounds to a small picnic ground near a boat-launch area on the lakeshore. Tables and grills are beneath the trees; a group shelter with eight tables can accommodate thirty-five persons. Modern restrooms are located between the picnic ground and the boat ramp.

Ebenezer Church Access Area provides a picnic shelter with twelve tables that can accommodate up to seventy-five persons, as well as two smaller shelters, each with four tables and a capacity of twenty-five persons. In addition, there are forty outdoor tables for picnickers. A playground for children and a central washhouse with restrooms are provided.

Sandy beaches on Jordan Lake are open to the public for swimming and sunbathing. They. are located at the Parkers Creek and Ebenezer Church access areas. The beaches are protected by lifeguards during the summer

Jordan Lake

months. Changing rooms and toilets are in washhouses at both locations. Windsurfing is permitted in a restricted area at Ebenezer Church Access Area. A swimming beach at Vista Point is for campers only.

Boating and **fishing** are popular activities at Jordan Lake. Public boat ramps with large parking lots for both vehicles and trailers are located at Crosswinds, Ebenezer Church, and Vista Point access areas. The largest is Crosswinds Boat Ramp, which has both four-lane and two-lane concrete ramps. Paved paths connect the ramps, the parking lot, and the two loading docks that are a short distance from the ramps. Modern restrooms are nearby. Drinking water is provided. Crosswinds Marina is a full-service facility, with fuel, supplies, and services for boaters, as well as a pair of two-lane ramps. At Vista Point Access Area, the road terminates at a parking area adjacent to a pair of two-lane ramps with docks for powerboats. In addition, two gravel-and-dirt ramps provide water access for sailboats. At Ebenezer Church Access Area, two-lane and four-lane ramps are available to boaters, with ample parking and restrooms nearby. The Parkers Creek Access Area road terminates just past the group camping area at a paved parking lot and a pair of two-lane boat ramps. This facility is available only to registered campers.

Fishing in Jordan Lake requires appropriate licenses, and fishermen must comply with applicable state regulations. Boating and fishing activities are supervised by the North Carolina Wildlife Resources Commission.

NEARBY

The B. Everett Jordan Lake Management Center, which houses the office of the Corps of Engineers, and the B. Everett Jordan Dam, which is located at the south end of the reservoir, are a short distance north of Moncure. The sites may be reached from U.S. 1 via SR 1012 and SR 1970, as indicated by the signs. Information and a colorful map of the Jordan Lake area may be obtained at the management center. From the parking lot, a paved walkway leads to a wooden observation deck at the edge of a bluff overlooking the lake. Visitors have an excellent view downstream of the dam across Haw River; upstream, the view is of the heavily wooded shorelines and the smooth water of Jordan Lake at the confluence of the Haw and New Hope rivers.

Recreational access areas on Jordan Lake in addition to those managed by the North Carolina Division of Parks and Recreation include boat-launch facilities at **Poe's Ridge** near Jordan Dam, a facility managed by the Corps of Engineers, and at **Farrington**, a facility managed by the North Carolina Wildlife Resources Commission.

Falls Lake State Recreation Area is north of Raleigh, 45 miles from Jordan Lake. A chapter on Falls Lake State Recreation Area is included in this volume.

KERR LAKE STATE RECREATION AREA

Address: Route 3, Box 800
             Henderson, N.C. 27536

Telephone: (919) 438-7791

Size: 2,563 total acres

Established: 1951

Location: Vance and Warren counties, north of Henderson. Nine separate
access areas may be reached via I-85, U.S. 1, or N.C. 39.
Bullocksville Access Area encompasses 455 acres; exit I-85 onto
SR 1237 to Drewry, then turn left onto SR 1366 to the entrance.
County Line Access Area encompasses 285 acres; exit I-85 onto SR
1237 to Drewry, turn left onto SR 1366, then right onto SR 1200 for 1.2
miles, then left onto SR 202 for 0.7 mile, then right onto SR 1361 to the
entrance.
Henderson Point Access Area encompasses 329 acres; exit N.C.
39 about 2 miles north of Townsville onto SR 1356, then continue about
3 miles and exit right onto SR 1359 to the entrance.
Hibernia Access Area encompasses 446 acres; exit N.C. 39 about 1
mile north of Townsville onto SR 1347, then continue about 2 miles to
the entrance.
Kimball Point Access Area encompasses 93 acres; exit I-85 onto
SR 1237 to Drewry, turn left onto SR 1366, turn right onto SR 1200 for
about 5 miles, then turn left onto SR 1204 and proceed 1 mile to the
entrance.
Nutbush Bridge Access Area encompasses 363 acres; exit N.C. 39
onto SR 1308 and travel about 1.5 miles to the entrance.
Satterwhite Point Access Area encompasses 282 acres, and **Satterwhite Marina** encompasses 28 acres; exit I-85 and U.S. 1 onto SR
1319 and travel about 6 miles north to the entrance.
Steele Creek Marina encompasses 282 acres; exit N.C. 39 about 0.5
mile north of Townsville onto SR 1346 and proceed about 1.5 miles to
the entrance.

Principal Attractions: A 50,000-acre lake on the North Carolina–Virginia border with boating access, fishing, and over 750 lakeshore campsites; commercial marinas.

Visitor Activities: Boating, fishing, swimming, and other water-based sports; camping; picnicking; nature study.

Season: Hibernia, Nutbush Bridge, and Satterwhite Point access areas are open for camping year-round; the other areas are open from May through October.

The John H. Kerr Dam, completed in 1952 by the United States Army Corps of Engineers, created a 50,000-acre reservoir in the Roanoke River Valley along the North Carolina–Virginia border. The construction of the dam followed a disastrous 1940 flood in which the river rose up to 27 feet above its normal level. The primary purposes of the project were flood control in the lower Roanoke River basin and the generation of electrical power, but the lake has become a major area for water-based public recreation. It is the site of the Governor's Cup Invitational Regatta each June, as well as of fishing tournaments and several other special events.

The North Carolina Division of Parks and Recreation leases 6,000 acres of land on the lakeshore. Part of this land is included in nine access areas adjacent to Kerr Lake. Each access area offers boating access to the reservoir and opportunities for camping, picnicking, and other recreational activities. The complex of park units at Kerr Lake has become one of North Carolina's most heavily visited recreation areas, with over a million visitors in 1986.

PLANT LIFE

Most of the nine access areas are in deciduous or mixed pine/hardwood forests typical of the lower Piedmont. Oaks, sweet gum, yellow poplar, and shortleaf and loblolly pines make up the canopy of most forests. In the understory, flowering dogwood is conspicuous in spring, when the beautiful, small trees bloom prior to the leafing out of the canopy.

The open lake is generally devoid of large plants. Stands of willows invade shallow lake margins, and small marshes develop in quiet coves. Kerr Lake has deep, open water that allows little opportunity for aquatic vegetation to develop.

ANIMAL LIFE

The lake has large populations of fishes, including largemouth bass, bluegill, crappie, chain pickerel, and catfishes. A reproducing population of striped bass is of special interest. The striped bass is an anadromous species that normally spends most of its life in the ocean, migrating into freshwater streams such as

Kerr Lake State Recreation Area • 313

the Roanoke River to spawn. Some adult striped bass were trapped in the reservoir when Kerr Dam was closed; those fish survived and were able to reproduce in the tributary streams emptying into the lake. Subsequently, the North Carolina Wildlife Resources Commission began to stock fingerlings in the reservoir, increasing the population. The river and its tributaries now constitute an important spawning area for the fish, and the landlocked striped bass are a major attraction at Kerr Lake. They feed, often in large schools, in the open lake on such smaller fishes as gizzard and threadline shad and may be caught by fishermen at all times of the year. The striped bass is one of the most sought-after trophy fishes in the state.

Screech owl, gray phase

The waters of Kerr Lake provide wintering habitat for several species of ducks, especially scaup and other divers. Wildlife in the uplands surrounding the reservoir is similar to that elsewhere in the Piedmont. Cliff swallows build their mud nests beneath bridges and feed on the abundant flying insects that inhabit the lake environment. Cliff swallows were first discovered breeding in the Carolinas in the 1960s, and they can now be found, along with barn swallows, nesting at many of the large reservoirs.

FACILITIES AND ACTIVITIES

A **campground** is located at each access area except Satterwhite Marina. A total of 754 campsites are available, 172 of which have on-site water and electrical hookups for RVs; no hookups are provided at Bullocksville Access Area. Each site is equipped with a table, a grill, and a tent pad. Central washhouses at each campground provide shower and toilet facilities. Dump stations are located at six of the campgrounds; there are none at Bullocksville Access Area and Steele Creek Marina. Most campsites are situated along the lakeshore, so campers have ready access to the lake. Each access area has at least one boat ramp, and campers often keep boats tied up at their campsites. Group campsites are available at Henderson Point, Hibernia, Kimball Point, and Satterwhite Point access areas. The campgrounds at Hibernia, Nutbush Bridge, and Satterwhite Point access areas are open year-round; the others are open from May through October.

A camping fee is charged. Sites may be reserved in person or by letter for a minimum stay of seven consecutive days, not to exceed fourteen days in a thirty-day period; otherwise, sites are assigned on a first-come basis. Detailed information about camping at Kerr Lake may be obtained by addressing an inquiry to the superintendent of the recreation area.

Picnic grounds are provided at each access area except Satterwhite Marina. Picnic tables and shelters are available; each shelter has drinking water, grills, and easy access to the lakeshore. Some shelters may be reserved by contacting a ranger. There are sandy beaches at most of the access areas. Swimmers should exercise caution, however, as no lifeguards are present.

Boat ramps that can accommodate both motorboats and sailboats are provided at each access area. Commercial marinas are located at Satterwhite Point and Steele Creek. **Boating** is one of the most popular activities on the lake. Boaters can follow a channel marked by buoys for a distance of 65 miles from Nutbush Bridge to Clarksville, Virginia; marinas in addition to those at state park access areas are at Palmer Point, Townsville Landing, North Bend Park, and Occoneechee Park along the way. Side trips into various unmarked tributary creeks are also possible.

Fishing is good all year, especially for largemouth bass, striped bass, and crappie. A North Carolina or a Virginia fishing license is required. Some public hunting is permitted on land around the reservoir distant from camping and recreational facilities; hunting is regulated by the North Carolina Wildlife Resources Commission.

Much of the woodland around the reservoir is managed to attract and encourage wildlife. Three short, unmarked **nature trails** are at Satterwhite Point, Bullocksville, and County Line access areas; because these trails are relatively obscure, visitors may need to ask directions at ranger stations.

NEARBY
Additional camping and recreational facilities are provided elsewhere around Kerr Lake. The United States Army Corps of Engineers maintains several access areas with campgrounds along the more than 800 miles of lakeshore in Virginia and North Carolina. Virginia has created two state parks—Staunton River State Park and Occoneechee State Park—on land adjacent to the reservoir. For information, write: Resource Manager, John H. Kerr Dam and Reservoir, Route 1, Box 76, Boydton, Va. 23917, or Division of Parks and Recreation, 1201 Washington Building, Capitol Square, Richmond, Va. 23219.

APPENDIX: Common and Scientific Names of Plants and Animals Mentioned in the Text.*

PLANTS

Alder
  (*Alnus* spp.)
Alumroot
  (*Heuchera* spp.)
American chestnut
  (*Castanea dentata*)
American elm
  (*Ulmus americana*)
American holly
  (*Ilex opaca*)
American lotus
  (*Nelumbo lutea*)
American olive
  (*Osmanthus americanus*)
Arrowhead
  (*Sagittaria latifolia*)
Aster
  (*Aster* spp.)
Atamasco lily
  (*Zephyranthes atamasco*)
Atlantic white cedar
  (*Chamaecyparis thyoides*)
Avens
  (*Geum radiatum*)
Bald cypress
  (*Taxodium distichum*)
Bamboo briar
  (*Smilax* spp.)
Basswood
  (*Tilia* spp.)
Bayberry
  (*Myrica pennsylvanica*)
Beachgrass
  (*Ammophila breviligulata*)
Bearberry
  (*Vaccinium erythrocarpum*)
Bear oak
  (*Quercus ilicifolia*)

Beauty berry
  (*Callicarpa americana*)
Beech
  (*Fagus grandifolia*)
Bellwort
  (*Uvularia grandiflora*)
Birdfoot violet
  (*Viola pedata*)
Bitter gallberry
  (*Ilex glabra*)
Black cherry
  (*Prunus serotina*)
Black gum
  (*Nyssa sylvatica*)
Black huckleberry
  (*Gaylussacia baccata*)
Blackjack oak
  (*Quercus marilandica*)
Black locust
  (*Robinia pseudo-acacia*)
Black needlerush
  (*Juncus roemerianus*)
Black oak
  (*Quercus velutina*)
Black walnut
  (*Juglans nigra*)
Black willow
  (*Salix nigra*)
Bloodroot
  (*Sanguinaria canadensis*)
Bluebeard lily
  (*Clintonia borealis*)
Blueberry
  (*Vaccinium corymbosum*)
Bluet
  (*Houstonia caerulea*)
Box elder
  (*Acer negundo*)
Bracken fern
  (*Pteridium aquilinum*)

*These represent only a small proportion of the plants and animals that occur in North Carolina parks.

Bradley's spleenwort
(*Asplenium bradleyi*)
Broad beech-fern
(*Thelypteris hexagonoptera*)
Broomsedge
(*Andropogon* spp.)
Bush honeysuckle
(*Diervilla lonicera*)
Buttercup
(*Ranunculus* spp.)
Butterwort
(*Pinguicula pumila*)
Cardinal flower
(*Lobelia cardinalis*)
Catawba rhododendron
(*Rhododendron catawbiense*)
Catbriar
(*Smilax* spp.)
Cattail
(*Typha* spp.)
Cherry bark oak
(*Quercus pagodaefolia*)
Chestnut
(*Castanea dentata*)
Chestnut oak
(*Quercus prinus*)
Christmas fern
(*Polystichum acrostichoides*)
Cinnamon fern
(*Osmunda cinnamomea*)
Climbing hempweed
(*Mikania scandens*)
Club moss
(*Lycopodium* spp.)
Crabgrass
(*Digitaria* spp.)
Cross vine
(*Anisostichus capreolata*)
Dangleberry
(*Gaylussacia frondosa*)
Devil's walking stick
(*Zanthoxylum clava-herculis*)
Duckweed
(*Lemna* spp.)

Dutchman's breeches
(*Dicentra cucullaria*)
Dwarf iris
(*Iris verna*)
Eelgrass
(*Zostera marina*)
Fall gentian
(*Gentinea autumnalis*)
False croton
(*Crotonopsis elliptica*)
False lily-of-the-valley
(*Maianthemum canadense*)
False Solomon's seal
(*Smilacina racemosa*)
Fetterbush
(*Lyonia lucida*)
Filmy angelica
(*Angelica triquinata*)
Fire cherry
(*Prunus pennsylvanica*)
Flame azalea
(*Rhododendron calendulaceum*)
Flowering dogwood
(*Cornus florida*)
Fraser fir
(*Abies fraseri*)
Fringe tree
(*Chionanthus virginicus*)
Galax
(*Galax aphylla*)
Gallberry holly
(*Ilex glabra*)
Giant cordgrass
(*Spartina cynosuroides*)
Goldenroot
(*Hydrastis canadensis*)
Goose berry
(*Ribes* spp.)
Grape
(*Vitis* spp.)
Grass pink
(*Calopogon pulchellus*)
Ground juniper
(*Juniperus communis*)

Groundsel tree
(*Baccharis halimifolia*)
Hackberry
(*Celtis* spp.)
Haircap moss
(*Polytrichum commune*)
Heart leaf
(*Hexastylis shuttleworthii*)
Hemlock
(*Tsuga* spp.)
Hobble-bush
(*Viburnum alnifolium*)
Honeysuckle
(*Lonicera japonica*)
Hornbeam
(*Ostrya virginiana*)
Huckleberry
(*Vaccinium* spp.)
Hypericum
(*Hypericum buckleyi*)
Indian pipe
(*Monotropa uniflora*)
Iris
(*Iris* spp.)
Ironwood
(*Carpinus caroliniana*)
Jack-in-the-pulpit
(*Arisaema triphyllum*)
Jewel weed
(*Impatiens capensis*)
Large-tooth aspen
(*Populus grandidentata*)
Laurel oak
(*Quercus laurifolia*)
Leatherwood
(*Dirca palustris*)
Lettuce saxifrage
(*Saxifraga micranthidifolia*)
Live oak
(*Quercus virginiana*)
Lizard's tail
(*Saururus cernuus*)
Loblolly bay
(*Gordonia lasianthus*)

Loblolly pine
(*Pinus taeda*)
Longleaf pine
(*Pinus palustris*)
Maidencane
(*Panicum hemitomon*)
Maidenhair fern
(*Adiantum pedatum*)
Marsh pennywort
(*Hydrocotyle umbellata*)
Mayapple
(*Podophyllum peltatum*)
Mistflower
(*Eupatorium coelestinum*)
Mockernut hickory
(*Carya tomentosa*)
Morning glory
(*Ipomoea* spp.)
Mountain ash
(*Sorbus americana*)
Mountain cranberry
(*Vaccinium erythrocarpum*)
Mountain galax
(*Galax aphylla*)
Mountain goldenrod
(*Solidago roanensis*)
Mountain laurel
(*Kalmia latifolia*)
Mountain lettuce
(*Saxifraga micranthidifolia*)
Mountain maple
(*Acer pennsylvanicum*)
Mountain pepperbush
(*Clethra acuminata*)
Mountain spleenwort
(*Asplenium montanum*)
Muscadine grape
(*Vitis rotundifolia*)
Netted chain-fern
(*Woodwardia areolata*)
Northern red oak
(*Quercus borealis*)
Ox-eye daisy
(*Chrysanthemum leucanthemum*)

Parrot feather
(*Myriophyllum brasiliense*)
Partridge berry
(*Mitchella repens*)
Pawpaw
(*Asimina triloba*)
Pepperbush
(*Clethra alnifolia*)
Persimmon
(*Diospyros virginiana*)
Pickerel weed
(*Pontederia cordata*)
Pignut hickory
(*Carya glabra*)
Pink lady's slipper
(*Cypripedium acaule*)
Pinxter-flower
(*Rhododendron nudiflorum*)
Pipsissewa
(*Chimaphila maculata*)
Pitcher plant
(*Sarracenia* spp.)
Pitch pine
(*Pinus rigida*)
Poison ivy
(*Rhus radicans*)
Pond pine
(*Pinus serotina*)
Post oak
(*Quercus stellata*)
Prairie willow
(*Salix humilis*)
Purple turtlehead
(*Chelone cuthbertii*)
Rattan vine
(*Ampelopsis* spp.)
Rattlesnake orchid
(*Goodyera pubescens*)
Red ash
(*Fraxinus pennsylvanica*)
Redbay
(*Persea borbonia*)
Red-berried elder
(*Sambucus pubens*)

Redbud
(*Cercis canadensis*)
Red cedar
(*Juniperus virginiana*)
Red maple
(*Acer rubrum*)
Red mulberry
(*Morus rubra*)
Red oak
(*Quercus rubra*)
Red spruce
(*Picea rubens*)
Rhododendron
(*Rhododendron* spp.)
River birch
(*Betula nigra*)
Rosebay rhododendron
(*Rhododendron maximum*)
Rose mallow
(*Hibiscus moscheutos*)
Rough-leaf loosestrife
(*Lythrum asperulaefolia*)
Royal fern
(*Osmunda regalis*)
Rusty woodsia
(*Woodsia ilvensis*)
St. John's wort
(*Hypericum prolificum*)
Salt grass
(*Distichlis spicata*)
Saltmeadow cordgrass
(*Spartina patens*)
Sassafras
(*Sassafras albidum*)
Saw-grass
(*Cladium jamaicense*)
Saxifrage
(*Saxifraga michauxii*)
Scarlet oak
(*Quercus coccinea*)
Scrubby post oak
(*Quercus margaretta*)
Sea oats
(*Uniola paniculata*)

Seashore mallow
(*Kosteletskya virginica*)
Seaside goldenrod
(*Solidago sempervirens*)
Sedge
(*Cyperus* spp.)
Sedum
(*Sedum* spp.)
Shagbark hickory
(*Carya ovata*)
Shortleaf pine
(*Pinus echinata*)
Silky willow
(*Salix sericea*)
Silverbell
(*Halesia carolina*)
Silverling
(*Baccharis halimifolia*)
Slough grass
(*Halodule beaudettei*)
Smilax
(*Smilax* spp.)
Smooth cordgrass
(*Spartina alterniflora*)
Sourwood
(*Oxydendrum arboreum*)
Southern lady fern
(*Athyrium asplenioides*)
Southern sugar maple
(*Acer floridanum*)
Spanish moss
(*Tillandsia usneoides*)
Sparkleberry
(*Vaccinium arboreum*)
Spring beauty
(*Claytonia virginica*)
Stonecrop
(*Sedum ternatum*)
Storax
(*Styrax americana*)
Strawberry bush
(*Euonymus americanus*)
Striped maple
(*Acer pennsylvanicum*)

Sugarberry
(*Celtis occidentalis*)
Sugar maple
(*Acer saccharum*)
Sundew
(*Drosera* spp.)
Swamp alder
(*Alnus serrulata*)
Swamp dogwood
(*Cornus stricta*)
Swamp rose
(*Rosa palustris*)
Sweet bay
(*Magnolia virginiana*)
Sweet fern
(*Comptonia peregrina*)
Sweet gum
(*Liquidambar styraciflua*)
Sweet pepperbush
(*Clethra alnifolia*)
Sycamore
(*Platanus occidentalis*)
Table mountain pine
(*Pinus pungens*)
Tag alder
(*Alnus serrulata*)
Titi
(*Cyrilla racemiflora*)
Trailing arbutus
(*Epigaea repens*)
Trillium
(*Trillium* spp.)
Trout lily
(*Erythronium americanum*)
Trumpet vine
(*Campsis radicans*)
Tulip tree
(*Liriodendron tulipifera*)
Tupelo gum
(*Nyssa aquatica*)
Turkey oak
(*Quercus laevis*)
Tway blade
(*Listera* spp.)

Umbrella tree
  (*Magnolia fraseri*)
Venus' fly trap
  (*Dionaea muscipula*)
Virginia creeper
  (*Parthenocissus quinquefolia*)
Virginia pine
  (*Pinus virginiana*)
Virginia willow
  (*Itea virginica*)
Water fern
  (*Azolla caroliniana*)
Water hickory
  (*Carya aquatica*)
Water-lily
  (*Nymphaea* spp.)
Water oak
  (*Quercus nigra*)
Wax myrtle
  (*Myrica cerifera*)
White oak
  (*Quercus alba*)
White snakeroot
  (*Eupatorium rugosum*)
Wild azalea
  (*Rhododendron* spp.)
Wild ginger
  (*Asarum canadense*)
Wild hydrangea
  (*Hydrangea arborescens*)
Willow
  (*Salix* spp.)
Willow oak
  (*Quercus phellos*)
Winged elm
  (*Ulmus alata*)
Wiregrass
  (*Aristida stricta*)
Witch hazel
  (*Hamamelis virginiana*)
Wood sorrel
  (*Oxalis* spp.)
Yarrow
  (*Achillea millefolium*)

Yaupon
  (*Ilex vomitoria*)
Yellow birch
  (*Betula lutea*)
Yellow buckeye
  (*Aesculus octandra*)
Yellow cow-lily
  (*Nuphar luteum*)
Yellow jessamine
  (*Gelsemium sempervirens*)
Yellow lady's slipper
  (*Cypripedium calceolus*)
Yucca
  (*Yucca* spp.)

ANIMALS

Invertebrates

Blue crab
  (*Callinectes sapidus*)
Common oyster
  (*Crassostrea virginica*)
Fiddler crab
  (*Uca* spp.)
Ghost crab
  (*Ocypode quadrata*)
Waccamaw helix
  (*Triodopsis soelneri*)
Waccamaw lance
  (*Elliptio* spp.)
Waccamaw mucket
  (*Lampsilis radiata*)
Waccamaw snail
  (*Amnicola* spp.)
Waccamaw spike mussel
  (*Elliptio waccamawensis*)

Fish

American eel
  (*Anguilla rostrata*)
Blue catfish
  (*Ictalurus furcatus*)

Bluefish
(*Pomatomus saltatrix*)
Bluegill
(*Lepomis macrochirus*)
Blue-spotted sunfish
(*Enneacanthus gloriosus*)
Bowfin
(*Amia calva*)
Brook trout
(*Salvelinus fontinalis*)
Brown bullhead
(*Ictalurus nebulosus*)
Brown trout
(*Salmo trutta*)
Carp
(*Cyprinus carpio*)
Catfish
(*Ictalurus* spp.)
Chain pickerel
(*Esox niger*)
Channel bass
(*Sciaenops ocellatus*)
Channel catfish
(*Ictalurus punctatus*)
Chubsucker
(*Erimyzon sucetta*)
Crappie
(*Pomoxis* spp.)
Croaker
(*Micropogonias undulatus*)
Darter
(*Etheostoma* spp.)
Flathead catfish
(*Pylodictis olivaris*)
Flounder
(*Paralichthys* spp.)
Gizzard shad
(*Dorosoma cepedianum*)
Golden shiner
(*Notemigonus crysoleucas*)
Green sunfish
(*Lepomis cyanellus*)
Hickory shad
(*Alosa mediocris*)

Killifish
(*Fundulus* spp.)
Largemouth bass
(*Micropterus salmoides*)
Long-nosed gar
(*Lepisosteus osseus*)
Muskellunge
(*Esox masquinongy*)
Pirate perch
(*Aphredoderus sayanus*)
Pumpkinseed
(*Lepomis gibbosus*)
Puppy drum
(*Sciaenops ocellatus*)
Rainbow trout
(*Salmo gairdneri*)
Redbreast sunfish
(*Lepomis auritus*)
Redear sunfish
(*Lepomis microlophus*)
Redeye bass
(*Micropterus coosae*)
Sauger
(*Stizostedion canadense*)
Sheepshead
(*Archosargus probatocephalus*)
Shellcracker
(*Lepomis microlophus*)
Silversides
(*Menidia* spp.)
Smallmouth bass
(*Micropterus dolomieui*)
Spot
(*Leiostomus xanthurus*)
Striped bass
(*Morone saxatilis*)
Sucker
(*Moxostoma* spp.)
Threadfin shad
(*Dorosoma petenense*)
Warmouth
(*Lepomis gulosus*)
White bass
(*Morone chrysops*)

White catfish
(*Ictalurus catus*)
White perch
(*Morone americana*)
White shad
(*Alosa sapidissima*)
Whiting
(*Menticirrhus* spp.)
Yellow perch
(*Perca flavescens*)

Amphibians

American toad
(*Bufo americanus*)
Bullfrog
(*Rana catesbeiana*)
Carolina mudpuppy
(*Necturus lewisi*)
Carolina treefrog
(*Hyla cinerea*)
Carpenter frog
(*Rana virgatipes*)
Chorus frog
(*Pseudacris* spp.)
Crawfish frog
(*Rana aerolata*)
Cricket frog
(*Acris* spp.)
Fowler's toad
(*Bufo woodhousei*)
Green frog
(*Rana clamitans*)
Marbled salamander
(*Ambystoma opacum*)
Mud salamander
(*Pseudotriton montanus*)
Northern dusky salamander
(*Desmognathus fuscus*)
Pigmy salamander
(*Desmognathus wrighti*)
Pine barrens treefrog
(*Hyla andersoni*)
Red salamander
(*Pseudotriton ruber*)

Slimy salamander
(*Plethodon glutinosus*)
Southern dusky salamander
(*Desmognathus auriculatus*)
Southern leopard frog
(*Rana sphenocephala*)
Spotted salamander
(*Ambystoma maculatum*)
Spring peeper
(*Hyla crucifer*)
Squirrel treefrog
(*Hyla squirella*)
Two-lined salamander
(*Eurycea bislineata*)
Wehrle's salamander
(*Plethodon wehrlei*)
Woodland salamander
(*Plethodon* spp.)

Reptiles

American alligator
(*Alligator mississippiensis*)
Banded water snake
(*Nerodia fasciata*)
Black racer
(*Coluber constrictor*)
Black rat snake
(*Elaphe obsoleta obsoleta*)
Canebrake rattlesnake
(*Crotalus horridus atricaudata*)
Carolina anole
(*Anolis carolinensis*)
Copperhead
(*Agkistrodon contortrix*)
Cottonmouth
(*Agkistrodon piscivorus*)
Diamondback terrapin
(*Malaclemys terrapin*)
Eastern box turtle
(*Terrapene carolina*)
Eastern fence lizard
(*Sceloporus undulatus*)
Eastern garter snake
(*Thamnophis sirtalis*)

Eastern hognose snake
(*Heterdon platyrhinos*)
Eastern mud turtle
(*Kinosternon subrubrum*)
Glass lizard
(*Ophisaurus* spp.)
Loggerhead turtle
(*Caretta caretta*)
Ringneck snake
(*Diadophis punctatus*)
Rough green snake
(*Opheodrys aestivus*)
Scarlet kingsnake
(*Lampropeltis triangulum*)
Scarlet snake
(*Cemophora coccinea*)
Six-lined racerunner
(*Cnemidophorus sexlineatus*)
Skink
(*Eumeces* spp.)
Snapping turtle
(*Chelydra serpentina*)
Southern hognose snake
(*Heterodon simus*)
Spiny softshell turtle
(*Trionyx spiniferus*)
Spotted turtle
(*Clemmys guttata*)
Timber rattlesnake
(*Crotalus horridus horridus*)
Yellowbelly slider
(*Chrysemys scripta*)

Birds

Acadian flycatcher
(*Empidonax virescens*)
American goldfinch
(*Carduelis tristis*)
American kestrel
(*Falco sparverius*)
American oystercatcher
(*Haematopus palliatus*)
American robin
(*Turdus migratorius*)

American wigeon
(*Anas americana*)
American woodcock
(*Scolopax minor*)
Bald eagle
(*Haliaeetus leucocephalus*)
Barn swallow
(*Hirundo rustica*)
Barred owl
(*Strix varia*)
Belted kingfisher
(*Megaceryle alcyon*)
Black-and-white warbler
(*Mniotilta varia*)
Black-billed cuckoo
(*Coccyzus erythropthalmus*)
Blackburnian warbler
(*Dendroica fusca*)
Black duck
(*Anas rubripes*)
Black skimmer
(*Rynchops niger*)
Black-throated blue warbler
(*Dendroica caerulescens*)
Black-throated green warbler
(*Dendroica virens*)
Black vulture
(*Coragyps atratus*)
Bobwhite quail
(*Colinus virginianus*)
Brown creeper
(*Certhia familiaris*)
Brown-headed nuthatch
(*Sitta pusilla*)
Brown pelican
(*Pelecanus occidentalis*)
Brown thrasher
(*Toxostoma rufum*)
Bufflehead
(*Bucephala albeola*)
Canada goose
(*Branta canadensis*)
Canada warbler
(*Wilsonia canadensis*)

Canvasback
(*Aythya valisineria*)
Carolina chickadee
(*Parus carolinensis*)
Chestnut-sided warbler
(*Dendroica pennsylvanica*)
Clapper rail
(*Rallus longirostris*)
Cliff swallow
(*Petrochelidon pyrrhonota*)
Common crow
(*Corvus brachyrhynchos*)
Common eider
(*Somateria mollissima*)
Common merganser
(*Mergus merganser*)
Common raven
(*Corvus corax*)
Common tern
(*Sterna hirundo*)
Common yellowthroat
(*Geothlypis trichas*)
Cooper's hawk
(*Accipiter cooperii*)
Dark-eyed junco
(*Junco hyemalis*)
Double-crested cormorant
(*Phalacrocorax auritus*)
Dunlin
(*Calidris alpina*)
Eastern bluebird
(*Sialia sialis*)
Eastern screech owl
(*Otus asio*)
Evening grosbeak
(*Hesperiphona vespertina*)
Field sparrow
(*Spizella pusilla*)
Golden-crowned kinglet
(*Regulus satrapa*)
Golden-winged warbler
(*Vermivora chrysoptera*)
Great blue heron
(*Ardea herodias*)

Great crested flycatcher
(*Myiarchus crinithus*)
Great egret
(*Casmerodius albus*)
Great horned owl
(*Bubo virginianus*)
Green-backed heron
(*Butorides striatus*)
Green-winged teal
(*Anas crecca*)
Gull-billed tern
(*Gelochelidon nilotica*)
Hooded merganser
(*Lophodytes cucullatus*)
Hooded warbler
(*Wilsonia citrina*)
Indigo bunting
(*Passerina cyanea*)
Kentucky warbler
(*Oporornis formosus*)
Laughing gull
(*Larus atricilla*)
Least flycatcher
(*Empidonax minimus*)
Least tern
(*Sterna albifrons*)
Louisiana waterthrush
(*Seiurus motacilla*)
Mallard
(*Anas platyrhynchos*)
Marsh hawk
(*Circus cyaneus*)
Marsh wren
(*Cistothorus plustris*)
Mourning dove
(*Zenaida macroura*)
Northern oriole
(*Icterus galbula*)
Northern parula
(*Parula americana*)
Osprey
(*Pandion haliaetus*)
Ovenbird
(*Seiurus aurocapillus*)

Painted bunting
(*Passerina ciris*)
Pileated woodpecker
(*Dryocopus pileatus*)
Pine siskin
(*Carduelis pinus*)
Pine warbler
(*Dendroica pinus*)
Pintail
(*Anas acuta*)
Prothonotary warbler
(*Protonotaria citrea*)
Purple sandpiper
(*Calidris maritima*)
Red-breasted nuthatch
(*Sitta canadensis*)
Red-cockaded woodpecker
(*Picoides borealis*)
Red-eyed vireo
(*Vireo olivaceus*)
Redhead
(*Aythya americana*)
Red-headed woodpecker
(*Melanerpes erythrocephalus*)
Red-shouldered hawk
(*Buteo lineatus*)
Redstart
(*Setophaga ruticilla*)
Red-tailed hawk
(*Buteo jamaicensis*)
Red-winged blackbird
(*Agelaius phoeniceus*)
Ring-necked duck
(*Aythya collaris*)
Rose-breasted grosbeak
(*Phercticus ludovicianus*)
Royal tern
(*Sterna maxima*)
Ruddy duck
(*Oxyura jamicensis*)
Ruffed grouse
(*Bonasa umbellus*)
Rufous-sided towhee
(*Pipilo erythrophthalmus*)

Sanderling
(*Calidris alba*)
Saw-whet owl
(*Aegolius acadicus*)
Scarlet tanager
(*Piranga olivacea*)
Scaup
(*Athya* spp.)
Snowy egret
(*Egretta thula*)
Song sparrow
(*Melospiza melodia*)
Spotted sandpiper
(*Actitis macularia*)
Summer tanager
(*Piranga rubra*)
Swainson's warbler
(*Limnothlypis swainsonii*)
Titmouse
(*Parus bicolor*)
Tree swallow
(*Iridoprocne bicolor*)
Tundra swan
(*Olor columbianus*)
Turkey vulture
(*Cathartes aura*)
Veery
(*Catharus fuscescens*)
Warbling vireo
(*Vireo gilvus*)
Whip-poor-will
(*Caprimulgus vociferus*)
White-breasted nuthatch
(*Sitta carolinensis*)
Wild turkey
(*Meleagris gallopavo*)
Willet
(*Catoptrophorus semipalmatus*)
Willow flycatcher
(*Empidonax traillii*)
Winter wren
(*Troglodytes troglodytes*)
Wood duck
(*Aix sponsa*)

Wood thrush
(*Hylocichla mustelina*)
Yellow-throated vireo
(*Vireo flavifrons*)
Yellow-throated warbler
(*Dendroica dominica*)

Mammals

Beaver
(*Castor canadensis*)
Big brown bat
(*Eptesicus fuscus*)
Black bear
(*Ursus americanus*)
Bobcat
(*Felis rufus*)
Bottle-nosed dolphin
(*Tursiops truncatus*)
Cotton rat
(*Sigmodon hispidus*)
Deer mouse
(*Peromyscus maniculatus*)
Eastern chipmunk
(*Tamias striatus*)
Eastern cottontail
(*Sylvilagus floridanus*)
Eastern mole
(*Scalopus aquaticus*)
Eastern pipistrelle
(*Pipistrellus subflavus*)
Evening bat
(*Nycticeius humeralis*)
Fox squirrel
(*Sciurus niger*)
Golden mouse
(*Ochrotomys nuttalli*)
Gray fox
(*Urocyon cinereoargenteus*)
Gray squirrel
(*Sciurus carolinensis*)
Hispid cotton rat
(*Sigmodon hispidus*)
House mouse
(*Mus musculus*)

Long-tailed weasel
(*Mustela frenata*)
Marsh rabbit
(*Sylvilagus palustris*)
Mink
(*Mustela vison*)
Mountain lion
(*Felis concolor*)
Muskrat
(*Ondatra zibethicus*)
Northern short-tailed shrew
(*Blarina brevicauda*)
Nutria
(*Myocastor coypus*)
Raccoon
(*Procyon lotor*)
Red bat
(*Lasiurus borealis*)
Red fox
(*Vulpes vulpes*)
Red squirrel
(*Tamiasciurus hudsonicus*)
River otter
(*Lutra canadensis*)
Silver-haired bat
(*Lasionycteris noctivagans*)
Southern flying squirrel
(*Glaucomys volans*)
Southern red-backed vole
(*Clethrionomys gapperi*)
Southern short-tailed shrew
(*Blarina carolinensis*)
Striped skunk
(*Mephitis mephitis*)
Virginia opossum
(*Didelphis virginiana*)
White-footed mouse
(*Peromyscus leucopus*)
White-tailed deer
(*Odocoileus virginianus*)
Woodchuck
(*Marmota monax*)

BIBLIOGRAPHY

De Hart, A. 1988. *North Carolina Hiking Trails.* 2d ed. Boston: Appalachian Mountain Club. A comprehensive listing of hiking trails in the state, with descriptions and essential data for hikers.

Fuller, K. 1977. "History of North Carolina State Parks, 1915–1976." In *Histories of Southeastern State Park Systems,* 125–43. Association of Southeastern State Park Directors. A brief summary of the historical development of the state's parks system.

Hall, C. 1981. *Southern Rock: A Climber's Guide.* Chester, Conn.: Globe Pequot Press. A directory of major rock-climbing opportunities in southeastern states, including descriptions and maps of established routes of ascent.

Jenner, M. G., C. R. Saint-Rossy, and C. J. Murray. 1986. *Guide to North Carolina Science Centers.* 2d ed. Durham, N.C.: North Carolina Academy of Sciences. A catalog of science centers in the state, with descriptions of their programs and facilities.

North Carolina Division of Parks and Recreation. 1988. *Systemwide Plan for the North Carolina State Parks System.* Raleigh, N.C.: Division of Parks and Recreation.

North Carolina Travel and Tourism Division. *North Carolina Camping and Outdoors Directory.* Raleigh, N.C.: Travel and Tourism Division. Source of brief information about the recreational resources of the state; part of a packet of materials available by writing North Carolina Travel and Tourism Division, Department of Commerce, Raleigh, N.C. 27611, or calling toll-free 1-800-VISIT NC.

Roe, C. E. 1987. *A Directory to North Carolina's Natural Areas.* Raleigh, N.C.: North Carolina Natural Heritage Foundation. A catalog with discussions of 108 of the state's most outstanding natural areas; provides information on locations and management.

Runkle, J., compiler. 1983. "A Guide to North Carolina State Parks." *tread softly: Carolina Conservation Quarterly* 1(3):25–59. A brief compilation of information about the state's parks, natural areas, and recreation areas.

Schumann, M. 1977. *The Living Land: An Outdoor Guide to North Carolina.* Chapel Hill, N.C.: Dale Press. A guide to diverse natural areas of the state managed by institutional, private, federal, and state agencies, including the Division of Parks and Recreation; the introduction is an eloquent statement of philosophy.

Tilden, F. 1962. *The State Parks: Their Meaning in America.* New York: Alfred A. Knopf. A discussion of the value of state parks and descriptions of selected parks in states throughout the nation.

Guidebooks to Plants and Animals

Plants

Batson, W. T. 1987. *Wild Flowers in the Carolinas*. Columbia, S.C.: University of South Carolina Press.

Holmes, J. S., and H. J. Green. 1983. *Common Forest Trees of North Carolina*. 15th ed. Raleigh, N.C.: North Carolina Department of Natural Resources and Community Development, Division of Forest Resources.

Justice, W. S., and C. R. Bell. 1968. *Wild Flowers of North Carolina*. Chapel Hill, N.C.: University of North Carolina Press.

Krochmal, A., R. S. Walters, and R. M. Doughty. 1969. *A Guide to the Medicinal Plants of Appalachia*. Washington, D.C.: United States Department of Agriculture.

Petrides, G. A. 1972. *A Field Guide to Trees and Shrubs*. Boston: Houghton Mifflin Company.

Radford, A. E., H. E. Ahles, and R. C. Bell. 1979. *Manual of the Vascular Flora of the Carolinas*. Chapel Hill, N.C.: University of North Carolina Press.

Animals

Eddy, S. 1969. *How to Know the Freshwater Fishes*. Dubuque, Iowa: Wm. C. Brown Company.

Gosner, K. L. 1978. *A Field Guide to the Atlantic Seashore*. Boston: Houghton Mifflin Company.

Kaplan, E. H. 1988. *A Field Guide to Southeastern and Caribbean Seashores*. Boston: Houghton Mifflin Company.

Manooch, C. S. 1984. *Fishes of the Southeastern United States*. Raleigh, N.C.: North Carolina Museum of Natural History.

Martof, B. S., W. W. Palmer, J. R. Bailey, J. R. Harrison, and J. F. Dermid. 1980. *Amphibians and Reptiles of the Carolinas*. Chapel Hill, N.C.: University of North Carolina Press.

Morris, P. A. 1975. *A Field Guide to Shells*. Boston: Houghton Mifflin Company.

Potter, E. F., J. F. Parnell, and R. P. Teulings. 1980. *Birds of the Carolinas*. Chapel Hill, N.C.: University of North Carolina Press.

Robins, C. R., and G. C. Ray. 1986. *A Field Guide to Atlantic Coast Fishes of North America*. Boston: Houghton Mifflin Company.

Ruppert, E. E., and R. S. Fox. 1988. *Seashore Animals of the Southeast*. Columbia, S.C.: University of South Carolina Press.

Webster, W. D., J. F. Parnell, and W. C. Biggs, Jr. 1985. *Mammals of the Carolinas, Virginia, and Maryland.* Chapel Hill, N.C.: University of North Carolina Press.

Photographs Taken by Walter C. Biggs, Jr.

Photographs taken by James F. Parnell

INDEX

Jones Lake, 59, 61, 63, 79
Jordan Dam, *See* B. Everett Jordan Dam
Jordan Lake, *See* B. Everett Jordan Lake

K

Kerr Dam, *See* John H. Kerr Dam
Kerr Lake, 313–15
Kimball Point Access Area, 312, 314
Kings Mountain National Military Park, 119
Kings Pinnacle, 113–14, 115, 117
Kron House, 163, 165–66, 173

L

Lake James, 221, 222–23
Lake Norman, 120, 121, 126
Lake Phelps, 91–92, 95
Lakeshore Trail, 124
Lake Tillery, 163, 166, 167, 170
Lake Trail (Crowders Mountain State Park), 117
Lake Trail (Jones Lake State Park), 65
Lake Waccamaw, 59, 73, 74–76, 95
Lake Wateree, 223
Lanier's Falls Trail, 195–96
Lassiter Swamp, 83, 89
Laurel Self-guided Trail, 168
Ledge Rock Access Area, 294
Ledge Springs Trail, 184
Linville Falls Recreation Area, 224–25
Linville Falls Trail, 225
Linville Gorge, 221, 225
Linville Gorge Wilderness Area, 225
Linville Mountain, 225
Linville River, 221, 222, 224–25
Linville River Access Area, 224
Little Creek Loop Trail, 195
Little Fishing Creek, 155, 158, 159, 160, 161
Little Pinnacle, 178, 183
Little Pinnacle Trail, 183
Live Oak Trail, 33

Lower Cascades, 149
Lower Cascades Trail, 149
Lower Falls, 266
Lower Falls Trail, 204
Lower Trail, 66
Luther's Rock, 232

M

Maple Hill Lodge, 216
Masonboro Island, 283, 285
Medoc Mountain, 155–57, 158
Merchants Millpond, 83, 84–85, 87, 88
Middle Falls, 266
Mill Creek, 17–18
Millpond Access Area, 88
Millpond Loop Trail, 87
Mitchell Falls, 240
Mitchell's Mill, 285–86
Mitchell's Millpond, 285–86
Moccasin Canal, 97
Moore's Creek National Battlefield, 70–71
Moore's Knob, 143, 144, 148–49
Moore's Knob Trail, 148–49
Moore's Wall, 143, 144, 152
Morgan Creek, 308
Morrow Mountain, 164–66, 171
Morrow Mountain Loop Trail, 169
Morrow Mountain Trail, 169
Mound Battery, 298–99
Mountain Trail, 184
Mount Craig, 238, 243
Mount Hallback, 238
Mount Jefferson, 227, 228
Mount Mitchell, 238–244
Mount Mitchell Trail, 243
Museum of Man, 186
Museum of North Carolina Minerals, 225, 246

N

Nags Head, 47, 48, 49–50
Nags Head Woods, 55

V

Vista Point Access Area, 306, 309, 311

W

Waccamaw River, 73, 75, 79
Wagoner Road Access Area, 249,
    253–54, 258
Washington, 35
Watercraft Center, 26
Wells Interpretive Center, *See* B. W.
    Wells Interpretive Center
Weymouth Woods, 277–81
White Lake, 63, 70, 80
Widow's Creek, 268, 269
Widow's Creek Falls, 268
Wilmington, 5–6, 11
Window Falls, 147
Window Falls Trail, 147

Wolf Rock (Hanging Rock State Park),
    144, 148
Wolf Rock (Stone Mountain State
    Park), 261, 262, 263, 267
Wolf Rock Loop Trail, 266
Wright Brothers National Memorial,
    54

Y

Yadkin River, 107, 108, 152, 163, 165,
    166, 176, 182, 185–86
Yadkin River Bridle Trail, 185
Yadkin River Section, 177, 179, 185
Yadkin River Canoe Trail, 110, 185
Yorkshire Center, 292

Z

Zeke's Island, 283, 304
Ziegle's Rock, 291